The Self

CW01476383

What is it to occupy a first-person stance? Is the first-personal idea one has of oneself in conflict with the idea of oneself as a physical being? How, if there is a conflict, is it to be resolved? *The Self* recommends a new way to approach those questions, finding inspiration in theories about consciousness and mind in first millennial India. These philosophers do not regard the first-person stance as in conflict with the natural—their idea of nature is not that of scientific naturalism, but rather a liberal naturalism non-exclusive of the normative.

Jonardon Ganeri explores a wide range of ideas about the self: reflexive self-representation, mental files, and quasi-subject analyses of subjective consciousness; the theory of emergence as transformation; embodiment and the idea of a bodily self; the centrality of the emotions to the unity of self. Buddhism's claim that there is no self too readily assumes an account of what a self must be. Ganeri argues instead that the self is a negotiation between self-presentation and normative avowal, a transaction grounded in unconscious mind. Immersion, participation, and coordination are jointly constitutive of self, the first-person stance at once lived, engaged, and underwritten. And all is in harmony with the idea of the natural.

Jonardon Ganeri is Professor of Philosophy within New York University's global network and Recurrent Visiting Professor of Philosophy at King's College London.

The Self

Naturalism, Consciousness, and the First-Person Stance

Jonardon Ganeri

OXFORD
UNIVERSITY PRESS

OXFORD
UNIVERSITY PRESS

Great Clarendon Street, Oxford, OX2 6DP,
United Kingdom

Oxford University Press is a department of the University of Oxford. It furthers the University's objective of excellence in research, scholarship, and education by publishing worldwide. Oxford is a registered trade mark of Oxford University Press in the UK and in certain other countries

© Jonardon Ganeri 2012

The moral rights of the author have been asserted

First published in 2012
First published in paperback 2015

All rights reserved. No part of this publication may be reproduced, stored in a retrieval system, or transmitted, in any form or by any means, without the prior permission in writing of Oxford University Press, or as expressly permitted by law, by licence or under terms agreed with the appropriate reprographics rights organization. Enquiries concerning reproduction outside the scope of the above should be sent to the Rights Department, Oxford University Press, at the address above

You must not circulate this book in any other form
and you must impose this same condition on any acquirer

Published in the United States of America by Oxford University Press
198 Madison Avenue, New York, NY 10016, United States of America

British Library Cataloguing in Publication Data
Data available

Library of Congress Cataloging in Publication Data
Data available

ISBN 978-0-19-965236-5 (Hbk.)
ISBN 978-0-19-870939-8 (Pbk.)

Links to third party websites are provided by Oxford in good faith and for information only. Oxford disclaims any resposibility for the materials contained in any third party website referenced in this work.

Acknowledgements

I would like to express my gratitude to the Arts and Humanities Research Council for the award of a Research Project Grant between 2008 and 2010, to the École des hautes études en sciences sociales for its invitation to be a Visiting Professor in May 2009, to Wolfson College Oxford, and to the University of Sussex. I would also like to thank Piotr Balcerowicz, Thomas Baldwin, Christopher Bartley, Ramkrishna Bhattacharya, David Chalmers, Christian Coseru, Georges Dreyfus, Eberhard Guhe, Julius Lipner, Chakravarthi Ram-Prasad, François Recanati, Peter Sahota, Manidipa Sen, Mark Siderits, Shalini Sinha, Richard Sorabji, Tom Tillemans, Jan Westerhoff, Dan Zahavi, and Francis Zimmermann. Chapters 3 and 4 are based on my article 'Emergentisms, Ancient and Modern', *Mind* (2011), 120.3: 671–703, and Chapter 15 on 'Cross-modality and the Self', *Philosophy and Phenomenological Research* 61 (2000), 639–58. An earlier version of Chapter 8 appears under the title 'Selfhood, Subjectivity, and the Use of the Word "I"' in Mark Siderits, Evan Thompson, and Dan Zahavi (eds.), *Self, No Self?* (Oxford University Press, 2010). I am grateful to the respective publishers. Finally, I am extremely grateful to Peter Momtchiloff, as well as to the other members of the OUP team, Sarah Parker, Eleanor Collins, Rowena Anketell, Daniel Bourner, and Bethan Lee.

"I have grown much too used to an outside view of myself, to being both painter and model, so no wonder my style is denied the blessed grace of spontaneity. Try as I may I do not succeed in getting back into my original envelope, let alone making myself comfortable in my old self."

—Vladimir Nabokov, *Despair*

"It's Borges, the other one, that things happen to ... I live, I allow myself to live, so that Borges can spin out his literature, and that literature is my justification ... Everything falls into oblivion, or into the hands of the other man. I am not sure which of us it is that's writing this."

—Jorge Luis Borges, "Borges and I"

Contents

Note on Diacritics and Pronunciation

I follow the International Alphabet of Sanskrit Transliteration (IAST) for the transliteration of Devanāgarī. Vowels are pronounced as in 'but' for a, 'father' for ā, 'fee' for ī, 'put' for u, 'boo' for ū, 'made' for e, 'bite' for ai, 'rope' for o, 'found' for au. The vowel ṛ is pronounced ri, as in 'pretty'. Consonants are pronounced as in 'chill' for c, 'try' for ṭ, the first t in the French *tout* for t, with aspiration indicated by an h as in 'ṭh', 'ch'; 'ship' for ś and ṣ, 'hiss' for s; jña is sometimes pronounced 'gya'. See Coulson (1976: 4–19) for details.

Key Philosophers Discussed

Dichaearchus (350-285 BCE). Pupil of Aristotle
Aristoxenus (fl. 335 BCE). Pupil of Aristotle

Kaṇāda (1st/2nd cent. CE). Author-compiler of the *Vaiśeṣika-sūtra*
Gautama Akṣapāda (2nd cent.). Author-compiler of the *Nyāya-sūtra*
Galen of Pergamon (129–216). Physician/Philosopher
Alexander of Aphrodisias (*c.*200). Aristotelian commentator
Plotinus (205–70). Founder of Neoplatonism
Porphyry (234–*c.*305). Pupil of Plotinus
Iamblichus (*c.*245–325). Syrian Neoplatonist

Asaṅga (4th cent.). Buddhist, Abhidharma /Yogācāra
Vasubandhu (*c.*316–96). Buddhist, Abhidharma/Yogācāra; Asaṅga's half-brother
Saṃghabhadra (4th cent.). Buddhist, Abhidharma; Vasubandhu's rival
Vātsyāyana (*c.*450). Nyāya commentator
Proclus (412–81). Neoplatonist

Dignāga (480–540). Buddhist, Yogācāra
Priscian (fl. 530). Neoplatonist who lives in Persia
Praśastapāda (*c.*530). Vaiśeṣika, reforms Kaṇāda's physics and metaphysics
Philoponus (490–*c.*570). Christian, critic of Arisotelian physics
Sthiramati (*c.*510–70). Buddhist, commentator on Vasubandhu
Uddyotakara (*c.*550). Nyāya

Dharmakīrti (600–60). Buddhist, Yogācāra/Sautrāntika. Dignāga's reinterpreter
Bṛhaspati (date unknown). Author-compiler of the *Cārvāka-sūtra*
Śaṅkara (*c.*710). Vedāntin
Kamalaśīla (*c.*740–95). Buddhist, Yogācāra/Sautrāntika/Mādhyamika
Bhaṭṭa Udbhaṭa (*c.*800). Independent, drawing on both Cārvāka and Nyāya
Jayanta (*c.*870). Nyāya
Vācaspati (*c.*960). Independent polymath, writing on Nyāya, Vedānta, etc.
Vyomaśiva (10th cent.). Vaiśeṣika
Śrīdhara (10th cent.). Vaiśeṣika
Bhaṭṭa Rāmakaṇṭha (*c.*950–1000). Śaiva
Udayana (10 cent.). Vaiśeṣika/Nyāya

Ibn Sīnā (980–1038). Islamic philosopher from Bukhara on the Silk Road; father from Balkh, ancient Buddhist Bactria

Prabhācandra (980–1065). Jaina

Ratnakīrti (11th cent.). Buddhist, Yogācāra

Raghunātha Śiromaṇi (*c.*1460–1540). First modern philosopher and inventor of the 'new reason', a radically reformed Nyāya-Vaiśeṣika (see Ganeri 2011)

Gadādhara Bhaṭṭācārya (*c.* 1604–1709), Navya-Nyāya

Jayarāma Nyāyapañcānana (fl. 1650s), Navya-Nyāya

Introduction

Perhaps the greatest mystery in philosophy is what it is to be a human being. Clearly we are animal creatures, with animal bodies and animal desires and appetites. Equally clearly we are beings with interiority, able to think of ourselves as ourselves, to occupy a first-person stance. Three influential depictions of our humanity have increasingly come to seem unworkable: the picture that we are immaterial souls associated with but separable from our animal bodies; the picture that we are nothing but especially complex networks of neural circuits; and the picture that we are simply causal flows of consciousness. Do the Indians, who thought long and hard about the question of what it is to be a human being, have any alternative advice? I believe so. I think that it is possible to derive from their discussion a powerful alternative answer to the question about our nature. The answer I will offer arises out of my reflection upon that discussion but is not the view of any single participant within it.

What is it to occupy a first-person stance? Is the first-personal idea one has of oneself in conflict with the idea of oneself as a physical being in the world? How, if there is a conflict, should it be resolved? This book aims to provide new ways of addressing these questions, drawing inspiration from theories about the self in first-millennium India. These philosophers do not regard the first-person stance as in conflict with the natural, their idea of the natural not that of scientific naturalism, but rather a liberal naturalism non-exclusive of the normative. A thought's being mine involves participation and involvement: it is a site of spontaneity.

It has nevertheless seemed to many that there is something suspect about the self. A self is that in virtue of which your thoughts are yours, and mine are mine. But, so it is said, the ownership of thought is not itself a natural relation, and only an analysis of subjectivity without selves can be naturalistically respectable, or else an analysis of ownership that makes it an attribute of the body. I believe that there is a deep residual influence of Descartes in this line of thought. It was Descartes the scientist who banished the self from the realm of nature; the doctrine of scientific naturalism threatens then to banish it altogether. Reclaiming the self is thus also a matter of reclaiming the idea of the natural.

It will, however, require much hard philosophical work before we are in a position to benefit from a discussion taking place in first-millennium India. Each of the principal naturalistic Indian philosophies of mind comes to us freighted with historical assumptions and packaged in extra-philosophical agendas. Thus Buddhist theory, which I will demonstrate includes an astonishingly rich and phenomenologically perceptive analysis of what is taken to be a universal human image of self, comes associated with an error-theory of first-person thought. Again, the naturalism of the Cārvāka, which developed in parallel with Buddhism but has received far less attention, presents a very penetrating and insightful third-person stance on our mental lives but combines it with an unacceptably impoverished understanding of the distinctiveness of first-person phenomena. Neither of these naturalist philosophies of mind, rich as they are, acknowledge the importance of unconscious processes or the emotions to the unity of self, and it is here that the third version of naturalism I will study, Nyāya-Vaiśeṣika, comes into its own. It will be in the work of this third group of thinkers that we find a full acknowledgement of the distinctive importance of the first-person stance within an entirely naturalistic and thoroughly non-Cartesian account of the mind. Once again we bring into view the philosophical vitality and significance of their picture of mind only when we disentangle it from a supra-philosophical conviction, this time one about the manner in which the self persists.

What will gradually emerge from this exercise in conceptual retrieval from historical sources are the materials for a *philosophical* explanation of the compatibility of naturalism with the existence of subjects of first-person phenomena. According to the theory about the self I shall eventually propose, the inhabitation of a first-person stance, the conscious presentation of oneself to oneself as a subject, and the unconscious ability internally to monitor and compare the contents of one's thought, sustain distinct elements in the notion of ownership. Three interrelated but mutually irreducible modalities of mineness—participation, immersion, and coordination—are jointly constitutive of a self: the self is a negotiation between self-presentation and normative avowal, a transaction grounded in unconscious mind. Selves are individuated by a relation of common ownership obtaining between clusters of acceptances, preferences, and intentions, delimited by normative emotional response and implying agency and sentience and so embodiment.

I now give an overview of the discussion. Part I, 'Naturalism and the Self', is methodological. Peter Strawson distinguishes two senses of the term 'naturalism', one of which he describes as strict or hard, the other liberal, the first grounding all explanation in the scientific, the second making an appeal to what is 'in our nature' as social human beings, that is to say, to whatever is 'a condition of our humanity'. In his promotion of liberal naturalism, John McDowell has recommended Aristotle and the medieval Aristotelian tradition—with its talk of second nature and of knowing and thinking as natural powers of human beings—as a corrective to too swift a deference to unenchanted nature. I agree that we are well advised to reflect again on more ancient conceptions of the natural, and one of the leading intuitions that will guide what follows is that an appeal to the naturalistic thought of first-millennium India is extremely promising. The reason for this is that, uninfluenced by Cartesianism, mindedness is not perceived as a relation in conflict with the idea of the natural. Rather than in second natural intentionality, however, spontaneity is located within the idea of ownership itself.

Indeed, I will show that the varieties of liberal naturalism in India are already responses to hard naturalistic ideas, and can therefore reasonably be drawn upon in a rejuvenated reaction now against too exclusive a commitment to scientific naturalism. I begin the book with a chapter simply charting the historical intellectual context, and one which in not describing and evaluating philosophical arguments is atypical of the book as a whole. In this Historical Prelude I identify a variety of forms of naturalistic thinking in ancient and first-millennium India, in particular Cārvāka Emergentism, early Buddhist trope dualism, and the minimal physicalism of Nyāya-Vaiśeṣika. It is from a stance grounded in liberal naturalism that the Buddha investigates the moral psychological properties of suffering and craving, which are to be understood within a manifestly normative framework of wrong belief and mistaken conception. The false move he identifies above all else is that of 'taking as one's own' (*upādāna*) particular states of mind, and in so doing fabricating an idea of self (*satkāya-dṛṣṭi*). This fundamental transition to a first-person stance is a move, for the Buddha invariably a bad one, in the space of reasons, the fabricated idea of self a mistake. Cārvāka thinkers argue that mental properties emerge when physical elements are organized in systems of appropriate complexity, just as the power to inebriate emerges in a mixture of yeast and barley. Their conception of a human being (*puruṣa*) is that of a physical body qualified by consciousness; it is the Strawsonian concept of a person, something to which both corporeal and psychological predicates are ascribed. The self in Nyāya and Vaiśeṣika, on the other hand, is best understood in terms of a unity of commitment, preference, emotion, and will, the unity of which is explained with reference to unconscious psychological mechanisms supervening on states of the physical body. What makes it a version of liberal naturalism is the account afforded of ownership: normative relations of endorsement and participation are constitutive of a thought's being 'mine', and so of the existence of a first-person stance.

In Chapter 1, I develop an analytical framework within which conceptions of self can be identified and classified. A conception about self supplies an answer to the question 'What am I?' Until very recently, virtually all western discussion about the self explored three conceptions: the Cartesian; the Humean or Reductionist; and the Materialist. These three are far from exhaustive, and indeed I identify eleven broad conceptions of self, grounding my classification in an orthogonal pair of distinctions: between adjectival and collective modes of exemplification, and between considerations about individuation and considerations about ownership. Thus, as well as the views just mentioned, Indian theory discusses what I will call Ownership, Pure Consciousness, and Phenomenal views, three types of (Buddhist) No Place view, the Tornado View and the Flame View. Within this taxonomy I situate several contemporary theories of self.

I then contrast two methodologies for thinking about the nature of self, neither of which I regard as fully satisfactory. The method of philosophical naturalism, which affirms a continuity between philosophy and natural science, leads to a conception of self as at best a reducible entity, reducible either simply to the body (Materialism) or else to an interconnected flow of mental particulars (the Humean view). Diametrically opposed to philosophical naturalism is an approach to the study of the self that rests on the use of imagination and intuition. Exercises of imagination lead to the discovery of a different kind of self, a self which consists essentially in thinking. The heart of the method is that if something can be imagined as separated from something else without being destroyed, then that other thing cannot be a part of its essence. This approach leads to broadly 'Cartesian' conceptions of self, and I will describe formulations of the *cogito* in the Islamic philosopher Ibn Sīnā and the Jaina Prabhācandra (both born in the year 980 CE). We learn from the Indian materialist Payāsi that any temptation to provide an explanation of the behaviour of the self by analogy with the behaviour of some physical entity or phenomenon is a trap, for such an attempt invariably ends up making the self sound like a mysterious crypto-physical being, a recherché denizen in the physical world.

The chapters of Part II, 'Mind and Body', have to do with embodiment, supervenience, bodily ownership, and physicalism. In Chapter 3, I distinguish between emergentist and epiphenomenalist strands in early Cārvāka theory, and I demonstrate that Cārvāka Emergentists are explicitly committed to supervenience. Emergentism seeks simultaneously to respect the idea that the mental is dependent on the physical and also to allow that it has causal autonomy with respect to it: these find expression in emergentism's commitment to a supervenience thesis and an irreducibility thesis. The leading idea in discussions about emergence is that systems of appropriate organizational complexity have causal powers which the components in the system, whether individually or together, do not. Jaegwon Kim has argued that the two key issues for the development of emergentism as a viable theory of mind are to give a positive characterization of the relation of emergence, beyond the mere denial of reducibility, and to solve the problem of downward causation, otherwise known as the exclusion problem. This is the problem that an instantiation of the supervenience base is apparently a sufficient cause for any effect attributed to an instantiation of the supervening properties. One seems forced to choose between reductionism (mental properties are 'nothing but' physical properties) and epiphenomenalism (mental properties are distinct from physical properties but the residue is inefficacious): genuinely novel emergent causal power is excluded.

From later Cārvāka discussion I derive in Chapter 4 a new theory of emergence. Emergence through 'transformation' (*pariṇāma*) is the idea that the emergence of mental states occurs only within a dynamical system, one whose physical states are in a constant process of flux produced by the fusion of elements and their microcausal powers. The microdynamic in this dynamical system jointly specifies the physical and mental state of the system at any given time, and does so only with reference to both the physical and the mental state of the system at earlier times. Because the domain is itself in a state of flux, the microdynamic will have variables taking mental property instantiations, physical property instantiations, and micro-entities as values. Supervenience functions simply as a constraining condition, one of the equations that define the system. This is a version of the Tornado View mentioned above. My claim is that the notion of transformation leads to a formulation of emergence in which the twin demands of dependence and autonomy are respected, and sense is given to the idea of downward causation. I find this solution especially in the work of Bhaṭṭa Udbhaṭa, whose theory I argue compares favourably with enactivist, realization, and fusion models of emergence.

I turn in Chapter 5 to the issue of the material constitution of the self and its identity over time. Animalism is the view that a person is identical with the human animal and not with either an immaterial soul or a psychological continuum. Jayanta, the ninth-century Nyāya philosopher, argues very tellingly against Animalism. His argument is that the manner of persistence involved in the preservation of first-person phenomena and other capacities constitutive of selfhood is not the same as that which characterizes the persistence of animal bodies. My aim is to show that the Animalism this argument targets is logically independent of the account of the emergence of the mental from the physical described in the last chapter, which therefore survives the critique unscathed.

A theory of self must do two things. It must tell us what kind of thing a self is: immaterial substance; suitably interconnected series of conscious experiences; the categorical basis of such a series; animal body; and so on (the question, 'What am I?'). But a theory of self must also give us materials to answer, within the specified kind, the question, 'Which one is me?' This question is often overlooked, but to neglect it is to court solipsism. The thought behind the difficulty I will call 'Attenuation' is that many theories of self fail precisely because their solutions to the first requirement imply that there is no answer to the second. In Chapter 6, I argue that avoiding Attenuation requires that selves are indeed essentially embodied: that, even if Animalism is false, one may well still want to maintain that selfhood requires embodiment; and perhaps more strongly, that selves are individuated according to bodily criteria, that an 'embodied mind' thesis is true. I distinguish that thought from another one, the idea that there is a 'core self' consisting in an invariant presence of bodily feeling.

There are two ways to account for the nature of the presented ownership constitutive of what I am calling 'immersion', the phenomenology of the first person.[1] One, just mentioned, sees it as fundamentally a relationship of bodily ownership: the theory of a core self as bodily feeling of presence to oneself is a bodily account of immersion. Other accounts develop an analysis out of a more detailed study of the intentional and phenomenal structure of self-consciousness and provide a subjective rather than a bodily account of immersion. I examine several remarkably rich and insightful analyses from Buddhist writers who propose subjective accounts of this sort. The chapters in Part III, 'Immersion and Subjectivity', are studies of Buddhist philosophy of mind in the work respectively of the early Vasubandhu, the later Vasubandhu, Dignāga, Dharmakīrti, and Ratnakīrti. I return to the relationship between first-person phenomena and embodiment only in Chapter 12. Although it is targeted primarily at Vedic and hard naturalistic ideas about self, in denying self the Buddhist aim is not merely to reject some given historical theory of self in the Indian discussion, but also to diagnose what they take to be a very deep but correctable error in our primitive conceptual scheme and in the phenomenology of self-awareness. It is incumbent upon them, therefore, to provide an accurate descriptive phenomenology of the first-personal, so as to be able to identify the error involved. One of the defining achievements of Buddhist theory consists in its demonstration that the unity of first-person phenomena is a compositional unity, and so that there can be unity without simplicity.

It is a key thesis of Buddhist philosophy of mind that there are proto-intentional psychological processes (*skandha*) through the joint operation of which intentional experience is constituted. The five psychologically primitive processes—embodied reacting, hedonic appraising, labelling or stereotyping, dispositional constructing, and conscious attending—belong

[1] On immersion, cf. Zahavi: 'The self is not something that stands opposed to the stream of consciousness, but is, rather, immersed in conscious life' (Zahavi 2005a: 125). Immersion, the presented mineness of experience, is synonymous with one of the meanings of the highly ambiguous term 'subjectivity'. Thompson defends a conception of the immersed self according to which 'the *I* picks out the stream from its own self-individuating phenomenal perspective' (Thompson 2011: 174).

individually to a level beneath that of intentionality. Proto-cognitive and proto-affective processes combine to constitute states of conscious intentional experience, experience which presents the world as one in which attention falls on objects which are perceptually registered as falling under schematic stereotypes, as organized in a hodological appraisal space of affordance and obstacle, in ways that shape the diachronic flow by readying for future experience. The great elegance and attraction of the theory, I argue in Chapter 7, lies in the fact that simultaneously it recognizes the irreducibility of the phenomenal character of experience, it admits the joint contribution of sensation and conceptualization in the constitution of experience, it acknowledges that experience is, as it were, saturated with affect, that appraisal is built into the fabric of experience, it maintains that every experience has, as a basic ingredient, a capacity or tendency to combine in various ways with various others, and it makes the attention intrinsic to experience.

In the next three chapters I identify three distinct Buddhist accounts of immersion, the place of first-person phenomena in the structure of self-consciousness: a mental files theory, a reflexive self-representational account, and a theory of quasi-subjects. I begin Chapter 8 by distinguishing between two concepts of self-consciousness. What is sometimes called a first-person perspective can consist of nothing more than a matter of having one's own mental life in view. What I am calling a first-person stance, in contrast, does require something more: it demands that one's mental life presents itself to one as 'mine', as owned by me. I develop an account, due to the later Vasubandhu, in which the phenomenal marking of experience with mineness (*kḷṣṭa-manas*) is based on drawing information from a mental file, the repository-consciousness (*ālaya-vijñāna*). Items in the repository do not themselves present with mineness, but comprise a sort of first-personal databank for the mind, information that can be drawn upon in the activity of bringing the states of the stream into self-conscious attention. The distinction between the mere occurrence of states with representational content and the availability of a first-person stance lies, according to this theory, in the way one's states access stored information about oneself, and in doing so 'root' the state in one's deep psychology. The phenomenal mineness of a mental state, the sense of ownership that comes with it, is strongly associated with its rootedness in deep strata of the psyche. I situate this theory in relation to contemporary work on the perspectival *de se*, the minimal self, and the idea of transient subjects, and show how it might explain the so-called 'immunity to error through misidentification' of first-person ascription. Vasubandhu also claims, however, that an error is involved in so thinking about one's thought as 'mine', and consequently in the use of the first person. I argue that this claim is logically independent of his constructive proposal.

I next discuss a development that took place in Buddhism in the sixth century, and subsequently had wide repercussions in the Indian discussion of self. Reflexivism is the thesis that self-consciousness consists in mental occurrences being reflexively conscious of themselves (*svasaṃvedana*). Dignāga's defence of reflexivism consists in part in a new 'two aspects' theory of representation, and in part in an argument that higher-order theories of self-consciousness are regressive. His argument is based on thinking about what is involved in the idea that one can have first-person access to the subjectivity of one's past mental life. With his theory that intentional content is comprised of both an object-aspect and a subject-aspect, Dignāga replaces the phenomenal mineness account of subjective immersion with a self-representational theory, in which a first-person perspective consists in turning the subject-aspect of one's thought into an object-aspect. The brilliance of Dignāga's argument consists in its demonstration that the possibility of having a first-person *perspective* on one's own mental past requires that a first-person *stance* consists in being reflexively self-aware. He is a presentist about first-person stances, their existence consisting in being reflexively self-aware in the present moment, and his argument is that this follows from our being nevertheless able to bring the subjectivity of our past thought into view.

Dharmakīrti, Dignāga's influential reinterpreter, expands the discussion with a sophisticated analysis of non-conceptual perceptual content. I argue in Chapter 10 that Dharmakīrti's account should be understood as a version of the so-called relational theory of sentience (as is also to be found in the work of Clark and Peacocke), and so, in particular, not as a sense-data theory. Dharmakīrti uses the theory to address the binding problem: how are flows of sensation bound into thought about robust objects with determinate identity conditions? The same question for him arises for self-consciousness: how are flows of reflexive self-awareness bound into I-thoughts, thought in which the self features as subject. The key insight is that reflexivity provides a principle by which to 'tie' together the subject-aspects of experiences in the content of self-conscious states.

This is an analogue for self-consciousness of the role performed by presented spatial location in solving the binding problem in perception, presented spatial location being what ties together the object-aspects in intentional experience.

Dharmakīrti argues nevertheless that binding generates only 'quasi-objects' and 'quasi-subjects', entities which lack full criteria of identity and for which the question 'Is this the same entity as before?' cannot be answered. Something goes wrong when a thought of the form 'I am happy' or 'I am in pain' occurs, that is, when there is a move up to first-person present-tense ascriptions of psychological states. What goes wrong is that such self-ascriptions imply that there is some determinate criterion for individuating flows of subjectivity when in fact there is none. Just as it is an illusion to think that one can keep track of waves in such a way as to give a determinate answer to the question 'Is this another wave or the same wave as before?', so the implication is that it is a mistake to think that when presented with a new occurrence of reflexive self-awareness there is any determined answer to the question 'Is this another, or is it me again?' Since the move up to genuine I-thought is precisely the move to forming a conception of oneself as oneself as a subject of consciousness, the fundamental Yogācāra Buddhist idea is that the claim that occupying a first-person stance requires I-thought involves an error.

The question that later Buddhist thinkers after Dignāga and Dharmakīrti will ask is an excellent one. An argument is formulated with great clarity that reflexivism cannot solve the *conceptual* problem of other minds, the problem of explaining how it is possible to form a conception of a mental life distinct from one's own or conceive that there can be a plurality of minds. Reflexivism, argues Ratnakīrti out of a suggestion made earlier by Jñānaśrīmitra, entails that there are no phenomenal or intentional boundaries between oneself and others within a stream of experience. I include in Chapter 11 a full translation of Ratnakīrti's closely argued text. The idea that reflexivism entails conceptual solipsism is confirmed by Kashmiri Śaiva philosophers, who appropriate Buddhist reflexivism but transform it into a constitutive theory of self: the self just is that which consists of reflexive self-representation. Abhinavagupta shows clearly that this view leads to solipsism, an implication he actually seems to welcome. These difficulties with reflexivist analyses of subjectivity constitute a partial vindication of the earlier phenomenal mineness theory. I will claim that, itself reformulated as a constitutive theory, it affords materials for a powerful analysis of the immersed self in terms of a compositional range of me/not-me constrasts.

My examination of Buddhist theory thereby concluded, I turn in Part IV, 'Participation and the First-Person Stance', to an analysis of the philosophy of mind in Nyāya and Vaiśeṣika thinkers. The leading idea in their work is that occupying a first-person stance has centrally to do with the bearing of reason of the whole of one's mental life. I discuss, first of all, Praśastapāda's five arguments against the thesis that mental states are properties of the body (and so against both materialism and property dualism). I call them the Unity, Spatial Parts, Persistence, Self-Knowledge, and Self-Reference arguments. The arguments are all attempts to give voice to a single thought: that the relationships of participation and endorsement that are implied by the idea of *owning* a mental state, and so of occupying a first-person stance, are fundamentally different in kind from any relation of physical exemplification. This phase in the argument is one of negative dialectic, its function to show that the apparent simplicity of the Cārvāka view, that mental properties are just properties of the physical body, comes at a high price when the debts of explanation it incurs are appreciated.

The hypothesis of two early Nyāya and Vaiśeṣika thinkers, Gautama and Kaṇāda, is that conscious states of mind nevertheless supervene on the body; more precisely, they supervene on the physical states of the body by virtue of an unconscious mechanism of comparison, selective attention, self-monitoring, information retrieval, and action-guidance. I claim in Chapter 13 that this metaphysical dependence discharges the requirement that the theory of mind be a 'minimal physicalism', and that it is compatible with freedom of will and autonomous agency. The procedural activity of the postulated unconscious mind constitutes a new aspect of the notion of ownership, one according to which a mental state is 'mine' only if its contents can be accessed and compared at the subpersonal level.[2] This mind (*manas*) is therefore properly describable as a self, a sort of 'underself'. Someone who is alienated from their commitments and desires, or, more extremely, who experiences them as alien insertions, is their owner only in a comparatively minimal sense. While their description of unconscious

[2] Distinct versions of such a subpersonal comparator mechanism are also postulated in Frith (1987, 1992); Campbell (1999); Spence (2001); Reisenzein (2009); and others.

procedure is excessively corpuscular, Nyāya-Vaiśeṣika philosophers are careful to recognize the importance of the idea of the unconscious mind.

Emotions have an indispensable place in the theory of self. According to a theory first advanced in detail by Kaṇāda's sixth-century reinterpreter, Praśastapāda, the core attributes of an emotion are an appraisal, an inclination to action, and a capacity to be felt. Pleasure, for example, is elicited by the appraisal of something as likeable or pleasant, is exhibited in an inclination to maintain a continuing relationship with the object, and is felt as agreeable or gratifying or favourable. Desire is elicited by the appraisal of something not at hand as potentially so, is exhibited in an inclination to create a relationship with it, and is felt as a 'calling out'. Emotions serve to indicate a relation of common ownership among the commitments, values, preferences, and intentions of a single subject. For a state to be owned is therefore precisely for it to engage the whole of one's being through its potential to make normative demands on any other owned state: this is part of what gives substance to the ideas of inhabitation, participation, and endorsement that attributions of ownership imply. Ownership entails embodiment because some of these demands can be satisfied only in action. The concept of ownership introduced in the analysis of emotion is different from that of phenomenologically immersed 'mineness' or unconscious procedural access. It is a normative concept of endorsement and sustains a third dimension of selfhood, the 'participant self'. It is the defining feature of a first-person stance that one occupies and endorses one's states of mind and is not merely a spectator of them, and so it is from this stance alone that the relationships definitive of liberal naturalism, the *pulls* of reasons and the *demands* for action, come into view.[3]

I substantiate the concept of a participant self in Chapters 15 and 16. The proposal is that items of mind exhibit rational demands only in the context of a subject. The best argument for there being subjects of consciousness is that if one's experience, intentions, preferences, and values are to bear

[3] Frankfurt's concept of identification provides a point of reference: 'The decision determines what the person really wants by making the desire on which he decides fully his own. To this extent the person, in making a decision by which he identifies with a desire, constitutes himself. The pertinent desire is no longer in any way external to him. It is not a desire that he "has" merely as a subject in whose history it happens to occur, as a person may "have" an involuntary spasm that happens to occur in the history of his body' (Frankfurt 1988: 170). Moran comments: 'As I understand it, in the activity of "identification" someone determines what shall be part of him as a person' (Moran 2002: 214). See also Velleman (2006).

rationally on one another they must stand in a relationship of common ownership and not merely one of common causation. Our philosophers develop this thought in two ways: through an argument first presented by Gautama at *Nyāya-sūtra* 3.1.1, that identity of content across sensory modalities requires a unitary subject; and through an argument first presented by Kaṇāda at *Vaiśeṣika-sūtra* 3.2.16, that the distinctness of distinct embodied mental lives implies there are distinct unitary subjects.

A unity argument infers the unity of the self from the possible integration of information from distinct sense-modalities and perhaps also memory. Several formulations are presented by Nyāya philosophers, some involving recognition, some binding, and some tracking. These are arguments only for unity: none of them sustains any conclusion about simplicity, immateriality, or eternality. I point out that although historically such additional conclusions were drawn, they are neither justified nor necessitated by the argument. Unity arguments are where the interrelatedness of the procedural, participant, and immersed selves is most fully expressed; or, to put it another way, where participation, immersion, and coordination find joint articulation in the idea of self. I will claim that the strongest version of the unity argument is one in which one considers what is required of someone who has the capacity to think of their perceptions in different modalities as perceptions of one and the same object. The conclusion of this argument is that it is necessary for self-consciousness and for the possession of a first-person stance that one conceives of oneself as an individual, and indeed as an individual who is dependent on a specific physical object, one's body. If a mistake is involved, it is not of the correctable sort, and so is not an 'error' in any normatively loaded sense of the term.

It follows from the Nyāya-Vaiśeṣika conception of self that there is a multiplicity of distinct individual selves. The account of how they are distinct distances the theory from any Cartesian conceptions of self, which are faced by the threat that in the limit 'there is absolutely nothing left to distinguish any Cartesian "I" from any other, and it is impossible to see any more what would be subtracted from the universe by the removal of *me*' (B. Williams 1973a: 42). Selves are individuated in terms of a common ownership relation obtaining between clusters of commitments, resolutions, and intentions, delimited by normative emotional response and implying agency and sentience and so embodiment. Historically it would be a decluttered version of the Nyāya-Vaiśeṣika view that would gain prominence in early modern India, perhaps because of the distinctive support it affords to an increasingly secular conception of autonomous agency. An early modern Nyāya thinker will recommend that once liberated the distinction between selves is dissolved, and he thereby preserves individuation by embodied mental life and rejects altogether an earlier doctrine of brute individual difference. This is to agree with a point I will make in Chapter 16, that any imagined state of discarnate existence is not the existence of a self, and does not represent the survival of any individual.

My thesis is that in a full account of human subjectivity three distinct dimensions in the concept of self are in play, corresponding to three elements in the notion of ownership, each having a naturalistically legitimate role in any viable conception of self. There is an *immersed self*, the aspect of first-person presentation in the content of consciousness, 'ownership' here referring to a phenomenologically given sense of mineness. There is a *participant self*, the inhabitation of a first-person stance, 'ownership' involving the relations of involvement, participation, and endorsement that sustain autonomy. Finally, there is an *underself*, the procedural monitoring of all the states, autonomous or alienated, that one embodies, 'ownership' now implying a relation of unconscious access to one's states of mind and their contents. Where my proposal differs from that of any classical author, Buddhist, Nyāya, or Cārvāka, is in attaching equal significance to immersion and participation, and indeed in seeing the interplay between them (mediated by and grounded in the underself) as constitutive of self.

Strawson is right, therefore, to say that 'our desires and preferences are not, in general, something we just note in ourselves as alien presences. To a large extent they *are* we' (P. F. Strawson 1992: 134). My desires and preferences are me because in accepting them I acknowledge their demands as my own, an acknowledgement that roots the desires and preferences in my whole being in such a way that any other state that is also me is subject to revision in the light of them, and vice versa. They are me because their conflict or congruence with other states of mine is what gives shape to my emotions as exhibited in inclinations to action and felt affect. They are me because in accepting them I make myself a participant in the commitments they incur, in the world as they represent it, both in its factual content and in the gerundival description of paths to be followed and goals to be shunned. They are me because I am aware of myself in them, an awareness that creates a range of me/not-me contrasts in such a way that the phenomenal presentation of the desire as my own consists in the call it makes on a body of information I have about myself, including my commitments, capabilities, and values. That is to say, they are me because my immersion in them consists in their rootedness in deep levels of my psyche, and not in the mere reflexivity of representation. They are me, in short, because I am engaged by them and alive to them. And this interplay between immersion and participation might require a Herculean effort of ratiocination were it not for the fact that my desires and preferences are also me because beneath the ground level of consciousness they are bound by subterranean roots to the rest of me, in unconscious procedures of comparison, monitoring, and feedback. So no effort is required, and no coercion: my desires and preferences are me because in respect of them, there is autonomy.

This book argues that the self is a negotiation between presented mineness and normative avowal, a transaction grounded in unconscious monitoring. Immersion, participation, and coordination are jointly constitutive of self, the first-person stance at once lived, engaged, and underwritten. And all is in harmony with the idea of the natural.

PART I

Naturalism and the Self

Historical Prelude: Varieties of Naturalism

Naturalism: Raw and Rich

An eschewal of the supernatural and a conviction that the methods of philosophy are continuous with those of the empirical sciences are the defining traits of naturalism.[1] While naturalism so defined is a term of wide scope, it has been particularly with Quine that philosophy has become increasing preoccupied with projects of 'naturalization', whose aim is to explain recalcitrant phenomena in an approved naturalistic vocabulary.[2] There have always been naturalists, but philosophers have also often thought of themselves as able to make use of *a priori* methods distinct from those of empirical investigation, and to appeal to 'intuition' as a way to test philosophical hypotheses (see Chapter 2). Philosophy has been thought of as a discipline prior to, or at least orthogonal to, science.[3] The most attractive strategy of naturalist explanation has been reductionist, according to which the phenomenon in question is shown to admit some form of reduction to the natural, and in particular to whatever is certified by an ideal science.

The conviction that such a project is feasible might be called 'the scientific turn' in philosophy. The great difficulty in establishing actual reductions, or even in demonstrating that a reduction is in principle possible, has caused those who have espoused it to move in one of several directions. One movement, clearly compatible with the scientific turn, is towards fictionalism whenever a reduction seems unavailable, leading to

[1] Papineau (1993; 2009: 1).

[2] Quine (1969).

[3] For a clear statement, Husserl (1984: 410; trans. Zahavi 2004: 337): 'Thus the "phenomenological reduction" is simply the requirement always to abide by the sense of the proper investigation, and not to confuse epistemology with a natural scientific (objectivist) investigation.'

a philosophical view that whatever is not already transparently natural is reducible to what is, and that whatever is not so reducible is a fiction, albeit a fiction with a utility which can itself be explained. There are now fictionalist accounts of mind, of morality, and even of mathematics.[4] An ameliorated version of the response recommends instead a weakening of what the naturalization project is taken to involve. Specifically, the claim is that it demands only that one can demonstrate there is 'supervenience' of the target phenomenon on natural science.[5] David Lewis sums up the aspiration thus:

> A supervenience thesis is, in a broad sense, reductionist. But it is a stripped-down form of reductionism, unencumbered by dubious denials of existence, claims of ontological priority, or claims of translatability. One might wish to say that in some sense the beauty of statues is nothing over and above the shape and size and colour that beholders appreciate, but without denying that there is such a thing as beauty, without claiming that beauty exists only in a less-than-fundamental way, and without undertaking to paraphrase ascriptions of beauty in terms of shape etc. A supervenience thesis seems to capture what the cautious reductionist wishes to say. (Lewis 1998: 29)

It has become clear, however, that supervenience does not itself constitute an explanatory relationship, and the requirement that supervening properties be naturalized therefore exerts a pressure to supplement a supervenience thesis with a further explanation of the metaphysical dependences that underpin it.[6]

A different movement altogether is to reach for a conception of naturalism that does not over-privilege the natural sciences. Peter Strawson distinguishes two senses of the term 'naturalism', one of which he describes as strict or hard, the other liberal,[7] the first grounding all explanation in the scientific, the second making an appeal to what is 'in our nature' as social human beings, that is to say, whatever is 'a condition of our humanity'

[4] e.g., Dennett (1992); Metzinger (2003); Nolan, Restall, and West (2005); Field (1989); Yablo (1998).

[5] So Heil (1992: 4–5): 'Naturalism in the philosophy of mind is the view that mental characteristics are determined by or supervene on features of agents comprehended by the natural sciences.'

[6] See Kim (1993, 1999, 2005).

[7] 'The term "naturalism" is elastic in its use . . . I shall myself draw a distinction between two main varieties, within which there are subvarieties. Of the two main varieties, one might be called *strict* or *reductive* naturalism (or, perhaps, *hard* naturalism). The other might be called *catholic* or *liberal* naturalism (or, perhaps, *soft* naturalism)' (Strawson 1985: 1). See also De Caro (2010).

(1985: 33). This movement regards the lesson to be learnt as being that the success of physics and other natural sciences has brought in its wake a philosophical programme of naturalization from too dogmatic an attachment to which we should now retreat. What we should retreat to, however, is not any form of supernaturalism, but rather to a more nuanced understanding of naturalism itself. John McDowell (McDowell 2004) has framed the discussion, with vocabulary borrowed from Sellars and ultimately from Kant, in terms of the distinction between a space of reasons and a realm of law, the one being the logical space 'of justifying and being able to justify what one says' (Sellars 1956: 298–9), the other being the dominion of an ideal physics and its explanatory framework. What is needed, he too argues, is a conception of the natural in which properly to locate a description of our humanity. McDowell has recommended Aristotle and the medieval Aristotelian tradition, with its talk of 'second nature' and of knowing and thinking as 'natural powers' of human beings.[8] He has expressed this view with particular clarity in some of his more recent writings:

> To avoid conceiving thinking and knowing as supernatural, we should stress that thinking and knowing are aspects of our lives. The concept of a life is the concept of the career of a living thing, and hence obviously the concept of something natural. But there are aspects of our lives whose description requires concepts that function in the space of reasons. We are rational animals. Our lives are patterned in ways that are recognizable only in an inquiry framed within the space of reasons. On these lines, we can see thinking and knowing as belonging to our mode of living, even though we conceive them as phenomena that can come into view only within a sui *generis* space of reasons. Thinking and knowing are part of our way of being animals. Thus the fact that we are knowers and thinkers does not reveal us as strangely bifurcated, with a foothold in the animal kingdom—surely part of nature—and a mysterious separate involvement in an extranatural realm of rational connections. (McDowell 2004: 95)

Later in the same essay, he elaborates the idea that a life is patterned by thinking and knowing: 'We do not in any way denigrate the reality of the

[8] Compare Halbig (2008: 72): 'The idea of a second nature as the basis for a relaxed naturalism has a fair claim on being the master idea not only of McDowell's richly suggestive *Mind and World* but also of his papers on subjects as diverse as metaethics, epistemology, philosophy of language and the theory of value.' See also Gubeljic et al. (2000). McDowell himself sees the appeal rather as dialectical therapy for a too deeply entrenched scientistic naturalism, and does not consider himself under an obligation to provide a constructive philosophy of nature.

mental if we say that the word "mind" labels a collection of capacities and propensities possessed by a minded being' (McDowell 2004: 104). The thought, then, is that there are capacities and propensities which can be recognized only in terms appropriate to the space of reasons, but which are nevertheless the capacities and propensities of living animal beings. In these two quoted passages, McDowell clearly is at pains to distance that thought from a fictionalist, a reductionist, or a supernaturalist philosophy of mind. A naturalistic theory of mind must show how properties or modalities whose recognition is the work of an inquiry framed within the space of reasons are also properties or modalities relevant to living animal beings. Concerning his use of labels like 'Greek naturalism', 'liberal naturalism', and 'relaxed naturalism', McDowell says:

> [T]he point of the labels is captured by this thought: by dint of exploiting, in an utterly intuitive way, ideas like that of the patterns characteristic of the life of animals of a certain kind, we can insist that such phenomena, even though they are beyond the reach of natural-scientific understanding, are perfectly real, without thereby relegating them to the sphere of the occult or supernatural. We can accept that a distinctively human life is characterised by a freedom that exempts its distinctive phenomena from natural-scientific intelligibility, without thereby being required to push it back into the region of darkness, the region supposedly occupied by phenomena that resist the light cast by natural science because they are occult or supernatural... What 'natural' means, as the root of 'naturalism' in, say, 'relaxed naturalism' as I use that phrase, is: not supernatural (not occult, not magical, ...). (McDowell 2008: 217–18)

The problem that has taxed the ingenuity of philosophers working with a hard naturalistic attitude has been the problem of mental causation. Specifically, if the mind is not merely an epiphenomenon, a causally inert by-product of the physical being, then it must have an involvement in the realm of law in virtue of being realized by, or at least supervening on, physical properties. The trouble is that the mind then seems not to have any distinctive causal work to do, all the causal work being already done by the physical realizers.[9] On pain of wholescale causal overdetermination, the

[9] The notorious 'exclusion' argument. Yablo (1992: 247–8): '(1) If an event x is causally sufficient for an event y, then no event $x^\star$ distinct from x is causally relevant to y (*exclusion*). (2) For every physical event y, some physical event x is causally sufficient for y (*physical determinism*). (3) For every physical event x and mental event $x^\star$, x is distinct from $x^\star$ (*dualism*). (4) So: for every physical event y,

attempt to avoid epiphenomenalism undermines itself. It has been suggested that a solution is to regard mental properties as irreducibly emergent properties of complex physical systems. Indeed, Aristotle's own theory of mind looks, on some readings, like an emergentist response to the epiphenomenalism of the earlier *harmonia* theory.[10] I will say much more about this in Chapters 3 and 4.

The question for a relaxed or liberal naturalism, then, is how an appreciation of the fundamental idea that a recognition of the mental is to be done 'only in an inquiry framed within the space of reasons' relates to the difficulty that any claim of dependence by the mental on the physical threatens the mind with causal irrelevance. McDowell implies that it is enough that we speak of the mind as a mode of a physical animal, but refrains from any definite account of the nature of these modes of being or ways of living. This reintroduction of scholastic Aristotelian terminology, the references to second natures and natural powers, is suggestive but remains obscure. I agree with McDowell that we need to retrace our steps and consider again more ancient conceptions. One of the leading intuitions which will guide what follows is that an appeal to the naturalistic Indian traditions is extremely promising here. Indeed, I will show that the varieties of liberal naturalism in India are already responses to hard naturalistic ideas, and can therefore reasonably be drawn upon in a rejuvenated reaction, now against modern versions of scientific naturalism. And conversely, attending to Indian theories about the self may be cathartic in revealing residual and largely unarticulated commitments to fundamentally Cartesian ways of conceiving the self in contemporary discussion, operative in the background as much of those who deny selves as those who endorse them.

True to his wide and hospitable outlook, Peter Strawson is happy to speak of two naturalist 'standpoints', and he tries, wherever possible, to accommodate the significance and validity of both hard/scientific and liberal/relaxed naturalism. I prefer for this reason to characterize the distinction as holding between raw and rich naturalisms, in a deliberate echo but without the evaluative overtone of the Indian terms *paramārtha* and

no mental event $x^{\star}$ is causally relevant to y (*epiphenomenalism*).' See Kim (1998, 2005) for supervenience formulations.

[10] Caston (1997, 2002).

saṃvṛti.[11] Scientific naturalism looks at nature in the raw, liberal naturalism sees nature richly attired in reason, norm, and value. Indian theory embraces a plurality of naturalisms, both raw and robed, about mind, life, and self.

Two Varieties of Hard Naturalism

The naturalist attitude is one of resistance to ontological or methodological proliferation. One dimension of this resistance is the rejection of anything supernatural, and the assumption of a naturalist attitude will therefore have different implications depending on what sort of supernaturalist is in the frame. A traditional conception of the supernatural has it that supernaturalism is 'the invocation of an agent or force that somehow stands outside the familiar natural world and whose doings cannot be understood as part of it' (Stroud 2004: 23), or again, more broadly, as implying the existence of 'entities that lie outside the normal course of nature' (Dupré 2004: 36). This is meant to include such things as spirits, angels, devils, ghosts, entelechies, and divine agencies. Scientific naturalism, by contrast, takes the supernatural to include anything not mentioned by or reducible to a complete fundamental physics. The ontology of such a physics may well include things that are immaterial and spatially non-locatable, but will exclude the intentional (meaning, reference, thought), the evaluative (moral and aesthetic properties, for example), the abstract (mathematical objects), and the secondary (colours, smells, tastes, sounds, and feels). There has clearly been a fundamental shift here, from an attitude in which naturalism's aim is to remove from view mysterious agencies whose presence cannot be detected and whose influence is unpredictable to a conviction that *all* the ordinary beliefs which comprise what Sellars called 'the manifest image' (Sellars 1956) are in some sense suspect or second-grade. This is, perhaps, a further indication that naturalism's guiding instincts have been usurped in its restricted form.

In India, naturalism began as a response to a different understanding of the supernatural. This was the view that the cosmos has *both* a ritual and a

[11] The so-called two 'truths', which are rather two sorts of objectivity: see Ganeri (2007: 57–60, 121–2, 126–32, 169–75). The evaluative overtone from which I want to distance myself comes in with the translation of the terms as 'ultimate' and merely 'conventional', with the implication that what is 'in our nature' as human beings can be seen from some transcendental perspective to be an error.

physical causal order. Ritual laws, according to this view, are causal laws which are independent of the laws of nature, exemplifying instead a non-natural nomology (*ṛta, apūrva, adṛṣṭa*). There is no necessity that they refer to any *agencies* outside the familiar natural world, though no exclusion of that possibility either. The characteristic of ritual law is to describe resemblance-mediated connections between small-scale and large-scale phenomena, between the microcosm and the macrocosm (Smith 1989). Ritual laws are also value-laden, in at least the following sense: someone who performs a ritual correctly, setting up a small-scale process in proper isomorphism with an intended large-scale effect, will benefit in a law-like fashion accordingly, that some good will come of their performance. Thus, in the time-honoured example, ritual law consists in formulae such as this one: 'One who performs the fire-ritual (*agnihotra*) will go to heaven (*svarga*).' The idea of ritual law is of causal law outside of the realm of natural law.[12]

Human lives differ in the degree to which they exemplify the parameters of well-being and quality of life, 'happiness' (*sukha*) and 'distress' (*duḥkha*).[13] The ambition of the Indian naturalist to provide an account of this dimension of variation among individual human lives which does not aver to the supernatural influence of ritual law, retributive forces, or divine agencies, an account which is fashioned instead on relevantly analogous phenomena in the rest of the natural world.[14] One important concept for hard versions of Indian naturalism is that of an 'individual nature' (*svabhāva*):[15]

[12] It is the endorsement of this idea by Mīmāṃsā which disqualifies it as naturalism. Other non-naturalist Indian theories canvas more straightforward advocacy of supernatural entities: the *brahman* of Vedānta, the *puruṣa* of Sāṃkhya, the *kevala* of Jainism. It is perhaps important to emphasize here, at the outset of our study, that the anti-naturalisms of Madhyamaka and Advaita Vedānta did not have the centrality or influence in Indian history of philosophy that Tibetan historiography, and 19th-cent. German Indology and Indian nationalism, would later respectively accord them. Contrary to a common misperception, much Indian theory falls within a broadly naturalist programme.

[13] I will provide a detailed analysis of these states in Ch. 14.

[14] Thus, the naturalism of the *Svasaṃvad Upaniṣad*, as summarized in the *Sāṃkhya-sūtra*: 'There is no incarnation, no God, no heaven, no hell; all traditional religious literature is the work of conceited fools. Nature, which is the originator, and time, the destroyer, are the rulers of things and take no account of virtue or vice in awarding happiness or misery to man' (cited in Riepe 1961: 26).

[15] Several writers propose *svabhāva-vāda* as a Sanskrit equivalent for the term 'naturalism' (Riepe 1961; Kulkarni 1968). My own use of the term 'naturalism', however, will encompass other varieties. The term *svabhāva* carries other meanings in addition to 'individual nature', including especially that of 'intrinsic property'. Madhyamaka Buddhism, beginning with Nāgārjuna, rejects *svabhāva* in both senses (Westerhoff 2009).

What fashions the sharpness of the thorns and the varied nature of beasts and birds? What fashions the sugarcane sweet and the margosa bitter? All this takes place as a result of individual nature.[16]

The fire is hot, the water cold, refreshing and cool the breeze of morn; by what came all this variety? From individual nature was it born.[17]

As well as explaining differences between different kinds of thing, the concept is also meant to explain differences between particulars within a kind, such as the ones found in the patterns of the tail-feathers on a peacock, or the various thorns on a single tree:

Of the many thorns of a jujube tree, one is sharp, another is straight, yet another is crooked; but its fruit is round. Say, who has made all this?[18]

What is the cause of the shape, the colour, the arrangement, the softness and so on of the stalks, the petals, the filaments and the pericarps of the lotuses? Who diversifies the feathers of the birds in this world? In just the same manner this whole universe is the product of the work of individual nature, to be sure.[19]

This further claim takes the idea of the nature of a thing beyond that of the natural kind to which it belongs. It is now an alternative mode of explanation of *individual* variations. The idea is that we should explain why *this* thorn is sharp but *that* one straight by referring to their distinct individual natures.[20] On some occasions the concept is made to extend to variations in psychological properties:

Just as a thorn is sometimes sharp, so too, without further reason (*ahetutā*), is pain.[21]

A hard naturalism which is grounded in the idea of individual nature exists along with another Indian variety of hard naturalism, one which rests upon the idea of there being a deterministic causal closure of the physical world (*niyati*). The main aim of this Ājīvika[22] naturalism is to demonstrate

[16] Anon. fragment, often quoted (fr. 6a; R. Bhattacharya 2002c: 77).

[17] Anon. fragment, often quoted (fr. 8; R. Bhattacharya 2002c: 78).

[18] Anon. fragment, quoted by Haribhadra, Guṇaratna (fr. 7; R. Bhattacharya 2002c: 78).

[19] Anon. fragment, quoted by Āryasūra (fr. 9; R. Bhattacharya 2002c: 77).

[20] This is also how the notion of *svabhāva* is used in the Āyurvedic texts like the *Caraka-saṃhitā* — with reference to the medicinal properties of particular mixtures of chemical ingredients.

[21] Anon. fragment, quoted by Hemacandra, Śāntarakṣita (fr. 17; R. Bhattacharya 2002c: 80). For further associations in the *Mahābhārata*, see R. Bhattacharya (1999a).

[22] Basham (1951); Hoernle (1956–60); Kaviraja (1990); Riepe (1961: 33–51). Hoernle suggests that the term 'ājīvika' originally signified something like a philosophical 'professional'.

that moral properties are epiphenomenal: there are, specifically, no causal laws in the form of regularities between good or bad conduct and the distribution of happiness and suffering. So-called laws of *karma* are precisely causal laws of this sort:

In this world, grief does not arise for a man even though he delights in evil courses, while for another person who does good, it does.[23]

The argument for this claim proceeds from the premise that the physical world is causally closed:

Whatever happens at any time, anywhere, is to be conceived as happening in the form of *niyati* only. Otherwise there would be no definite sequence of causes and effects or a fixed pattern of anything, owing to the absence of a regulating law (*niyāmaka*).[24]

This use of an argument from causal closure earned Ājīvika the nickname 'causalism' (*kāraṇa-vāda*). The principle seems to be that everything supervenes globally on the total physical state of the world. There can be no alterations, and a forteriori no alterations in the distribution of pleasure, pain, and the other parameters of human well-being, without some alteration in the total state of the physical world. *Niyati*, it has been said, is an 'all-embracing metaphysical principle . . . [such that] causal processes could not be conceived in isolation from the entire system' (Jayatilleke 1963: 149).

The association of naturalism with determinism is not obviously incompatible with its simultaneous association with an idea of individual nature. Indeed, the ancient sources sometimes present the doctrine of individual nature too as implying a denial of free will.[25] It was a contemporary of the Buddha, Gośāla, who first proposed Ājīvika naturalism. Another contemporary of the Buddha, Ajita Keśakambalin, developed still a different version of hard naturalism: he denies that pleasure and pain exist at all. That is to say, he is an eliminativist rather than an epiphenomenalist.[26]

[23] Anon. fragment, quoted by Śīlāṅka (source: Jayatilleke 1963: 147).

[24] Anon. fragment, quoted by Guṇaratna (source: Jayatilleke 1963: 146).

[25] 'All this takes place through individual nature. There is no scope for action according to one's wishes. What is the use of efforts of will (*prayatna*)?' Anon. fragment, quoted by Haribhadra, Guṇaratna, and others (fr. 6; R. Bhattacharya 2002c: 76). Cf. frs. 2, 3, 12, 19. Strictly speaking, this is a fatalist consequence of determinism.

[26] 'There is no almsgiving, sacrifice, or oblation. A good or bad action produces no result. This world does not exist, nor does the other world' (*Dīgha* i. 57; Walshe 1995: 96). R. Bhattacharya (1999b) has

That we are in the territory of a theory of human nature and of the self is visible from a text which is actually our oldest mention of the hard naturalistic ideas I have been reviewing:

Governed by what do we live in pleasure and pain, each in our respective situation? Should we regard it as time, as individual nature (*svabhāva*), as causal determinism (*niyati*), as chance (*yadṛcchā*), as the elemental reals (*bhūta*), as the source of birth (*yoni*), or as the person (*puruṣa*)? Or is it a combination of these? Perhaps it is not [any of these], because there is the self (*ātman*). Even the self is not in control, because it would itself be the basis (*hetu*) of pleasure and pain.[27]

Individual differences in the quality of human life supervene upon facts about the physical elements, or biological facts, or psychological facts, or some combination; and are either deterministically fixed by causal history, or subject to chance; and are regulated by Time, or by individual nature. The first of these claims is a version of physicalism, the second a biological or ecological naturalism. In the third, the autonomy of the mental is respected, and the distribution of pleasure and pain held to supervene on facts about individuals' psychology, or on a combination of psychological, biological and physical facts. The remaining claims are causal closure hypotheses: that the distribution of pleasure and pain is completely causally determined by past history, or that its causal history involves chance and indeterministic causal relations (including as a special case the extreme claim that all is chance).[28]

We have here physicalist, animalist, and reductionist theories of self. One late pre-modern author, Guṇaratna, ties the discussion explicitly to a question about the metaphysics of self, identifying six views about the self, among which are explicitly identified doctrines of causal determinism and individual nature.[29]

A methodological naturalism is evident in these discussions. Observations about the working of the natural world lead to the construction of parallel

convincingly demonstrated that the phrase 'this world does not exist' is to be taken to mean that happiness does not exist in this world. See also Jayatilleke (1963: 98–9).

27 *Śvetāśvatara Upaniṣad* 1cd–2 (trans. Olivelle 1998: 415, slightly revised).

28 Fink (2008: 61–4) draws attention to comparable ideas in Plato (*Laws* 888e–892c).

29 Guṇaratna (1969: 14–24; trans. 1990: 293–8).

explanations about the functioning of mind and morality, in a more or less seamless fashion. There is a continuity between the methods by which the natural world is investigated and understood and the methods of philosophy. It is a restricted or hard naturalism, in which individual nature (*sva-bhāva*) replaces individual ritual duty (*sva-dharma*) in the explanation of human nature, value, and action.

Three Varieties of Liberal Naturalism

Underlying the Vedic conception of ritual law is the idea that it subsumes *all* moral law. The Vedic conception effectively substitutes the Sellarsian distinction with a different one—between a realm of ritual law and a realm of natural law. One naturalist response, as we have just seen, is to take the rejection of ritual law to be equivalent to an embrace of hard determinism.

A different idea is available in the work of philosophers whose ideas came to be known as Cārvāka and, alternatively, as Lokāyata. They are described as followers of a certain Bṛhaspati.[30] These thinkers argue that mental properties emerge when physical elements are organized in systems of appropriate complexity, just as the power to inebriate emerges in a mixture of yeast and barley:

> Earth, fire, air, and water are the elementary reals (*bhūta*).
> Their combination is called the 'body', 'senses', and 'objects'.
> Consciousness (is formed) out of these [elementary reals].
> As the power to intoxicate (is formed) out of fermenting ingredients.[31]

This is intended to accompany and subserve a rejection of Vedic ritual law, and of everything supernatural:

[30] Haribhadra says that the philosophy 'was manufactured by Bṛhaspati in order to deceive Indra' (Haribhadra I. 110; cf. R. Bhattacharya 2001: 51), implying that he is a mythical figure. Al-Bīrūnī, on the other hand, is happy to consider him as the author of the *Cārvāka-sūtra*.

[31] *Cārvāka-sūtra* I.2–5. The known fragments of Bṛhaspati's lost *Cārvāka-sūtra* are collected and provisionally sequenced in R. Bhattacharya (2002a). Bronkhorst (2008: 297) considers that, as late as 800 CE, Cārvāka 'still constituted a living tradition which had not yet disappeared'. Several Cārvāka philosophers have now been identified by name: Payāsi, Javāli, Bṛhaspati, Kamalāśvatara, Purandara, Aviddhakarṇa, Bhāvivikta, Udbhaṭa.

There is no after world because of the absence of any other-worldly being
Due to the insubstantiality of consciousness in the after world.
Religious acts are not to be performed.
Its instructions are not to be relied on.[32]

Observations about natural emergence in the causal powers of chemical mixtures lead Cārvāka thinkers to a position that hopes to save naturalism from epiphenomenalism. Cārvāka naturalism is incompatible with the doctrine of individual natures, if individual nature is conceived of as distinct from and additional to the material elements.[33] What is important is the possibility that, although having emerged from the material, mental properties are not merely reducible to it. Pleasure and pain are also emergent properties from matter.[34] Although their opponents take their atheism and anti-supernaturalism to imply that they must be either immoral hedonists or altogether amoral, Cārvāka naturalists are also represented, more sympathetically, as recommending autonomy and justice not founded on religious conviction.[35] What makes the Cārvāka view a liberal rather than a hard naturalism is, as I will show in detail in Chapters 3 and 4, that the supervenience of the mental (including, in particular, the first-personal) on the physical does not sustain a reduction, so that a full inventory of reality must

[32] *Cārvāka-sūtra* 4.3–5.2. Tucci (1929: 686) (summarized in Riepe 1961: 58) identifies twelve key Cārvāka principles, his list including the rejection of God, of the soul, of sacred scripture, of *karma*, of post-mortem existence, and of the efficacy of ritual.

[33] For clear evidence that two doctrines encode quite distinct varieties of Indian naturalism, see R. Bhattacharya (2001). See also Kaviraja (1990).

[34] I suggest that prior to the *Cārvāka-sūtra*, Cārvāka doctrine consisted in the identification of self with body; afterwards, in the emergence of the mental from the physical with or without such an identification. Udbhaṭa, described by Cakradhara as 'roguish' (*dhūrta*) but also as 'well-educated' (*suśikṣita*) (Cakradhara 1982–4: i. 100, 52), later introduced what would now be termed 'downwards causation', saying that the mental is *for*, and not just *from*, its emergence base. The development of Cārvāka might be thought to have these phases: 1) self is identical to body (Payāsi); 2) self is an emergent aspect from body (Bṛhaspati); 3) self is that in virtue of which emergent mental aspects are unified (Udbhaṭa). The transition from the first to the second phase responds to a Persistence Argument (see Ch. 5), and from the second to the third is responsive to the Unity Argument (Chs. 5, 12, 15). I discuss the emergence theory in Chs. 3 and 4.

[35] Cārvāka might have had an affiliation with political theory and statescraft (*arthaśāstra*). So Abū-l-Fażl: They regard paradise as a state in which man lives as he chooses, free from the control of another, and hell the state in which he lives subject to another's rule . . . They admit only of such disciplines as tend to the promotion of external order, that is, a knowledge of just administration and benevolent government' (al-Faḍl 1873–1907: iii. 217). See R. Bhattacharya (1997). Bongard-Levin (1978) argues that the mathematical astronomer Āryabhaṭa (b. 476), one of the 'nine jewels' in the court of Candragupta, was sympathetic to Cārvāka four-element theory and empiricist methodology. Affinities exist between the Cārvāka and the Hellenistic school of Empirics.

include both the supervenience base and all that is emergent, irreducibly supervenient, upon it.[36]

A second variety of liberal naturalism is associated with still another ascetic of the time, Gautama, later to become known as the Buddha. The Buddha comes very close to acknowledging that there is a space of reasons distinct from the realm of ritual law. It is from a stance grounded in the space of reasons that he investigates the moral psychological properties of suffering (*duḥkha*) and craving (*tṛṣṇā*), which are to be understood within a manifestly normative framework of wrong belief and mistaken conception (*avijñāna*). These unhealthy ways of being are symptomatic of false moves in the course of a life led well. The false move he identifies, above all else, is that of 'taking as one's own' (*upādāna*) what is not, in particular states of pleasure and pain, and in so doing fabricating a false idea of self (*satkāya-dṛṣṭi*). A human life is now thought of in the following way. There are five interwoven sequences of processes, one of which is directly physical, passive sensory reacting (*rūpa*), and the other four more distinctively psychological: affective appraising (*vedanā*), labelling (*saṃjñā*), dispositional readying (*saṃskāra*), and conscious attending (*vijñāna*).[37] The picture is strongly anti-substantialist; for example, the body is described as resembling a mass of foam, and affect as being like a bubble. The flow of mental processes is said to be patterned according to a twelve-step chain beginning with misconceptions and ending with suffering. One thinks mistakenly that something would be good, imagines it, thinks of oneself as doing or having it. One then experiences it and finds it pleasant, one starts to need it for oneself, is driven by wanting it, and when one does not have it, one suffers.

In this description of an interwoven psychological process, concepts have been used whose function is to provide or reject justifications. Presented with reasons, one forms a conception of oneself as possibly benefited by something: this is a fundamental transition into a value-laden first-person

[36] Compare Baker (2011). Baker there characterizes naturalism as 'the ontological view that science can provide a supervenience base that accounts for all reality' (2011: 161), and finds in it no materials for a reconciliation with the first-person perspective. She then notes the possibility of a view, which she calls 'supervenient evolutionary emergentism', in which emergents are not reducible to the supervenience base, and comments that 'a full account of reality would include the original subvenient base together with the emergent items' (2011: 167 n. 2). In Baker (1998) she is willing to classify views of this sort as a variety of naturalism, albeit a 'weak naturalism' as opposed to the strict scientific naturalism that is the target of her more recent paper.

[37] I will interpret this picture of a human life in Ch. 7.

perspective.[38] It is a move, for the Buddha invariably a bad one, in the space of reasons, formulated in an idiom that is causal but does not preclude seeing the transition as involving reason-giving and justification.[39] The final step too is described as a transition to a condition of suffering, a value-laden way of making reference to a psychological event. It is thus only using terms whose sense is evaluation-laden that the reference to elements in a causal chain is made. There is no way to describe the causal chains constitutive of the flow of a life in a vocabulary wholly grounded in the realm of natural-scientific law. A certain mental event is picked out with the phrase 'suffering' or 'distress' (*duḥkha*), and it would be of little relevance to be told to which neurophysiological happening, if any, it is token-identical. What is relevant is that the twelve-step process comes into view when described in normative terms, and that is why the Buddha is able to assert that we should do better in our individual lives by refraining from the transitions it describes. That is what makes it a liberal naturalism, one which consists precisely 'in describing patterns in our lives that are intelligible only in terms of the relations that structure the space of reasons' (McDowell 2004: 103). The Buddha's denial of the reality of self within this framework has been taken by much of the historical Buddhist tradition to consist in a denial that the phenomenologically apparent self is genuine (see Chapters 8, 9, 10), the Buddha therefore disagreeing with Hume's claim that there is no presented mineness and so no introspectible self, but rather arguing that what is presented is a *mere* appearance (or at any rate, something better off not presented).[40] A different possibility, and to my mind a plausible one, is that what his denial consists in is a rejection of the idea of what I will later call a participant self.[41]

[38] See Chs. 8, 9, 10, and 11.

[39] McDowell has argued, against Rorty, that we should not think of the distinction between the realm of law and the space of reasons as obtaining between a space of reasons and a space of causes, because to do so would 'preempt the possibility that reasons might be causes' (McDowell 2004: 92).

[40] There is something potentially incoherent in portrayals of the Buddha's view as being that the self is an illusion. The error alleged to be involved in the phenomenology of first-person phenomena is not well described as being that they are illusory, because an appearance is not an illusion of an appearance. I will show in later chapters that historical Buddhist thinkers are much more careful in their description of the error allegedly involved in first-personal self-conscious thought.

[41] Ekstrom (1999, 2005) presents a theory of the participant self in the spirit of Frankfurt but without his problematic commitment to higher-order volition. Her view is that a self is constituted by 'a collection of preferences and acceptances . . . along with the capacity or faculty for forming and reforming that [collection]', where a preference is a desire formed by a process of critical evaluation, and acceptance marks the 'endorsement of a proposition formed by critical reflection with the aim of

A third variety of liberal naturalism from India is the one developed by philosophers in the overlapping schools of Vaiśeṣika and Nyāya. Frauwallner has described Vaiśeṣika as a 'nature-philosophy' (1973: ii. 12–13), averring perhaps to its atomist theory of the physical world. What is clear is that their views about the mind are thoroughly non-Cartesian. A study of their ideas is therefore extremely valuable, both as a retrieval of an important resource for thinking about the mind and as an aid in diagnosing suppressed Cartesian assumptions still at work. The mind is not transparent to itself; there are both affective and cognitive processes below the level of consciousness; the self is essentially embodied; content is external.[42] Within the Nyāya-Vaiśeṣika framework, moreover, phenomena that can seem extremely puzzling, such as the psychopathology known as thought insertion, have an intuitive philosophical explanation. So thoroughly non-Cartesian is their conception of mind that a Tibetan writer mistakenly portrayed them as claiming that the self is itself material. Klong chen pa:

> According to the Naiyāyikas, the self is of a material essence. For them, the idea that the self cognises is due to the mind becoming aware of objects (*artha*) that are supported by the self. This is similar to the way visual consciousness occurs based on the eye seeing colour. Thus it is taught: 'Moreover the self is here, in possession of qualities like desire and anger. It is the support, that which engages with all, the enjoyer. The self is asserted to be of a material essence.'[43]

A more recent Tibetan thinker, Ju Mipham, clarifies what should be understood by Klong chen pa's claim that the self is 'material':

> In this system [of the Vaiśeṣika, the word] 'matter' should not necessarily be understood as a materiality that is established by particles, but rather as a general term for all that is not cognition. The self, as asserted by the Vaiśeṣika, is pervasive, similar to space and direction, and its essence is not cognition.[44]

assenting to what is true' (2005: 55). In describing the self as a collection of preferences and acceptances along with a faculty for critical reflection, her view is thus that there is nothing more to the participant self than a bundle, which, if supplemented by a metaphysical view about bundles, will converge on the view I am suggesting makes sense of the position of the historical Buddha as depicted in the early Nikāya (though not of much of the later Buddhist tradition).

[42] See Chs. 12, 13, and 14.

[43] Klong chen pa (1308–63), *The Treasury of Wish-fulfillment* (Klong chen pa 1968).

[44] Ju Mipham (1846–1912), *Commentary on Śāntarakṣita, Madhyamakālaṃkāra* 35 (Mipham 2004: 313). I am grateful to Thomas Doctor for bringing these passages to my attention and for both translations.

Two good points are emphasized here. First, the Nyāya self does not consist in conscious cognition, it is not thought of as something whose essence is to be conscious. So it is not a Cartesian *res cogitans*, an essentially thinking thing. Rather, and this is the second point, it is that by virtue of which there is a mental life. Mipham's argument is that the self of the Vaiśeṣikas can be said to be 'matter' insofar as it is not something that consists in thinking, but it does not follow that it is 'material' in a corpuscular sense of the term. Mipham accurately notices that the theory of these thinkers is neither hard naturalist nor is it a theory that constitutes the self in terms of the purely phenomenal. As I will show in much greater detail in later chapters, the self in Nyāya and Vaiśeṣika is best understood in terms of a participant notion of the ownership of thought, emotion, experience, and intention, whose phenomenological and intentional structure is explained with reference to unconscious subpersonal mechanisms of comparison, attention, and coordination, the whole supervening on states of the physical body.[45] What makes it a version of liberal naturalism, above all, is the account afforded of the unity of the self and the nature of its ownership of psychological states. Owning a mental state involves endorsement and so implies the possibility of exercising a rational claim on any other of one's mental states. In their account the normative demands of the emotions are intrinsic to the idea of ownership.

This historical survey of the variety of naturalisms in ancient India completed, I now commence the book proper with a taxonomy of conceptions of self. I will then, in each of the subsequent parts, attend in detail to the *philosophical* reconstruction of the three liberal naturalist accounts whose historical origins I have just sketched.

[45] See Chs. 14, 15, 16, and the Conclusion.

1

Conceptions of Self: An Analytical Taxonomy

Two Distinctions about 'Having'

A conception about self supplies an answer to the question 'What am I?' Part of that answer is the specification of a relationship between me and the mental states that are mine, between an individual and a mental life. Another part of the answer is the specification of a relationship between me and the physical states that are mine, between an individual and a body. A third part specifies the relationship between an individual and their physical environment and social relations. In this chapter, I will present a new taxonomy of the possible views that might be taken of these relationships, which I will construct on the basis of two distinctions in the ways a self might be thought to be related to a mental life, physical body, and wider environment: a distinction between collective and adjectival modes of exemplification,[1] and a distinction between the individuation and the ownership of mental states.[2] A collective property is a property of a totality which is not necessarily a property of any item within it. According to one view, being a self is a collective property of the totality of mental states that is the stream or flow of a mental life. There are reductionist, emergentist, and constitutive versions of this conception, and Sellars's 'Principle of Reducibility' is helpful in distinguishing between them (cf. Haskar 1999). What the principle asserts is that

[1] This distinction is closely related to Broad's distinction between Centre and No-Centre theories (Broad 1925: 566).

[2] This distinction is closely related to a distinction P. F. Strawson draws between what he calls 'having$_1$' and 'having$_2$' (Strawson 1966: 96).

if an object is *in a strict sense* a system of objects, then every property of the object must consist in the fact that its constituents have such and such qualities and stand in such and such relations, or roughly, every property of a system of objects consists of properties of, and relations between, its constituents.[3]

A reductionist version of the first view claims that this Principle is true of selves: every property of a self must consist in the fact that mental states have such-and-such qualities and stand in such-and-such relations. An emergentist version denies that the principle is true of selves: selves have properties which do not consist in the fact that mental states have such-and-such qualities and stand in such-and-such relations. According to the constitutive version of the view, the relationship is instead one of constitution. Constitution is not a relation either of reduction or emergence, because it is a broad rather than a narrow relation. A pot is a piece of clay that stands in a distinctive set of relationships with a potter and a utility, some of which are such that if they did not obtain, the piece of clay would not count as a pot at all, others are such as to license the description of the pot as good, bad, unfinished, or broken. Similarly, it might be held that a self is a mental life that stands in a distinctive set of relationships with a social world of law and ethics. Some of the relationships are such that if they did not obtain, the mental life would not count as a self at all; others are such as to license the description of the mental life as healthy, well-rounded, dysfunctional, fragmented, and so on.

The second way a self might be thought to relate to a mental life views the relationship as being the same as the relationship between a piece of rope and a knot, or surface and a dent; that is, rather than a self being thought of as a collective feature of a mental life, the mental life is viewed as *adjectival* on a self.[4] It takes as central the existence of a certain sort of metaphysical dependence between a self and a mental state, such that the mental state could not exist without the self it is the state of. Parfit has suggested that the idea of adjectival dependence be analysed as follows: Xs are adjectival on Ys only if Xs are essentially of or in Ys, and there could not be Xs without Ys,

[3] Sellars (1963: 27).

[4] Shoemaker (1996: 10): 'But an experiencing is something whose existence is "adjectival on" a subject of experience. The ontological status of an experiencing, or an episode of being appeared to, is similar to that of a bending of a branch or a rising of the sun.'

and an X of one Y could not have been an X of a different Y (Parfit 1999: 239). The view conceives of the self in a manner that apparently courts the possibility that there is a self even when there is the most rudimentary or fragmented mental life, and even the possibility of a self when there is no mental life at all, just as there can be a piece of rope which is unknotted or a surface that is not dented (dents need surfaces, but surfaces don't need dents).

One might feel that what a self is reducible to, emergent from, or constituted by is not (or not only) a mental life but rather the collection of states and properties of a physical body. Similarly, rather than claim that experiences are adjectival upon subjects of experience, one might want to say that a subject of experience is something whose states are metaphysically dependent on bodies. So this first distinction generates a range of possible relationships, collective and adjectival, involving the body, the stream of experience, and the self.

There is an orthogonal way for a distinction to be drawn, one in terms of a distinction between individuation and ownership. By 'individuation' I mean here the metaphysical problem of providing an 'ontological assay' (Moreland 1998: 251) of the situation so as to specify what makes it the case that there is a plurality of individuals; rather than any epistemological or linguistic concern. The previous discussion has provided materials for two methods of individuation, one by way of the specification of a relationship to a collection and the other in terms of adjectival dependence. It is a distinct idea to say that my experiences are *mine*—that they are not occurrences happening to me, insertions in my mental life, but, in a sense, are me. The thought is expressed very well by Peter Strawson in a passage I will frequently return to:

> Our desires and preferences are not, in general, something we just note in ourselves as alien presences. To a large extent they *are* we. The point gains force from the very fact of exceptions to it: i.e. from the presence in some subjects, sometimes, of dispositions and desires which they do experience as intrusive compulsions. In respect of them, there is no sense of freedom. (P. F. Strawson 1992: 134)

Ownership too might formally be thought of either in terms of collection or of adjectival dependence, and it is not inevitably the case that the question about ownership which this consideration introduces is resolved by the same considerations as resolve the question of individuation or metaphysical dependence. Holding the distinct considerations about individuation and about ownership apart, we can see that there is potentially an elision in Shoemaker's affirmation that 'an experiencing is something whose existence is "adjectival on" a subject of experience', in that it presumes that what I am calling questions of ownership and questions of individuation are resolved with reference to the same set of facts.[5]

The distinction between the question of whom a mental state is a state of (the question of ownership) and what it is metaphysically dependent upon (the question of individuation) is marked in Indian theory with the widespread technical use of a pair of terms: one is said to be the location or 'place' (*ādhāra*)[6] of experience; the other is its support or 'base' (*āśraya*).[7] Thus, according to what I will later call an Ownership View, states of mind are owned by selves and dependent on bodies; selves present a 'place' of ownership for experiences whose individuative 'base' is in the body.

To say that the self provides the place of ownership and the body the base of individuation is *not* to say that the self or the body is a mere 'container' or 'receptacle' for the mind. The expressions 'place' (*ādhāra*) and 'base' (*āśraya*) are used in a technical, non-colloquial, sense. Some classical criticisms fail to recognize that the terms are being used in these technical senses, and trade on their common or colloquial meanings.[8] Nor is it right to conflate the ideas of 'place' or 'base' with that of 'substratum'—at least not as that notion is used in substratum theories of individuation, according to which the substratum is a bare particular (Bergmann 1967; Moreland 1998; Sider 2006). To do so would be a symptom of a deep residual Cartesianism, in which matters of individuation and matters of ownership are conflated. In an Ownership View, by contrast, what makes it the case that there is a plurality of subjects of experience is a question answered with reference to metaphysical dependences implicated in embodiment and not with reference to any proposal such as that subjects of experience are bare

[5] Lowe (1996: 6) offers an epistemological argument for the distinction: 'That these experiences are my experiences is arguably known to me as a necessary truth; but that these experiences are associated with this body, though perhaps known to me, does not seem to constitute a necessary truth.'

[6] For an example of this use of the term *ādhāra*, Kumārila: *śaktyādhāraprakḷptau vā nā 'tmano 'nyaḥ prakalpyate* | (*Ātmavāda* 72ab).

[7] Many examples of this use of the term *āśraya* will be given later, esp. in Chs. 7 and 12.

[8] Such criticisms involve the dialogical fault technically known as *vāk-chala*, trading on an equivocation involving a homonym.

particulars. A distinction drawn by Connell (1988: 90) between two ways in which something can be thought to have a property is helpful here. While bare particulars exemplify properties by way of a simple attributional tie, substantial individuals are constituted by capacities and potentialities which serve as the grounds for the properties they instantiate; Connell speaks of the property being 'rooted in' the individual. My own view is that ownership is 'rooted' in the deep psyche of the individual and in their propensities to endorsement, and individuation is determined by the essentially embodied character of a capacity for normative emotional response. I am not assuming that ownership is a primitive concept; indeed, I believe that it comprises various strands, closely intertwined in normal psychologies but capable of separation in pathological ones.[9]

This distinction between ownership and individuation is closely related to a distinction P. F. Strawson draws between what he calls 'having$_1$' and 'having$_2$' (Strawson 1966: 96). His 'having$_1$' is 'really a kind of causal dependence', whereas *base* is perhaps best understood as a supervenience-supporting relation of metaphysical dependence; his 'having$_2$' is a 'peculiar non-transferable kind of possession', while *place* leaves it at least an open matter whether, in cases of thought insertion, subjects transfer ownership in any relevant sense when they deny that a thought is their own. I will say more about thought insertion in later chapters. Strawson does not himself endorse the distinction between 'having$_1$' and 'having$_2$', but those who regard first-person phenomena as a challenge for naturalism (Baker 1998, 2011; see also Chapter 3) believe that not to do so is a mistake. I give a precise definition of the concepts of *base* and *place* on p. 261, with the help of theoretical apparatus it would be distracting to introduce here, and again on p. 327 within the conceptual framework of the book as a whole.

Buddhist and Real Self Views

With the help of this pair of distinctions, we can now construct a taxonomy of views about self. First, there are those views in which indeed no distinction is drawn between the two sorts of 'having':

[9] See Campbell (1999, 2002); Bortolotti and Broome (2009). In the Conclusion I cite a case study where immersion and participation come apart.

Type I: One-dimensional Views

Cartesian View	Self is both place and base
Materialist View	Body is both place and base
Reductionist View	Stream is both place and base

The Cartesian View[10] makes the self both the owner of experience and that upon which it adjectivally depends. This, rather than dualism, is the defining characteristic of Cartesianism as a theory in the philosophy of mind. Any theory which retains the feature basic to Cartesian theories, the undifferentiated identification of the self as place and base, however different from Descartes's theory of mind in other respects, is still fundamentally Cartesian. In such a view the self is indeed a substratum or bare particular.

The Materialist View is that mental and physical properties are exemplified in a single domain of entities. This view encompasses both type-identity theory and property dualism (hard naturalism—'materialism' with a lower case—is but one version of this view). It is also Strawson's view about persons as the exemplars of both M- and P-predicates. It includes a range of Indian formulations, from Animalism to Cārvāka Emergentism.[11]

The Reductionist View is the view that a stream of experience collectively provides mental states with both an identity and an owner; it is the view of Parfit and also of Hume.[12]

Then there are views which endorse the idea of a self as the owner of experience, but deny that it plays the double role which the Cartesian View assigns it:

Type II: Real Self Views

Ownership View	Self is place, body is base
Phenomenal View	Self is place, stream is base
Pure Consciousness View	Self is place, there is no base

[10] It can sound odd using the name 'Cartesian' when discussing Indian theory from before the time of Descartes, but it should be remembered that this is merely a well-established label for a given philosophical view. A synonym, perhaps preferable, is the Substantial Ego View.

[11] Sorabji (2006: 267) says that the owner is 'the embodied person'. Martin (2008: 225) diagnoses Sorabji's view as a type of non-reductive materialism.

[12] Parfit (1984, 1999); for Hume see Ch. 2.

There are again several versions of the Ownership View. One is the Constitution View, which takes the relation between body and self to be a constitution relation.[13] A second type of Ownership View is a Natural Self View, which I mentioned earlier in this chapter.[14] A third version is that the self is an invariant sense of embodied self-presence. We might call this the Minimal Ownership View; I will discuss it in Chapter 6.[15] What all versions of the Ownership View have in common is the importance given to the body as that upon which a mental life is metaphysically dependent, but without a reduction of self to body.

The Phenomenal View is the view that the self is an entity imminent in, but not identical or reducible to, the stream, which is the collective base; for example by being emergent from it, or constituted by it.[16] A popular analogy is the relationship between a serpent and its coils. One version is the sort of view William James favoured, namely that there is really just a succession of selves one after another but no enduring self:

> The consciousness of Self involves a stream of thought, each part of which as 'I' can remember those which went before, and know the things they knew... It is a *Thought*, at each moment different from that of the last moment, but *appropriative* of the latter, together with all that the latter called its own.[17]

[13] This is the view of Baker (2000). An Indian thinker considers and criticizes the view: he says that if a body is to a self as a piece of gold is to a crown, then it will share the self's properties, but the properties of matter are not those of the self (Prabhācandra 1990: 117,9–15). Baker, perhaps the most influential contemporary constitution theorist, seeks to address this objection with the doctrine that there is a distinction between *non-derivative* and *derivative* modes of property occurrence (Baker 2000: 46–58; 2001: 164).

[14] This is the Nyāya-Vaiśeṣika View; see Chs. 12, 13.

[15] A view of this sort is recorded in the Upaniṣads and seemingly attributable to some of the most ancient naturalists in India: *Bṛhadāraṇyaka* 2.4.12, identified as Cārvāka by Jayanta (1982–4: ii. 202). It is also a view of several classical phenomenologists and even of one prominent neuroscientist. The phenomenologists include Husserl, Merleau-Ponty, and Henry (Gallagher and Zahavi 2008: 203). The neuroscientist is Damasio (1999: 7, 10, 127).

[16] Haskar (1999); Dainton (2008). Several theories of self in the phenomenological tradition fall naturally into this group. Sartre, according to Williford (2011), has a reflexive Phenomenal View. Zahavi's Minimal Self View (Zahavi 2005a) is either an Ownership View or a Phenomenal View, depending on the precise significance accorded to embodiment (see further Ch. 8). Peacocke (2014) advances a Phenomenal View. He states that "we ought to recognize a wider range of theoretical options on what subjects of consciousness are" and says that he "will be arguing for a fourth option ... distinct from the three classical views that subjects are either Cartesian egos, or Strawsonian persons, or are constructed entities, built from various other mental and non-mental entities, in the spirit of Hume" (ibid. 2). While the acknowledgement of a possibility other than any Type I View is welcome, Peacocke fails to notice the full range of options identified here from the Indian discussion.

[17] James (1890: Ch. 10). One 1st-millennium author attributes such a view to the followers of the Buddha (but I think is mistaken to do so): 'The Buddhists think that the many moments of consciousness (*vijñāna*) that exist in a single body constitute [each of them] a self. In order to deny such an assertion, [it is said that] for each body there is one [self] not many' (*tathā hy ekasmin śarīre 'nekaṃ vijñānam ātmeti śākyā manyante* | *tatpratiṣedhārthaṃ pratiśarīram eko nānekaḥ* | (Vyomaśiva 1983: i. 155,9–11)). Cf. also Kant's

A Pure Consciousness View retains the idea of ownership but denies that experience is metaphysically dependent on anything. The only way for this to be possible is for it to own itself: self simply is pure consciousness, self-owning and not dependent on anything.[18]

Suppose instead that we give up on the idea that there is any such thing as the ownership of experience. This idea, we can now see, permits three variants:

Type III: No Place (Buddhist) Views

No Place View 1	Body is base, there is no place
No Place View 2	Stream is base, there is no place
No Place View 3	There is no base, there is no place

The No Place View is that the happenings of the mind are not owned. The mind's ontology is one of tropes not properties. There is nothing that owns mental tropes and they don't aggregate to form subjects (it is the fundamental wrong move to think that any of the mental items, or the collective stream, *is* a subject). So the notion of a *place* for mental states is an idle one, but the notion of individuating *base* is still available. One No Place View grounds mental occurrences in the body, retaining psycho-physical supervenience. A second retains from Reductionism the idea that streams are individuative. A third No Place view denies that there is anything which individuates mental occurrences. They do not supervene on bodies, nor are they metaphysically adjectival to streams, although they may stand in causal relations of one sort or another. They are not well individuated, metaphysically speaking.

Because place is denied, and not merely self, and because I am aware of no other philosophers who think this, I will designate Type III conceptions 'Buddhist'.[19] The first No Place View is that of Abhidharma Buddhism. Yogācāra, also known as the Mind-Only (*cittamātra*) or the Cognition View

famous 'elastic balls' metaphor (*Critique* A 363–4 n.). Galen Strawson has championed a variant of the account, which he calls the 'transience' or 'string of pearls' theory of self. He says that a self lasts for only as long as an active conscious experience does, perhaps two or three seconds (G. Strawson 1999a; 1999b; 2009: 9).

[18] The 'witness consciousness' of Advaita Vedānta and the *rigpa* of Tibetan Dzogchen are varieties of this conception. It has been claimed that traces of the conception can be detected in early Buddhism (Albahari 2006).

[19] Strawson's 'no-ownership' doctrine, which he reconstructs from hints he finds in Wittgenstein and Schlick but is reluctant to ascribe to anyone, is evidently a variety of the first sort of No Place View: 'The 'no-ownership' theorist may be presumed to start his explanation with facts of the sort which illustrate the unique causal position of a certain material body in a person's experience ... but experiences are not owned by anything' (P. F. Strawson 1963: 9–6).

(*vijñānavāda*) is a version of the second view. So too is Sautrāntika.[20] Madhyamaka Buddhism is a No Place View of the third sort.

Although Type III views are all defended by Buddhists, not all Buddhists advance a Type III view. The 'Pudgala Realist' (*pudgala-vāda*) view of Vātsiputrīya Buddhism is that what they call *pudgala* is not identical to the stream, which is the base, but neither is it wholly different.[21] Theirs is a view I will shortly describe and designate the Flame View. They use the term *pudgala* to mean something that is emergent from a dynamical system. Vasubandhu, writing as an Abhidharma Buddhist, denies that dynamical systems have emergent macrostates, and so asserts that there are no *pudgalas* in the Pudgala Realists' sense. I will say more about No Place Views in the next section.[22]

Tornado and Flame Views

There are two views not so far defined:

Type IV: Stream is Place

Tornado View	Body is base, stream is place
Flame View	Stream is place, there is no base

These views rest on the idea that dynamical systems of sufficient complexity can exhibit new properties, emergent macro-properties. A provisional working definition of emergence is this:

A property *P* of a mereologically complex object *O* is emergent if

[20] This is what makes it possible for a philosopher like Dharmakīrti to integrate Sautrāntika and Yogācāra.

[21] I avoid the usual translation of *pudgalavāda* as 'Personalism' so as to avoid confusion with the very different western doctrine which goes by that name. Indeed, I argue in Ch. 7 that the translation of *pudgala* as 'person' is problematic: 'psycho', 'pneuma', or even 'spirit' are perhaps all better.

[22] Lowe (1996: 8) distinguishes between what he calls 'psychological constructivism' and a 'non-entity theory'. According to the former, the self 'is nothing *over and above* the states of which is it the subject, but is not therefore *nothing at all*, since it is a perfectly respectable entity whose identity and persistence conditions are entirely expressible in terms of relationships between those states'. According to the non-entity theory, 'there is literally no such thing as the self, as philosophers have attempted to conceive it, and indeed that there is no object of first-person reference, because "I" is not really a referring expression at all'.

1. [Supervenience] *P* supervenes on the properties of the parts of *O*,
2. [Non-Structurality] *P* is not had by any of *O*'s parts and is not a structural property of *O*, and
3. [Autonomy] *P* has a direct determinative influence on the pattern of behaviour of *O*'s parts.[23]

The purpose of the third clause is to give sense to the idea that emergence produces properties that are causally autonomous, but it is open whether some other formulation of the autonomy requirement is better. There are two ways in which a view about emergence can depart from the provisional definition. One is to drop the autonomy requirement altogether. The claim then is that it is possible for a mereologically complex object to have properties which do not confer on it new causal powers not derivable from the object's parts and arrangement, and yet are not merely structural properties of the system of parts. And indeed, non-linear dynamical systems theory has demonstrated exactly how it is possible for this to happen. We define a microdynamic which governs the evolution in time of the system's microstates. The relevant feature of certain dynamical systems is that, although every state at any time is in principle derivable from the initial conditions, there is no implementable procedure for conducting the derivation in real time. One influential suggestion is that the only way to make predictions is through simulation.[24] Other suggestions are possible. What matters is that the emergent macrostates have no properties not in principle derivable from a structural description of the system, together with a specification of its initial conditions. This is what is generally known as 'weak' emergence.

The second alternative way to depart from the provisional definition is to drop supervenience. Again, the literature has proposals for non-supervenience-based versions of dynamical emergence.[25] An interesting

[23] Bedau (1997: 376), adapted from O'Connor (1994). See Ch. 3 for refinements.

[24] Thus Bedau (1997: 377–8): 'I define weak emergence as follows: Macrostate *P* of *S* with microdynamic *D* is weakly emergent if *P* can be derived from *D* and *S*'s external conditions but only by simulation.' Rueger (2000a) provides an analysis of synchronic and diachronic emergence in a similar framework.

[25] O'Connor (2000) now claims that only such models, and not supervenience-based emergence models, can provide a good account of emergence.

proposal is that the component parts of a system undergo 'fusion' as the system evolves.[26]

When it is the physical body, and not the stream, which provides both the microstates of the system and the place of ownership, these suggestions are all versions of the Cārvāka View. The idea that the provisional definition is the correct way to formulate emergence reflects Udbhaṭa's understanding, according to which the autonomy must be an autonomy of causal powers. The second proposal is most closely associated with the classical Cārvāka of Bṛhaspati, in which it is considered sufficient for emergence that mental properties are *from* the material elements, but not *for* them. A proposal of the third sort is in those later Cārvāka philosophers who say that the micro-constituents themselves undergo a 'transformation' (*pariṇāma*) in the course of the time evolution of the system.[27]

Type IV views, however, take the role of ownership to be discharged by the experiential stream, not the body. The first of the two views is a description of mind for which an appropriate analogy would be the cyclone or tornado. Thus Bedau (1997: 375):

> Some [examples of emergence] involve inanimate matter; e.g. a tornado is a self-organising entity caught up in a global pattern of behaviour that seems to be autonomous with respect to the massive aggregation of air and water molecules which constitute it. Another source of examples is the mind: our mental life consists of an autonomous, coherent flow of mental states (beliefs, desires, etc.) that presumably somehow ultimately arise out of the swarm of biochemical activity among our brains's neurons. Life is a third rich source of apparent emergence. For example, the hierarchy of life embraces ecosystems composed of organisms, which are composed of organs, which are composed of cells, which are composed of molecules, but each level in this hierarchy exhibits behaviour that seems autonomous with respect to the behaviour found at the level below.

[26] Humphreys (1997a) defines a fusion operator for property instances, where 'By a fusion operation, I mean a real physical operation' (1997a: 10). In his (2000), he extends the treatment to fused objects, such as the overlapping wave-functions of two electrons in close proximity, and offers a partial analogy: 'Consider poker chips in a casino. The basic units are red chips, and as soon as you have accumulated two red chips you can trade them in for a blue chip that is worth two units. The blue chip is not composed of two red chips and you cannot count its two components because it does not have any, but it behaves exactly as if there were two such units present' (2000: 28–9). On the claim that there is no supervenience, see also Humphreys (1996, 1997b).

[27] I discuss classical Cārvāka, and the risk of epiphenomenalism it courts, in Ch. 3, and the theory of transformation as well as Udbhaṭa's concept of 'assistive causation' in Ch. 4.

We would then think of the mind as a tornado-like occurrence within a dynamical flow of experience. What characterizes the Tornado View, above all, is the thought that mind is an emergent macrostate of the non-linear dynamical behaviour of aggregated particles, here mental events.[28] The term 'disturbance' has been used as a collective noun for the sorts of entity in question (Karmo 1977), a term which captures the idea of a single process running through a succession of metaphysical supports, just as a cyclone does with volumes of air.

The second view is characterized by a rather different thought. The idea now is that the micro-elements are in a process of fusion and mutation, and that it is the emergent macrostates yielded by this process of mutation which we want to identify as corresponding with mind. An analogy better than that of the tornado, therefore, is the flame, pictured as something emergent from a process in which the constituent material is continuously in flux. It would be a mistake to describe this view in terms of particles shifting their patterns of aggregation, because here the micro-elements do not persist in time. The 'reconfigurations' they undergo are of a metaphysical and not merely a spatio-temporal nature.[29]

This begins to sound like a No Place View, but there is a crucial distinction. No Place theorists deny that the stream provides a place of ownership. It is therefore a mistake to identify the emergent macrostates which are described in the Tornado and Flame Views as genuinely self. The Buddhist View is a different theory altogether. It is a dynamical theory in which at each moment in time there is a different set of micro-constituents, and there is a microdynamic which governs the time evolution of successive sequences of sets of micro-constituents.[30] This is different from the Tornado View, because there is no enduring set of particles analogous to the molecules of air and water in the tornado. And it is different from the Flame View, because there is no macrostate, no emergent non-structural property analogous to the flame itself. The way of the mind is to be a dynamical

[28] See Rueger (2000a, 2000b) for clear discussion, using the van der Pol oscillator as an example. The work of Vareli and Thompson (Vareli, Thompson, and Rosch 1991; Thompson 2007) on evolving autopoetic systems uses weak emergence to model biological systems, then extended to the theory of mind. What this yields is in effect a synthesis of Cārvāka and Tornado Views, with the cell rather than the flame as the guiding analogy.

[29] See Jayanta's analysis of change—the so-called *pākaja* theory—in Ch. 5, which he explicitly attributes to flames.

[30] Vasubandu (1973) (AK 1.39, trans. 1988–90: 108), where he says that each moment in the stream is the base (*āśraya*) of the next.

system of trope-cluster sequences. Qua tropes, they have no place: they are not owned by anything or anyone, not even by the streams themselves. The view that there is such an emergent macrostate is that of Vātsiputrīya Buddhists. They use the term 'person' (*pudgala*) to designate this macrostate (see further Chapter 7); they have a Flame View.

We can now see more clearly why a Buddhist View is a demanding one, and has to be described with considerable care if its distinctness from other more familiar views is not to be obscured. For other views too seem *at first glance* to deny that there is a self: neither the Materialist nor Reductionist View, nor the Tornado or Flame View, mentions one. In every case, however, it is open to stipulate that what the term 'self' really means, in any of these views, is whatever it is that the view takes to be the place: the body or the stream.[31] It makes no difference whether we describe the Reductionist View as the view that there are streams but not selves, or as the view that the self in fact is the stream. These are just notational variants of the same philosophical position. Again, some Cārvākas will put their view as being that there is no self but only the body, others that the self is the body. Similarly, it makes no difference whether we say that there are no selves but only flames or that the self is in fact the flame. There is a simple bijection between the two discourses.[32] The Buddhist View is not simply that there is no *self* distinct from body or stream, it is that there is no ownership of experience at all. To deny this is to deny that there is anything that could be even a surrogate for a self. The first variety of the Buddhist View retains the thought that the time evolution of trope-cluster sequences supervenes on the physical body. The second variety considers it to be determined by relations internal to the stream itself. The third, and most

[31] See e.g. Kumārila: *ye cehā 'jñātanānātvās teṣāṃ deheṣv ahaṃ matiḥ | tatrāpyātmā 'bhimānenety ahaṃ buddhir dhruvā 'tmani ||* (*Ātmavāda* 132a–d).

[32] Precisely the same point applies to Metzinger's claim that 'No such things as selves exist in the world: Nobody ever was or had a self. All that ever existed were conscious self-models that could not be recognised as models' (Metzinger 2003: 1; see also Metzinger 2011). At face value, his view is a version of the Yogācāra View, that there is no place but a base in the phenomenal stream. However, he sees himself as having naturalized the discussion about self, and that implies that his true view is that it is the body which is the base. Metaphysically, Metzinger's view is therefore a Materialist View, with a claim about the special content of some mental states (that they represent a 'phenomenal self-model'). Buddhists are liberal naturalists, and their 'no self' doctrine should not be conflated with the hard naturalism of Metzinger's.

challenging view, is that there is neither supervenience on something physical nor internal determining relations.[33]

There are no other views than these eleven. This is because the very idea of a self is that of a place, and the very idea of a body is that of a base. So there are no views in which the self is a base but not a place, and no views in which a body is a place but not a base. That is enough to exclude five of sixteen possibilities, leaving the eleven views identified. Necessarily, every conception about self falls into at least one of these eleven.[34]

No Place Views can be paired against Real Self Views in accordance with what, if anything, is taken to be the base, the individuating ground for experience. These three pairings in effect constitute three research programmes in the philosophy of self, in the form of three sets of potential dialogues between Real Self and No Place conceptions about self. Research programmes taking the form of a dialogue between Pure Consciousness and Madhyamaka views were actively pursued in India in the second half of the first millennium.[35] Activity in the research programme whose shape is that of a dialogue between Yogācāra or Sautrāntika and Phenomenal views has begun only in the last few years, as the result of a fruitful encounter between Buddhist scholars and phenomenologists.[36] It will be natural for these dialogues to include Reductionist Views as dialogue partners, for they share the idea that mental lives are based in the stream.[37]

I am interested in views which take it that mental lives are essentially embodied. My inquiry belongs within a research programme of a third sort, that is a dialogue between Ownership Views and the first sort of No Place View. It is to be expected that philosophical dialogues in this third research programme will include as a conversation partner certain Materialist Views, for they too ground mental lives in the body. I will

[33] I will reflect on these claims in Chs. 7, 8, and 9, and in Chs. 10 and 11 consider the arguments for and consequences of an additional idea, that any of these Buddhist Views require experience to be reflexively self-aware.

[34] Several synthetic views can easily be generated, for example by taking the conjunction of stream and body to be the base.

[35] Ganeri (2007) is a study of just this dialogue. The chapters of that book alternate between presentations of Madhyamaka and Vedānta so as to bring out the *dialogical* nature of the encounter. The work of Candrakīrti is particularly central here.

[36] Coseru (2012); Siderits, Thompson, and Zahavi (2011). It is natural for Dharmakīrti and Śāntarakṣita to be focal points in such endeavours.

[37] See Parfit (1984, 1999); Siderits (2003).

investigate Cārvāka, Buddhist No Place, and Nyāya-Vaiśeṣika Ownership views. Before turning to this programme, however, there is more to be said about views of the first type distinguished above, and in particular the correlation between them and the kinds of methodological inquiry that lead to them.

2

Experiment, Imagination, and the Self

In the country once described as 'the philosophical laboratory that was India' (Stcherbatsky 1923: 68), the use of two different kinds of philosophical experiment led to the discovery of two different kinds of self. The method of philosophical naturalism, which affirms a continuity between philosophy and natural science, led to a conception of self as a reducible entity, reducible either simply to the body or else to an interconnected patterned flow of mental particulars. Animalist and psychological continuity accounts of the self are these theories' modern successors. Diametrically opposed to philosophical naturalism was an approach to the study of the self that rests on imagination. Exercises of imagination led to the discovery of a different kind of self, a self which consists essentially in thinking. The heart of the method is that if something can be imagined as separated from something else without being destroyed, then that other thing cannot be a part of its essence. In discussing these methods, I will therefore be focusing on the Materialist, Reductionist, and Cartesian views about self as defined in the last chapter, the three Type I views. The centre of gravity of the Indian analysis of self lies, as I have indicated, elsewhere, in the exploration of views belonging to Types II, III, and IV.

Methodological Naturalism

Quine describes methodological naturalism as a consequence of the 'abandonment of the goal of first philosophy', which has come about because of the recognition that 'it is within science itself, and not in some prior philosophy, that reality is to be identified and described' (Quine 1981: 72).

The suggestion goes back to Hume. In the introduction to the *Treatise*, Hume proposes that the old methods of 'metaphysical reasonings' be replaced with a new 'experimental philosophy'. This new philosophy applies the methods of the sciences to a study of human nature:

For to me it seems evident, that the essence of the mind being equally unknown to us with that of external bodies, it must be equally impossible to form any notion of its powers and qualities otherwise than from careful and exact experiments, and the observation of those particular effects, which result from its different circumstances and situations. (Hume 1978: p. xvii)

Hume's failed attempt, using this method, to detect a self is one of the most famous and influential experiments in the history of philosophy:

For my part, when I enter most intimately into what I call myself, I always stumble on some particular perception or other, of heat or cold, light or shade, love or hatred, pain or pleasure. I never can catch myself at any time without a perception, and never can observe anything but the perception. (Hume 1978: 252)

Hume concludes from this experiment that a self must be something 'whose different and co-existent parts are bound together by a close relation', and not something which is 'perfectly simple and indivisible'. In the notorious Appendix, he summarizes the view that he has advanced in the body of the *Treatise* thus:

When I turn my reflection on myself, I never can perceive this self without some one or more perceptions; nor can I ever perceive anything but the perceptions. It is the composition of these, therefore, which forms the self. (Hume 1978: 634)

With regard to all objects, not just the self, he draws a contrast between 'the doctrine of philosophers', by which he means a natural philosophical or scientific attitude, and 'the doctrine of the vulgar', the ordinary opinion of common sense: 'When I view this table and that chimney, nothing is present to me but particular perceptions, which are of a like nature with all the other perceptions. This is the doctrine of philosophers. But this table, which is present to me, and the chimney, may and do exist separately. This is the doctrine of the vulgar' (1978: 634). Hume seems to think, therefore, that his experiment establishes that there is no self understood in the 'vulgar' sense as something simple and indivisible. The same method also establishes that there is no table in the vulgar sense. In the case of the table, of course, the coexistent parts are perceptions of the constituent material parts from which the table is made, the sorts of thing one would see if one were to look at the table through a very powerful microscope. Introspection, for Hume, is a kind of microscope for the mind, and the mental particulars which it detects—sensible qualities, emotions, thoughts—are the mental parts from which a self is made.

It might now seem that it is only in a rather contrived sense that Hume can say that he does not observe a self, in the strange 'philosophical' sense in which he would also say that one does not observe a table: one does not observe a table as something 'simple and indivisible' separate from its constituent parts and their properties. Yet one does observe a table and one does so *in virtue of* the pattern of coexistence of its parts. In that same sense, we might think that one does observe a self when one introspects mental particulars: one observes a self *in virtue of* the pattern of coexistence of those mental particulars. Hume's anxiety in the *Appendix* is the result of his belief that he can find nothing in perception corresponding to such a pattern of coexistence, and so can form no idea of a self as anything other than a clump and succession of discrete perceptions. He elsewhere remarks that 'The difficulty, then, is how far we are *ourselves* the objects of our senses. 'Tis certain there is no question in philosophy more abstruse than that concerning identity, and the nature of the uniting principle, which constitutes a person. So far from being able by our senses merely to determine this question, we must have recourse to the most profound metaphysics to give a satisfactory answer to it; and in common life 'tis evident these ideas of self and person are never very fix'd nor determinate. 'Tis absurd, therefore, that the senses can ever distinguish betwixt ourselves and external objects' (Hume 1978: 189–90).

This anxiety, it seems to me, is an inevitable product of Hume's scientific naturalism. For as I emphasized in the Historical Prelude the patterns of coexistence that 'bind together in a close relation' the individual mental happenings are patterns that must be articulated in a vocabulary unavailable to the Humean naturalist. Hume's experiment is a failure. It is a failure because what he set out to detect is not something that *could* be detected within the design specification of the experiment he conducts. His scientific method, of microscopic inspection and introspection, never could detect a self, if by that what is meant is what binds the mental particulars together into one. So Shoemaker rightly says that 'whether we interpret "perceive" in the broad sense or in the narrow sense, the [Humean] view that we have introspective perception of individual mental happenings but not of a self is indefensible' (Shoemaker 1996: 24). The problem with Hume's naturalism is that his method is blind to the facts which are constitutive of selfhood. He speaks about individual 'perceptions' but not to what it is for a subject to own a perception. A concept of self affords an explanation of the sources—real or illusory—of the distinction between what is mine and what is another's.

If certain ancient reports are to be believed, experiments in self-detection had been performed long before Hume. There are accounts of a naturalistically inclined individual called Payāsi, who, like Hume, devised experiments with which he hoped to demonstrate that there is no self considered as a discrete existence separable from the body.[1] His application of experimental techniques that are used to investigate the natural world was much more radical than Hume's. One proposal is to catch someone and place him in a large vessel, which is then to be sealed and covered with a damp skin, over which is to be laid a second covering of damp clay. The vessel is then to be put in an oven until the person is dead, and the jar is opened. We are told to 'watch carefully: maybe we can see his soul escaping. But we do not see any soul escaping.' Another proposal is to pummel the hapless individual to see if any soul can be beaten out of him; another to weigh him before and after killing him; and another, more gruesome still, to peel off layers—cuticle, skin, flesh, sinews, bones, and marrow—until the soul is exposed. The last experiment is reminiscent of one described in *Chāndogya Upaniṣad* 6.12.1-2, where a banyan fruit is cut up in order to find its inner essence, first the skin, then the flesh, then the seeds. It is again a method of dissection and microscopic inspection, that is to say, one appropriate to a reductive naturalism.

Payāsi's interlocutor Kāśyapa, a companion of the Buddha, does not in any case dispute the claim that no soul is detected. What is disputed is whether anything follows from this. Kāśyapa asks, 'How *could* you see the soul of a dead man entering or leaving his body?' He says that to thrash a dead body in order to extract the soul which had animated it is as silly as

[1] The story of Payāsi is recorded in both Buddhist and Jaina sources: *Dīgha Nikāya* D. ii. 316–57: *Payāsi Sutta* (trans. Walshe 1995: 351–68); *Rāyapaseṇiya* 667[47]–817[84]: *Paesi-kahāṇayaṁ* (trans. Bollée 2002).

thrashing a trumpet to get at the music one had heard emanating from it. Kāśyapa makes his point as follows:

It seems that when the trumpet is accompanied by a man, by effort, and by the wind, then it makes a sound. But when it is not accompanied by a man, by effort, and by the wind, then it makes no sound. In the same way, when this body has life, heat and consciousness, then it goes and comes back, stands and sits and lies down, sees things with its eyes, hears with its ears, smells with its nose, tastes with its tongue, feels with its body, and knows mental objects with its mind. But when it has no life, heat or consciousness, it does none of these things. (D. ii. 338)

We should remember that Buddhists, as much as Hume, reject the conception of the self as something simple and indivisible. The reason that Kāśyapa dismisses Payāsi's experiments is methodological: no such experiment could confirm or disconfirm anything about the self. It is naïve to think that the experimental methods used to investigate the natural world are so simply applicable to the study of human nature. The natural-scientific stance of the experimenter Payāsi does not manage to pick out selves at all. Indeed, any attempt to form an adequate conception of a self from such a stance will necessarily end up describing something whose properties are entirely mysterious:

Those who maintain that the soul is something different from the body cannot tell whether the soul is long or small, whether globular or circular or triangular or square or hexagonal or octagonal, whether black or blue or red or yellow or white, whether of sweet smell or of bad smell, whether bitter or pungent or astringent or sour or sweet, whether hard or soft or heavy or light or cold or hot or smooth or rough. Those therefore who believe that there is and exists no soul speak the truth.[2]

Philosophical naturalism regards the propositions of philosophy as able to be formulated in terms which make it possible to use the methods of natural science to test and verify them. But this leads to a distinctive kind of philosophical anxiety, which has its roots in a sense that one's subject matter has slipped through one's fingers. The terms of reference themselves guarantee that the self has disappeared out of view.[3]

[2] The view of a Cārvāka naturalist, as reported in the Jaina *Sūtrakṛtāṅga* 2.1.11 (trans. Jacobi 1895: 340).

[3] Shoemaker (1996: 9): 'The very conception of mental facts that provide us with a stock of mental particulars to serve as objects of introspective awareness tends to make it appear that the self, or mental subject, cannot itself be an object of introspective awareness.'

Hume belongs in the same camp as Payāsi, that is the camp of a hard or restrictive naturalism. The Buddhists do not: although they too describe the combination of mental particulars, their terms of reference are rooted in an intentional rather than a scientistic stance. The bonds that bring the mental particulars into close relation are thoroughly normative and evaluative. This different approach is implicit in the description Kāśyapa provides, a description of what McDowell referred to as 'the career of a living thing', something patterned in ways only recognizable in terms drawn from the language of the space of reasons. Kāśyapa says that agency, perception, and consciousness are distinctive of a living, conscious, thing. Buddhist thinking about the self has often been compared with that of Hume, and the comparison is not unhelpful in so far as it reveals how the assumption of a naturalistic attitude leads, in both cases, to a relational conception of self in preference to a substantialist one: the self, insofar as it exists at all,[4] exists in the relationship between mental particulars, rather than as the substratum in which they inhere (in terms of the distinction drawn in the last chapter, both are collection rather than adjectival accounts). What I am arguing is that Hume and the Buddha nevertheless differ in a critical respect. Hume's account is located entirely in the realm of law: he speaks of 'that chain of causes and effects, which constitute our self or person'. Early Buddhist theory of mind, by contrast, is one of liberal naturalism. The point might be made by observing that for at least some Buddhists, what is described are not chains of causes and effects at all, but rather cluster-sequences in their phenomenological presentedness—'dependent origination' (*pratītya-samutpāda*) is then an account of temporal ordering within the structure of appearance, not a proto-Humean regularity theory of causation (a claim I will say more about in Chapters 7 and 11).

In the Jaina version of the story, Payāsi, now spelt 'Paesi', supposes that the soul, if it is something distinct from the body, must nevertheless explain variations as if it were something physical:

[4] Cf. Martin and Barresi (2006: 137): 'After Hobbes, but still in the seventeenth century, Spinoza, Boyle, and Locke also proposed relational views of personal identity. To thinkers in earlier centuries, a relational theory of personal identity had not suggested that the self might be a fiction. To eighteenth century thinkers it did.' This shift might in fact have come about as a result of new exposure to Buddhist sources from China.

Then prince Paesi spoke to Kesi thus: 'Now are the souls of an elephant and an ant of the same size?' 'Certainly, Paesi, the souls of an elephant and an ant have the same size.' 'But are not the actions and activities, afflictions, food, intake, evacuation, inhaling, exhaling, well-being and beautiful appearance of an ant more modest than those of an elephant, and in just the same way the actions and activities, afflictions, food, intake, evacuation, inhaling, exhaling, well-being and beautiful appearance of an elephant more impressive than those of an ant?' 'Certainly, Paesi.' How then, Venerable Sir, is the soul of an elephant of exactly the same size as that of an ant?' (*Paesi-kahāṇayaṁ* 772 (74) [187]; trans. Bollée 2002: 147)

In reply, Kesi seeks to change the metaphor through which the soul is conceived:

'Paesi, suppose there is a hall in a building . . . Someone with a light or lamp enters the hall of that building. He then completely shuts the door openings everywhere, so that they are tight, impervious, without gaps or apertures. Right in the middle of this hall, let him light a lamp. Now this lamp would illuminate, light, brighten and irradiate this hall inside but not outside. Further, if this person were to cover this lamp with a bushel, then it would illuminate the bushel inside, but neither outside it nor outside the hall . . . In just the same way, Paesi, the soul, too, is reborn in such a body as it is bound to by the *karma* of its previous existence. It animates it, be it small or big, by innumerous soul units. Therefore, Paesi, you should believe that the soul and the body are different and not identical.' (*Paesi-kahāṇayaṁ* 772 (74) [187]; trans. Bollée 2002: 147)

Kesi tries to show that even the physicalist has ways to explain the varying sizes of souls without identifying the soul with the body. The contrast between the respective responses of Kāśyapa and Kesi is in fact extremely instructive. In inviting his interlocutor to explain how the soul can behave like an ordinary physical thing, Payāsi sets a trap, since any attempt to provide an explanation of the behaviour of the self by analogy with the behaviour of some physical entity or phenomenon always ends up making the self sound like a mysterious crypto-physical being, a recherché denizen in the physical world. The temptation is to bring the self into the orbit of natural scientific intelligibility with similes about billiard balls, force fields, centres of gravity, mirrors, or, as in Kesi's case, light dispersal.[5] But to

[5] Dennett (1992) draws an analogy between selves and centres of gravity, but glosses it with a fictionalist account of theoretical entities. Scientific realism disagrees with Dennett about the status of theoretical entities, and first-person realism disagrees with him about the status of selves (cf. e.g.

surrender to the temptation is also to surrender any hope of explaining the self in terms that are *appropriate* to it, that is, in a vocabulary drawn from a liberal naturalism. Kāśyapa too uses a simile, and to that extent also falls into the trap set by Payāsi, but is not himself committed to the existence of selves. A defender of the claim that selves exist in nature must be vigilant about conceding, however implicitly, that physicalism provides the only criteria for what exists and what is natural. We can understand McDowell's assertion that his appeal to Aristotelianism is only *therapeutic* as the claim that having an alternative model of mind in view offers a defence against the temptations of Payāsi's Trap, the temptation to be drawn into a naturalization agenda. The Buddha's strategy was perhaps the best of all: to remain silent in the face of such impossible questions.

The *Cogito*: Augustine, Ibn Sīnā, Prabhācandra

In contrast with methodological naturalism stands the thought that philosophy can proceed in isolation of empirical inquiry, but appeal instead to what we might call exercises of imagination. This is exemplified above all in the provision of conceivability proofs that the self is *in essence* something non-bodily. A stronger claim is that it is *actually* separable from the body. Proofs of this sort are offered by three philosophers belonging to three very different philosophical traditions. The Christian philosopher Augustine appeals to the principle that to know a thing with certainty one must know with certainty its essence. The *cogito* proves that one does know with certainty oneself, and therefore one knows with certainty one's own essence. One does not know for certain whether one is anything bodily, however, and so one is not essentially bodily:

> In no way is anything rightly said to be known so long as its essence is not known. Hence so long as the mind knows itself, it knows its essence, and when it is certain about itself, it is certain about its essence. But it is certain about itself, as the points made above establish. It is not at all certain whether it is air or fire or any body, or anything bodily. So it is none of those things. (*On the Trinity* 10.10.16; trans. Sorabji 2006: 221)

Velleman 2005). In a strange echo of Kesi's talk about the spread of light from a lamp, Haskar (1999, 2001) recommends an analogy between selves and magnetic fields.

How might one demonstrate *a priori* that I and my body are discriminable in essence? The Bukharan philosopher Ibn Sīnā (980–1038 CE; aka Avicenna) also suggests a method. Ibn Sīnā says that one can imagine a man coming into existence flying through the air but having no sensory perceptions. This man knows that he exists, but not that his body exists. So he is not, in essence, his body:

> We say that one of us must imagine himself as if he were created all at once and as a whole, but with his sight covered so that he cannot see anything external, and created falling through the air or a vacuum, but falling in such a way that he encounters no air resistance nor anything else that would allow him to have any sensations, and with his limbs separated from one another so that they do not meet or touch. Then consider whether he will affirm the existence of his essence [or: of himself]. For he will not have any doubt in affirming existence for his essence, yet he will not along with this affirm [the existence of] the extremities of his limbs, nor his innards, his heart, his brain, or anything external to him. Instead, he will affirm [the existence of] his essence, without affirming that it has length, breadth, or depth. Nor, if in that state he were able to imagine there to be a hand or other body part, would he imagine that it was a part of himself or a condition for his essence [or: himself]. (Al-Shifâ: *Soul*, I.1, trans. Peter Adamson, in Sorabji 2006: 224)

It has been argued (Sorabji 2006: 226–7) that Augustine and Ibn Sīnā have a common source in the Neoplatonist thinker Porphyry. Porphyry appeals to the following idea: if something can withdraw itself from something else without being destroyed, then that other thing cannot be a part of its essence. He is reported to have said that 'the intellect is most aware of itself and does not get destroyed when it separates itself from the body' (*Sentences* 41).

Thirdly, I have found a remarkable version of this very influential argument in an Indian author, the Jaina philosopher Prabhācandra (980–1065 CE). Prabhācandra, who was born in the same year as Ibn Sīnā, argues as follows:

> It is not appropriate to deny that the self is known, since this is given in first-person acts of awareness (*ahampratyaya*) of the form 'I apprehend in awareness such things as a jar.' For in these, the thing is presented as object (*karmatayā*), while the self is presented as agent (*kartṛtayā*). It is not the case that the agent is the body or the sense-faculties or anything else, since they, just like the jar, are presented as objects.

> And also because one experiences first-person acts of awareness even when the body and the sense-faculties are not presented. [Consider] someone whose body is concealed by a cloak made of thick and dark cloth, and the working of whose senses is withdrawn (*uparata*); they are unaware of their body as endowed with such features as being heavy or clear-skinned. What this proves is that a first-person act of awareness, directly experiencing [the self] after being reflexively self-aware (*svasaṃviditaḥ punas tasyānubhūyamāno*), has as its ground (*ālambana*) something other than the body or the sense-faculties or their objects (*viṣaya*). Thus it is proved by reason that the self is a distinct and permanent substance. (Prabhācandra 1990: 119,18–120,4)

> Now, it is true that if the self were presented as without the body then it would be something distinct and permanent, just as fire [is presented] without water. Surely, though, this is not the case: it is always presented with it, at least in ordinary life. In this statement, what is the meaning of the phrase 'without the body' (*śarīra-rahita*)? Does it mean 'distinct by nature [essentially distinct]' (*svabhāva-vikala*), or does it mean 'located in a different place, having left the place of the body' (*taddeśaparihāreṇa deśāntarāvasthita*)? It is in the first sense that the self is presented as without the body; for the self is by nature consciousness and immaterial (*amūrta-caitanya-svabhāva*), and so by definition not the body, which by nature is unconscious stuff with colour and so on (*rūpādi-mad-acetana-svabhāva-śarīra-vilakṣaṇa*) (1990: 120,10–16).

One can imagine oneself with one's senses disabled and one's body masked (or drugged). So one can imagine oneself without one's body, not in the sense of floating freely from it, but in the sense that to think about oneself is not necessarily to think about one's body. From this exercise in imagination, what is alleged to follow is that the body and the self have distinct natures or essences (*svabhāva*), whether or not they can actually exist separately from one another. There are powerful resemblances both to Ibn Sina's *flying man* and to Augustine's *cogito* in this argument by Prabhācandra. There is a comparison too with Descartes's later and much more famous argument for a 'real distinction' between mind and body.

The general pattern of these exercises in *a priori* metaphysical reasoning is roughly as follows. We do not, in self-reflection, identify the self as having bodily properties. We do, in self-reflection, identify the self. So the self is something which is identified as having non-bodily properties. Sidney Shoemaker has claimed that the argument breaks down because introspection is not a matter of identifying a self at all. The fallacy, he says, is in the move from our failure to identify the self as having bodily properties to the supposition that we do identify it as having non-bodily properties. He finds this point in Wittgenstein's comment: 'We feel . . . that in cases in which "I" is used as subject, we don't use it because we recognize a person by his bodily characteristics; and this creates the illusion that we use this word to refer to something bodiless, which, however has its seat in our body. In fact *this* seems to be the real ego, the one of which it was said "Cogito, ergo sum"' (Shoemaker 1996: 18). But in assimilating the use of imaginative exercises to an introspective model of inner observation, this criticism misses the point. It is not a search for self-knowledge but an exploration of what is possible in the imagination. If there is a challenge to this method of philosophizing, it can only come from a denial that imaginability entails metaphysical possibility.

We might summarize the various conclusions from the thought experiment as follows. According to Augustine, one can be self-aware in the absence of any *knowledge* about one's own body. According to Ibn Sina, one can be self-aware in the absence of a *concept* of one's body. According to Prabhācandra, one can be self-aware in the absence of *perceptual experience*, and in particular in the absence of current proprioceptive perceptions of one's body. Against such claims, one might try to argue that one cannot have self-awareness without thinking of oneself as embodied, or at least that one cannot be self-aware in the absence of (the possibility of) proprioceptive perceptions. I will return to these possibilities on several occasions below.

Naturalism and the First-Person Stance

The empiricist methodology of the hard naturalist runs aground on its assumption that the perception of individual experiences is less problematic than the perception of individual selves.[6] The alternative, a method based

[6] 'It seems to me that whether we interpret "perceive" in the broad sense or in the narrow sense, the view that we have introspective perceptions of individual mental happenings but not of a self is indefensible . . . And I think that this puts the Humean denial in an interesting new light. For it completely undermines the view, which motivates "bundle", "logical construction", and "no subject" theories of the self, that from an empiricist standpoint the status of the self (the subject of experience) is suspect compared with that of such things as sensations, feelings, images, and the like' (Shoemaker 1996: 24).

on exercises of imagination, runs aground too, but at a different place. The problem is that I seem to be able to imagine what is metaphysically impossible. For it is metaphysically impossible for one object to be identical to another one, and yet it would seem that I can imagine being someone else.[7] Similarly, although I can imagine being without a body, it does not follow that it is metaphysically possible that I should be able to be bodiless (this indeed is one motivation for separating questions of individuation and ownership).

Bernard Williams concludes from these points that exercises of imagination cannot be trusted as a method for establishing what is possible: 'At least with regard to the self, the imagination is too tricky a thing to provide a reliable road to the comprehension of what is logically possible' (1973a: 45; cf. 1973b: 70–3). I seem to be able to imagine myself existing without any given one of my actual characteristics, and this leads me to

> the idea that it is not necessary to being *me* that I should have any of the individuating properties that I do have, this body, these memories, etc. And for some of them, such as the body, we may think that it is not necessary to have one at all; and, quite readily, we might not have any memories. (1973a: 41)

This process leads, in the limit, to that notion of self which Williams describes as an 'attenuated "I" ', and he rightly observes that a fundamental difficulty with a so severely attenuated 'I' is that 'there is absolutely nothing left to distinguish any Cartesian "I" from any other, and it is impossible to see any more what would be subtracted from the universe by the removal of *me*' (1973a: 42). What has gone wrong, according to Williams, is that two different modes of the imagination have become confused with one another in these imaginary exercises, the mode according to which one imagines of a certain thing, not myself, that it has such-and-such characteristics, and the mode in which one imagines being such-and-such oneself.[8] Williams derives the idea of the 'attenuated I' from Strawson, who put the point in even more vivid terms:

[7] Bernard Williams raises the point in his important essay, 'Imagination and the Self' (Williams 1973a).

[8] Could we escape the problem by drawing a distinction between imagining being someone else and imagining *oneself* being someone else (Vendler 1979: 172–3)? No, because the same difficulty simply repeats itself at a higher level, the level of self-ascribing content to *oneself* in imagination (Recanati 2007: 204).

> In order to retain his idea of himself as an individual, he must always think of himself as disembodied, as a *former* person . . . Since he has, as it were, no personal life of his own to lead, he must live much in the memories of the personal life he did lead; or he might, when this living in the past loses its appeal, achieve some kind of attenuated vicarious personal existence by taking a certain kind of interest in the human affairs of which he is a mute and invisible witness . . . In proportion as the memories fade, and this vicarious living palls, to that degree his concept of himself as an individual becomes attenuated. *At the limit of attenuation there is, from the point of view of his survival as an individual, no difference between the continuance of experience and its cessation.* (P. F. Strawson 1963: 116, my italics)

I will describe any theory which falls to this objection 'Attenuated'.

That there is a *prima facie* tension between naturalism and a genuine acknowledgement of the first-person position is evident in an important and instructive argument, one which is again due to Prabhācandra. Prabhācandra seeks to demonstrate that hard naturalism is incompatible with the existence of reflective self-awareness. He offers first an analogy: the matter of the body cannot reflect itself, any more than a mirror can.[9] Developing the argument,[10] he claims that it is characteristic of self-awareness for a first-person present-tense self-ascription to be a truth-apt mental state in the content of which the self features.[11] This content does not have as its objective ground (*ālambana*) the body, because such states do not require the perception of anything external to themselves in order to occur.[12] In support of that claim, he mentions the thought experiment we discussed above, which purports to show that one can be in such a psychological state even when in circumstances of complete sensory deprivation. And he spells out what he thinks is the difference between the content of such a state and the content of an empirical perception: in the first case, the self is cognized but *not by way of* something else.[13] If a state is both a genuine awareness of

[9] Prabhācandra (1990: 110, 11–12): '[The Cārvākas say this:] Let it be that consciousness lacks any internal form; being matter transformed, it cannot be aware of itself, any more than a mirror [can reflect itself].' Śaṃkara makes the same point with a different analogy: nothing material can revert on itself, any more than an acrobat can climb on his own shoulders (1917, *infra* 3.3.54).

[10] Prabhācandra (1990: 111,19–113,3); and again, with some elaboration, in Prabhācandra (1991: 348,22–349,8).

[11] *sukhyahaṃ duḥkhyaham icchāvān aham ityādyanupacaritāham-pratyayasyātmagrāhiṇah pratiprāṇi saṃvedanāt* |

[12] *nāpi śarīrālambanaḥ bahiḥkaraṇa-nirapekṣāntaḥ-karaṇa-vyāpāreṇotpatteḥ* |

[13] *na cārthāntarasyārthāntara-svabhāvenāpratyakṣatvaṃ doṣaḥ* | There is a suggestion here of the phenomenon of 'immunity to error through misidentification' (Shoemaker 1968: 557), prominent in discussions

the self and yet different from any perceptual experience, then the conclusion (which he states explicitly only at 1991: 349,3–4) is that it must be admitted that there is something distinct from the body, which can serve as the objective referent in first-person self-ascription of psychological properties, and as their owner (*jñānavān*).[14] Notice that Prabhācandra does not make his argument rest on a difference in the epistemology of mental and physical properties (that is, on what I will call in Chapter 12 the Self-Knowledge Argument), but on a difference in the very way that first-person self-ascription and ordinary experience have content.

More recently, Hermann Weyl sees the tension as testing both scientific naturalism and Husserl's phenomenology:

> It is time now to point out the limits of science. The riddle posed by the double nature of the ego certainly lies beyond those limits. On the one hand, I am a real individual man . . . carrying out real and physical and psychical acts, one among many. On the other hand, I am 'vision' open to reason, a self-penetrating light, immanent sense-giving consciousness. (Weyl 1954a; in Bell 2004: 178)

Again,

> Here finally arises in its full seriousness the metaphysical question concerning the relation between the one pure I of immanent consciousness and the particular lost human being which I find myself to be in a world full of people like me (for example, during the afternoon rush hour on Fifth Avenue in New York). Husserl does not say much more about it than that 'only through experience of the relationship of the body does awareness take on psychological reality in man or animal'. (Weyl 1954b; in Bell 2004: 178)

Weyl's description of the problem makes it clear that it is neither the standard mind-body problem nor the so-called 'hard problem' about consciousness, although it is related to both. More recently still, Lynne Rudder Baker has identified it as the crucial test of naturalism:

> Can the first-person perspective be accommodated by naturalism? The answer depends on what is meant by 'naturalism.' If naturalism requires only that there be no appeal to anything supernatural or immaterial, then the first-person

about self-knowledge and self-reference, that no *identification* is involved in the 'use as subject' of the first-person pronoun. The same point is made by Rāmakaṇṭha in his discussion of reflexive awareness (for textual references, see Watson 2010 nn. 11, 34).

[14] *ataḥ śarīrātirikaḥ kaścid etasya ālambanabhūto jñānavān artho 'bhyupagantavyaḥ* |

> perspective is naturalistic. A capacity for a first-person perspective seems no less likely to have been produced by evolution than a capacity for speaking a language or a capacity for solving differential equations. Call this sense of naturalism 'weak naturalism.' There are more robust construals of 'naturalism,' however, incompatible with the relaxed ontological pluralism that seems plausible to me. A more robust naturalism would be the view that what exists is only what is countenanced by the natural sciences. This more robust ontological naturalism is often allied with various projects of 'naturalisation.' These projects aim to provide full and sufficient explanations of various intentional, semantic, and mental phenomena in nonintentional, nonsemantic and nonmental terms. It is this robust naturalism, in both its ontological and epistemic versions, to which I suggest that the first-person perspective presents a challenge. (Baker 1998: 342–3; cf. 2013 for fuller elaboration)

My aim in what follows is to seek alternative conceptions of the commitments and ambitions of naturalism; or, to put it the other way round, to ask what naturalism must be, in order for the *prima facie* incompatibility between naturalism and the first-person perspective to be resolved. I will retrieve from first-millennium Indian thought three answers to that question, each having its own terms of reference, each facing its own challenges. The fundamental motivation behind this Indian revitalization of naturalism is to escape from being driven into an oscillation between empiricist enthusiasm and unconstrained exercises of imagination.

The argument of Prabhācandra seems to force a naturalist to make a choice between one of three possibilities. The first is to try to argue that the self which features in the content of first-person psychological judgement is indeed the human being, and to provide an explanatory theory of content, presumably one in which a distinction is drawn between the *de re* and the *de se* modes under which the body is presented in thought. The second is to deny that such judgements are genuinely truth-apt, but instead to give a fictionalist, error-theoretic, or other irrealist explanation of the first-person stance. The third is to try to argue that there is indeed a way to make sense of the asymmetry between the first-person and the third-person positions within a naturalist outlook.

I will correspondingly explore three naturalist accounts. The Cārvāka identify a human being (*puruṣa*) with a sort of entity capable of bearing both physical and psychological attributes, where psychological attributes are emergent properties of complex physical structures. There is here, though, no explanation of the asymmetry between the first-person and the third-person stance. Buddhists seek to explain that asymmetry by way of a phenomenological investigation into self-consciousness, offering a way to ground a distinction between viewing our mental lives in a third-person or 'theoretical' perspective (*manovijñāna*) and viewing it as imbued with a sense of mineness (*manas*). To this attractive analysis, they bring, however, an additional commitment to an error-theory about the first-person stance. The third view is that of Nyāya and Vaiśeṣika philosophers, who look upon human subjectivity as the owning of conscious thought, emotion, and intention, itself explained by unconscious causal psychological mechanisms, all of which supervene on neurophysiological states of the physical body, and the totality of which is a human being. I will gradually defend a view which combines a closely related conception of the asymmetry between the first- and third-person stances with a more perceptive analysis of the phenomenology of the first-person stance and with a theoretically sophisticated understanding of the third-person relation between mental and physical properties.

Where does this leave us with respect to the eleven conceptions of self distinguished in the last chapter? Cartesian, Animalist, and Reductionist Views have just been examined, and the research programme within which they fall found to be methodologically problematic. More exactly, the Cartesian View suffers from what I will henceforth call the Attenuation Problem, the problem that *place* of ownership by itself is not individuative of selves.[15] Animalism and the Reductionist View suffer from what I will call the Persistence Problem (see Chapter 5). Difficulties over Attenuation and Persistence motivate a move away from Type I conceptions. The programme to investigate views which deny that self has any metaphysical base—Madhyamaka and the Pure Consciousness (Advaita Vedānta) View—cannot be thought of as a naturalist one in any sense. The Flame and Torrent views are best investigated using methods of mathematical modelling which have been developed to study those biological and ecological phenomena which constitute non-linear dynamical systems. This research programme has therefore tended to become associated with a 'naturalization' agenda, although it is not strictly forced to be. The Yogācāra and Phenomenal views, both of which take the stream to be the metaphysical base of first-

[15] For a clear statement of Attenuation, P. F. Strawson (1963: 100): 'One cannot identify others if one can identify them *only* as subjects of experience, possessors of states of consciousness.'

person phenomena, are for that reason best seen as pure phenomenologies. The critical issue they face is that there can be gaps in phenomenal consciousness. So the trio of views, Cārvāka Emergentism, Buddhist Abhidharma, and the Ownership View of Nyāya-Vaiśeṣika—having in common the fact that they all take first-person phenomena to have a metaphysical base in the physical body—form an integral group. The taxonomy of the last chapter gives us very good reasons for reading these three conceptions about self together.

PART II

Mind and Body

3

Emergence

Emergence: The Core Issues

As a position in contemporary philosophy of mind, emergentism developed out of the early work of a number of British philosophers.[1] Each special science (chemistry, biology, psychology, and so on), it is claimed, describes a range of causal powers that emerge from but are irreducible to the causal powers of physical particles:

British Emergentism maintains that some special science kinds from each special science can be wholly composed of types of structures of material particles that endow the kinds in question with fundamental causal powers. Chemical elements, in virtue of their minute internal structures, have the power to bond with certain others. Certain biological organisms, in virtue of their minute internal structures, have the powers to breathe, to digest food, and to reproduce. *And certain kinds of organisms, in virtue of the minute internal structures of their nervous systems, have 'the power of cognising, the power of being affected by past experiences, the power of association, and so on'* (Broad 1925: 436). The property of having a certain type of structure will thus endow a special science kind with emergent causal powers. Such a structure will have an emergent causal power as a matter of law, but the law will not be 'reducible to' or 'derivative from' laws governing lower levels of complexity and any boundary conditions involving the arrangements of particles. (McLaughlin 1992: 50–1; my italics)

Generalizing, the satisfaction of two conditions is typically regarded as necessary for any theory to be emergentist:

[1] J. S. Mill (1843), and then Lewes (1875), Morgan (1923), Alexander (1920), and Broad (1925).

1. Mental properties *supervene* on physical properties.[2]
2. Mental properties confer on their instances causal powers *irreducible* to the causal powers conferred by the properties supervened on.[3]

One idea, perhaps the leading one in discussions about emergence, is that systems of appropriate organizational complexity have causal powers which the components in the system, whether individually or together, do not. Emergentism hopes to give sense to the idea that mental properties are metaphysically *dependent* on physical properties but yet possess causal *autonomy* with respect to them.[4]

Jaegwon Kim (Kim 2006a; cf. also 2006b) agrees that any version of emergentism is committed to a supervenience thesis and an irreducibility thesis, and specifically that the core emergentist idea that emergent properties contribute new causal powers neither explicable by nor predictable from the basal properties is a denial of functional reducibility. The two key issues for the development of emergentism as a viable theory, he argues, are i) to give *a positive characterization* of the relation of emergence, beyond the mere denial of reducibility; and ii) to solve *the problem of downward causation*, otherwise known as the exclusion problem or the supervenience problem. This is the problem that an instantiation of the supervenience base is apparently a sufficient cause for any effect attributed to an instantiation of the supervening properties. One seems forced to choose between reductionism (mental properties are 'nothing but' physical properties) and epiphenomenalism (mental properties are distinct from physical properties, but the residue is inefficacious): genuinely novel emergent causal power is excluded.

As I will demonstrate here, the philosopher of mind Bṛhaspati and at least some of his successors are emergentists. Responsive to the key issues Kim has identified, theirs is a powerful articulation of a conception of the mind's dependence on, and autonomy from, the physical.

[2] e.g. Van Cleve (1990), O'Connor (1994), McLaughlin (1997), Kim (1999, 2006a, 2006b), Chalmers (1996, 2006), Shoemaker (2007), Macdonald and Macdonald (2010). O'Connor (2000) and Lowe (1996) have, however, defended non-supervenience-based accounts.

[3] I will discuss a conception of emergence which denies this, 'weak emergence', below.

[4] As Mark Bedau observes, 'emergent phenomena are Janus-faced; they depend on more basic phenomena and yet are autonomous from that base' (Bedau and Humphreys 2008: 6), describing dependence and autonomy as the two hallmarks of emergence (ibid. 155).

Cārvāka Naturalism

There are references in the Indian texts to a group of renegade freethinkers whose views about human life are radically at odds with then-prevailing belief. These worldly intellectuals deny the existence of anything that smacks of the supernatural—such as transcendental beings, immaterial souls or heavenly other-worlds. Life, they say, is for living here on earth. And they have a most interesting account of what human life itself consists in. A human person is a material body, made, like everything else, out of the four elements—but one in which thought, reason, intelligence and consciousness arise as the physical elements are transformed, in exactly the same way that the process of fermentation leads to the emergence of the power to intoxicate in a mixture of appropriate ingredients. The views of these philosophers, who were known as Lokāyata ('worldly'), or more commonly Cārvāka, and whose central figure is the enigmatic Bṛhaspati, have been deeply unfashionable, their treatises destroyed or left to rot, their ideas subject to fierce and hostile criticism. That they were, nevertheless, still known in sixteenth-century India is evinced by the report of Abū-l-Fażl, who describes their theory for the benefit of the Mughal Emperor Akbar, saying that 'they regard paradise as a state in which man lives as he chooses, free from the control of another, and hell the state in which he lives subject to another's rule . . . They admit only of such disciplines as tend to the promotion of external order, that is, a knowledge of just administration and benevolent government' (al-Faḍl 1873–1907: iii. 217). No truck is given here to religion and other 'inner' spiritual disciplines.

Our search for fresh foundations for naturalism gives us new reasons to examine the views of these thinkers. Their most important contribution, I will claim, is the doctrine that psychological states are emergent physical states. A separable claim is that the self is identical to the physical body. This second issue has to do with the material constitution of the self and its identity over time, and the view is a version of Animalism, the claim being that a person is identical with the human animal and not with either an immaterial soul or a psychological continuum. I suspect that this view represents an earlier phase in the development of Cārvāka, to be associated with the likes of Payāsi rather than with Bṛhaspati and his followers (see also Chapter 5).

According to Bṛhaspati, consciousness is due to the four constitutive principles of matter, just as the power to intoxicate is due to the ingredients in the wine.[5] What we call a human body, or a sense-organ, or a physical object, is just a combination (*samudāya*; an assemblage) of earth, fire, air, and water; indeed, these four kinds of matter are all there is. A person is a human body endued with thinking, and individual lives differ one from another as bubbles differ in water. New work on the reconstruction of Bṛhaspati's text allows us to conjecture that it begins as follows:

1.1 Next then we will examine the nature of the reals.
1.2 Earth, fire, air and water are the reals.
1.3 Their combination is called the 'body', 'senses', and 'objects'.
1.4 Consciousness (*caitanya*) [is formed] out of these [elementary reals].
1.5 As the power to intoxicate [is formed] out of fermenting ingredients.
1.6 A human being (*puruṣa*) is a body qualified by consciousness.
1.7 [Thinking is] from the body alone.
1.8 Because of its presence when there is a body.[6]

Two initial observations: First, Bṛhaspati's commitment to physicalism might seem to be unambiguous. He says that earth, water, fire, and air are real, nothing else, and that what we call an object, a body or a sense-organ is just an aggregation. The science of the four elemental reals just is what for him was the science of physics, and everything which exists, it is asserted, is identical to the elements or to some combination of them. Second, Bṛhaspati appears to commit himself to the completeness of physics in his further claim that all variation in the world is due to variation in 'origin' (*janma*). The varied patterns which are seen in the eye of a peacock's tail feathers come about as a result of details in their provenance, and the same explanation works for all other-worldly variation:

2.1 The world is varied due to variations in origin.
2.2 As the eye in the peacock's tail.[7]

[5] For a list of the various sorts of mental state or capacity that Indian thinkers have classified under the description 'consciousness' (*caitanya*), see Ch. 5.

[6] *athātas tattvaṃ vyākhyāsyāmaḥ* | *pṛthivyāpastejovāyur iti tattvāni* | *tatsamudāye śarīrendriyaviṣayasaṃjñaḥ* | *tebhyaś caitanyam* | *kiṇvādibhyo madaśaktivat* | *caitanyaviśiṣṭaḥ kāyaḥ puruṣaḥ* | *śarīrād eva* | *śarīre bhāvāt* | (R. Bhattacharya 2002a: 603–4).

[7] *janmavaicitryabhedāj jagad api vicitram* | *mayūracandrakavat* | (R. Bhattacharya 2002a: 604).

I take this to mean that there is a complete physical causal history for every change or difference, that is, as a version of the thesis that every physical effect (every 'variation') is determined by antecedent physical causes (its 'origin'). In spite of the choice of example, I do not take this to be a reference to the doctrine of individual nature (*svabhāva*).

Bṛhaspati's philosophy of mind can be resolved into a pair of theses:

> [Thesis 1] A human being consists in a living body made out of the four elements which, in that combination, instantiates mental properties.

It is striking that the term 'self' is not used here at all, but only the term 'human being' (*puruṣa*).[8] The difficulty is to extract further resolution from a second thesis:

> [Thesis 2] It is *due to* the combination of the elements in the body that mental properties are instantiated.

The trouble is with the ablative, which I have translated, as neutrally as possible, as 'due to'. Is the claim that thinking consists in the elements combined in a certain way, i.e. that it is *made from* them (an ablative of composition); or that it is the claim that *because of* the elements there is thinking (an ablative of explanation); or is it the claim that thinking is *produced out of* them (an ablative of causation)? Later sources will disambiguate this ablative in two different ways, as well as offering a distinct three-way disambiguation of the statements taken as a group. These disambiguations generate a range of philosophical positions about the mind-body problem. From among the ensuing positions one can retrieve materials for a distinctive variety of emergentism.

Epiphenomenalism

Among these various possibilities one suggestion is that Cārvāka philosophy of mind is a form of epiphenomenalism. According to this possibility the

[8] Bṛhaspati reserves for the term *puruṣa* the same sense that P. F. Strawson does the term 'person', that is with reference to specimens of a type of entity 'such that to each individual of that type there must be ascribed, or ascribable, *both* states of consciousness and corporeal characteristics' (Strawson 1963: 104). Writers in the philosophy of Sāṃkhya attach a quite different significance to the term.

mind is a by-product of the material body, lacking in causal powers of its own. The question has a long history, and indeed goes back to the first presentation of Bṛhaspati's thought to a European audience. In a famous and widely circulated lecture given to a public meeting of the Royal Asiatic Society in London, 3 February 1827, Henry T. Colebrooke conjectured of Bṛhaspati that '[a]mong the Greeks, Dicaearchus of Messene held the same tenet' (Colebrooke 1837: 429). Dicaearchus (*c.*350–285 BCE) was a member of the Lyceum and a defender of the *harmonia* theory, put forward by Simmias in the *Phaedo*, that the soul is a 'tuning' (*harmonia*) or 'tempering/ blend' (*krasis*) of the body, that a blend of hot, cold, fluid and dry material is to the soul what the tuning is to the lyre (*Phaedo* 86b7–c2). Dicaearchus wrote a dialogue, now lost, about the soul, which is mentioned by several later authors. One important source is Cicero, who reports:

> In the remaining two books, [Dicaearchus] introduces a certain Pherecrates, an old man from Phthia, said to be a descendant of Deucalion, who maintains the following. The soul is nothing at all and this name completely vacuous—animals and animate things are so-called in vain [*anima* meaning 'soul'], for there is neither soul nor spirit in either man or beast. That whole power by which we act or are aware extends evenly through all living bodies and is not separable from the body. In fact, [that power] is nothing, nor is there anything else, apart from the body just alone by itself, so configured that it lives and is aware by the tempering of its nature. (*Tusculanarum disputationum.* 1.10.21)

This is certainly the source relied on by Colebrooke, for he describes the tenet in question, the one which he finds also in Bṛhaspati, as being 'that there is no such thing as soul in man; that the principle, by which he perceives and acts, is diffused through the body, is inseparable from it, and terminates with it' (Colebrooke 1837: 430). The view which Sextus Empiricus attributes to Dicaearchus is that thinking is 'nothing apart from the body disposed in a certain way' (*Adversus mathematicos* 7.349). Plutarch introduces a very similar view, without attributing it: 'Or is this the case? Namely, that the substance of the soul isn't anything at all; rather, it is the tempered body which possesses the power of thinking and living' (*Against Colotes* 1119ab).

The analogy with the tuning of a musical instrument is helpful because it reminds us that there are three different things we must keep apart: (i) the blend itself; (ii) the dispositional properties and causal powers that the body has, and for which the blend is the categorical base; and (iii) the effects of the blend either on the body or on other things. One might think of a block of ice, with crystalline structure, brittleness, and a capacity to cool other things. Reviewing ideas about the *harmonia* theory, Victor Caston observes that the idea was understood by Dicaearchus as a claim that the soul just is the blend (Caston 1997, 2001). Dicaearchus is described as holding that the soul is an attunement of the elements of matter that comprise the body, rather than as a power ascribable to the body in virtue of the attunement.[9] Denying that the attunement has any causal powers of its own, Dicaearchus is an epiphenomenalist.[10]

Certain classical Indian thinkers likewise will interpret Bṛhaspati as identifying the mind with a combination of elements in the body, making him an epiphenomenalist like Dicaearchus (mind has no causal powers over and above those of the body), while others will claim that his view is that the mind is a distinct power which emerges from the combination but is not identical to it. There is textual evidence of this disagreement among the Indian Cārvāka philosophers of mind. Referring to the basic thesis, that it is due to the physical elements that there is thinking, we are informed that:

> Here, some commentators explain that thinking arises from (*utpadyate*) the elements, while others say that it is made manifest (*abhivyajyate*) [by them]. (Kamalaśīla 1968: 633,15–634,1)

[9] Aristoxenus, another supporter of the *harmonia* theory, and someone who went with Alexander the Great to India, took the tuning to be of the organs and limbs rather than of the four elements within the body.

[10] Caston (2001: 185): 'He accepts Aristotle's claim that a *harmonia* cannot have causal powers. But he does not think that this is a reason to reject the *harmonia* theory; if anything, it is a reason to change our views about the soul. He thinks that while there are mental events, they are completely inefficacious—their alleged effects are to be accounted for solely in terms of the powers of the body. Dicaearchus' position is that of the modern epiphenomenalist.' Caston mentions a passage from Plutarch's *On Desire and Grief* which attributes the view, apparently to Dicaearchus, that 'Some straightforwardly extend belief and calculation into the body, saying that the soul is not a cause at all, but that it is rather by the difference, quality, and power of the body that such things come about' (ibid: 185; cf. Caston 1997: 345). In his discussion of the thesis that the soul is a *harmonia*, C. C. W. Taylor indeed distinguishes these four interpretations:

> [1.] the soul is identical with the ratio or formula according to which the elements are combined to form the living man;
> [2.] the soul is identical with the mixture or combination of those elements according to that formula;
> [3.] the soul is some entity produced by the combination of those elements according to that formula, but distinct alike from them and from the formula itself;
> [4.] the soul is identical with a state of the bodily elements, viz., the state of being combined according to that formula. (Taylor 2008: 74–5)

Again:

Some people restore the connecting verb [in 'due to the elements, thinking'] with 'is manifested' (*abhivyajyate*), but others with 'comes into being' (*prādhurbhavati*). (Prabhācandra 1991: 342,2–3)

This second source goes into much greater detail than any of the others in explaining the concept 'manifestation' in place here. He tells us that a manifestation is something which 'puts together well' or 'refines' and 'perfects' (*saṃskāraka*) what is already there, rather than bringing into being something that was not there before (Prabhācandra 1990: 226,12–13). As such, the manifestation is not a separate thing, over and above the four elements, even though it is does have a distinctive characteristic of its own (1990: 225,25); it is not a 'distinct reality' (*tattvāntara*) (1990: 115,13). In this, there is certainly an affinity with the Greek word *harmonia*, which 'derives from a verb for "fitting together," for joining things so as to adapt or accommodate them to each other . . . ', such that tempering 'is the balancing of one against another so as to produce a dynamic whole' (Caston 1997: 321–2). So the manifestation account, in thinking of states of mind as refinements of the body, is a close cousin of the *harmonia* theory as that theory was understood by Dicaearchus.

Other philosophers, notably Galen and Alexander, are drawn to a different reading of the *harmonia* theory, that the *harmonia* gives rise to new causal powers—and our source too distinguishes such a view among the possible interpretations of Bṛhaspati's claim that consciousness arises from the physical elements in the right combination. This same source indeed provides us with a helpful threefold classification of physicalist solutions to the mind-body problem. A physicalist must claim that the lack of distinction between self and body consists in either i) their identity (*svabhāva*), or ii) the self being a quality or state (*guṇa*) of the body, or iii) the self being an effect (*kārya*) of the body (Prabhācandra 1990: 120,22–3). This division might be brought into correspondence with the one we have seen in connection with the *harmonia* theory: the mind is either identical to the tempered body, or to the tempering itself, or to a power caused by that tempering. It might also be said to correspond with the modern distinction between reductionism, epiphenomenalism, and emergentism. I will refer again to the idea that the self is a quality of the body in Chapter 6; here I am interested in the first and third possibilities.

Supervenience

The notion of supervenience is explicitly formulated in the Indian discussion, particularly in critics' descriptions of what Cārvāka naturalism is committed to. The supervenience claim is that fixing the body's physical state fixes its mental state: two bodies cannot be distinguishable in terms of their mental properties and yet be indistinguishable in terms of their physical properties. The Latin term *super-venire* is a rendering of the Greek *epi-ginesthai* and *ginesthai epi*, terms which are used, in a sense close to the modern one, by Alexander and Philoponus. Philoponus in particular uses the notion in contrast with the idea that psychological characteristics simply result from (*apotelesma*) and follow (*hepesthai*) the blend of chemical ingredients, in such a way as to allow mental states to react back on the body.[11] Donald Davidson was the first contemporary philosopher to promote the idea. He did so as follows:

> Mental characteristics are in some sense dependent, or supervenient, on physical characteristics. Such supervenience might be taken to mean that there cannot be two events exactly alike in all physical respects but differing in some mental respects, *or that an object cannot alter in some mental respects without altering in some physical respects*. (Davidson 1980: 214; my italics)

We can see supervenience as having two components: *dependence* ('nothing can have mental-properties unless it also has physical-properties'), and *determination* ('nothing can be just like a given thing as regards its physical-properties without also being just like it as regards its mental-properties'). In short, 'every mental-property, some physical-property', and 'same physical-properties, same mental-properties' (Van Cleve 1990: 221).

Supervenience, I have said, is explicit in the formulations we have of Indian physicalist philosophy of mind. It is not to be found in what one might think of as the obvious place, however. The obvious place is a certain standard argument for physicalism, one at which Bṛhaspati hints in his

[11] I owe this information to Richard Sorabji; see further his (2003; 2005: i. 194, 201, 202; 2010: 33–4).

laconic formulae 1.7–1.8. Other sources present the argument in similar terms:

Thinking is a quality of the body, because it is present when there is a body and absent when there is none.[12]

I will call this the *covariance argument*. Its premise is that there is a relation of 'presence and absence' between states of the body and states of the mind, and its conclusion is that mental states are states of the body. This relation has two components, 'covariance in presence' (*anvaya*) and 'covariance in absence' (*vyatireka*). The basic pattern, as Cardona (1967–8, 1981) has shown, is:

Covariance in presence: When B occurs (*tadbhāve*), A occurs (*tadbhāvāt*).
Covariance in absence: When B is absent (*tadabhāve*), A is absent (*tadabhāvāt*).

Here, A = mind or mental property, and B = body or physical property. On scrutiny, it is clear that we do not yet have a supervenience relation. The two halves of the rule of presence and absence resolve themselves as follows:

[Presence:] (Necessarily,) anything which has certain physical properties is thinking.
[Absence:] (Necessarily,) anything which is thinking is a physical thing (i.e. if *x* does not have physical properties, then *x* does not have any mental properties).

It is clear why this does not specify a relation of supervenience. If this is all there is to covariance, then the covariance of the physical with the mental and the mental with the physical lacks the determination component of the supervenience definition. It does not have 'same B-properties, same A-properties' feature, but only the weaker 'every A-property, some B-property'. More particularly, while supervenience is an asymmetric relation between A and B, covariance is entirely symmetric. The covariance argument is at best enthymematic, but it is unclear what suppressed premise is in the background of appeals to this argument.

Some of our sources, however, introduce the new thought that the body is the 'material cause' of thinking (*upādāna-kāraṇa*), and it turns out not only that the operative notion of 'material cause' does imply supervenience, but

[12] Gautama (1997: 203,3): *Nyāya-sūtra* 3.2.46. See also *Brahma-sūtra-bhāṣya* 3.3.53 (Śaṇkara 1917).

that this is made explicit. The idea is that, just as a sculptor could not change the features of a statue without making changes to the material out of which it is made, so too one cannot alter mental states without there being some alteration in their physical basis: we would now call this a relation of constitution. Our sources tell us that it is part of the notion of material cause that alterations in the material cause are implied by alterations in that which it is the material cause of. In other words, the idea of a material cause carries with it the idea of a supervenience base. Having established this principle, the critics of Cārvāka naturalism go on to argue by *reductio* that thinking does not have the physical body as its material cause: if it did, then the mental would supervene on the physical, but it does not. Here is one important text:

> Is it possible that the elements of matter be the 'cause' of thinking, either as the material cause or as a co-operating cause? Certainly not as the material cause, because even when they alter [thinking] does not. If one thing does not alter when another does, that other is not its material cause; the relation between a horse and a cow illustrates this. Thinking is not altered when the material elements that have been transformed into a body alter. This is not [merely] an undemonstrated assertion, for it is well known that thinking which is otherwise engaged is unaltered even by the stab of a knife, which feels [to the preoccupied thinker] no different from a rub of sandal-paste. In exactly the same way, there can be alterations in thinking without alterations in the [elements comprising the body]. This too is not an unfounded claim, since the joyful emotion one feels when near to a lovely woman alters without one's body changing state. (Prabhācandra 1991: 344,9–15)

Another source is if anything even clearer:

> Nor is the 'material cause' view correct. For it is well known that the particular cause regarded as the material cause is one such that an alteration in the effect is impossible unless one brings about an alteration in it . . . That is why someone who wants to alter something alters it only by altering its material cause, and in no other way. For when the material cause is present and its power is unimpeded, nobody can prevent the occurrence of its subsequent effect. (Kamalaśīla 1968: 642,23–643,5.)

What this shows is that when someone claims that the relation between mind and body is one of 'material causation', better described as a relation of constitution, that is indeed to make a supervenience claim.

A modal operator is used explicitly in these two formulations, and we are in a position to consider whether the supervenience involved is strong or weak.[13] Inverting the conditional, the claim here is that if *x* is the material cause of *y* then it is not possible to bring about an alteration in *y* without an alteration in *x*. What has been said is that if *x* undergoes an alteration, then it is *impossible* to prevent the alteration in *y*.[14] So the force of the statement is that there are no circumstances in which the intended alteration in *y* does not occur and yet the alteration in *x* does; i.e., necessarily, if *x* undergoes alteration *G*, then *y* undergoes alteration *F*. Presuming that the entire claim has the status of a 'rule' or 'law' (*niyama*), and so that there is a second, wide scope, necessity, we can conclude that what is being attributed to the naturalist who sees the relation between mind and body as one of 'material causation' is a strong supervenience thesis.[15] Our source, not himself a naturalist, points out that to deny strong supervenience of mind on body is not to commit oneself to denying that there are any circumstances in which physical changes necessitate alterations of the mind.

What we have so far established is that the classical theory endorses supervenience, the first requirement for a theory of emergence. Mark Bedau argues that we should distinguish between *strong* and *weak* conceptions of emergence in the following way.[16] Strong emergence involves 'a requirement that emergent properties are supervenient properties with irreducible causal powers' (Bedau 2008: 158; cf. O'Connor 1994). Weak emergence involves a less demanding requirement, which in Bedau's

[13] In the modal rather than the possible worlds formulation, given two families of properties A and B, A *weakly* supervenes on B if and only if necessarily, if anything *x* has some property *F* in A, then there is at least one property *G* in B such that *x* has *G*, and everything that has G has *F*; and A *strongly* supervenes on B if and only if necessarily, if anything *x* has some property *F* in A, then there is at least one property *G* in B such that *x* has *G*, and *necessarily* everything that has *G* has *F*.

[14] Compare with Kim's formulation of what he calls the principle of downward causation: 'To cause any property (except those at the very bottom level) to be instantiated, you *must* cause the basal conditions from which it arises' (1999: 24; my italics).

[15] The locative absolute, like the genitive absolute of Greek, can have a conditional, causal, temporal or circumstantial force. Caston has observed that the genitive absolute is used, in ancient formulations of supervenience, with conditional force, expressing an antecedent (1997: 335). Here, the locative absolute is being used in the same way. Caston has also pointed out that 'Aristotle... might have made his claim with the outermost necessity operator left implicit; philosophers often overlook this operator when speaking more loosely' (Caston 1992). Something similar applies here. An agreement in presence and absence is elsewhere described as a 'rule' or a 'principle' (*niyama*) (cf. Uddyotakara: 'Material things which possess weight fall because of it: this is a [case of] a rule'). It follows that the supervenience relation in emergence is here affirmed to carry nomologically rather than modally strong necessity (agreeing here with Noordhof 2010: 71–2 about the type of supervenience involved in emergence).

[16] See Bedau (1997, 2008); cf. Rueger (2000a, 2000b).

account is the requirement that 'emergent properties can be derived from micro-level information but only in a certain complex way'. The complexity requirement is what distinguishes weak emergent causal powers from the resultant properties of the system: one cannot *deduce* weakly emergent phenomena from one's knowledge of the basal conditions, but only *simulate* them.[17] As I noted in the last chapter, weak emergence uses dynamical systems theory to demonstrate how systems can come to present emergent properties without the strong requirement. The worry is that if mental properties are only weakly emergent, then they will be epiphenomenal. In the next chapter, I will consider two ways in which the classical theory of Bṛhaspati is modified in later Cārvāka, precisely in response to this worry. It is a worry which was present in the minds of the classical thinkers themselves.

Let me bring this phase in the discussion to a close by returning to Colebrooke and the lecture on Cārvāka naturalism he gave in London in 1827. It is striking now how many of the ideas that were to find a place in British Emergentism are already here. The first of the British Emergentists, J. S. Mill, used the example of chemical change to illustrate his idea of a 'heteropathic law' in *A System of Logic* (Mill 1843). Mill goes on to say that 'All organised bodies are composed of parts, similar to those composing inorganic nature, and which have even themselves existed in an inorganic state; but *the phenomena of life, which result from the juxtaposition of those parts in a certain manner*, bear no analogy to any of the effects which would be produced by the action of the component substances *considered as mere physical agents*' (Bk. III, Ch. 6, §1; my italics). It seems likely that Mill, a person whose duties as a senior official of the East India Company included correspondence with Colebrooke, and who belonged with him to a circle of London literati based around the Royal Society, would have heard Colebrooke's lecture or read it when it was published in 1837, the very

[17] Chalmers (2006: 252–3) considers a definition of weak emergence based on complexity ('Weak emergence is the phenomenon wherein complex, interesting high-level function is produced as a result of combining simple low-level mechanisms in simple ways') but prefers a more overtly epistemological definition, resting on notions of *interest* and *unexpectedness* ('A weakly emergent property of a system is an interesting property that is unexpected, given the underlying principles governing the system'). Chalmers recommends that strong emergence is best characterized as 'non-deducibility even in principle', and suggests that consciousness is the only strongly emergent phenomenon, all other examples of emergence being weak. The conception of emergence I am developing is stronger than Chalmer's 'weak emergence', but weaker than his 'strong emergence'.

time he was working on *A System of Logic*. Colebrooke's work enjoyed in general an extremely wide circulation—even Hegel had some of his writings, and his translations of Sanskrit texts about mathematics were very well known to De Morgan and Boole.[18] I cannot help but wonder whether Bṛhaspati did not after all have a role in the emergence of British Emergentism.

[18] Colebrooke's primary source for Cārvāka, Rāmatīrtha's commentary on the *Vedānta-sāra*, was first published in 1828. It was translated into German by Othmar Frank in 1835 and into English by Ram Mohun Roy in 1832. Two influential British Indologists, J. R. Ballantyne and A. E. Gough, published translations in subsequent decades. Cārvāka was thus readily available to English-speaking audiences in the early 19th cent.

4

Transformation

Causation and Mind

A central element in mature Indian emergentism is the notion of a 'transformation' (*pariṇāma*). In many later sources the Cārvāka naturalist is represented as holding the view that there is a transformation of those elements which are in the combination making up the body. Not mentioned in the earliest statements, it is appropriate to regard it as a development; and we can now begin to see what the motivations for such a development are. It is here that we should look for a positive characterization of the emergence relation.

Emergentism begins with the idea that systems which achieve appropriate levels of organizational complexity instantiate causal properties which are not exhibited by the components, whether as individuals or in aggregate. It is expressly stipulated that no familiar compositional model will render intelligible the emergence of these new properties. They are not scalar sums, as the mass of a whole is the scalar sum of the masses of its component parts, nor are they vector sums, as the sum of a collection of forces results in a single new force. Nor are they mixtures, as the mixture of the colours of the parts results in the colour of the whole. The capacity to think is different in kind from any of the capacities or properties of the four elements, no matter how they are combined and synthesized. This is why Mill speaks of *heteropathic* laws and Broad of *trans-ordinal* laws; of which Bṛhaspati's 'thinking is from the elements' is alleged to be an instance. The emergentists' much-favoured example is chemical synthesis: for example, the emergence of salt and water from a reaction involving two quite different compounds, or, as our author said, the emergence of alcohol's powers from a process whose ingredients are sugar, yeast, barley, and water.

Searle argues that micro-neuronal features are *causally* sufficient for the instantiation of macro-mental features, and that this is what it is for the mental to 'causally supervene' on the physical. Mental properties are 'system features [which] cannot be figured out just from the composition of the elements and environmental relations; they have to be explained in terms of the causal interactions among the elements' (Searle 1992: 126). Searle claims that this is enough to describe them as emergent properties of the system but distinguishes *his* concept of emergence (which he calls 'causal emergence') from what he describes as a 'more adventurous' conception, according to which an emergent feature such as consciousness could cause things that could not be explained by the causal behaviour or the neurons: 'The naïve idea is that consciousness gets squirted out by the behaviour of the neurons in the brain, but once it has been squirted out, it then has a life of its own.' The difficulty with Searle's account is that *neither* of his two conceptions of emergence is adequate: 'causal emergence' is too weak a notion, failing to sustain a robust explanation of the autonomy of emergent features, while the 'more adventurous' conception fails to do justice to the requirement that emergent features are dependent on the micro structures from which they emerge.[1] Relatedly, the idea that the relation between mental and physical properties is one of 'material causation' (*upādāna-kāraṇa*) is not held, by later Cārvāka naturalists, to suffice for a satisfactory characterization of emergence. They recommend a conception of emergence distinct from either of the two distinguished by Searle.

It is a deeply held intuition that nothing completely new can come into existence—nothing can come into existence which cannot be understood in terms of the nature of fundamental components and the ways they can be combined. What had formerly seemed mysterious about chemical reaction no longer surprises us, with our much better understanding of the nature of chemical bonds and the structure of atomic matter. The Cārvāka hypothesis about transformation can be seen as a way to reconcile this attachment to homopathic law with the key features of emergentism. Without a transformation in the micro-base, a homopathic theory of the emergence of psychological capacities is driven inevitably in the direction of panpsychism, for (so the thought goes) a complex could not think if the elements don't, any more than a whole could have a mass if all its parts were massless. The

[1] Causal emergence has also been recommended in O'Connor and Wong (2005); Wong (2006).

panpsychist alternative to emergentism has indeed been taken seriously by a number of philosophers in recent times,[2] but our sources provide two strong counter-arguments. One is that any object at all should then have psychological capacities, and we are lacking a clear criterion why only some do and others do not. The other is that, within a single body, there will be many sites of awareness, but no 'governing principle' orchestrating them:

Even as the power to intoxicate resides to a small measure in each part of the intoxicating liquor, so too [the Cārvāka must claim that] thinking is to a small measure in the parts of the body. And then many things will be thinking in one body. But it is impossible for the respective aims of many thinking entities to act in conformity, any more than many flying birds, bound by a single cord but disposed to move in conflicting directions, are able to cross even the distance of a span, even though the capacity is there for them to do so. So too the body would be unable to do anything. (Vācaspati 1980: 767,21–4; cf. 1996: 531,13–19.)[3]

It is in order to provide a non-panpsychist but not epiphenomenalist explanation of mental causation that the transformation theory is introduced. Let us suppose that the blending or combining of the elements 'transforms' them in such a way that in their transformed state their combination, according to homopathic principles, instantiates psychological properties. Then it will be true to say that mental properties are reducible to the properties of the transformed physical base but equally true that they are irreducible to the properties of the untransformed base.

One of our sources says that the view is that 'matter, although insentient in its inert state, will be bestowed with consciousness when in a body transformed' (Jayanta 1982–4: 201,26-202,1; see Chapter 5). Another says that it is the view that thinking, although not observed in the material earth out there, is present in the elements as transformed in the form of a body (Śaṅkara 1917: 765,7-8). As so expressed, the idea seems to be that the

[2] Nagel (1979: 181–95); G. Strawson (2006); Van Cleve (1990). Nagel's argument for panpsychism goes as follows: Human beings are complex systems composed entirely of matter [Materialism, Anti-Dualism]. Mental properties are not logically implied by any physical properties [Anti-Reductivism]. Human beings do have mental properties [Anti-Eliminativism]. There are no emergent properties [Anti-Emergence]. *Therefore*, the basic physical constituents of the universe have mental properties [Panpsychism].

[3] This anticipates what Seager (1995) calls the 'combination problem' and Stoljar (2001) the 'structural mismatch problem' for panpsychism. Chalmers (2010: 136) comments that 'the combination problem is easily the most serious problem for [in his taxonomy] the type-F monist view, and at this point, it is an open question whether or not it can be solved'.

elements themselves acquire new causal powers when they are in a certain state, namely the state of jointly composing a body, powers that they did not have beforehand when they were in other combinations with other elements. This is different from the view that the body as a whole has powers which none of its parts have individually. It is instead the view that the parts themselves have new powers *conditionally* upon their membership of the whole.

There is a resonance of this idea in the way Galen distinguishes between resultant and emergent properties. He says:

> Consider the first elements. Even though these substrata are unable to perceive, a body capable of perceiving can at some point come into being, because they are able to act on each other and be affected in various ways in many successive alterations. For anything constituted out of many things will be the same sort of thing the constituents happen to be, should they continue to be such throughout; it will not acquire any novel characteristic from outside, one that did not also belong to the constituents. *But if the constituents were altered, transformed, and changed in manifold ways, something of a different type could belong to the composite that did not belong to the elements*.... Consequently, something heterogenous cannot come from elements that do not change their qualities. But it is possible from ones that do... Therefore, it is necessary that that which is going to sense be constituted either (i) from first elements capable of sensation or (ii) from ones incapable of sensation, but naturally such as to change and alter.[4]

Here Galen distinguishes two possibilities. One possibility is that the power to sense is an additive, resultant property, a possibility which leads directly to panpsychism. The other possibility is that the power to sense is an emergent property, and Galen's commitment to the principle that 'something heterogenous cannot come from elements that do not

[4] *On the Elements according to Hippocrates*, 1.3, 70.15–25, 72.19–21, 74.14–17; trans. Caston (1997: 355-7); my italics. Although rightly seeing in the passage an early anticipation of the distinction between emergent and resultant properties, Caston curiously does not remark on the role to which Galen accords the concept of transformation. Neither does Kim, who quotes the passage in Kim (2006b), but glosses it in such a way that the idea of transformation entirely disappears: 'Galen is saying that a composite object made up of simpler constituents, when these constituents enter into special complex relationships ("act on each other and be affected in various ways"), can come to exhibit a novel property ("something of a different type") not possessed by its constituents' (2006b: 189). It seems to me that Caston and Kim are too keen to read Galen here as anticipating *modern* understandings of emergence, and in doing so fail to notice an idea which an examination of the Indian theory makes vivid.

change their qualities' leads to the conclusion that the elements must be transformed.

The early British Emergentists also use the word 'transformation', but seem to mean something rather different by it. Thus Samuel Alexander:

> physiological complexes of a sufficient complexity carry mind or consciousness. They may be said to be 'transformed' in the consciousness they carry . . . the parts are used up to produce something different from them and transcending them, but, used up as they are, they are not altered or superseded but subserve. In this special sense there is a 'transformation' of the parts in building up a higher existence, *but the parts remain what they were.* (Alexander 1920: 370; my italics.)

Alexander clearly asserts that in his view the 'parts remain what they were'. Carl Gillett (2006) has proposed that one reads this as the claim that an emergent property partly determines which causal powers are *contributed* by the base properties, that the base properties contribute causal powers in a way that is conditional upon the fact that they realize an emergent property. What distinguishes the Indian transformation theory from Samuel Alexander's is its claim that the emergent property determines not only what causal powers the base properties 'contribute', but what causal powers they actually possess. The idea is that the parts have new powers in virtue of being parts of the whole, and which are, therefore, intelligible only in reference to the whole to which they have come to belong. What powers an element has is conditional on what combination it is in. Emergence by transformation is the idea that the elements have cognitive powers only when in the frame of a living body, powers they do not have in other sorts of combination or in no combination at all.

What this brings into view is the availability of a conception of emergence distinct from either of the two conceptions distinguished by Searle. The proposal motivating the transformation theory is that, when micro-entities come together in appropriately complex systems of organization, the micro-properties they instantiate are transformed so as to give rise to novel causal powers in the macro-entity they constitute. The emergence of conscious states is not merely a fact about our inability to predict the behaviour of very complex systems, nor is consciousness something which is just 'squirted out'. It is a fact about the properties and powers of micro-entities when they belong to macrophysical structures.

Downward Causation as Assistive Causation

Downward causation is causal influence going down from the higher level of the mental to the lower level of the physical. The exclusion problem presents the very notion with seemingly insuperable difficulties. Kim's preferred way to formulate the problem is to begin with mental-mental causation (Kim 1998: 41-3). Suppose that M is a mental property, that it has causal powers, and that one of its instantiations is the cause of the instantiation of a second mental property M*. M* supervenes on, but is not reducible to, a physical base P*, a set of physical properties. The instantiation of M can cause an instantiation of M* only by causing an instantiation of its physical base P*. This is the downward causation. But M too has a physical base P, whose instantiation is sufficient for the instantiation of M. If an instantiation M is causally sufficient for an instantiation of P* and hence of M*, then so too is an instantiation of P. There is an overdetermination in the causation of instantiations of M*. This is a reductio of the supposition that M has causal powers.

Anxieties about downward causation are evidently at work in the remarkable proposal of a ninth-century independent thinker Bhaṭṭa Udbhaṭa, who acquired a reputation as a very 'cunning' interpreter of Bṛhaspati.[5] He observes that in the sentence 'Due to the elements (*bhūtebhyaḥ*) there is thinking', the grammatical case can be construed as ablative or as dative, and he proposes that the force of the dative has to be acknowledged. The source of our knowledge about his proposal is this brief passage:

The ancient naturalists like Bhāvivikta and others interpreted [*sūtra* 1.4] as asserting 'Thinking is from the elements', because the ablative has been employed in the expression '(from) the elements.' But Udbhaṭa interprets the expression as being in the dative, meaning thinking is to or for the elements; [he says that] thinking is autonomous (*svatantra*) and is an assistant (*upakāraka*) to the material elements which

[5] Udbhaṭa seems to have attempted to adapt Cārvāka emergentism so as to accommodate Nyāya insights about the unity and autonomy of the self (his commentary on the *Cārvāka-sūtra* being a sort of metaphrasis). Solomon (1977–8: 990) describes him as a 'progressive Cāvāka', a description contested, however, by R. Bhattacharya (2010b), who thinks he is better understood as 'a Naiyāyika who wears a Cārvāka hat' (the phrase is due to Prabal Kumar Sen). I prefer to think of him as trying to construct a plausible naturalist philosophy of mind out of both Cārvāka and Nyāya materials, something Shukla (1984) has also attempted. See also Bronkhorst (2008); Del Toso (2011).

constitute the body. (Cakradhara 1982–4: ii. 257; cf. R. Bhattacharya 2002a: 606, Bhā.9.)

Thinking is now not simply an effect of the combinations of material elements, transformed or otherwise, but also functions as a cause with respect to them. Thinking is 'autonomous' (*svatantra*), and it 'assists' the elements. The important notion of 'assistive' (*upakāraka*) causation supplements that of material causation (*upādāna*). Udbhaṭa's distinction between two concepts of causation offers him the hope to be able to explain how the mental can display an appropriate autonomy and yet be emergent.[6]

One of our sources offers an analogy by way of explanation of the new idea. He says that a traveller will start a fire from sparks generated by rubbing sticks together, but will then use the flames to keep new material burning. Similarly, mental properties emerge through transformation from matter, and are thereafter jointly responsible along with matter for future mental states.[7]

Another of our sources discusses the idea in the course of a careful examination of the Cārvāka naturalist account of the causation of one mental event by another, which is also, as I noted above, the context in which Kim prefers to formulate the problem of downward causation. A mental event at one time causes a mental event at a later time. How? Two possibilities are considered. The first is this:

Now suppose one says that [for the mental event] at the later time, the body acts as an assisting cause and not as a material cause. How so? The body is an assisting cause in that it helps bring about the later effects of the thinking which has it as its material

[6] The proposal has contemporary supporters. Dretske (1988), for instance, has proposed a distinction between what he calls 'structuring' and 'triggering' causation. We will see other contemporary proposals later.

[7] Prabhācandra (1990: 118,11–15). The idea is mentioned by Jayarāśi (1940: 57–88). Lowe (1996: 82) develops an account of 'autonomous mental causation' based on the idea that agents engage in 'enabling' or 'facilitating' causation rather than 'initiating' causation. More recently he has sought to defend a volitionist account of agency within an emergentist framework with the help of a distinction between event causation and what he calls 'agent' or 'substance' causation (Lowe 2008). He says that his view 'may also fairly be described as an *emergentist* position, in that it regards the causal powers of persons as *complementing* and *supplementing*—rather than either being reducible to or existing entirely independent of—those of their bodies' (2008: 92), and that it is 'a form of emergentism in the philosophy of mind, according to which non-physical mental events states are causally autonomous and yet are themselves ultimately the products of prior physical evolution' (ibid. 41). That description seems exactly what the traveller analogy captures. In spite of this similarity, an essential point of difference exists: there is in Cārvāka naturalism no suggestion that subjects qua individual substances are agent causes.

cause in the present. So that is how thinking is causally effective but not independent of the body. (Kamalaśīla 1968: 646,8–11)

The fundamental issue, that of reconciling autonomy with dependence, is very clearly identified here. The proposal is that mental events are jointly produced by earlier mental events in tandem with the physical bases of the earlier events. In terms of Kim's formulation of the problem of downward causation, the proposal is that M and P are individually necessary and jointly sufficient for M*, just as the fire and fuel at one time are jointly productive of fire at the next. What is difficult to understand, in this proposal, is why P is not itself sufficient, if M supervenes on P. The argument seems already to assume that M has a causal power not shared with P, but this is exactly what we are trying to explain.

A revised proposal follows:

The body, assisted by the earlier mental event, is the material cause of the later mental event. (Kamalaśīla 1968: 646,20–1)

The new idea is that the physical base P* of the newly produced mental event M* has M as an assistive cause. I suggest that what this new proposal does is to combine the idea of assistive causation with the earlier idea about transformation. The point of the proposal, then, is that, as is suggested by the analogy of lighting and maintaining a fire, the earlier emergent mental event contributes to the transformation of the physical base of later emergent mental events. The transformation of the micro-elements is, at later stages in a mental process, partly subject to causal input from mental properties at earlier stages.

This idea is clearly to be distinguished from an idea which Kim attributes to Sperry, that there is what he terms 'synchronic reflexive downward causation' (1999: 26), in which a macro feature such as a pain exerts a causal influence on *its own* micro-constituents, the basal neural process such as a C-fibre firing. In the view being articulated here, the only downward causation is diachronic, while the synchronic relation (the 'material causation' relation) is constitutive. The diachronic downward causation introduced is similar to that for which Paul Davies coins the phrase *level-entanglement*, and illustrates as follows:

Consider a computer that controls a microprocessor connected to a robot arm. The arm is free to move in any direction according to the program of the computer.

Now imagine a program that instructs the arm to reach inside the computer's own circuitry and rearrange it, for example, by throwing a switch or removing a circuit board. This is software-hardware feedback, where software brings about a change in the very hardware that supports it (Davies 2006: 43)

One way to unpack the idea further is as follows. It is granted that both P and M are sufficient causes of P*, but the proposal is that P* does not represent a physical state specifiable as basal to M* in any way *other than as* the base of M*. Prior mental states assist in the production of later ones by delimiting regions of the physical world along lines and boundaries that the physical world, by itself, does not acknowledge. A sort of context principle is in play: only in the context of the presence of a mental property does it make sense to ask for the region of the physical which that mental property supervenes upon. A transformation account of emergence explains why this should be so, for the physical base P is itself the product of a transformation of the constituent elements consequent upon their constituting the emergence base for preceding mental properties, rather than merely an assemblage of micro-physical entities in a complex pattern.

The proposal insists that mind-mind causation has an explanatory priority over bottom-up physical causation in the specific and restricted sense that the physical causes of mental states can be identified only because of mind-mind interactions. Broad says that the only peculiarity of a trans-ordinal law is 'that we must wait till we meet with an actual instance of an object of the higher order before we can discover such a law; and that we cannot possibly deduce it beforehand from any combination of laws which we have discovered by observing aggregates of a lower order' (Broad 1925: 79). Its irreducibility consists in our inability to specify the physical base or 'material cause' of the higher level property instantiation other than as the basis of the instantiation of that higher level property. The reason for this is that patterns of diachronic assistive causation are responsible for patterns of transformation in the basal conditions.

The Emergence of Consciousness

In a more contemporary vocabulary, my interpretation of the later Cārvāka theory is as follows. The emergence of mental states occurs only within a dynamical system, one whose physical states are in a constant process of flux produced by the fusion of elements and their microcausal powers. The microdynamic in this dynamical system jointly specifies the physical and mental state of the system at any given time, and does so only with reference to both the physical and the mental state of the system at earlier times.[8] This must happen in such a way that the initial conditions mention only physical states—that was the point of the analogy with the traveller and the fire. At each moment in time a mental state has a physical realizer on which it supervenes, but this is a purely formal covariance, since there is no way to identify the subvening physical state other than through the description 'the physical state upon which M supervenes'. Supervenience functions simply as a constraining condition, one of the equations that define the system. Because the domain is itself in a state of flux, the microdynamic will have variables taking mental property instantiations, physical property instantiations, and micro-entities as values.

The choice of an analogy involving fire to illustrate the view is no coincidence, then. In terms of the discussion in Chapter 1, the model borrows from ideas that lie behind both the Tornado View and the Flame View. It postulates that there are privileged dynamical systems which display *strong* emergence, systems in which the emergent properties are not merely complexity effects. Perhaps, as Chalmers (2006: 253) suggests, the weak emergence one finds in normal dynamical systems is sufficient for all natural phenomena except mind. Perhaps there is only one sort of dynamical system with the requisite feature, and that is the embodied mind. Bedau (2008: 158) claims that strong emergence is irrelevant to natural science, and that might be exactly why the mind is resistant to natural scientific intelligibility. It is Payāsi's Trap again, an attempt to understand the mind by way of a false analogy with a natural phenomenon, in this case the sort of complex non-linear dynamical system one regularly finds in biology, ecology, and cosmology. The claim, in other words, is that the right mathematics needed to model embodied conscious minds need not be mathematics that finds

[8] This is akin to a notion of *systemic causation*: 'Mental properties emerge because one of the capacities of emergent systems is to help generate new emergent systems. That is, *systemic causation* involves the creation of stable diachronic patterns (systems distributed over space and time) in which the stability and integrity of such patterns is maintained across constant changes in the micro-base of such systems' (Silberstein 2006: 205).

application anywhere *else* in the natural world. And after all why should it?—there *is* something special about minds.

This is, therefore, the point at which our view parts company with the 'enactive' model of Francisco Varela. Varela recommends that we see the relation as one of emergence through self-organization: 'The aggregates would arise as one moment of emergence, as in a resonating network where strictly speaking there is no all-or-nothing separation between simultaneous (since the emergent pattern itself arises as a whole) and sequential (since for the pattern to arise there must be a back-and-forth activity between participating components)' (Varela, Thompson, and Rosch 1991: 98), adding that 'in a culture that did not have access to scientific notions of circular causality, feedback/feedforward, and emergent properties, nor to logical formulations for handling self-reference, the only recourse for expressing an emergent may have been to say that a process is both cause and effect' (1991: 119). This is a dynamical systems model with weak emergence.[9] I have, of course, been at pains to show that the culture had full access to a good range of relevant concepts. Varela's neurophenomenological project is the naturalization of all aspects of mind using a type of dynamical systems model common to the description of the behaviour of physical systems.

The account I am recommending also differs from an analysis of emergence suggested by Sidney Shoemaker (Shoemaker 2002, 2007). Shoemaker develops a line of thought, which indeed he claims to find in C. D. Broad, in terms of a notion of 'micro-latent' causal powers. A micro-latent power is defined as follows:

> The component entities have powers that, collectively, determine the instantiation of the emergent property when they are combined in an emergence-engendering way. But these being cases of emergence, these cannot all be powers that manifest themselves when the components are not combined in emergence-engendering ways. Some of them must be 'latent' powers. Or, since these powers do not remain latent when their possessors are combined in emergence-engendering ways, let us speak of them as 'micro-latent' powers. We can contrast these with the 'micro-manifest' powers which these same entities manifest when they are not combined with other entities at all, or are configured in ways that are not emergence engendering. (Shoemaker 2007: 73)

[9] Thompson (2007: app. B) attempts to sidestep the exclusion problem within a framework of weak emergence.

Shoemaker claims that emergence should be understood in terms of the existence of micro-latent causal powers which manifest themselves when the elements are combined in what he calls 'emergence-engendering' ways, thereby giving rise to a 'micro-emergent' state of affairs. He argues that the distinction between micro-latent and micro-manifest powers is sufficient to solve the exclusion problem for downward causation:

Supposing that micro-entities have micro-latent powers, when a group of micro-entities that are among the constituents of a macro-entity are configured in an emergence-engendering way there will be one microphysical state of affairs consisting of these particles being configured as they are and having the micro-manifest powers they have, and another micro state of affairs consisting in all of this plus their having the micro-latent powers they have. The first micro state of affairs, which can be called a micro-physical state of affairs, will be a part of the second, which can be called a micro-emergent state of affairs. It will be the latter that has the causal clout required for downward causation. And it will be the latter that is the instantiation of the one micro-structural property, an emergent one, that the macro-entity has in virtue of certain of its micro-constituents being propertied and related as these micro-entities are. (Shoemaker 2002: 63)

Such a proposal does indeed give sense to a notion of transformation: we might say that the transformation of the elements consists in the *activation* of their micro-latent powers. Shoemaker does, I believe, articulate the notion of transformation which the early British Emergentists Broad and Alexander had in mind. However, the two accounts differ with respect to the assumption that micro-physical states of affairs persist and coexist in emergence engendering circumstances with emergent micro-properties. Shoemaker's is a description of emergence for which an appropriate analogy would be the cyclone or tornado.[10] The alternative view is characterized by a rather different thought. The idea is instead that the micro-elements are in a process of mutation, and that emergent macrostates are consequent upon

[10] Thus Bedau (1997: 375): 'Some [examples of emergence] involve inanimate matter; e.g. a tornado is a self-organising entity caught up in a global pattern of behaviour that seems to be autonomous with respect to the massive aggregation of air and water molecules which constitute it. Another source of examples is the mind: our mental life consists of an autonomous, coherent flow of mental states (beliefs, desires, etc.) that presumably somehow ultimately arise out of the swarm of biochemical activity among our brains's neurons. Life is a third rich source of apparent emergence. For example, the hierarchy of life embraces ecosystems composed of organisms, which are composed of organs, which are composed of cells, which are composed of molecules, but each level in this hierarchy exhibits behaviour that seems autonomous with respect to the behaviour found at the level below.'

this process of mutation. An analogy better than that of the tornado, therefore, is the flame, pictured as something emergent from a process of in which the constituent material is itself continuously changing, and in ways causally determined by emergent macrostates. It would be a mistake to describe this view in terms of particles shifting their patterns of aggregation or their 'emergence engendering' distribution.[11]

In this respect transformation theory approaches the 'fusion emergence' account of Paul Humphreys. Humphreys defines a fusion operator for property instances, where 'By a fusion operation, I mean a real physical operation' (1997a: 10). In his (2000), he extends the treatment to fused objects, such as the overlapping wave-functions of two electrons in close proximity, and offers a partial analogy: 'Consider poker chips in a casino. The basic units are red chips, and as soon as you have accumulated two red chips you can trade them in for a blue chip that is worth two units. The blue chip is not composed of two red chips and you cannot count its two components because it does not have any, but it behaves exactly as if there were two such units present' (2000: 28–9). Yet the transformation theory diverges from that account too, in that its ambition is to preserve supervenience within a generative model of emergence. Humphreys is explicit that the technical notion of 'fusion' he introduces cannot sustain supervenience (Humphreys 1996, 1997b). His 'fusion' operation applies to property instances, and is characterized by what Wong (2006) describes as 'basal loss':

> What is most distinctive in fusion emergentism is Humphreys's property fusion operation, which takes property instances (at the ith level) and generates an emergent property instance (at the i+1st level) with novel causal powers. When property instances at the generating ith level are fused, the individual property instances are destroyed and are nonindividuable within the emergent fusion existing at the i+1st level. Call this the basal loss feature of fusion emergentism. (Wong 2006: 345)

This feature of the technical operation Humphreys calls 'fusion' is essential to his strategy with respect to the exclusion argument, for it is the *necessitated* destruction of the base in fusion which for him blocks overdetermination.

[11] Shoemaker's attempt to argue that a causal-powers metaphysics is consistent with non-reductive psycho-physical realization is criticized in O'Connor and Churchill (2010).

Transformation emergence, however, is distinguished from fusion emergence in its technical guise in wishing to endorse what is the majority view, that emergence is a supervenience-based relation, and in therefore considering that this formal notion of 'fusion' cannot correctly describe the relationship of metaphysical dependence involved in emergence.[12] More precisely, there is no commitment to the *necessity* of 'basal loss' in the transformation theory, although it will sometimes, perhaps often, be present as a contingent feature of emergence-engendering dynamical systems. Fusion, in a transformation theory, is not a function that can be defined in advance, but is rather something that is 'solved for' in the dynamical system, when that system is subject to the general constraint afforded by supervenience.

Hard naturalist theories of mind, ancient as well as modern, seek to do justice to two compelling but apparently incompatible scruples. One is that ours is a physical world, everything happening within it open to physical explanation. The other is that mindedness is a matter of causal significance, that it makes a causal difference that there are minds. The more we feel the pull of one of these scruples, the more mysterious becomes the other. A robust commitment to physicalism leaves the mind looking like an epiphenomenal by-product of natural processes, a causally inert shadow. But a view of the mind as possessing aetiological autonomy threatens to re-enchant the physical world with supernatural causes and effects. The attraction of emergentism is that it offers a way to escape the dilemma. An emergentist tries to prise free the soundly motivated scruples about the dependence and autonomy of the mental from too-rigid theory, to see the problems as symptoms of the fact that an insight has been poorly encoded in doctrine. Such is precisely, I have argued, how the philosophy of Bṛhaspati came to be seen. Later philosophers feel the tension that is created between the demands of dependence and autonomy, and seek proposals that help one to see a way for these demands to be compatible. What I have sought to bring to view is the *general form* that such a proposal will take.

Without wishing to diminish the points of contact that certainly exist between transformation theory and the accounts of Varela, Shoemaker, and Humphreys, I nevertheless want to affirm that it is a distinct theory with

[12] For an extended critical discussion of Humphreys, particularly his understanding of the demands imposed by causal overdetermination, see Wong (2006).

distinctive and important virtues. In particular, I believe that it makes clear what the key issue for emergence really is. The metaphor of the traveller and the fire leads to a conception of body as a dynamical system, flame-like in its mode of persistence, and fully able to sustain an intertwined mental life, as long as there is an initial 'spark' of mindedness. Once we have located this maximally material and minimally mental spark, the model of assistive causation shows how to move to an account of an embodied stream of consciousness. Then, by a second application of the same metaphor, we are led to a conception of a stream of thought as a dynamical system, flame-like in *its* mode of persistence, and fully able to sustain an intertwined first-person life as long as there is an initial 'spark' of self-awareness. Once we have located this spark of minimal self-awareness, the model of assistive causation shows how to move to an account of an embodied and enstreamed self. Further recursion on the model generates higher-order first-person thought, and arguably at some point must settle on reflexive self-awareness, attractors in the dynamical system. The entire description, I must stress, is a purely formal model of self-consciousness, and not an account of the actual psycho-biological genesis of mind. It is a conceptual argument, and is genealogical in the type of explanation it affords. The question is: does anything correspond in fact to the initial sparks of mindedness and self-awareness which the formal model posits in theory? Rather than either of Kim's, I suggest that *this* is the core issue upon which the prospects for emergentism rest.

I have argued that a theory of emergence is at the core of the Cārvāka conception of human beings as the bearers of physical and psychological characteristics. I will return in later chapters to various aspects of this analysis of emergence, in particular to the thought that reflexivity enters, not as a general account of subjectivity, but only in specified circumstances (Chapter 9, Conclusion), and to the more general idea that mental properties are irreducibly supervenient on the physical (Chapters 12, 13). Cārvāka philosophers also have a theory of self: that the self is just the human being (*puruṣa*), i.e. a version of Animalism. In the next two chapters, I am going to argue first that Animalism is false, but second that selves are necessarily embodied; indeed, I will find in some of our philosophers a commitment to what is now known as the 'embodied mind' thesis, that bodily attributes, such as the species of animal one is a member of, fundamentally shape the character of the mind one has.

5

Persistence

My account in the two preceding chapters was based on the fragmentary remains of Bṛhaspati's *Cārvāka-sūtra*, and on the description of the theory in the work of two philosophers with a doxographical interest in fairly representing their opponents' views, the Buddhist Kamalaśīla and the Jaina philosopher Prabhācandra. Unlike many critics, these philosophers did not misrepresent the Cārvāka view as an identity theory of mind, in which states of mind are type-identified with physical states.[1] I argued that the doctrine is rather that psychological states are emergent from physical states but not themselves type-identical to physical states. Some contemporary philosophers have claimed that emergence in anything other than a weak sense is incompatible with physicalism,[2] and if that is right then Cārvāka in its developed form is not properly described as a version of physicalism. Other contemporary philosophers, however, think that any theory which affirms that mental states and processes supervene on physical states and processes is a form of physicalism (Lewis 1983: 361; Kim 1998: 191; cf. Wilson 2005), and I have argued that Cārvāka indeed commits itself to a supervenience thesis.

I turn now to the claim that the self is identical to the physical body (*dehātma-vāda*). The issue has to do with the material constitution of the self and its identity over time, and the view is a version of what would now be called Animalism, the claim being that a person is identical with the human animal and not with either an immaterial soul or a psychological continuum. This was explicitly Payāsi's position and at first sight it is also implied by

[1] The identity theory of mind attracted contemporary attention in the work of Place (1956), Feigl (1958), and Smart (1959). Arguments against it will be considered in Ch. 12.

[2] Thus e.g. J. J. C. Smart (2008: 1): 'The physicalist will deny strong emergence in the sense of some philosophers, such as Samuel Alexander and possibly C. D. Broad. The latter remarked that as far as was known at that time the properties of common salt cannot be deduced from the properties of sodium in isolation and of chlorine in isolation. Of course, the physicalist will not deny the harmless sense of 'emergence' in which an apparatus is not just a jumble of its parts.' See also Smart (1981).

Bṛhaspati (*Cārvāka-sūtra* 1.6). The Materialist View is that the body is the place or owner of experience, and it follows that it is a matter of indifference whether one says that the body is the self or that there is no self but only a body. Jayanta Bhaṭṭa, the ninth-century Nyāya philosopher, argues very tellingly against Animalism, and so against the Materialist View, and I will discuss his argument in comparison with the ideas of a contemporary critic of materialism, Roderick Chisholm. My eventual aim is to show that the Animalism this argument targets is logically independent of the account of the emergence of the mental from the physical, which therefore survives Jayanta's critique unscathed.

I might note that contemporary philosophers in India have independently sought to defend the 'self-as-body' hypothesis. Badrinath Shukla presented his rather drastic reworking of classical Nyāya as a form of Animalism in an oral presentation in Sanskrit before a meeting of pandits in Sarnath, October 1984. The text was later translated into English and published.[3] Ananta Kumar Bhattacharyya defended the hypothesis in an article that was written in Bengali and published in the journal *Darśana* in 1958; an English translation of this article too is now available.[4] Debiprasad Chattopadhyaya and Ramkrishna Bhattacharya have done much to retrieve Cārvāka from an ungenerous fate.[5] To these philosophers, as much as to Abu al-Faḍl, this naturalist theory seems to sustain a secular and egalitarian theory of human nature and society. My view (for which see Chapter 16 and the Conclusion) is that the autonomy of the individual is better preserved in an Ownership View, one which does not, however, give any encouragement to the idea that there can be life after death.

Cārvāka Naturalism Redescribed

Jayanta presents both a reconstruction of Cārvāka naturalism and a refutation (Jayanta 1982–4: ii. 201–18). I find in Jayanta an astute *philosophical*

[3] See Shukla (1984) for details of both.

[4] See A. K. Bhattacharya (1958–9) for details of both. Ananta Kumar Bhattacharyya has been described as 'among the foremost of the recent great traditional Indian scholars of Bengal'.

[5] Chattopadhyaya (1959); Chattopadhyaya and Gangopadhyaya (1990); R. Bhattacharya (2009).

appreciation of the theory he is criticizing, an appreciation which is perhaps influenced by Udbhaṭa's revisionary commentary on the original Cārvāka sources (R. Bhattacharya 2010b). The view he describes is, nevertheless, different from any of the Cārvāka views I described in earlier chapters in a crucial respect, and there are in particular two curiosities in his presentation of the position. I will summarize his argument before quoting the text. Jayanta tells us first that the position is that there are no good reasons to think of the self as a separate entity. Such a self cannot be *perceived* as an object among others by the external senses, and neither is it perceived in introspection in the way that particular mental states like pleasure and pain are.[6] Nor is a *deduction* available, not only because of a general methodological suspicion with respect to the deduction of unobservable entities[7] but also because none of the marks alleged to prove a separate self do actually entail its existence.[8] People have postulated a self in order to explain certain mental functions that are characteristic of selfhood, especially the memory of one's own past experience and the conscious identification of an object across sensory modalities.[9] The body itself is responsible for these activities; so the self just is the body.

Neither can one appeal to the ancient religious *scriptures* to prove the existence of a separate self, for such scriptures have no particular authority. In any case, one can actually find in one of those scriptures an endorsement of the naturalist theory, for it is asserted there that the self is 'a single mass of cognition' (*vijñāna-ghana*), which has 'risen up out of these elements and is dissolved into them'.[10] But since there is no self able to dissociate itself from the body and transmigrate, all the talk in the scriptures of an 'after-world' (*paraloka*) is completely empty, and all action aimed at reaching such a world is a waste of time.

[6] Cf. the discussion in Ch. 2 on Payāsi and Hume.

[7] The Cārvāka position is that empirically grounded induction is admissible, but not the use of inference to make purely speculative deductions about unobservables and supernatural realities. In this they are similar to the Empirics in Greece and Rome, who permit the use only of epilogisms. See Kamalaśīla on *Tattvasaṃgraha* 1481–2 and cf. Gokhale (1993); R. Bhattacharya (2000; 2010a: 28–30).

[8] This refers to a set of five arguments, Unity, Spatial Parts, Persistence, Self-Knowledge, and Self-Reference, which I discuss in Ch. 12.

[9] See Ch. 15.

[10] *etebhyaḥ bhūtebhyaḥ samutthāya tānyevānu vinaśyati* (Bṛhadāraṇyaka Upaniṣad 2.4.12; cf. 4.5.13).

The full text of Jayanta's reconstruction of Cārvāka naturalism reads as follows:

> A dialogue about liberation will not result in an agreeable outcome
> Without considering whether the self does indeed exist or does not.
> Accordingly the Cārvāka, who deny that there is another world,
> Think that there is no self other than the body inlaid with consciousness.

No self as such is known by perception, because it cannot be distinguished by the external senses [which perceive things] like pots, nor by the internal sense [which perceives things] like states of pleasure. Nor is inference a source of knowledge according to the Cārvāka. There is anyway no suitable mark from which to deduce a self. There will be a capacity for thinking in the material elements themselves, when they acquire a preeminence of power produced by a special kind of transformation. For example, *guḍa*, *piṣṭa* and similar things undergo a transformation into alcohol and have a power to intoxicate they did not have earlier. Likewise, matter, although insentient in its inert state, will be bestowed with consciousness when in a body transformed. At the end of a period of time, as a result of disease or such like, it loses that special attribute and the elements go back to a state devoid of consciousness. But since, during that period of time, consciousness has not yet departed, the elements themselves will undertake to conduct the range of functions like memory and [cross-modal] identification (*pratisandhāna*). So how could a self be proved?

The scriptures have validity only as a matter of convention and wishful thinking; how can they prove the [eternal] self? And anyway there is indeed this scripture: '[the self] is a single mass of cognition, which is risen up out of these elements and is dissolved into them.' So in the absence of an eternal self suitable for the other world, enough of this talk about another world, which is a waste of effort![11]

Jayanta says that the view is that the matter which constitutes the body is not initially conscious, but it acquires the potential for conscious thought on undergoing a particular transformation of elements, where this is to be understood as an entirely natural process, exactly resembling the way that the matter of sugar, flour, water, and yeast acquires the potential to inebriate as it is transformed in the process of fermentation. When eventually disease or some other cause leads the body to lose this particular transformation of elements, it ceases again to be conscious.

[11] Jayanta (1982–4: ii. 201,18–202,8).

Is the Self Physical?

I said that there are two curiosities in Jayanta's presentation. The first has to do with the way he sets up the issue. What Jayanta does is to specify a range of functions or capacities which constitute the distinctive role of the self. He then goes on to characterize the Cārvāka view as being that the body is perfectly able itself to perform those functions. So the argument is given the following form:

1. The self is that in virtue of which the functions of memory, cross-modal object identification, and so on are discharged.
2. The body is what discharges these functions.
3. Therefore, the body is the self.

What is interesting is the strong resemblance this bears with the 'functional reduction' strategy of Jaegwon Kim (Kim 1998: 97–103; 2005: 98–108). Kim says that what a physicalist should do is first to give a functional definition of some given mental state and then identify the physical state or process which 'realizes' the defined function. A functionalist argues, first of all, that mental properties can be defined by the causal tasks they perform, and second that physical states can be identified which actually perform those causal tasks. These physical states are then said to 'realize' the mental properties. Being in pain, for example, is functionally analysed as a state standardly caused by tissue damage and trauma, and which in turn causes groans, grimaces and avoidance behaviours. And it turns out that, in human beings, the firing of C-fibres is what 'realizes' that causal role (see Kim 1998: 106). If this is so, then one has achieved a 'functional reduction' of pain to a certain brain state. Jayanta seems to characterize Cārvāka naturalism precisely as involving a commitment to a functional reduction strategy.

The second curiosity is this. The term Jayanta has used to describe the relationship between consciousness and the body is *khacita*, which means 'inlaid' or 'set' or 'studded', as a piece of metal might be studded with diamonds. The relevant *Cārvāka-sūtra*, on the other hand, reads: 'A human being is a body endowed with consciousness', where the term used is *viśiṣṭa*, 'endowed with, qualified by'. Jayanta's choice of the term 'inlaid' seems to suggest that he takes the view to involve property dualism. However, when he specifies the Cārvāka view further, he states that it is the view that the material elements themselves are capable of carrying out the activities that are characteristic of consciousness: '[D]uring that period of time [in which] consciousness has not yet departed, the elements themselves will undertake to conduct the range of functions like memory and [cross-modal] identification (*pratisandhāna*).' As I have said, this further description encourages the conjecture that Jayanta understands Cārvāka to be a sort of functionalism. What is under discussion here are higher-order cognitive functions, in particular the ability to remember one's own past experiences, and the ability to reidentify a particular presented through one sense-modality with the same particular presented through another sense-modality. Other philosophers argue that these cognitive functions could be discharged only by a self considered as an endurant. The distinctive physicalist move, according to Jayanta, is first to say that cognitive functions like these can be taken to provide a functional definition of what it is to have a self, and second that they do have a basis in the physical body, i.e. that there are bodily states and processes which perform the causal work specified in the functional definition. It will be in that sense that consciousness is 'set' or 'inlaid' into the body. So my view is that the use of this term should be understood as indicative of *a realization relation* rather than as implying that mental properties are *implanted* into the physical body.

Here is a list of the various capacities which Indian philosophers have at one time or another associated distinctly with consciousness:

- The capacity to ascribe to oneself mental and physical attributes, that is, to think thoughts that are expressed in first-person present-tense ascriptions of psychological states: 'I am happy', 'I am thinking about going out.' [*ahaṃ-pratyaya*]
- The capacity to be reflexively self-aware, that is for one's thoughts to be aware of themselves as well as their intentional objects. [*sva-saṃvedana*] The content of reflexive self-awareness is held by some to be non-conceptual.
- The capacity to reidentify objects both over time and across sensory modalities, that is to think thoughts that are expressed as 'This object which I now am touching is the same as this object which I am now looking at' [*anusandhāna*] and 'This object which I am now looking at is the same as that object which I saw yesterday.' [*pratyabhijñā*]

- The capacity to have occurrent thoughts with intentional content, including those associated with perception, reason and linguistic understanding. [*jñāna*]
- The capacity to have occurrent memories. [*smṛti*]
- The capacity to have occurrent desires, dreads, pleasures, and pains. [*icchā, dveṣa, sukha, duḥkha*]
- The capacity to anticipate the future, to imagine how it might be, to make resolutions. [*saṃkalpa*]
- The capacity to have dispositional traces, such as those associated with long-term non-occurrent memory. [*saṃskāra; bhāvanā*]
- The capacity to *feel* emotions such as love, hate, regret, and sorrow; the feeling of the emotion being distinct from the emotion itself. [*vedanā*]
- The capacity to sense proprioceptively one's body. [*rūpaṇa*]
- The capacity selectively to attend to objects in one's surroundings or to one's own mental state. [*vijñāna; manas*]

The claim (made explicitly by Jayanta) is that some subset of this list of capacities is constitutive of having a self. What functional reductionism claims is that the capacities which are constitutive of a self have a physical realization in the body. If I am right in what I have been arguing in this section, then Jayanta interprets Cārvāka naturalism as a kind of functional reductionism.

As I have already shown at length, Cārvāka in its later articulation is rather a variety of non-reductive emergentism. The proposal that consciousness comes into being along with a transformation of the physical elements, that it arises out of them, and that it ceases to be when that particular transformation is dissolved, does encourage us, as we have seen, to understand the theory as a kind of emergentism, because emergentists too claim that 'novel' properties emerge when matter organizes itself into systems of appropriate complexity. The crucial aspect of emergentism as a distinct approach in the philosophy of mind is the further claim that the 'novel' properties are not explicable or deducible solely on the basis of information about the lower level properties of the base elements. In claiming this, emergentism seeks to present itself as an alternative to mechanistic theories of mind. A mechanist too will accept that the physical properties to which mental properties are meant to be reducible are properties instantiated only by complex physical systems, in other words that these are properties which qualify the whole system without qualifying any or every constituent part. Such properties, however, are thought of as like the behavioural properties of a mechanical clock, which are entirely predictable given a sufficiently detailed description of the parts and the mechanism by which they are related.

According at least to Kim, reductive functionalism is actually a better strategy for the physicalist than non-reductive emergentism. The position Jayanta ascribes to the Cārvāka, even if it deviates from their actual view in the way I have suggested, is still an extremely powerful and persuasive one (one cannot say that Jayanta has misrepresented the view simply in order to gain a polemical advantage).

The argument I will consider now does not depend on these details. Its target is the thesis that a self is a body that thinks, as opposed to either a distinct individual or a consubjective stream of experience. Before turning again to Jayanta's text, it will help us to contextualize his argument with one drawn from contemporary theory.

A Persistence Argument Against Animalism

One of the most interesting and influential objections to any standard version of materialism is Roderick Chisholm's (1979) argument from *entia successiva*. An *ens successivum* is an entity which is made from different things at different times. Chisholm argues that my physical body is an entity of such a sort, but that I am not. He concludes that whichever entity it is that I am, it is not my physical body. His presentation of the argument is brief enough for me to be able to repeat it in full:

The body that persists through time—the one I have been carrying with me, so to speak—is an *ens successivum*. That is to say, it is an entity made up of different things at different times. The set of things that make it up today is not identical with the set of things that made it up yesterday or with the set of things that made it up the day before. Now one could say that an *ens successivum* has different 'stand-ins' at different times and that these stand-ins do duty for the successive entity at the different times. Thus the thing that does duty for my body today is other than the thing that did duty for it yesterday and other than the thing that will do duty for it tomorrow. But what of me? Am *I* an entity such that different things do duty for *me* at different days? Is it *one* thing that does my feeling depressed for me today and *another* thing that did it yesterday and still *another* thing that will do it tomorrow? If I happen to be feeling sad, then, surely there is no *other* thing that is doing my feeling sad for me. We must reject the view that persons are thus *entia successiva*. Our reasoning can be summarised. Suppose (i) that I am now sad. Then (ii) if there is an *ens successivum* that bears my name and is now sad, then it is sad in virtue of the fact that one of its stand-ins is now sad. But (iii) I am not sad in virtue of the fact that some *other* thing is doing my feeling sad for me. Therefore (iv) I am not an *ens successivum*.

The key premise in Chisholm's argument, and one for which he does not offer additional reasons, is that nothing stands in for me when I am the owner of a mental state. I will argue in the next chapter that the premise gets its plausibility precisely because it is formulated in the first person, and makes a claim about what is involved in having a first-person perspective. When I am in pain, it is the fact that the pain is *mine*, not just that a pain is occurring, which makes what Chisholm says seem right. In any case, the argument is clearly directed at the concept of 'place', in the terminology of Chapter 1.

I will not, for the moment, consider whether contemporary materialists have available to them a good response.[12] Instead, I want to use Chisholm's argument to help us understand better the argument which Jayanta offers in order to refute Animalism. Again, I will describe the argument and then quote the text.

Jayanta presents a variation of Chisholm's argument. They agree that if the self is identical to the body then both must be *entia successiva*. Chisholm's next move is to say that the body may well be an *ens successivum*, but the self certainly is not. Jayanta's move is to say that the body is certainly not an *ens successivum*. Both conclude that the self is not the body.[13] Jayanta argues against the claim that the body is something which has different states (*avasthā*) at different times. His first argument is that nothing endures through the sorts of organic change which characterize human physiology. The claim rests in part on his commitment to a particular theory about chemical reaction, the theory that chemical reactions involve the complete disintegration into atoms of the reacting elements followed by their reconstitution. Thus, consider what happens when a pot is baked in a kiln and, as

[12] See Zimmerman (2003).

[13] So (1) If Animalism is true then body and self are both *entia successiva*. Chisholm: (2) Self is not an *ens successivum*. Jayanta: (2) Body is not an *ens successivum*. (3) So Animalism is false.

a result, the clay of which it is made changes colour from yellow to red. Suppose further that the process is one in which every part of the pot changes colour, not only the external surface. The theory of chemical change in question says that this can be the case only if the structure of atoms within the pot is broken down, permitting the atoms individually to change colour, before regrouping into a pot. The pot does not, strictly speaking, survive the process of firing intact, but disintegrates and is re-formed. This is a model of how individuals can persist through *substantial* change as well as *qualitative* change, and I will refer to it again later in the book.

Jayanta's argument relies also on a commitment to mereological essentialism, according to which a whole does not survive the loss or gain of even a single part. The two commitments enable Jayanta to deny that there is any such thing as a human body which exists at various different times: he denies that the human body is an *ens successivum*. Indeed, the commitment to mereological essentialism is largely motivated by the wish to be able to argue against the endurance of the human body and so against Animalist criteria of personal identity.

Here is the text:

What we say is that the body is not the substratum of such states as desire, because it is different according to the different stages of a life—childhood, youth, old-age, etc.

For an object seen by one cannot be remembered by another
Nor a desire for it arise in someone other than the one who remembers it.
So one should affirm some substratum for the single chain of effects
Which begins with an initial perception and finishes in a desire.

The body is different according to the different life-states, childhood and so on, and so it cannot be the substratum. The case is just as with distinct experience-streams. Just as Yajñadatta does not remember what is seen by Devadatta, so the body of the youth would not have remembered what has been experienced by the body of the child.

[The Cārvāka replies:] The states alone are different; the body is the one who has those states (*avasthātṛ*) and it indeed is the same. The proof of this is the re-identification (*pratyabhijñā*) [of the body at different times]. Nor is this re-identification explicable in another manner, such as is the case with the re-identification of a finger-nail which was cut off and grew again; for there can be no annihilation [of the body from one time to the next]. In the case of a pillar, one certainly refutes the doctrine that it is [a sequence of] moments by appeal to re-identification; and the case is precisely the same here too.

[Jayanta:] It is incorrect [to say that the two cases are alike], since in the case of a pillar, no cause of distinctness (*nānātva*) is observed, but here difference is seen in terms of colour, size and condition [of the body in different life-stages]. The re-identification is an error for which resemblance is responsible. In a boy, a youth, and an old man the size and so forth are indeed not observed to be the same.

On account of the processing of food too, it is known that the body is different.
Digestion would otherwise not follow the course of chemical change.
Consuming curd and milk would not nourish it.
But it is seen to become red upon the ingestion of gold.
Since some parts waste away and others arise new,
How is it possible for the whole to be the same?

[Jayanta now provides a long analysis of different theories of chemical change (*pākaja*).] Therefore what we say is that the body is not one and the same, for it is seen that there are differences in size and so on [at different times]. Our firm view is that re-identification with respect to it is akin to the re-identification of a flame and such like.[14]

Bodies do not endure; they persist through time the same way flames do. Jayanta's next argument is a *reductio* of the very idea of an *ens successivum*. He argues that the one who has different states at different times cannot be *identical*, at a time, to a state. That would imply, by the transitivity of identity, that every state is *identical* with every other state (both states being identical to the one who *has* the state). On the other hand, if the body and its stand-in are distinct entities at a time, then they should be able to be cognized distinctly, and this of course is never the case.[15] Jayanta's position is that there is no enduring body; there are only body-stages:

What was said, namely that the stages of life are many but there is a single one who has those states (*avasthātṛ*), viz. the body, this is incorrect also because it is indefensible on either of two alternatives, that of identity and that of difference [between stages and the body]. Suppose that the stages are not distinct from the body; then it is impossible for there to be a mutual difference between one stage and another stage. Suppose instead that the stage is distinct from the body; then it should be possible to point out a way to perceive them as different. But that is not the case ...

[14] Jayanta (1982–4: ii. 214,3–217,16; omitting 215,5–217,5).

[15] Some philosophers have likewise tried to block Chisholm on the grounds that the so-called stand-ins are not really distinct entities at all.

So the body, because it is different [at different times], is akin to a distinct experience-stream in lacking the capacity for acts of memory or [cross-modal] identification, and so is not the place of states of desire and the like.

In this argument, Jayanta anticipates some recent work in the philosophy of identity over time. The claim that the human body does not endure might seem extreme, but is a version of what is now called 'four dimensionalism' (Sider 1997, 2001). The normal understanding of that view is that an object is a 'worm' in space-time, with only a temporal *stage* of the object existing at any given time. In the terminology of David Lewis, the claim is that bodies *perdure* but do not *endure*. Sider defends the more radical idea that 'it is better to identify everyday objects with the short-lived temporal parts, and analyze talk of persistence over time with a temporal version of counterpart theory' (1997: 197 n.). Jayanta's view about bodies is in this more radical vein.

To support these remarks, Jayanta says that a human body has the same metaphysical status as a flame. The metaphor of the flame is well chosen, and the analysis of persistence through chemical change (*pākaja*) presented by Jayanta is in fact a very good statement of the Flame View, the view that the micro-elements are in a process of fusion and mutation, and that it is the emergent macrostate yielded by this process of mutation which one should *identify as the place of experience*. The view distinguishes two different metaphysical relationships both expressed by the locative. It says that the flame is 'in' the changing body of burning gas in the same sense that the ripple is in the water, a sense which will permit the entity in question to propagate by being in different bodies of material at different times. We are not inclined to say of such entities that they are independent existents whose location we have specified, as when we do when we say that the car is in the garage. We might then take the fact that the relationship which a flame has to a volume of gas is quite different from that which is alleged to obtain between a material object and its stand-ins as grounds to deny that disturbances are *entia successiva*—the swirl of gas is not a 'stand-in' for the flame itself, but the matter through which it persists.

Schematically, the argument is this:

1. The experiential capabilities that are functionally definitive of a self are of such a nature that only an enduring entity, wholly present at different times, could realize them.
2. The body is not an endurant.
3. Therefore, the self is not the body.

This argument leads Jayanta to the position that there must be an enduring categorical basis for a range of experiential capacities. He singles out two such capacities in particular: the capacity to remember just *one's own* past experiences, and the capacity to correlate perceptions in different sense-modalities in order to judge 'This object that I am looking at is the same as the object that I am touching.' If it is to discharge these functions, Jayanta asserts, a self must be an endurant, but the material human body is, as we have put it, four-dimensional.

Less committally, the argument requires only that the manner of persistence involved in the preservation of first-person phenomena is not the same as that which characterizes the preservation of physical objects. Jayanta puts the argument in a way which dramatizes the difference, but for it to succeed one need be committed neither to endurantism about selves nor to mereological essentialism about bodies. A view I will mention in Chapter 11 is that selves do not endure but persist by way of overlapping stretches of the so-called 'specious present'; that is clearly not a viable manner of persistence for a material object.

This argument against Animalism is targeting its most basic claim, namely that the body is the place, that which *owns* experience, i.e. that psychological properties are properties of the physical body. The form of the argument is clear: Whatever is the place has a certain property. The body does not have this property. Therefore, the body is not the place. The Materialist View is the only view to claim that the body is the place, and so this is an argument against that view. Bodies simply are not the right sort of things to be places; they do not exist in the right way. Prabhācandra's argument was formally the same (Chapter 2), except that for him the property in question was 'being something which one can imagine oneself separated from'.[16] It is a tautology that one cannot imagine oneself separated from the place, i.e. from oneself. Yet one can imagine oneself separated from the body. So, again, the body is not the place. This is a weaker argument, however, if only because Leibniz's Law does not hold for intentional properties. Finally, Jayanta's argument rests only on a claim about the way that bodies persist, and ought therefore to work just as well against any view which takes the place to be something which persists that way. Jayanta claims indeed that bodies persist the way streams or flames do, so his argument applies equally to the Reductionist,

[16] Jayanta himself records a version of this argument (Jayanta 1982–4: i. 157.1–7).

Tornado, and Flame views. What is worth stressing is that it does not engage with Buddhist Views, for these are views which deny that there is a place. This is a very revealing observation, for it can be read as suggesting that the Buddhist Views are designed from the outset to be immune to the Persistence Argument. The Persistence Argument leaves all Real Self Views and all Buddhist Views unscathed. Indeed a Buddhist presentist will welcome the argument as confirmation of their view that nothing can ground the persistence of first-person phenomena at all.

Powerful as Jayanta's argument is, there remains at least one reason for wanting to identify the self with the body. That is simply that we do think of ourselves as having an identity which is both physical and mental: it is I who was born on a certain date, who walked to work, ate lunch, and so on. I do seem to be the bearer of both physical and mental properties. Again, and relatedly, Jayanta's view has the apparently unattractive consequence that the first-person 'I' is not a univocal expression, but rather that it is used in two distinct ways, one to refer to the categorical basis of one's experiential capacities ('I remember seeing that film') and differently when one attributes physical properties to oneself ('I walked to work', 'I am getting fat'). Perhaps an explanation can be found for this strange behaviour of the first-person pronoun, but it is additional *prima facie* evidence in favour of the identity between the self and the body. In Chapter 8 I will consider the Buddhist answer, which is that the use of 'I' is always mistaken; and in Chapter 12, I will describe a Nyāya proposal that the use of 'I' with reference to the body is modulated, metonymic upon its use with reference to the self.

A theory of self must do two things. It must tell us what kind of thing a self is: an immaterial substance; a suitably interconnected series of conscious experiences; the categorical basis of such a series; and so on. But a theory of self must also give us materials to answer, within the specified kind, the question: 'Which one is me?' This question is often overlooked, but to neglect it is to court solipsism. We do self-ascribe physical predicates, and bodies are identifiable entities in public space. The Cārvāka inspired thought is that the alternatives fail precisely because their solutions to the first requirement imply that there is no answer to the question, 'Which one is me?' The claim is that no solution to what I earlier called the Attenuation Problem can come from a *purely* first-person stance. I will say more about this in the next chapter, and begin to press the case for the view that selves are essentially embodied.

6

The Self as Bodily

The Strong First-Person Requirement

The ability to possess what has been called a strong first-person perspective is the capacity 'not just to have thoughts expressible by means of "I", but also to conceive of oneself as the bearer of those thoughts' (Baker 1998: 330). The distinction between weak and strong first-person phenomena is, Baker argues, reflected in the difference between *making* a first-person reference and *attributing* the first-person reference to oneself. Weak first-person phenomena are in play whenever one responds to one's environment in a way that demands an egocentric perspective: ducking when one sees a projectile heading in one's direction, for example. If asked, I might say I ducked because the ball was coming towards me, thereby making a first-person reference. But it is important to notice that animals too have a perspectival awareness, an awareness of their environment which locates them within it. What they lack is the ability to conceive of themselves, in the way that I do if, for example, I wonder whether I should have ducked, thereby *attributing* to myself the first-person thought 'Should I have ducked?' Animal selves are perspectival, human selves are strongly first-personal.[1] I prefer to use the phrase 'first-person stance' for what Baker calls the strong first-person perspective, reserving the phrase 'first-person perspective' for its use, as in Shoemaker (1996), for the idea of having one's own mental life in view.

I will call the thesis that a self is something which can conceive of itself as itself, and so entertain a first-person stance, the 'strong first-person requirement' on selfhood. Jayanta's reference to memory and identification can be read as introducing such a requirement. When he says that a self must be able to remember its own past experiences, it is not enough simply that

[1] Peacocke's distinction between 'perspectival' and 'reflective' self-consciousness is closely related (Peacocke 2010); see also Albahari (2006); Henry and Thompson (2011).

some past experience causes a given present memory, for example a memory of being rained on. What he has in mind is the strong first-person sense, as in 'I remember that I *myself* was getting wet', in which I attribute to myself a memory expressed in the first person. Similarly, as I will show in detail in Chapter 15, the point about cross-modal identification is not merely that a sufficiently sophisticated cognitive system can correlate information from different sense-modalities (the *under*-self), but that a subject of experience can think of itself as seeing and touching the very same object: 'This thing which *I* am now looking at is just the same as the thing which *I* am now touching' (the *participant* self).

The existence of this requirement also explains why Chisholm is right to say that the concept of a self precludes the possibility that when I feel sad, it is in virtue of some other thing doing my feeling sad for me. Chisholm's point is that owning a mental state, for example feeling sad, is not something one does, as it were, by proxy, in the way that one can vote in an election by having someone else place one's vote. The reason Chisholm is right to claim this is that such a possibility is incompatible with having a first-person stance, in which one thinks of one's feelings *as one's own* and not as the feelings of a stand-in: I am the one who is feeling sad. Someone who conceives of their feeling sad *as their own* could not think of themselves as feeling sad in virtue of something else feeling sad for them. The point is, as P. F. Strawson importantly observes, that our ownership of our thoughts and feelings is internal to our sense of self: 'Our desires and preferences are not, in general, something we just note in ourselves as alien presences. To a large extent they *are* we' (P. F. Strawson 1992: 134).

A phenomenon has been thought to present Animalist criteria for personal identity with insuperable difficulties is the possibility that I might go from one body to another and survive the transfer. What I want to demonstrate is that the bodily transfer objection actually turns on very similar issues to do with first-personal phenomena.

Is Bodily Transfer Possible?

Philosophers who think that the diachronic identity of the self is that of an enduring psychological entity and those who think that it consists in relations of psychological continuity agree about one thing: it is possible for me to transfer to another physical body and still survive, and that the Animalist thesis that the self is the body is therefore false. We are familiar with Shoemaker's brain-state transfer device and Parfit's teletransporter, both of which transfer all the information in one's psychology from one brain or body to another.[2] Such thought experiments are intended to show that it is conceivable that I can continue in another body, or at least that criteria of bodily identity are not criteria of personal identity.

Peter van Inwagen (1997) presents a formal argument that bodily transfer is incompatible with Animalism. His argument is based on a very simple idea: that if two objects are distinct, then they cannot become identical. If I am identical to my body, and am then transferred into another body, then that other body is identical to me after the transfer but distinct from me before. Two distinct things have become identical. Van Inwagen's argument is vitually the same as the one Jayanta uses to refute the idea that one can be identical to a life-stage at one time and a distinct life-stage at another; and that is not surprising, because Jayanta's view about the persistence of bodies implies that at each life-stage I have a distinct body. Why should we accept the principle that distinct entities cannot become identical? Van Inwagen says:

> In the present case, the objects under consideration have different histories. For example, you are here now and the physical object that you are going to become after the information has flowed from one brain to another is now over there—and each of them is in only one of these two places, not in both simultaneously. If you are this organism now at t_1 and will be that organism over there later at t_2, that organism over there will, by a simple application of Leibniz's Law, be able to say, truly, 'At t_1 I was right here and it is not the case that at t_1 I was right here.' (1997: 310)

Given that many philosophers have regarded bodily transfer as a distinct possibility, the fact that it is incompatible with Animalism seems to put still further pressure on that view.

Such considerations have also been a decisive motivation in the development of accounts whose aim is to supersede that of the Cārvāka. Buddhists have told stories about survival in a new body to support their view that it is

[2] See Parfit (1984: 199); Shoemaker (1984: 108–11); cf. B. Williams (1973b: 79–81).

a mistake to identify oneself with one's mere body. In one story, the parts of the body are replaced one by one until there is a completely new one, a process which induces a question about survival:

Once a man who was ordered to go to some distant place, found himself passing the night in a deserted house. In the middle of the night a demon who was carrying a dead man on his shoulders, came and set it down next to him. Then a second demon came along in pursuit of the first and began to angrily reproach him saying, 'That dead man belongs to me; why was it you who carried it here?' The first demon replied, 'It is my property, it's me who took it and I carried it off myself'. The second demon responded, 'It was really me who carried that dead man here'. The two demons, each taking hold of the corpse by a hand, fought over it. The first demon said, 'There is a man here whom we can interrogate'. The second demon then asked him, 'Who carried this dead man here?' The man thought to himself as follows: 'These two demons are very strong; whether I tell the truth or I lie, my death is certain; in neither case would I escape. How would it be good to lie?' He then declared that it was the first demon who had carried [the corpse]. Then the second demon, in a rage, grabbed him by the hand, tore it off and threw it to the ground. But the first demon took an arm of the corpse and attached it to him. In the same way he replaced the two arms, the two feet, the head and the sides of the body [with parts of the corpse]. Then the two demons together devoured the body of the man which they had replaced [with that of the corpse], and after wiping their mouths departed.

The man then reflected thus: 'The body that was born of my father and mother, I have seen with my own eyes being entirely devoured by those two demons. Now my present body is entirely constituted by the flesh of someone else. Do I quite clearly have a body, or do I no longer have a body? If I think I have one, it is entirely the body of another. If I think that in fact I don't have one, here is a body that is perfectly visible'. When he had thus reflected, his mind grew greatly troubled and he became like someone who has lost their senses. The next morning he returned to the road and departed. Arriving in a kingdom in a highly puzzled state, he saw a group of monks by a Buddhist stūpa; he didn't know what else to ask them than whether his body existed or not. The monks asked, 'Who are you?' He responded, 'I don't really know whether I am a person or I am not a person'. He then told the assembly at length about what had happened. The monks then said, 'This man recognises for himself the non-existence of the 'I'. He will easily attain the state of liberation'. Addressing him, they said to him, 'Your body, from the beginning until today, was never a self, and it is not that this has only now come to be the case. It is only because the four great elements are assembled together that you thought, 'This is my body'. Between your body at other times and that of today there is no difference.'[3]

The possibility of psychological linkages across bodies is also considered by the Nyāya commentators, in connection with a problem about neonate emotion. *Nyāya-sūtra* 3.1.18–26 argue that a neonate experiences the emotions of fear (*bhaya*), sorrow (*śoka*), and delight (*harṣa*), emotions which, it is claimed, are constitutively such as to follow on the heels of a memory of some experience in the past. Praśastapāda analyses the respective emotions as follows (see further Chapter 14). Delight is the experience of pleasure one has on fulfilling a longing for something one desired. Fear is an inability to rid oneself of the wish to flee in the presence of what will lead to something one does not desire. Sorrow is the unfulfillable longing for something which one desires and from which one is separated. Elsewhere, desire itself is analysed as an unfulfilled longing for something one wants but does not have. Emotions like these are complex psychological events, and only occur as part of a richly woven psychological life, involving, in particular, remembered past experiences and anticipated future ones. Applied to the question of neonates, the further argument canvassed is that we know these emotions are felt by newly born infants, because we see that they flinch, cry, and smile; therefore, even a neonate must have memories of experiences from another body.

What I want to point out is something very interesting about the analyses that have been given of the states of fear, sorrow, and delight. In each case, a first-person stance is involved. One does not feel delight unless one is aware that *one's own* longing has been fulfilled; one does not feel afraid unless one cannot rid oneself of the wish to flee from that which one does not *oneself* welcome. Discussing these cases, Prabhācandra the Jaina comments: 'Those who have not had prior experiences of the results following from what is desired or undesired would not, in a law-like manner, wish to seek or avoid them. That to which the prior experience is ascribed, it is the self, a distinct existence' (Prabhācandra 1991: 3478,1–3). Many emotions are first-person

[3] Pseudo-Nāgārjuna (1994: 738–40). See Ganeri (2007: 212–15) for further discussion of this passage. The example resembles Parfit's spectrum argument (Parfit 1984: 237), and more especially Stone's modification (Stone 1988: 522). Parfit's view is that what such arguments show is that the man's question as to whether he was the same person as before is an empty one.

involving, and their alleged reach across bodies seemingly again calls for selves to have identity conditions distinct from bodies.

If bodily transfer is a genuine possibility, then so is the possibility of fission. Thought experiments involving fission have dominated discussion about personal identity. It is therefore of some interest to note that the alleged impossibility of twins sharing psychological links with their common parents is cited by Prabhācandra as a reason in favour of independent selves over psychological streams: 'It cannot be the case that repeated exposure to an object by one person leads it to be recognized by someone else. If such were the case, then each child would recognise [objects experienced by its parents] and judge "This has been experienced by me." Moreover, each child would recognise objects experienced by the other' (Prabhācandra 1990: 119,10-14).

The Embodied Self

Even if Animalism is false, one might still want to maintain that selfhood requires embodiment, and perhaps even more strongly, that selves are individuated according to bodily criteria. That is to say, one might take the lesson to be not that one of Reductionism or Cartesianism must be true, but rather that questions of individuation and ownership must be kept apart. One Nyāya philosopher, Vācaspati, points to a particular difficulty in the earlier-mentioned theory about neonate emotion: if a newborn's desires are the result of its remembering pleasures from its previous life, and if it is possible for an elephant to be reborn as a human being, then why is it that we do not find baby human beings with the desires of elephants, such as the desire to eat certain sorts of leaves?

[Objection:] If the desires of a neonate are the result of remembering past experiences, then in the case where a self that occupied a human body in its past life is born into an elephant's body, the desires of the elephant cub would be for such things as are sought after by human beings.

[Reply:] The answer is that the character of the child's desires depends on the body he has at the time; and the desires in the elephant cub would be those in accordance with the experiences undergone by that self in a remote previous life when in an elephant's body. (Vācaspati 1997: 476,17—477,2, on *Nyāya-sūtra* 3.1.26; trans. Jha 1984: 1170, modified.)

There is a recognition here that the nature of one's appetites, and other dimensions of one's experience, are subject to bodily criteria. This is the so-called 'embodied mind' thesis (Lakoff and Johnson 1999; Shapiro 2004; Gallagher 2005).[4]

A further argument is that it is not after all conceivable that I could be exactly as I am, enjoying the very same inner phenomenology and with the very same first-person stance, but in a different body (or different type of body). Thomas Nagel famously argues that a human being can form no idea what it would be like to be a bat, with its echo-mediated acquaintance with the world. The best one can do is to imagine one's own body having a bat-shape; thus, recalling what we said before about the imagination, we must distinguish between imagining having a different body and imagining oneself as differently bodied (Nagel 1974). Commenting now on the *Brahma-sūtra-bhāṣya*, Vācaspati suggests that the self is not the body because a very skilled *yogī* can assume the physical form of a tiger, and also because one can dream that one is a tiger—but in either case 'although one conceives of oneself as assuming another body, one continues to recognise the seat of one's concept of *I* (*ahaṃkāra*).'[5] If Nagel is right, not even the most skilled *yogī* could know what it is like to be a tiger, and I take it that what Vācaspati means by the preservation of the 'seat of one's concept of *I*' in this example is that one can dream of *oneself* inhabiting a tiger's body, but one cannot dream being a tiger: my dream of being in a tiger's body is that of having all my experience, conditioned by my human embodiment, simply transplanted there.[6] The seat of one's concept of *I* is just the grounds of one's occupancy of a first-person stance, and the point is that one could never inhabit a tiger's first-person stance: the identity conditions of one's occupancy of a first-person stance are at least in part bodily. If some version of an

[4] Lakoff and Johnson describe the embodied mind thesis as a 'challenge to western thought'. Presumably they have in mind the Abrahamic/Cartesian picture of the mind as potentially able to exist in separation from the body. The Nyāya conception of embodied self is similarly in tension with the more 'Cartesian' view of the Jainas.

[5] *yogavyāghravat svapnadaśāyāṃ ca śarīrāntaraparigrahābhimāne 'py ahaṃkārāspadasya pratyabhijñāyamānatvam ityukam* | (Vācaspati 1980: 766,30–1).

[6] See also Kumārila 1929: *Ātmavāda* 59a–62d.

'embodied mind' thesis for first-person stances is correct, then that is an argument against any conception of self which does not presume the body to be the individuative base. It is evident from this example that occupying a first-person stance is a matter of one's whole bearing; it is not simply an issue about a special sort of content that some mental states happen to have, so-called 'phenomenal content'. The analyses of the first-person stance in three Indian thinkers, Vasubandhu, Praśastapāda, and Vātsyāyana, are all sensitive to this point.

One naturalist text affirms that there is no possibility of bodily transfer at the moment of death:

> Upwards from the soles of the feet, downwards from the tips of the hair on the head, within the skin's surface is the human being (*jīva*), or what is the same, the self (*ātman*). It lasts as long as the body lasts, it does not out-last its destruction. With that ends life. Other men carry the corpse away and burn it. When it has been consumed by fire, only dove-coloured bones remain, and the four bearers return with the hearse to their village. Therefore there is and exists no [immaterial] soul.[7]

This text is important because it neither denies that there is self nor does it identify it with the body. It affirms that the self and the body are co-persistents, that the self does not outlast the body. So there is here the beginning of a possibility that a broadly naturalist perspective is consistent with conceptions of self other than Animalism. A naturalist who is not an Animalist might wish to argue instead that psychological traits which require specifically embodied individuation criteria are constitutive aspects of selfhood. According to what I am calling the strong first-person requirement, nothing is a self which lacks the capacity to conceive of itself as itself. So then the question is whether there is any aspect of mind which is subject to specifically embodied individuation criteria and can also ground the satisfaction of the strong first-person requirement. If there is, then the claim that this is a self represents a way to endorse the embodied mind thesis without identifying the self with the body. This is not the Nyāya Vaiśeṣika View, but it is one which has enjoyed considerable support.

[7] Quoted in the *Sūtrakṛtāṅga* 2.1.15 (trans. Jacobi 1895: ii. 339–40).

Core Self as Bodily Presence

C. D. Broad draws a distinction between those theories about the unity of mind which 'ascribe the unity of the mind to the fact that there is a certain particular existent—a Centre—which stands in a common asymmetrical relation to all the mental events which could be said to be states of a certain mind' and those 'No-Centre' theories which do not.[8] Among the theories which do propose such a Centre, it is common to take it to consist in something like a Pure Cartesian Ego. Broad notices, however, that there is room for a theory that is neither a Pure Ego theory nor a No-Centre theory. That is to say, he anticipates the existence of what I am calling Type II, or Real Self, conceptions of self. According to Broad,

> [T]he most plausible form of this theory would be to identify the Central Event at any moment with a mass of bodily feeling. The longitudinal unity of a self through a period of time would then depend on the fact that there is a mass of bodily feeling which goes on continuously throughout this period and varies in quality not at all or very slowly. (Broad 1925: 566)

The claim that there is a more or less static sense of 'bodily feeling'. It answers Chisholm, because there is nothing which stands in for it. It gives the naturalist just quoted much of what they want, a self essentially individuated by the body. And it answers Jayanta in so far as it is an endurant, wholly present at different times. On the assumption that bodily feeling supervenes on states of the body, such a view takes the body to be the individuative base, but not identical to the self. It is, we might say, a Minimal Ownership View.

William James too said that there is what he called 'the nucleus of "me"', which consists in 'bodily existence felt to be present' (James 1890: i. 400). As James was aware, though, this 'nucleus of "me"' is not yet a self, and Broad's proposal is not a viable one. One obvious problem is that nothing in Broad's suggestion implies that the changing body of a single individual will sustain the same or even a very similar somatic field. A more serious problem is that the presence of a continuous mass of bodily feeling is compatible with the inability to discharge any of the higher-order functional tasks alleged to be

[8] This distinction is closely related to the one with which I began Ch. 1, the distinction between collective and adjectival conceptions of self.

constitutive of having a self. The theory of self we are looking for is one for which having a first-person stance—an ability to conceive of my mental life as my own, including the ability to think of the states that depend on my having the body I do as *my own* bodily states—is a necessary condition on selfhood.

According to the suggestion of Jayanta, a naturalist might derive support for their view from certain Upaniṣadic passages where the self is portrayed as 'a single mass of cognition, which is risen up out of these elements and is dissolved into them'. The self is spoken of there as being without a core or a surface, but as pervading the subject in the way that salinity pervades brine water or salt crystals. The implication is that it is something which is diffused throughout one's experiential life: 'When a chunk of salt is thrown in water, it dissolves into that very water, and it cannot be picked up in any way. Yet, from whichever place one may take a sip, the salt is there! In the same way this Immense Being has no limit or boundary and is a compact mass (*ghana*) of cognition (*vijñāna*)' (*Bṛhad. Up.* 2.4.12). The picture is of the self as being an invariant mode of self-awareness which saturates the entirety of one's inner life, a constant hum of presence to oneself.

A similar idea is prominent in the phenomenological tradition. Michel Henry says, for example, that 'The interiority of the immediate presence to itself constitutes the essence of ipseity' (Henry 1975: 38). It is available in Gabriel Marcel's notion of a body-mediated sense of participation, which he called the feeling of being 'at home' in oneself (Marcel 1949). Zahavi demonstrates that the idea that there is what he calls 'a pre-reflective sense of mineness' in experience is part of the thought of several classical phenomenologists. He goes on to argue that 'it is also possible to identify this pre-reflective sense of *mineness* with a minimal, core, self' (Zahavi 2005a: 125). The term 'core' refers to the version of the idea found in Damasio's neuroscientific posit of a 'core consciousness' (Damasio 1999: 7, 10, 127).

Leibniz said that music is a *sensation* of counting without being aware that one is counting, and here the phenomenon falls under a similar description: the self is a feeling of being present to oneself without being explicitly aware that one is present to oneself. This would explain the much-discussed diaphanousness of the self, its elusiveness to conscious attention. As Ryle once said, someone who tries to catch the self 'has failed to catch more than the flying coat-tails of that which he was pursuing. His quarry was the hunter' (Ryle 1949: 187). If the self is at core what lies beneath attention, then to try to make it into an object of attention is to engage in an act which is pragmatically self-defeating, like trying to step on one's own shadow. Beneath whatever one does succeed in bringing to one's attention there is a sensation of self-presence, and that, so it is claimed, should be identified as the essentially embodied core self.

For this to be a workable proposal as a theory of self, and not merely as a datum within human phenomenology, one would need to be able to claim that it is precisely because of the 'presence to oneself' that one is in a position to think of one's states as one's own, that the capacity for a first-person stance is *underwritten* by it—although, being a capacity, it need not presently be exercised in order to be present. I will consider in several later chapters whether more can be said about this notion of 'underwriting' (recalling also Vācaspati's use of the term 'seat'). Yogācāra Buddhists too acknowledge that something underwrites the capacity in question, which they see as a sort of first-person mental file (*ālaya-vijñāna*) but deny is identical with a self (Chapter 8).[9]

The worry is that the core or minimal self is too minimal to count as a self. A core self does not seem to do one of the things that a respectable concept of self must, and that is to individuate thinkers. The property 'being a thought of one's own' is a property like 'being a divisor of itself', which is equally true of every number; the reflexive pronoun is just a place-holder. Zahavi says that 'the particular first-person givenness of the experience makes it mine and distinguishes it for me from whatever experiences others might have' (2005a: 124). This choice of words suggests that first-person givenness is individuative of individual selves, but it is not clear that it actually is. What does the real work here is an embodiment criterion; it is because of their having distinct bodies that individuals are individuated. That is what prevents this variety of Minimal Ownership View from collapsing into a Pure Consciousness View.[10] A Core Self theorist therefore does best to insist that the 'presence to oneself' in virtue of which I can

[9] Zahavi makes it a 'minimal demand to any proper theory of self-awareness' that it 'be able to explain the peculiar features characterising the subject-use of "I"; that is, no matter how complex or differentiated the structure of self-awareness is ultimately shown to be, if the account given is unable to preserve the difference between the first-person and third-person perspectives, unable to capture its referential uniqueness, it has failed as an explanation of self-awareness' (1999: 13).

[10] This point is acknowledged, in Gallagher and Zahavi (2008: 184): 'If my self-experience is, in the primary instance, of a purely mental nature, i.e. if my body does not figure essentially in my self-ascription of (some) psychological states, while my ascription of mental states to others are based

think of my experience as my own is rooted in the body ('risen up out of the elements'), that it is fundamentally embodied, but without identifying it simply with somatic or proprioceptive sensation. An embodied feeling of presence-to-self is, at least potentially, able to distinguish distinct individual selves, because it is distinct from one body to another.[11] So the hope is that a Minimal Ownership View solves the twin problems of Attenuation and Persistence.

For at least one contemporary Animalist, the proposal is nevertheless untenable, because the posited sense of 'presence-to-self' simply does not exist:

> [Some say this:] 'The "I" experience, as we can all feel, is quite distinct from bodily experiences of pain or joy. Therefore, the "I" experience must be grounded in something, which is quite distinct from both body and unconscious mind (*manas*).' This is not tenable: we do not believe in the possibility of any experience which may be characterised as the experience of the pure 'I'; neither do those who believe in the doctrine of self (*ātman*). According to us self-as-body theorists, this person is no different from the body, which is the actual referent of the term 'I'. We do not understand why one should unnecessarily look for another referent. (Shukla 1984 [1991: 11].)

Shukla's scepticism about the very existence of the posited invariant sense of self-presence is to be taken very seriously, but I do not share his confidence that a Strawsonian concept of a person is what is needed instead. What we need rather is a way to respect the asymmetry between the first- and the third-person stances in a manner compatible with naturalism. What we need is precisely a 'doctrine of self', a more robust version of the Ownership View.

There are two ways to account for the nature of presented mineness or what I am calling immersion. One, which we have just been examining, sees it as fundamentally a relationship of bodily ownership. The core self as bodily feeling of presence to oneself is thus one possible account of the immersed self, and this seems to be the account preferred by the Nyāya-Vaiśeṣika insofar as they countenance the idea at all. Other accounts develop an

solely on their bodily behaviour, what, then, should guarantee the ascription of the same type of states to others?'

[11] As in Merleau-Ponty's claim that subjects realize their ipseity in their embodied being-in-the-world (Merleau-Ponty 1962: 408).

analysis out of a more detailed study of the structure of self-consciousness and provide a subjective rather than a bodily account of immersed ownership. I now examine in detail several remarkably rich and insightful analyses from Buddhist writers of subjective immersion, separating out the constructive analysis from the further claim that immersed ownership is an illusion. I will argue that one such analysis is mistaken—the theory that self-consciousness consists in every moment of consciousness being reflexively self-aware, and I will instead prefer an analysis of self-consciousness in terms of the existence and function of what I will call phenomenal 'mineness-markers'.[12] I will seek to establish that this theory of self-consciousness is independent of Buddhist No Place Views about self, and the consequent Buddhist claim that genuine first-person thought rests on a mistake. I will return to the relationship between first-person phenomena and embodiment only in Chapter 12.

[12] Non-Buddhist thinkers in India do indeed use reflexivist analyses of immersion as the basis for a constructive account of the immersed self (See Watson 2006). Zahavi's (2005a) analysis is based on a Phenomenal View; still another analysis of subjective immersion bases it instead on a Pure Consciousness View, that of the Advaita 'witness consciousness' (Fasching 2011; Albahari 2006). Although there is no Indian precedent, I will recommend a theory of the immersed self likewise developed out of Vasubandhu's analysis of immersion.

PART III

Immersion and Subjectivity

7

The Composition of Consciousness

A Trope Metaphysics of Mind

I now want to examine a theory of mind which has had an unparalleled influence in many parts of the world over a period of many centuries. The theory in question rests on the following idea. Individual mental particulars such as particular moments of conscious experience have a compositional structure. Mental particulars are built out of five sorts of basic kinds of psychological activity, namely:

1. embodied reacting (*rūpa*)
2. hedonic appraising (*vedanā*)
3. labelling or stereotyping (*saṃjñā*)
4. dispositional constructing (*saṃskāra*)
5. conscious attending (*vijñāna*)

This is the starting point for all Buddhist views about mind, and perhaps in particular that of Abhidharma Buddhism.[1] We need to address several difficult questions. What sort of thing (*dharma*) are the five basic sorts (*skandha*) sorts of? What is the relationship between the five basic psychological sorts and the four 'elemental' physical sorts (*mahābhūta*)? What is the relationship between individual thoughts, items of intentional conscious experience, and the five sorts? What is the relationship between persons and the five sorts? Finally, of course, is the question of what account is to be given of first-person phenomena and in particular the idea of *self*, a question I will fully address only in

[1] Ganeri (2016). Waldron (2003: 53) claims that Abhidharma has four characteristic features: '(1) It depends upon a *phenomenological* analysis of experience in descriptive terms; (2) it is *metapsychological* in the sense of being a self-conscious, systematic analysis of experience; (3) it is a comprehensive description of experience in *systemic* terms, that is, in which all of its items are mutually defined and distinguished from one another; and (4) finally, Abhidharma thinkers considered an analysis of experience in terms of dharmas as the *only ultimate* account of "how things really are".'

the next chapter. The scheme used to be portrayed as designed to delineate the structure of human personhood as an interwoven stream of five types of personality-factor. Gethin, however, corrects this portrayal: "To explain the *skhandhas* as the Buddhist analysis of man, as has been the tendency of contemporary scholars, may not be incorrect as far as it goes, yet it is to fix upon one facet of the treatment of the *skhandhas* at the expense of others ... At the most general level [they] are presented as five aspects of an individual being's experience of the world" (1986: 52).

Just what *sort* of thing are these basic items out of which mental particulars are fashioned? I have proposed that the constituents are best understood as tropes (Ganeri 2001: Ch. 4). There are several understandings of what a trope is, and so I will specify that a basic psychological item is a trope in the sense neither of a property-particular such as the property of being a particular shade of blue, nor in the sense of an exemplifier or instantiation of such a property, such as the particular object which has that shade of blue, but rather as something ontologically more fundamental than either objects or properties, and in terms of which both objects and properties can be defined. So the colour blue is a combination of all particular blues, the blue of this vase, the blue of the sky at this moment in time, the blue of that particular splash of paint; and a vase is a combination of a certain particular blue, a certain particular shape, a certain particular texture, and so on.[2] Likewise, in our theory of mind, an individual conscious experience is a 'trope-cluster' of mental tropes of the five types listed above: a particular registering, a particular appraisal, a particular stereotyping, reading and attending jointly constitute a given individual conscious state. The term 'trope' is not a particularly fortunate one, and contemporary trope-theorists have urged instead the use of 'qualiton' (Bacon 1995). This is also a better rendering of the Buddhist term *dharma*.

It is stipulated by our thinkers that the basic constituents do not change over time, and it follows that all change involves a going out of existence or a coming into being of constituents. Everything is in fact subject to change; so the basic constituents have only a circumscribed temporal span (*anityatā*).[3] The basic constituents are nevertheless not identical to events, although events, like everything else, are made from them. Jaegwon Kim, for example, has argued that an event is the exemplification by an object of

[2] This is classical trope-cluster theory, first proposed in Stout (1921) and D. C. Williams (1953). For reviews of contemporary work in trope-theory, see Bacon (1995), Simons (1994), Chrudzimski (2004).

[3] The term *anityatā* is often translated as 'impermanence' but does not in itself imply that the constituents exist only for a moment (*kṣaṇa*). That is, however, the view of Buddhist presentism.

a property at a time. This is true of qualitons too, but it is a truth entailed by their nature, rather than a definition. Donald Davidson, conversely, has claimed that an event is a basic occurrence capable of falling under different types, and, in particular, he has defended a view which he calls 'anomalous monism', the thesis that every mental event is also a physical event (i.e. that the same event falls under both a mental and a physical type), but that there are no psycho-physical laws between mental and physical properties. Our fundamental constituents of the mental differ from Davidsonian events in two respects: complexes of Davidsonian events do not constitute objects or properties; and not all of the basic Buddhist constituents fall under *both* a mental and a physical type. Davidson's theory is meant to explain how mental events can have physical causes, but ends up vulnerable to a version of the notorious exclusion problem: the event's participation in causal relations is determined by its physical type, leaving the fact that it also falls under a mental type causally irrelevant. The theory of anomalous monism does not, in the end, offer any solution to the problem of mental causation.

A trope-based analysis has been shown to do better. Heil (1992: 136–9) distinguishes between supervenience as a relation between properties (types) and realization as a relation between tropes (tokens). Allowing that mental trope could have been realized by a different physical token, Heil identifies realization with a constitution relation, and the point is then that a mental trope inherits the causal powers of the neurological trope which constitutes it. The error in the exclusion argument is seen to lie in that in eliding supervenience and realization, it equivocates on the notion of property (type vs. trope). In a similar spirit Robb (1997) notices that because mental types are not physical types, *sui generis* psycho-physical causal law is consistent with the token-token identity of psychological and physical events.[4]

Some Buddhists will agree that mental tropes supervene on physical tropes; but there are also Buddhist trope dualists who reject supervenience, and there are Buddhist trope idealists, who claim that all tropes are mind-dependent. Those who endorse supervenience will nevertheless dissent from the above description in one crucial respect. Instead of assuming that basic psychological tropes are already intentional, a mental state's intentional properties are explained by its composition from more fundamental and proto-intentional tropes. It is a key thesis of Abhidharma psychology that there are proto-intentional psychological processes through the joint

[4] See also Macdonald (1989); Macdonald and Macdonald (2010: 150–5).

operation of which intentional experience is constituted. The psychologically primitive processes—registering, appraising, stereotyping, readying, and attending—belong individually to a level beneath that of intentionality. Rather than struggling to account for intentionality in terms of causal relevance (as in Heil 1992: 139–47), the Buddhist view distinguishes between a trope-based solution to the exclusion problem and a compositional account of intentionality. In this, they can draw support from the methodology of contemporary neuroscience. Thus neuroscientist Richard Davidson:

> The challenge that faces the study of emotions is similar to that once faced by investigators studying cognition—the decomposition of complex emotional phenomena into more elementary constituents. Cognitive scientists do not study 'cognition' as a whole. Rather, they have developed specific paradigms to isolate more elementary stages of information processing. It is these more elementary components that will most likely yield to an analysis in terms of underlying neural systems. (Davidson 2003: 131)

Proto-cognitive and proto-affective processes, themselves realized in underlying neural systems, combine to constitute states of conscious intentional experience, experience which presents the world as one in which *attention* falls on objects which are perceptually *registered* as falling under schematic *stereotypes*, as organized in a hodological *appraisal* space of affordance and obstacle, in ways that shape the diachronic flow by *readying* for future experience.

In this theory the relationship between the basic mental constituents is described as being one of 'joint occurring' (*sahabhū*), and as an 'enveloping' (*anu-pari-vartante*).[5] I believe that trope-clustering provides the right theoretical model to understand the relationship these terms indicate. The binding of qualitons is through neither causal-psychological continuity nor relations of co-consciousness, but rather by trope-composition. It is perhaps possible to think of the tropes (*dharma*) in this theory as particular psychological powers, a definite and particular instance of the power to register, for instance, and of individual intentional thoughts as the joint sum of a cluster of such powers. Buddhist tropes, while *logically* prior to the

[5] For references, see Stcherbatsky (1923: 36, esp. n. 3); Waldron (2003: 57–8).

intentional states they constitute, are not prior *in existence*. They exist only in the states they constitute, just as quarks exist only in elementary particles.[6]

It is a good question whether the Buddhist theory is compatible with what David Lewis calls 'Humean supervenience':

> Humean supervenience is . . . the doctrine that all there is to the world is a vast mosaic of local matters of particular fact, just one little thing and then another . . . We have geometry: a system of external relations of spatio-temporal distances between points . . . And at those points we have local qualities: perfectly natural intrinsic properties which need nothing bigger than a point at which to be instantiated. For short, we have an arrangement of qualities. And that is all. There is no difference without difference in the arrangement of qualities. All else supervenes on that. (Lewis 1986: p. ix)

A 'local quality' or 'natural intrinsic property' is one whose instantiation at a point is metaphysically unconstrained by what other properties are instantiated.[7] If Humean supervenience is compatible with Buddhist philosophy of mind then there is a metaphysical possibility that a particular mental item, say one of feeling hopeful, is instantiated at a point in space-time without any other instantiations of particular mental items. Assent or dissent to the contention that Buddhist items of mind are local mental qualities seems to be a dividing line between Abhidharma and Yogācāra on the one hand, and Madhyamaka on the other. I will describe in Chapter 10 the view of the Yogācāra philosopher Dharmakīrti, who does indeed appear to treat a mental trope as local mental quality. The difference between Abhidharma and Yogācāra, one might conjecture, is that the 'mosiac of local matters of particular fact' on which all else supervenes is, in Abhidharma, ultimately a mosaic of local physical qualities, while in Yogācāra it is a mosaic of local mental qualities.

As I said in Chapter 1, this is dynamical theory in which at each moment in time there is a new, perhaps partially overlapping, set of micro-constituents (now identified as tropes), and there is a microdynamic which governs the time evolution of successive sequences of sets of

[6] Thus Martin (1980: 8): 'An object is not collectable out of its properties or qualities as a crowd is collectable out of its members. For each and every property of an object has to be had by that object to exist at all.' That is why I distinguished between collection and ownership in Ch. 2.

[7] Loewer (1996: 177): 'Call a property "Humean" if its instantiation requires no more than a spatio-temporal point and its instantiation at that point has no *metaphysical* implications concerning the instantiations of fundamental properties elsewhere and elsewhen.'

micro-constituents.[8] It is not a Tornado View, because there is no enduring set of particles analogous to the molecules of air and water in the tornado, and it is not a Flame View, because there is no macrostate, no emergent non-structural property analogous to the flame itself. Pudgala Realists however (on whom see below) do think that there is precisely such a state. Insofar as the constituents carry with them nothing corresponding to ownership, there is in this picture of the mind nothing playing the role of a self. It follows that there is also no account yet of a first-person stance, and I will look in the next chapter at the remedy to this lacuna in later Buddhist theory.

Macro and Micro

In an Abhidharma version of the theory, the fundamental physical constituents (*bhūta*) are not the four sorts of material element, earth, fire, air, and water, but rather four sorts of trope: the hard, the hot, the moving, and the gluey.[9] Each of these is, at it were, an independent parameter, so the theory is different from an ancient Greek one—that there are four elemental qualities, the hard and the soft, the wet and the dry—in which the independent parameters are only two. Physical objects are amalgams of these various kinds of basic physical power, constituted so as to present resistance, 'obstancy' (*pratighāta*).

The sensible qualities and the sensing systems are held to constitute a domain of dependently or derivatively physical things (*bhautika*; AK 1.9ab, 12-14). There is indeed textual evidence that the notion of dependence involved at this level is such as to support supervenience:

> This means that the primary elements are, with regard to the derived elements, the cause of arising, the cause of alteration (*vikāra*), the substratum (*ādhāra*), the cause of duration, and the cause of development. (Vasubandhu, *Bhāṣya* on AK 2.65b; trans. 1988–90: 309.)

Alteration in sensible qualities is caused by changes in the physical base, which is just to say that sensible quality supervenes on the primarily physical.

[8] In Buddhist technical vocabulary, the set at a time is called *rāśi* (lit. a mass, an amount, a heap, a sum), the sequence is called *santāna* (lit. continuous flow, uninterrupted series), and the microdynamic is called *pratītya-samutpāda* (lit. following-on joint production).

[9] Vasubandhu (1973: AK 1.12, 4.3-4).

Vasubandhu adds that the sensing of such qualities depends on the functioning sensory system. Colour sensations, for example, have the faculty of sight as their 'base' (here Vasubandhu explicitly uses the term *āśraya*), something that is simultaneous with them and upon which they depend: 'The base of a sensation is its sense-organ, for sensation changes according to the modality of the sense organ' (AK 1.45ab; trans. 1988–90: 125). A sense-organ, here, is not something like a nose, but rather a specific quality or capacity which a certain complex of matter has; we would now speak, for example, of the olfactory aspect of the exteroceptive system. Sensory acquaintance is an essentially physical process of being-impacted-upon by one's physical surroundings, a 'registering'. The sensory qualities are those qualities that get registered by the somato-sensory and proprioceptive systems.

That this relation of 'base' itself sustains supervenience is further suggested by Saṃghabhadra's comment. Saṃghabhadra says that changes in the quality of the sense-organ produce similar changes in the quality of its corresponding sensations.[10] Alterations in the physical substrate are correlated with corresponding alterations in the sensations themselves. It is also indicated by what is said about the apperception of one's inner mental states. This too, it is claimed, must have a 'base', which is described by some as an internal sense-organ and by others as something still more robustly physical, 'heart-stuff' (*hṛdaya-vastu*). Saṃghabhadra (E375) confirms the point, saying that apperception is indirectly affected by changes in the body. In the next chapter, I will describe the far more sophisticated theory about the base of self-consciousness that one finds in Vasubandhu's later, post-Abhidharma, works.

I will offer a final, but difficult, piece of textual evidence, from Buddhaghosa. Buddhaghosa seems to suggest that the sensibles like red or blue are emergents:

> Just as a magician turns (*dasseti*) water, which is not crystal, into crystal, and turns a clod that is not gold into gold, and shows them—and being himself neither a spirit or a bird shows himself as a spirit or a bird—so too, being themselves not blue-black, the four elements of the physical turn themselves into the blue-black 'dependently physical', being themselves not yellow . . . not red . . . not white, they turn themselves into the white 'dependently physical' and show that. (Buddhaghosa, *Visuddhi-magga* 1977: 366-7; trans. Ñāṇamoli 1964: 98.)

[10] Saṃghabhadra E375a (1999: 675).

The idea that the physical elements, not intrinsically coloured, turn themselves into sensible colours and in this way show themselves sounds at first sight like an emergence account of the relation between macro- and micro-properties. The analogy with a magician seems to suggest that all is not as it appears, but when Buddhaghosa repeats the same passage elsewhere, he explains it this way:

> Thus because of their illusory resemblances to the juggler's counterfeiting are they called 'primary elements.' . . . These material forms are not found standing mutually inside or outside; they just exist depending one on the other. Thus, because they have unimaginable footing, and resemble the counterfeiting of phenomena by spirits, they are called 'primary elements'. (Buddhaghosa, *Atthasālinī* 599; trans. 1921: ii. 294.)

So what colours disguise is their derivate nature: they show themselves as if they were just primary elements. It is not that they are themselves mere appearances.[11] In these passages Buddhaghosa is searching for the right language to articulate the relation between macrostates and microstates, a relationship for which contemporary philosophers have used terms like 'realization', 'supervenience', and 'constitution'. In confirmation of the point made earlier, it is clear that he regards this as a token-token relationship.

I want finally to mention two anomalies about registering, whose preservation in our theory is the manifestation of considerable insight. They both have to do with the idea of macro-physical attributes. One of these anomalies concerns the sense of touch. Our philosophers argue that, while the other sensibles are straightforwardly derivative from the base of the four primary physicals, tangibility (*spraṣṭavya-dhātu*) is different. It has a mixed status, partly basic, partly derivative. This seems to me to be a recognition of the fact that touch is in some way a more fundamental sense than the others, a more immediate form of contact with the world.

Another interesting claim is that there are particularly deep dispositions of character (*avijñapti-rūpa*) which are produced by one's past actions and behaviour patterns, and which are, as Vasubandhu puts it, 'dependent upon the primary elements, as a shadow exists dependent on a tree, as the brilliance of a jewel exists dependent upon the jewel'.[12] That too is a supervenience-based dependence relation, though less robust than before,

[11] I will return to this point in Ch. 10, while discussing whether qualia are genuinely intrinsic, or actually relational but presenting themselves as intrinsic.

[12] Vasubandhu (1973: AK ad 1.13; trans. 1988–90: 71). Further textual references: Lusthaus (2002: 523). Vasubandhu himself does not defend this Abhidharma doctrine.

and some of our philosophers are led to include these fundamental character traits within the category of the derivatively physical itself. This is a very curious inclusion, among the category of the physical, of something seemingly mental. It is said to be the physical trace of one's psychological habits.[13] The idea might be that habits of mind *determine* patterns of emergence from the primary matter, which do not occur naturally, but only in their presence, a thought echoing the point I made earlier in relation to the joint production of mental states in Cārvāka emergentism.

To summarize. Embodied reacting leads to a physical process of somatosensory impact (*sparśa; phassa*) with the physical surroundings. The sensibles are features which supervene upon aspects of the physical environment in dependence on the somato-sensory system. Sensations of touch are closer to the ground than the other kinds of sensation; and there are ways in which deep habits of behaviour and thought *carve* themselves into one's physical make-up, and hence inform one's future mental states. In Chapter 10, I will describe the more developed account of sentience in a later Buddhist thinker, Dharmakrti. In translating *rūpa* as "reacting" or "registering", my aim, following Gethin (1986), is to construe the notion in a way that does not commit Buddhists to a concept of normatively inert matter, to avoid the danger of reading into the compound *nāma-rūpa* a naïve metaphysical dualism of mind and matter. *rūpa* is that which by being "molested" or "deformed" (*ruppati*) solicits a response and enables "touch" (*sparśa; phassa*) under its minded aspect; *nāma* is mindedness in its various forms and capacities, proto-conceptual and phenomenal, that which conforms and asks the world to conform, i.e. "bends" (*namana*). These are two aspects of a single entity, a minded human being; they are also two aspects within items of perceptual experience; and they are also two aspects in intentional action—for it is important always to remember that Abhidharma terminology refers to functions and capacities, and is not restricted to specific classifications of entities. So *rūpa* means "lived body" in the context of a taxonomy of human beings, but mere matter in the context of a taxonomy of the physical world; in the context of a taxonomy of experience, again, it means those aspects of experience which are comparatively more passive.

[13] For a partially analogous proposal that background beliefs produce occurrent thoughts only by way of producing subpersonal 'motor instructions', see Campbell (1999: 617).

See further Kramer (2013): even the merely imagined (*parikalpita*) has *rūpa*, which can hardly be matter.

The Elements of Content

As well as registering our surroundings, we do other things: we *subsume* what we register into a scheme of classification, for example by classifying a red sensation as red; and we *appraise* what is registered—as harmful, helpful, or indifferent, as worth pursuing or avoiding. The three activities of registering, stereotyping and appraising run in tandem, interlinked in relations of mutual feedback and anticipation. The physical world presents itself as a structured space of opportunities and dangers. Repeated exposure to such a world leads us to form dispositions of response; we *ready* ourselves for future encounters. In this way, particular registrations acquire new dispositional propensities with respect to one another, as a particular smell might come to dispose one to particular feelings. We also *attend* to what is registered, selecting certain features from the totality.[14]

The fundamental Abhidharma insight is that these types of mental activity are individually beneath the level of the intentional, and indeed jointly constitutive of it. These proto-intentional mental activities belong to a level below that of belief-desire psychology. They represent a level of mental functioning from which beliefs and desires are distilled. Bernard Williams has hinted at such a picture of the mind:

> It is far from being true that every thought swimming around in one's mind is already the content of a belief as opposed to some other mental state such as a guess, a fancy, or (very importantly) a wish. We may have a picture of discrete beliefs lodged in a person's mind, waiting to be expressed... But in many other cases, it is not merely that we do not know what we believe (though this is of course often true), but *that a given content has not come to be a belief at all.* (Williams 2002: 82, my italics.)

This fundamental insight about the way thoughts and intentions are formed, which Moran calls a 'deliberative stance',[15] can easily be obscured in the

[14] It is frequently stressed in the texts that *vijñāna* involves the attention (*āvartana*); see Waldron (2003: 29, 51); Coseru (2012: Ch. 3). I explore this relation between attention and consciousness in detail in Ganeri (2016).

[15] Moran uses the terms 'theoretical stance' and 'deliberative stance' to mark 'the difference between that inquiry which terminates in a true description of my state, and one which terminates in the *formation* of an attitude' (Moran 2001: 63).

rendering of Buddhist terminology. Conventional translations need to be read with this in mind: *rūpa* being rendered as 'matter' or 'materiality'; *vedanā* as 'feeling'; *saṃjñā* as 'cognition', 'perception', or 'recognition'; *saṃskāra* as 'constructing activity' or 'formation'; and *vijñāna* as 'consciousness'. Candrakīrti's classical gloss, on the other hand, is particularly insight-He paraphrases each term with an active noun, *rūpa* becoming *rūpaṇa*, 'embodied reacting'; while *vedanā* becomes *anubhava*, 'experiencing'; *saṃjñā* becomes *nimitta-udgrahana*, the taking up of an object's mark; *saṃskāra* becomes *abhisaṃskaraṇa*, 'shaping one's dispositions'; and finally *vijñāna* becomes *viṣaya-prativijñapti*, the going towards an object in thought (taking aim at, attending).[16] These five sorts of mental activity are jointly constitutive of thinking. Again, I find this to be in basic agreement with current neuroscientific approaches to the study of cognition.[17]

Many contemporary Abhidharma scholars, we may note, are highly critical of older renderings of *skandha* terminology: see Gethin (1986), Reat (1987), Johansson (1979), Harvey (1995), Karunadasa (2010), Davis and Thompson (2013). The translation of *saṃjñā* as "perception", for example, is discredited by both Harvey and Gethin on textual grounds and can no longer be used in modern scholarship. Similarly, the older claim that Buddhist theory is a compositional theory only of persons and not of mental particulars is refuted within the tradition by no less a figure than Buddhaghosa, who identifies precisely this as marking the transition from the Suttas to Abhidharma (*Sammoha-vinodanī* 200–1). In Ganeri (2016) I agree with Bodhi (2007: 78) and Karunadasa (2010: 101) that the compositionality of the mental is more conveniently formulated with respect to the list of "concomitants" (*caitta, cetasika*) than the partially overlapping and coordinate list of "aggregates" (*skandha*). According to Buddhist theory, a manifest item of the mental—an individual experience, a belief or desire, a thought—is a qualiton-cluster: of embodied reacting, hedonic appraising, labelling,

[16] Candrakrti, *Prasannapadā* (1960: B 343,20). Candrakrti is not an Abhidharma author, but his gloss on the basic meaning of these pan-Buddhist terms is insightful.

[17] Recent work in neuroscience uses a model of semantic and affective priming, together with focal attention, where semantic features include '1. the integration of multiple features of the object into a single "object" code; 2. the identification of this object; and 3. the categorization of the object' (Storbeck and Clore 2007: 1221). There are clear congruencies with the ideas of appraising, stereotyping, readying, and attending. Storbeck and Clore note that findings in neuroscience 'suggest that categorization tends to occur prior to identification' (2007: 1224), while 'affect is a potential moderator of all kinds of cognitive operations', something which is 'inherently integrated' in cognition (2007: 1230).

dispositional constructing, and conscious attending constituents. The great elegance and attraction of the theory indeed lies here. For, simultaneously,

- it recognizes the irreducibility of the phenomenal character of experience;
- it recognizes the joint contribution of sensation and conceptualization in the constitution of experience, something that is known to Kantian scholarship as the Discursivity Thesis;[18]
- it acknowledges that experience is, as it were, 'saturated' with affect, that appraisal is built into the fabric of experience;[19]
- it recognizes that every experience has, as a basic ingredient, a capacity or tendency to combine in various ways with various others; and
- it makes the attention intrinsic to experience.

Sensation and conception are said to combine into thought through a relation of 'co-ordination' (*sārūpya*). Stcherbatsky finds in this relation an analogy with Kant's schematism: he says that it is 'intended to supply a bridge between pure sensation and reason'.[20] In Chapter 10 I will look at Dharmakrti's much more detailed analysis of the idea that there is a bridge between sensation and thought, and at his further argument that an illusion is involved in the construction of objects as intentional contents of conscious thought, that intentionality is an illusion, a fictitious by-product of the composition of tropes. One of the most important questions for the Buddhist account is whether this further claim is defensible.

Kim has described the phenomenal character of experience as the 'mental residue' which even his fully worked out reductive physicalism is unable to reduce (Kim 2005: 170). That residue is what has led some philosophers of mind to defend a property dualism (most notably, Chalmers 1996). Our philosophers tell us that phenomenal character is not the only residual problem for physicalism. Another has to do with the activity of mental disposition-formation, and is designated *citta-saṃprayukta-saṃskāra* or *experiential readying*. The idea of experiential readying is the idea of what gives shape to the experience as one that is, for example, a looking forwards in anticipation, backwards in memory, or onto the present in attention or

[18] Allison (2004, Ch. 4).

[19] For evidence that affect and cognition are not subserved by separate and independent neural circuits, see Davidson (2003); Storbeck and Clore (2007).

[20] Stcherbatsky (1923: 56 n. 1; cf. 64–6).

concentration; and for these thinkers it is important that it give moral shape to the experience as well, an idea that encompasses moral and emotional psychology.[21] The claim that experiential readying is an irreducible but natural aspect of the mind is part of what makes this theory a variety of liberal rather than hard naturalism. Indeed, the Buddhist concept of experiential readying might be seen as a close cousin of Aristotelian second nature.

Conscious intentional thought, then, has a compositional structure. In the next two chapters I will examine two theories about the structure of first-person phenomena and self-consciousness, one drawn from the post-Abhidharma work of the later Vasubandhu and one from the Yogācāra thinker Dignāga. I want to end this chapter by considering how the ideas so far presented illuminate the vexed question of the status of the notion of a 'person' (*pudgala*) in Buddhist theory.

Pudgala: Flame or Stream?

The use of the term *pudgala*, often translated as 'person', is puzzling in early Buddhism. The concept *pudgala* is not yet that of an occupant of a first-person stance, nor indeed is it quite that of an entity whose identity over time is in question. Nor is it precisely the idea of a participant in moral space or the political order. Its most fundamental designation is with respect to something putatively more than the mere stream of psycho-physical happenings that seems to be all there is to a human being according to the standard Buddhist picture. The so-called 'Pudgala Realists' (Pudgalavādins or Vātsiputrīyas; see Chau 1999; Priestley 1999) are emergentists: they claim that the *pudgala* is an inexplicable product of diachronic aggregation. Like the Cārvāka naturalists I spoke about in earlier chapters, they too point to examples from the natural world to illustrate their theory. For them, the choice example is the relation between fire and the fuel in which it burns: the fire is dependent on the fuel, but not in the same way that the shape of a heap of sand is dependent on the grains. Their view is that, like fire, there is something which is dependent upon but yet irreducible to the constituent

[21] Among the higher-level dispositional states grounded in experiential readying, for example, are: courage, equanimity, humility, moral repugnance, dispassion, freedom from lust, hatred, harm, mental suppleness, good habits of mind; and, of course, the opposites of all of these.

ingredients of a psycho-physical stream. They thus use the term *pudgala* to refer to the macrostate of a dynamical system which is subject to a microdynamic (*pratītya-samutpāda*, 'combined origination in dependence') by which its total collective state at one time determines its state at the next.

The taxonomy of Chapter 1 provides us with a clear way to understand this position. It is a Flame View. The Flame View is that the micro-elements are in a process of mutation, and that the emergent macrostates yielded by this process of mutation are to be identified as corresponding with mind, just as a flame is something emergent from a process in which the constituent material is continuously changing. This is different from any No Place View, since No Place Views deny that there is any emergent macrostate. To that extent other Buddhists are justified in regarding Pudgala Realism with deep suspicion. A Flame View theorist thinks that there is something other than the stream: emergent upon the underlying dynamical system, there are macrostates which take the stream as their owner. The theory is best understood as the thesis that a *pudgala* is an emergent from the dynamical system that is the interlaced stream of the five sorts of mental particular. It is not clear whether they think that the emergence in question is weak, and the emergent *pudgala* epiphenomenal, or strong, and the *pudgala* causally autonomous. On the other hand, the Flame View is still a far cry from any Real Self view. A Real Self view might hold that the self is an emergent from the neurophysical base, but will also hold that mental states are adjectivally dependent on it, not as with the Pudgala Realist that the *pudgala* is irreducibly dependent on the collective stream. Based on this analysis, I think that *pneuma*, *psyche*, or even *spirit* would all be better translations of *pudgala* than *person*.

Vasubandhu strongly opposes the claim that any such thing exists. The exact nature of his disagreement, however, requires stating with care. His view is that nothing corresponds to the Pudgalavāda use of the term *pudgala*. That is because he has a No Place View, and such views deny that there are emergent macrostates of the sort posited. Equally clearly, however, he does not deny that streams, the underlying dynamical systems themselves, exist, and it might seem that there is nothing to prevent one using the term to denote that. He has indeed been called a 'Buddhist Reductionist', seeming to imply that he reduces 'persons' to streams; but again, he clearly does not hold what I have called the Reductionist View (the view of Parfit, for example). This is because he has a No Place View, and so, in particular, denies that mental particulars have owners, even ownership by the stream. It is problematic in the extreme to correlate Buddhist controversy as to the status of the *pudgala* with western discussions of personal identity. I think it is possible to make sense of all this, but only if we proceed with caution.

C. D. Broad defined emergent qualities as 'qualities which are possessed by groups having such-and-such a structure and such-and-such constituents but are *not deducible* from a knowledge of the structure of the group and the qualities of its constituents' (Broad 1925: 581). In another place, he said that 'an emergent quality is roughly a quality which belongs to a complex as a whole and not to its parts' (1925: 23). The adverb 'roughly' here is important, because another category of quality shares with emergent qualities that same feature, so-called structural properties. Something's shape, for instance, need be the shape of none of its parts, but we would not count it as an emergent property. This is because it is entirely explicable ('deducible') how something's shape depends on and is a result of the arrangement and shape of its parts. There are thus three ways for a property to be a property of a complex (or whole or aggregate) without necessarily being a property of any of its constituents or parts:[22]

1) *Scalar sums.* For example, the mass of an object is not the mass of any of its proper parts. The mass of the whole is a scalar sum of the masses of the parts.
2) *Structural resultants.* For example, the shape of an object is not the shape of any of its proper parts. The shape of an object is a structural property, deducible from knowledge of the parts and their arrangement.
3) *Emergents.* For example, arguably, the biological or psychological properties of an organism emerge from the nature and arrangement of its parts, but are not deducible from knowledge of their nature and arrangement.

Kim has argued that the right way to understand the non-deducibility condition characteristic of emergent properties is as a condition that rules out functional reduction (Kim 2006a; see Chapter 3 above). What marks out scalar sums and structural properties is that they are *functionally* reducible to the constituents. The mass of a heap of sand is a function of the masses of the grains; indeed, the function is simply addition. The shape of a table is also a function of the shapes and positions of its parts; in this case, the

[22] Armstrong (1978: ii. 69); O'Connor (1994).

function is a more complex structural one. What distinguishes emergents then, if there are any, is that they are not functionally reducible to their constituents. Kim is a reductive physicalist who takes the reduction of the mental to the physical to consist in the functionalization of mental properties and the identification of their physical realizers.

There is a different and older concept of reduction, still in play and also relevant to our understanding of Buddhist *pudgala* theory. This is the model developed by Ernest Nagel, which sees reduction as consisting in the nomic derivation of the laws of the theory to be reduced from the laws of the reducing theory. Such derivations need auxiliary empirical premises called 'bridge-laws', which correlate the predicates in the reduced theory with those of the reducing theory:

Bridge Law Requirement. If theory T is to be reduced to T★, for each primitive predicate M of T there must be a bridge law of the form M↔N, providing M with a coextensive predicate N of T★.[23]

When the theory to be reduced is a theory of mind, the bridge law might, for example, correlate the predicate '. . . is a pain' with a predicate from the theory of neuroscience, such as '. . . is a C-fibre firing'. It might then seem that under a Nagel reduction, any statement in the reduced theory can be translated into an equivalent statement in the reducing theory. One might think, for example, that if the theory of macroscopic middle-sized objects permits of a Nagel reduction to a theory of atoms and their interactions, then our talk about tables and chairs will be translatable into talk about their constituent atomic swarms. And then one might be led to the conclusion that tables and chairs really are nothing over and above swarms of atoms, or even that swarms are all there really are, and that middle-sized objects exist only in name and not in reality. It is in this context that David Lewis draws a distinction between the *cautious* and the *incautious* reductionist: the cautious reductionist does not confuse the 'nothing but' clause in a reductionist thesis with a denial of existence (Lewis 1998: 29; quoted above, p. 20).

These distinctions are what we need to make sense of Vasubandhu's view about *pudgalas*. Vasubandhu insists that *pudgala* is just a name we use for a resultant combination of mental particulars. He states that whatever exists

[23] Kim (2005: 98).

but is not fundamental physical stuff is such as to disappear when broken up in actuality or in thought:

That of which one does not have a cognition when it has been broken is real in a concealing way (*saṃvṛti-sat*); an example is a pot. And that of which one does not have a cognition when other [elemental qualities (*dharma*)] have been excluded from it by the mind is also conventionally real; an example is water. That which is otherwise is ultimately real (*paramārtha-sat*). (Vasubandhu 1975: 334) [AK 6.4]

The examples Vasubandhu gives are a pot and a body of water. A pot, clearly, is something which none of its proper parts are: it disappears if broken into its parts. A body of water seems, on the face of it, to be a stranger example, since water is a fundamental type of elemental material. I propose that what is going on is that he is mentioning something which is a scalar sum (a body of water) and something which is a structural resultant (a pot), and that the implication is that this exhausts the ways in which combining elements can create something new. Vasubandhu's point is then that the 'new' properties of the pot are not at a higher metaphysical level than those of its constituents. Although such objects have properties which their constituents do not have, they are merely resultant properties (they satisfy Sellars' Principle of Reducibility).

When Vasubandhu turns to an attack on Pudgala Realism, only in an appendix to the main work,[24] he says that the case is exactly the same as with the pot and the water in his earlier example, and he further adds that a *pudgala* is also like a heap or a river.[25] Vasubandhu's thought seems to be this. If the term *pudgala* refers to anything, it must refer to something which has a property that none of its constituents have. The lesson from the earlier discussion is that any such property is either a scalar sum or a structural resultant. There is therefore simply no room for the Pudgala Realist theory, namely that being a *pudgala* is an emergent property. To put it another way, Vasubandhu's argument is that if it is a *conceptual truth* about *pudgala*s that they are emergent, then there are no *pudgala*s. What Vasubandhu is claiming is there are no *pudgala*s *as pudgala*s *are conceived of by the Pudgala Realist*. His alternative idea is that the only legitimate use of the term *pudgala* is to refer

[24] Vasubandhu (1973: 1189–1234); trans. Duerlinger (2003); Kapstein (2001: 347–74); discussion in Ganeri (2007: 160–73).

[25] *prajñaptisat pudgalo rāśidhārādivat* (Vasubandhu 1973: 1205).

to a structural property of the stream. Those entities *are* reducible to their constituent qualitons, just as a heap or a flow is reducible to its constituents.

A different reading of Vasubandhu has it that what he argues is that all talk of *pudgala*s is mere talk. According to the alternative view, being a *pudgala* is not a property at all, let alone a resultant one. It is a fiction, a mere convention. On this reading, he is at best an *incautious* reductionist, someone who says that the reduced entities do not *really* exist at all. The point at issue is whether one attributes to him an elimination thesis, according to which the existence of a reduction entails that the terms of the reduced theory are not genuinely referential, or an identity thesis, which says that what best explains the existence of the reduction is that reduced entities are identical to their reducing counterparts, so that *pudgala* is identical to a diachronic clustering of mental particulars. The availability of cautious reductionism, a middle way between eliminativism and emergentism, is most clearly noticed by Vasubandhu's contemporary, Saṃghabhadra. The best thing to say about Vasubandhu himself is probably that he did not fully distinguish between these two alternative ways of resisting Pudgala Realism. When he denies that there are *pudgala*s what he is denying is that there is anything corresponding to the Pudgalavāda conception of an emergent entity, not *eo ipso* asserting that they are mere fictions. To say that a *pudgala* is nothing other than a stream of mental particulars is not of itself to say that it is nothing at all. Vasubandhu is an eliminativist about the illegitimate use of *pudgala* and a Nagel reductionist about its legitimate use, with a degree of *caution* that is unclear. Saṃghabhadra is more clearly a cautious Nagel reductionist about the legitimate use.

What is clear is that the Buddhist *pudgala* is not a Strawsonian person, something to which both corporeal and psychological predicates are ascribed. The Strawsonian concept is rather that of the Cārvāka *puruṣa*:

> A human being (*puruṣa*) is a body qualified by consciousness.[26]

For Vasubandhu we may if we wish designate the stream itself with the term *pudgala*. That does not make his a Reductionist View, in the terminology of Chapter 1, because the stream is not a self and not a surrogate for a self: there is no self. Neither Abhidharma nor Vātsiputrīya Buddhism has a Reductionist or a Real Self conception of self. The choice is between a No Place

[26] *Cārvāka-sūtra* 1.6: *caitanya-viśiṣṭaḥ kāyaḥ puruṣaḥ* | (R. Bhattacharya 2002a: 603–4).

View and a Flame View, and Vasubandhu is correct to see in Pudgala Realism a doctrine that concedes the utility of the concept of a place of ownership.

The difficulty for Pudgala Realism is to demonstrate that it can actually sustain a plausible concept of ownership, one which makes sense of the claim that something which is emergent from the items in the stream can also serve as their owner, and to do so without a commitment to synchronic downward causation. Ownership Views, which separate out questions of ownership from questions of emergence (the emergence base being, if anything, the physical body), and Buddhist (No Place) Views, which deny that there is any such phenomenon as ownership to begin with, both escape the need to confront that difficulty.

Buddhists are committed to providing an analysis of first-person phenomena, in order accurately to diagnose the source of the error they believe to be involved, and in the theory so far there is scant trace of one. In the coming chapters I will introduce three such accounts, a mental files account based on what I will call 'mineness-markers', a reflexivist self-representational account, and a quasi-subject theory. In every case, a level of subjectivity is identified and the source of its erroneous misconstrual as genuinely first-personal located. It is of course open for a theorist who is not committed to an error-theory about first-person phenomena to regard the analysis of subjectivity as providing the basis of a non-erroneous account of the first person, and so to transform the Buddhist analysis of immersion into a theory of the immersed self; and there are historical precedents for precisely such moves. On the other hand, it is also open to a theorist to object to the underlying analysis itself on theoretical grounds, as providing an adequate analysis of subjectivity. There are precedents for that move too.[27]

[27] The Buddhist theory of 'two truths' is sometimes appealed to here as a way to bracket the error-theory and affirm the truth of the underlying analysis 'at the conventional level'. My own view is that the doctrine of two truths is best interpreted as a distinction within the concept of objectivity (see Ganeri 2007: 39–60, 97–124).

8

Self-Consciousness

Two Concepts of Self-Consciousness

Buddhist philosophy of mind has it that conscious thinking is a synthesis of five more basic forms of mental activity: the processes of embodied reacting, hedonic appraising, labelling, dispositional constructing, and conscious attending. It is important that they can say that one is also able to attend to what is going on in one's mind. Thus they are led to include within attending a mode of conscious self-attention (*mano-vijñāna*). It is a way of being self-aware, of attending to one's own psychological state. It is also a problem.

The theory of mind claims that attending to one's surroundings is modality-specific: attending to what one sees is different from attending to what one hears or touches, smells or tastes. Attending to what is going on in one's mind is something different again, and Vasubandhu therefore distinguishes in all six varieties of attention.[1] Presumably, the idea is that there is a distinction not merely in the objects of attention (since then one could distinguish arbitrarily many different types), but that these six represent six different ways of bringing one's attention to bear, so to speak. It does not seem right, however, to say that it is the act of bringing one's attention to bear upon one's states of mind which makes them present themselves *as one's own*. That is the point of Strawson's insight that 'our desires and preferences are not, in general, something we just note in ourselves as alien presences. To a large extent they *are* we' (P. F. Strawson 1992: 134). In the chapters that follow I will describe Buddhist attempts to describe this distinction within the intentional structure of consciousness, the term 'self'

[1] *ṣaḍvijñānadhātavaś cakṣurādyāśrayā rūpādyālambanāvijñāptayaḥ* | (*Pañca-skandhaka* 135; in Vasubandhu 2008).

in these chapters used to designate what I have called the *immersed* self. In every case, Buddhist thinkers do two things at once: they provide a constructive analysis of the immersed self, and they associate with it an error-theory. It is important to retain a clear grasp of the distinction between these two dimensions in the Buddhist project. I find in the constructive analyses much of philosophical importance, but do not share the view that the immersed self is an illusion or error or fiction.

Asaṅga, Vasubandhu's elder sibling, is careful not to say that it is only when we attend to our mental states that they come to carry the impression of being us or ours. Therefore, to the six varieties of conscious attention he adds a seventh item, which he calls simply 'mind', or else, to stress its role in generating the illusion of self, an 'afflicted mind' (*kliṣṭa-manas*).[2] It is, he seems to think, a still more basic mode of being self-conscious, arguing that there must exist a *pre-attentive* modality of self-consciousness, which is distinctively associated with a sense of ownership, as well as being the *base* of conscious reflection and something which contributes to the persistence of one's sense of self:

How does one know that *manas* in the sense of 'afflicted mind' (*kliṣṭa-manas*) exists? Without it, there could be no uncompounded ignorance, i.e. a basic ignorance not yet associated with all the diverse defilements but standing as their base (*āśraya*). Besides, conscious self-attention (*manovijñāna*) must also have a simultaneous support, as do the sensory consciousnesses which have such supports in their material organs. Such a simultaneous support can only be the 'afflicted mind'. Also, the very etymology of the word 'manas' has to do with 'mine,' which can be explained only by the afflicted mind. Also, without it there would be no difference between the non-identifying trance and the cessation trance, for only the latter is free of afflicted mind. Also, the sense of an existence of self is always present in unskilful states: there must be some special consciousness to account for the persistence of this sense. The

[2] This is a new sense for the term *manas*, which in its traditional use in Abhidharma is either simply synonymous with thinking (*citta*, *vijñāna*), or, in some authors, the name of a postulated 'inner' sense-faculty. Kramer (2008) translates *kliṣṭa-manas* as 'notion of I', and observes that the incorporation of this new concept represents a modification in the traditional system of the five *skandhas*, a modification that is evident in Sthiramati's commentary on Vasubandhu's *Pañcaskandhaka*. Galloway (1980) translates *kliṣṭa-manas* as 'passional consciousness', and derives interesting information about the notion from Guṇaprabhā's commentary on the *Pañcaskandhaka*; see further below. Dreyfus and Thomson (2007: 112) translate *kliṣṭa-manas* as 'afflictive mentation', and comment that '[t]his is the inborn sense of self that arises from the apprehension of the store-consciousness as being a self. From a Buddhist point of view, however, this sense of self is fundamentally mistaken. It is a mental imposition of unity where there is in fact only the arising of a multiplicity of interrelated physical and mental events.'

afflicted mind is always always associated with the four afflictions: the view of self-existence (*satkāyadṛṣṭi*), the conceit 'I am' (*asminmāna*), attachment to self (*ātmas-neha*), and ignorance (*avidyā*); but is itself ethically neutral.[3]

The later Vasubandhu develops the new theory still further.[4] He says that this new factor 'mind' is a way of being aware, associating it with the activity of thinking (*manana*), and adding that it takes the repository-consciousness (*ālaya-vijñāna*) as its foundation.[5] Repository-consciousness is a sort of first-person mental file.[6] Vasubandhu says that 'mind' undergoes a transformation (*pariṇāma*) into something that we metaphorically call a self, but that this transformation is the work of cognitive fabrication (*vikalpa*), and there is in fact no such thing:

For the metaphorical designation of self and tropes, which functions in several ways, rests upon the transformation of consciousness.

[3] *Mahāyāna-saṃgraha* 1.6–7; trans. Anacker in Potter (1999: 461) from extant Chinese and Tibetan translations. Cf. Waldron (2003: 147). Waldon explains: 'Each type of sensory cognitive awareness has its own simultaneous support (*sahabhū-āśraya*), that is, the material sense-faculties upon which their proper functioning depends. Mental cognitive awareness (*mano-vijñāna*), however, has no simultaneous support since traditionally its support is the previous moment of mind' (Waldron 2003: 148).

[4] In the course of doing so, his own philosophical position develops too, from Abhidharma to Yogācāra, a development that sees him reject the trope dualism of Abhidharma and instead come to regard everything as dependent on mind for its existence (*citta-mātra*). While his *Pañcaskandhaka* is seemingly Abhidharma, the *Triṃśikā-vijñapti-kārikā* is Yogācāra. The exact details of Vasubandhu's intellectual development remain an open question: see Hirakawa *et al.* (1973); Gold (2011). At the end of Ch. 11 I will claim that a reinterpretation of the earlier theory as a phenomenological psychology rather than a metaphysics of mind renders it available to a Yogācāra perspective.

[5] Guṇaprabhā, commenting on Vasubandhu's *Pañcaskandhaka*, says: '[Vasubandhu:] "In reality, the consciousness (*manas*) has the storehouse perception for its phenomenon." Guṇaprabhā: "This means that it phenomenalises [sees] the storehouse perception as a self." Vasubandhu: "It is that which is associated with the constant delusion of self (*ātmamoha*), view of self (*ātmadṛṣṭi*), egoism of self (*ātmamāna*), and lust for self (*ātmarāga*), and so on." Guṇaprabhā: "It is explained as operating always, and arises as good (*kuśala*), bad (*akuśala*), and indifferent. His saying 'It is of one class' means that it has an afflicted (*kliṣṭa*) nature. 'It is continually produced' means that it is momentary." ' (Quoted in Galloway 1980: 18.)

[6] The history of the concept of the repository-consciousness is complicated. Originally conceived as a vehicle for the continuity of consciousness when all six types of attention are absent, it was a technical solution to what would otherwise be a difficulty in the Yogācāra theory of individual persistence (Dainton 2008 grapples with the same problem in a modern context). Dreyfus and Thompson (2007: 112) say of it that '[t]his continuously present subliminal consciousness is posited by some of the Yogācāra thinkers to provide a sense of continuity in the person over time. It is the repository of all the basic habits, tendencies and propensities (including those that persist from one life to the next) accumulated by the individual'. Schmithausen comments that 'it may well be that *ālayavijñāna* was, initially, conceived as a kind of "gap-bridger", but hardly in such a way that its occurrence in ordinary states had been denied' (1987: §2.13.6). See also Waldron (2003).

Based on it [sc. the repository-consciousness], there functions the consciousness called *manas*, which consists in thinking (*manana*) having that [repository-consciousness] as its base.

This transformation of consciousness is a cognitive fabrication, and what is cognitively fabricated by it [the transformation] does not exist.[7]

The import of the use of the terms 'cognitive fabrication' (*vikalpa*) and 'metaphorical designation' (*upacāra*), in connection with the self, is that the end result of the transformation of pre-attentive self-consciousness is the sort of first-person present-tense psychological ascription one would express in the words 'I am *F*'. The transformation has made the self into a conceptual thought content; but the expression of that thought content uses a word, 'I', in some way that is not one of genuine literal reference. So the claim is that three distinct phenomena are involved in achieving a first-person stance:

1. Conscious attention to one's own states of mind (*manovijñāna*).

This must have a base (*āśraya*). The base is:

2. A pre-attentive mode of being self-aware (*manas*).

That is subject to transformation (*pariṇāma*). What it is transformed into is:

3. First-person present-tense ascription of a psychological state (*ahaṃ-pratyaya*)—thinking 'I am *F*', for some psychological predicate *F*.

My possession of a first-person view, a view on my own mental life, has to be underwritten. What underwrites it is the fact that my mental life presents itself to me, in a primitive and pre-attentive way, as being *mine*. This same primitive mode of being self-aware is rendered in such a way that it now seems to justify me in making assertions of the form 'I am *F*'. In fact it is never the case that assertions of such a form are true of a self: uses of 'I' never literally refer. The proposal is thus that there is a pre-attentive mode of self-consciousness because of which my experiences present themselves to me as *mine*; that first-person present-tense ascription of a psychological state draws

[7] *ātmadharmopacāro hi vividho yaḥ pravartate* | *vijñānapariṇāme 'sau* || 1a–c || *tasya vyāvṛtir-arhatve tad-āśritya pravartate* | *tad-ālambaṃ manonāma vijñānaṃ mananātmakam* || 5 || *vijñāna-pariṇāmo 'yaṃ vikalpo yad-vikalpyate* | *tena tan-nāsti* || 17a–c || (*Triṃśikā-vijñapti-kārikā* in Vasubandhu 1925; trans. Richard Robinson, in Lusthaus 2002: 275–91). See also Anacker (1984: 186–7).

upon additional conceptual resources, ones not available on the basis of primitive self-consciousness alone; and that first-person psychological ascriptions do not actually involve genuine reference to a self.

Phenomenal Mineness and Mental Files

We now have, for the first time, the materials for a concrete proposal about how a No Place View might provide an account of self-consciousness and the first-person stance. In an updated vocabulary, it goes something like this. A stream of mentality, a mental life, can certainly include within it items of conscious attention to its own states. Items in the stream, however, do not simply float free, as it were, but are anchored. In the case of vision, the anchoring consists of the supervenience of a mental item on the micro-states of the visual sense faculty, particularly neurophysiological happenings in the visual cortex and retinal receptor cells. Attending to a shade of red is a matter of bringing into focus a phenomenal quality, as a sentient response to the impact of the physical surroundings. When the stream attends to its own states there is an analogue of the idea of a stimulus, and an analogue of the idea of an anchor. The analogue of a stimulus is simply that items in the stream make themselves felt, just as do things in the physical surroundings. The awareness of something red can itself become something consciously attended to. Although taking its cue from something less tangible, the notion of conscious attention in play is the same as before, and this does not in itself introduce, or require the introduction of, items of a new type into the stream. The analogue of an anchor, on the other hand, does require something new. If one were to say that items of consciously attending to other items in the stream simply supervene on the same neurophysiological bases as items of sensory attention, then they would themselves be not merely analogous to sensory attention but further instances of it. Their special quality would not be accounted for (and we would be in danger of entertaining something like a perceptual model of self-awareness). This special quality consists in the fact that it is the stream attending to *itself*, and not to the world. So there must be something within the stream itself which can serve as the primary anchor to these special items of conscious attention. This intermediary, this new and additional type of item in the stream, is something whose existence is hypothesized in order to make sense of the possibility of intrastreamal attention. These items are intertwined in the flow of the stream, and in their phenomenal appearance present themselves as a feeling of 'mine'. They are the extra ingredient which gives the stream the phenomenal quality of being self-conscious, and not merely conscious. They are themselves anchored in yet another set of items, items of information pertaining to that particular stream (the repository-consciousness, *ālaya-vijñāna*; an individual's mental file), and which may or may not itself be supervenient on aspects of neurophysiological activity. Items in the repository do not themselves carry a feeling of mineness, but inform the quality of mineness which attaches itself to the stream's conscious self-attention. They comprise a sort of databank for the mind, information that can be drawn upon in the activity of bringing the states of the stream into conscious attention.

Here is a first detailed picture of what the occupancy of a first-person stance looks like from a Buddhist perspective. Nothing owns experience, it has no place, and to compensate for this the idea of a base is expanded in such a way that there are new items in the base on which the stream's attention to itself rests. The new items in the base are pre-attentive moments which encode a feeling of 'mineness', although there is nothing to which the items in the stream are truly said to belong. In what follows I will call items of this newly hypothesized sort of mental trope, the new *manas* of Asaṅga and Vasubandhu, 'mineness-markers'. The distinction between the mere occurrence of states with representational content and the inhabitation of a first-person stance consists, according to this theory, in the way one's states access stored information about oneself, and in doing so 'root' the state deeply in one's psychology (I have in mind here the distinction mentioned in Chapter 1 between bare attribution ties and grounded exemplification; Connell 1988: 90). The phenomenal mineness of a mental state, the *sense* of ownership that comes with it, is strongly associated with its rootedness in deep strata of the psyche.

The ability, not just to have a world in view, but also to reflect upon the fact that one does, seems to be an essential part of what it means to be conscious. Sidney Shoemaker says (using the phrase 'first-person perspective')[8] that

[8] My use of 'first-person stance' instead of 'first-person perspective' is intended to signal the distinction between merely having one's own mental life in view and thinking of that life as one's own, thinking from a first-person position.

It is essential for a philosophical understanding of the mental that we appreciate that there is a first-person perspective on it, a distinctive way mental states present themselves to the subjects whose states they are, and that an essential part of the philosophical task is to give an account of mind which makes intelligible the perspective mental subjects have on their own mental lives. (Shoemaker 1996: 157.)

It is to this task that our Buddhists address themselves when they say that conscious attention to one's own mental life (*mano-vijñāna*) must have a base, which they claim is a pre-attentive mode of being self-aware (*manas*) (in other words that occupying a first-person stance is a prerequisite for having a first-person perspective in the sense just mentioned). There is no question of having a view on one's mental life without that mental life presenting itself to one *as one's own*. In a much-quoted passage, Peter Strawson says:

It would make no sense to think or say: This inner experience is occurring, but is it occurring to *me*? (This feeling is anger; but is it I who am feeling it?) Again, it would make no sense to think or say: I distinctively remember that inner experience occurring, but did it occur to me? (I remember that terrible feeling of loss; but was it I who felt it?) There is nothing that one can thus encounter or recall in the field of inner experience such that there can be any question of one's applying criteria of subject-identity to determine whether the encountered or recalled experience belongs to oneself—or to someone else. (P. F. Strawson 1966: 165.)

If I cannot be mistaken about whose inner experience it is that I am experiencing, this is because no *identification* of a subject, and so no possibility of *misidentification*, is involved at all. Buddhist philosophers seek to explain what is known as the 'immunity to error through misidentification relative to the first-person pronoun' of self-ascriptions[9] by acknowledging that when my experience presents itself to me as my own, no representation of myself as a subject takes place. Asaṅga and Vasubandhu postulate instead the existence of a primitive mode of self-awareness, an awareness of my inner life as mine. This is what makes it possible for me to have a first-person, rather than merely a third-person, view on my mental life.

[9] 'To say that a statement "*a* is Φ" is subject to error through misidentification relative to the term "*a*" means that the following is possible: the speaker knows some particular thing to be Φ, but makes the mistake of asserting "*a* is Φ" because, and only because, he mistakenly thinks that the thing he knows to be Φ is what "*a*" refers to' (Shoemaker 1968: 557).

The Immersed Self

Vasubandhu speaks of a transformation of basic self-awareness into explicit self-ascription, a transformation based on cognitive fabrication and justifying an only metaphorical use of the language of self. What is difficult is to understand how it can be thought mistaken to make the transition from being aware of oneself as being in a certain mental state to explicitly formulating the thought that one is, and indeed asserting that one is. Vasubandhu's thesis is that this transition demands some new conceptual resource (one which is not in fact available). Is that thesis true?

Zahavi, for one, does not see any difficulty with the transition. He says:

> Contrary to what some of the self-sceptics are claiming, one does not need to conceive of the self as something standing apart from or above experiences, nor does one need to conceive of the relation between the self and experience as an external relation of ownership. It is also possible to identify this pre-reflective sense of *mineness* with a minimal, core, sense of self.... In other words, the idea is to link an experiential sense of self to the particular first-personal givenness that characterises our experiential life; it is this first-personal givenness that constitutes the *mineness* or *ipseity* of experience. Thus, the self is not something that stands opposed to the stream of consciousness, but is, rather, immersed in conscious life. (Zahavi 2005a: 125.)

Zahavi's minimal self precisely consists in a 'pre-reflective sense of mineness', and it appears to follow that to refer to oneself in the first person nothing more is required than that one's experience be given 'immediately, noninferentially and noncriterially' (2005a: 124) as mine. He also says, however, that 'this form of egocentricity must be distinguished from any explicit I-consciousness. I am not (yet) confronted with a thematic or explicit awareness of the experience as being owned by or belonging to myself. The mineness is not something attended to; it simply figures as a subtle background presence' (2005a: 124). So there is, after all, a transition—but it is a transition which involves only paying attention to the mineness inherent in my experience, not in the exercise of any new conceptual resource. Zahavi's emphasis on the idea that the relation of ownership is not external shows that this is an account of the 'immersed self', the self as a phenomenal given within a mental life.

This idea seems to be wholly expressible in the framework I have been presenting. One can consciously attend to items in the stream, and 'mineness-markers' (items of *manas*) are among them. In directing one's attention to those items, one is bringing into focus the mineness of the experiences based on them. Zahavi's 'minimal self' therefore just is Vasubandhu's 'mind' (*manas*), and that raises in stark terms the crucial question: What is to prevent someone from identifying the 'mind' (*manas*) hypothesized by Vasubandhu as a self? Zahavi describes the self, in its most minimal condition, as the mineness imminent in experience. This sounds very much like a Phenomenal View, but elsewhere Zahavi emphases the importance of embodiment, and in fact his theory is a Minimal Ownership View.[10] Indeed, it looks like the view described at the end of Chapter 6, the idea that self is an embodied background sense of presence to oneself. I located that view as having Indian origins in the naturalist who said that the self 'has no limit or boundary and is a compact mass of cognition' (*Bṛhad. Up.* 2.4.12). The entire weight of Vasubandhu's commitment to a No Place View seems now to rest on the single fact that Buddhist mental constituents are tropes in flux, and as such do not constitute a single 'compact mass'. In his attempts to give a realistic account of self-consciousness, has Vasubandhu conceded too much? Or does the similarity rather confirm something I suggested at the end of Chapter 6, that Zahavi's 'minimal self' is too minimal to count as a genuine self?

Recanati also has an account of the transition we are interested in. He draws a distinction between implicit and explicit *de se* thoughts, a *de se* thought being 'a *de re* thought about oneself, that involves a particular mode of presentation, namely a first-person mode of presentation' (Recanati 2007: 169). He continues:

As Frege wrote in 'The Thought', 'every one is presented to himself in a particular and primitive way, in which he is presented to no one else'. I call the 'special and primitive' mode of presentation which occurs in first-person thoughts 'EGO' or

[10] Gallagher and Zahavi (2008: 184): 'If my self-experience is, in the primary instance, of a purely mental nature, i.e. if my body does not figure essentially in my self-ascription of (some) psychological states, while my ascription of mental states to others are based solely on their bodily behaviour, what, then, should guarantee the ascription of the same type of states to others? How would we ever come to be in possession of a truly general concept of mind that is equally applicable to different subjects?' I will come back to the conceptual version of the problem of other minds in Ch. 11.

rather 'EGO_x' where 'x' stands for the name of the person thinking the thought. (2007: 170.)

Explicit de se thoughts are *de se* thoughts 'the content of which involves an "identification component" through which the object thought about is identified as oneself'. When a subject looks at themselves in a mirror and thinks 'My legs are crossed', they identify themselves under the concept EGO, and ascribe to themselves a property: I am that person whose legs are crossed. An *implicit de se* thought involves no such identification. Recanati says that 'implicit *de se* thoughts are identification-free, and they are *de se* only externally: no concept EGO occurs as part of the *lekton* [roughly, the content]. The *lekton* is a personal proposition, without any constituent corresponding to the person to whom a property is ascribed' (2007: 176). In an implicit *de se* thought, one simply thinks of one's legs as crossed, a thought that is true because it is indeed one's own legs which are crossed. The distinction is reflected linguistically in the contrast between the anaphoric construction 'He expects *that he will be late*' and the gerundival construction 'He expects *to be late*' (cf. Perry 1998; the distinction Williams draws, mentioned in Chapter 2, between two sorts of imagining is clearly related). The claim is that it is precisely because no identification of a subject is involved that implicit *de se* thoughts are immune to error through misidentification.

Recanati argues that the concept EGO involved in the notion of an explicit *de se* thought is itself explained by this notion of an implicit *de se* thought. He says:

> The notion of an implicit *de se* thought in which the self is not represented is important . . . to understand the concept of self that occurs in explicit *de se* thoughts. Indeed, the ability to entertain implicit *de se* thoughts is arguably a necessary condition for anyone to evolve the concept EGO. That is so because, as suggested by Evans, Perry, and myself following them, the concept EGO is best construed as a repository for information gained in a first-person way . . . Now a piece of information is gained in the first-person way if and only if it is the content of an implicit *de se* thought. It follows that the first step in an elucidation of the concept of self is a correct analysis of the functioning of implicit *de se* thoughts. (2007: 177.)

The above theory of 'mineness-markers' seems to me to present one such analysis of implicit *de se* thought. A mineness-marker certainly contains no representation of the self, and it has as its 'foundation' (*ālambana*) all the information contained in the repository-consciousness. It is a first-personal way of accessing that information. The description 'repository for information gained in a first-person way' might seem like a good description of the joint contribution of 'mineness-markers' and repository-consciousness, a mental file containing first-person information. Moreover, as we have seen, Vasubandhu speaks of a 'transformation' of mineness-markers into a concept of self, and that echoes with the claim Recanati is making about the evolution of the concept EGO. Finally, Recanati claims that the ability to entertain implicit *de se* thoughts is a necessary—though not necessarily a sufficient—condition for the evolution of the concept EGO, and this too is parallel to something Asaṅga and Vasubandhu are keen to stress; indeed, it is the primary motivation for introducing the idea of mineness-markers in the first place. For, as Asaṅga says, 'That [*manas*] has the mode of taking the repository-consciousness as its object and conceiving it as "I am" (*asmīti*) and "I" (*aham iti*)'.[11] Note that the concept EGO, as a repository of information gained in a first-person way, does potentially individuate thinkers, for no two such repositories need be alike. This concept of self is much less 'minimal' than Zahavi's. Once again the question presents itself: Is there anything to stop one identifying the hypothetical repository-consciousness as a self?

Both Vasubandhu and Recanati agree that there are explicit *de se* thoughts involving the concept SELF, but while Recanati thinks that the truth conditions of such thoughts are such that they are often true, Vasubandhu thinks that they are always false. He thinks this because he thinks that the concept SELF, which may well have evolved in the manner described, is an *empty* concept, like the concept PHLOGISTON or the concept PEGASUS. It is clearly stated that the evolution of the concept brings with it all manner of moral defilements, and one form of justification for that claim is that the concept itself rests on a mistake. Sthiramati's comment on the first verse of Vasubandhu's *Triṃśikā* bears the point out: he says that the concept SELF presents only an apparent (*nirbhāsa*) referent, just as the perception of someone with an eye disease presents only apparent hairs and circles. It is 'metaphorically designated' (*upacaryate*) because it is said to be there when it is not, as if one were to use the word 'cow' when

[11] Asaṅga, *Yogācārabhūmi* (quoted in Waldron 2002: 42).

there is no cow (but only an ox).[12] A resemblance with something that does exist leads to the misuse of a term for something that does not.

With Strawson's assertion that 'no use whatever of any criteria of personal identity is required to justify [a person's] use of the pronoun "I" to refer to the subject' (P. F. Strawson 1966: 165), Vasubandhu would appear to dissent. Strawson's point is that we don't need any extra conceptual resource in order to make explicit self-references, and in particular we don't need a criterion of identity. The pronoun 'I' is not a term which we can correctly use only if we have successfully identified its referent, because if it were then there would be the possibility of error through misidentification relative to it. Strawson infers that 'I' refers to its subject *without* there being a criterion of identity. Vasubandhu's view seems to be that the use of the pronoun 'I' *never* refers to a subject of experience. Perhaps what he would do would be to agree with Strawson's argument but contrapose it. His point would then be that all genuine reference involves the identification of a referent, and given that there is no question of such an identification in the case of the first person, the pronoun 'I' *cannot* be a genuine referring term. In saying that it is instead a 'metaphor' (*upacāra*), there might seem to be a gesture at the possibility of a different, non-referential, account of its use. To say 'I feel hopeful' is, it might be thought, to speak non-referentially of the existence of a hope which presents itself pre-attentively as mine (see also Tzohar 2011). This is not in fact Vasubandhu's strategy, but rather that of the later Buddhist philosopher Candrakrti. I will pursue this point further in the next section.

The Use of 'I' as a Metaphor

Can one hear an echo of the Buddhist idea in the following remark, the very remark, as it happens, out of which P. F. Strawson constructed the 'no ownership' View (1963: 95 n. 1):

> One of the most misleading representational techniques in our language is the use of the word 'I,' particularly when it is used in representing immediate experience, as in 'I can see a red patch.' It would be instructive to replace this way of speaking

[12] *tam ātmādinirbhāsam rūpādinirbhāsaṃ ca tasmād vikalpād bahirbhūtam ivopādāyātmādyupacāro rūpādidharmopacāraś cānādikālikaḥ pravartate vināpi bāhyenātmanā dharmaiś ca | tad yathā taimirikasya keśoṇḍukādyupacāra iti | yac ca yatra nāsti tat tatropacaryate | tad yathā bāhīke gauḥ |* (Sthiramati 2007: 42).

by another in which immediate experience would be represented without using the personal pronoun. (Wittgenstein 1975: 88.)

In another place, Wittgenstein speaks of 'two different cases in the use of the word "I" (or "my")', the use 'as object' and the use 'as subject' (1960: 66–7). The use 'as object' is the use to which it is put when we refer to ourselves as human beings, embodied entities in a public space, the use it has when, for example, one person says to another, 'I am just going to the shops to get the paper' or 'I have twisted my ankle'. The use 'as subject' is its use in representing immediate experience. Having distinguished between these two uses, one strategy would be to identify one of these uses as the primary use, and analyse the other use as being in some way derivative upon the first. A derivative use is metonymic and modulated; that is, the term is used to refer to something else, which stands in some relation to the primary referent. Among the contemporaries of Asaṅga and Vasubandhu are Vaiśeṣika philosophers, who argue that the primary use of 'I' is to refer to a self (*ātman*), and that its use to refer to oneself as an embodied being, in statements like 'I am sturdy', is an act of modulated meaning, that is, reference to something which stands in an 'is-the-body-of' relation to the primary reference.[13] I will comment more fully on their views about self-reference in Chapter 12.

A variant on this approach is recommended by Galen Strawson. Strawson argues that the two uses are *both* genuinely referential, and *neither* is primary—in short, that 'I' is not univocal. One use is to refer to what he describes as a 'thin subject', which is 'an inner thing of some sort that does not and cannot exist at any given time unless it is having experience at that time' (2008: 156). The other use is to refer to the human being 'considered as a whole':

Are we thin subjects? In one respect, of course, we are thick subjects, human beings considered as a whole. In this respect we are, in being subjects, things that can yawn and scratch. In another respect, though, we are in being subjects of experience no more whole human beings than hands or hearts: we are—literally—inner things, thin subjects, no more things that can yawn or scratch than eyebrows or thoughts . . . —But 'What then am I?' Am I two different sort of things, a thin subject and a thick subject? This is ridiculous . . . My answer is that 'I' is not

[13] On this notion of pragmatic 'modulation', see Ganeri (1999) and Recanati (2004).

univocal. We move naturally between conceiving of ourselves primarily as a human being and primarily as some sort of inner subject (we do not of course naturally conceive of ourselves as a *thin* subject). Sometimes we mean to refer to the one, sometimes to the other; sometimes our semantic intention hovers between both, sometimes it embraces both. (G. Strawson 2008: 157–8.)

Strawson (2007: 543) is clear that he thinks of the relation between the two uses as one of whole to part. Vasubandhu, although he does not say so here, would perhaps be content to endorse as 'conventional' (*saṃvṛti-sat*) the use of the first person in statements like 'I am going to the shops', a use governed by the token-reflexive rule that 'I' refers to the speaker. When 'I' is used in the expression of first person present-tense ascription of a psychological state, however, his claim is that the reference to an inner self fails, that this use erroneously imports a subject-predicate model and imposes it upon one's inner experience. In other words, his view of this use of 'I' is that there is a combination of metonymy and error-theory. When 'I' is used metonymically to refer to the inner subject, something always goes wrong, and what goes wrong is that there is nothing at the far end of the metonymic relationship for it to refer to.[14]

According to the formulation we have reached, then, 'I' does not function as an expression of genuine reference but is rather one of *disingenuous reference*: it is a referring expression without a referent, its use creating the false impression that there is one. The pragmatic context of use triggers the substitution of a literal semantic value with a derived or modulated value. That is, I suggest, the best way to understand Vasubandhu's claim that it is a 'metaphor'.[15] Vasubandhu's claim is thus that the error involved has to

[14] This, indeed, is a view which Strawson considers but rejects: 'If it turns out that the best thing to say about selves is that there are no such things, then the best thing to say about "I" may well be that it is univocal after all, and that the apparent doubleness of reference of "I" is just the echo in language of a metaphysical illusion. If this is right, then "I" is not in fact used to refer to selves as distinct from human beings even when its users intend to be making some such reference and believe that they are doing so. On this view, the semantic intentions of "I"-users sometimes incorporate a mistake about how things are. I disagree' (2007: 543).

[15] We might similarly understand Simone Weil's famous claim that 'to say "I" is to lie'. To use the word 'I', the thought would be, is disingenuously to speak as if there is an inner subject of experience to which it refers. 'I'-users' semantic intentions involve an error. One must distinguish, however, between correctable errors for which one is culpable and 'errors' that are intrinsic to the very nature of human experience and linguistic practice. 'Errors' of the second sort are not the curable targets of Buddhist therapy. I will say more about this in Ch. 10.

do with the pragmatics, it being a mistake to suppose that the modulated value in fact exists.

I alluded at the end of the last section to a different possibility altogether. It might be the case that the mistake which 'I'-users make is not a pragmatic one but rather that it involves a mistake about the semantic role of 'I' itself. Perhaps what goes wrong in the use of 'I' in representing immediate experience is that speakers take themselves to be making a referential use of an expression, and in doing so mistake its true logical role. It would be as if someone thought that 'perhaps' is a referring expression, and then imagined that there must be something in the world that it designates. The new suggestion is attractive because it does not make the argument hinge on a prior metaphysical claim about the non-reality of selves, which then stands in need of further, extra-linguistic, justification. Rather, once we are clear about the logical role of 'I', we see that looking for a referent is as misguided as looking for the referent of 'perhaps'. And indeed, this is what Wittgenstein seems to say about the 'use as subject' of the word 'I', its use in a sentence such as 'I have a pain'. For Wittgenstein, denying that 'I' is a referring expression, when used as in first-person present-tense ascriptions of psychological states, is the only way to explain the phenomenon of immunity to error through misidentification:

> [T]here is no question of recognising a person when I say I have a toothache. To ask 'are you sure that it's you who have pains?' would be nonsensical . . . And now this way of stating our idea suggests itself: that it is as impossible that in making the statement 'I have toothache' I should have mistaken another person for myself, as it is to moan with pain by mistake, having mistaken someone else for me. . . . To say, 'I have pain' is no more a statement about a particular person than moaning is. (Wittgenstein 1960: 66–7.)

The suggestion that there is a non-referential account of the use of 'I' was developed in one direction by Anscombe (1975). Anscombe, however, does not distinguish two uses, and argues that the first person does not refer even cases like 'I have a broken arm'. Other writers have tried, following the lead of Shoemaker, to argue that immunity of error does not commit one to a non-referential account of 'I', and indeed to reconcile immunity with the idea that 'I' refers univocally to the embodied human being.[16] In an

[16] Shoemaker (1968); McDowell (2009).

insightful remark about Anscombe, Campbell suggests that the best way to understand her position is as claiming that the patterns of use involving the first person do not require justification in a 'semantic foundation':

An alternative reaction would, of course, be to say that we ought to abandon the search for a semantic foundation for our use of the first person. There are only the patterns of use, and no explanation to be given of them. This was essentially G. E. M. Anscombe's position in her famous paper, 'The first person,' in which she claimed that the first person does not refer. This claim is generally rejected, simply because philosophers have thought that when there is a use of the first person, there is, after all, always someone around who can be brought forward as the referent. But this is an extremely superficial response to Anscombe's point. Her claim is best understood as making the point that the ascription of reference to the first person is empty or idle; it does no explanatory work. In fact it may be that Anscombe misstated her own point by putting it as the dramatic claim that 'I' does not refer. A better way to put the point might have been to insist that in the case of the first person, the pattern of use is fundamental, and is given no explanatory justification at all by knowledge of the reference of the term. It would have been consistent with this point to accept that it would be legitimate to introduce a disquotational or deflationary notion of reference. (Campbell 2004: 218.)

I have argued at length elsewhere that something along these lines is just the move made by the Mādhyamika philosopher Candrakīrti.[17] His position, I claimed, is that we can give a fully explanatory use-theoretic account of the role of the first person in performances of self-appropriation, an account in which it is otiose to assign a reference. Asaṅga and Vasubandhu, on the other hand, say that in the movement from a pre-attentive self-awareness to an explicit use of 'I', a transformation of some sort is involved, one which involves conceptual work (*vikalpa*), and that the use of 'I' is metaphorical or metonymic. Their view is that the use of 'I' is indeed referential, and that the use as object and the use as subject are to be understood as making reference to, on the one hand, the human being, and on the other, an inner subject of experience, this second use being derivative from the first. There is, however, no subject of experience and so the subject use of the first person is an error.

The mineness-markers and repository-consciousness theory of Asaṅga and Vasubandhu constitutes a new and extremely valuable explanation of

[17] *Prasannapadā* B 212,25–6; *Madhyamakāvatāra* 6. 162–3. See Ganeri (2007: 200–3).

self-consciousness and the first-person stance. Their further claim that the first person itself, the word 'I', is used metaphorically or metonymically in reporting the contents of the first-person perspective, rests on a prior commitment to the non-existence of a subject of experience. Only this permits them to claim that its use is one of what I have called 'disingenuous reference', a pragmatic failure in the speaker's intentions to identify a modulated value for the term. I have also distinguished a different strategy, which is to begin with the observation that such reports are immune to error through misidentification and to argue that it follows that in the proper account of the use of the word 'I' in first-person present-tense ascriptions of psychological states, the assignment of a referent is explanatorily superfluous. There are still other Buddhist diagnoses of the mistake that is alleged to be involved in the transition to self-conscious thought about oneself as subject (see Chapter 10).

A Descriptive Metaphysics of the Self

Vasubandhu and Asaṅga propose what is in many ways an extremely attractive account of self-consciousness and the first-person stance. It sees the mind as a dynamical system of interlocking and mutually constituting psychological activities with mechanisms for self-monitoring. It explains how the system can be conscious of its own internal states without any commitment to the dubious doctrine of an inner sense-organ, and it does so in a way that treats seriously the fact that, as Strawson put it, our thoughts and desires '*are* we' and are not just things happening to or within us. Not least, this thoroughly non-Cartesian description seems able to offer the promise an explanation of thought insertion and yet balance it with an account of the general immunity to error of self-ascription. That is a sensational accomplishment.

Along with this theory is the concomitant claim that the use of 'I' in first-person present-tense ascriptions of psychological states is erroneous. What my study has established, however, is that the two claims are logically distinct. Vasubandhu does not argue for the second claim, he simply presupposes that it is correct. For later Buddhists, the danger that his theory might indeed be seen to be consistent with a Real Self View seems to have been sufficient motivation to reject Vasubandhu and look for a different model of self-consciousness—and the accounts of Candrakīrti, which I have discussed elsewhere (Ganeri 2007), and Dignāga, which I am about to consider, are both models in which the danger is much less evident. From a contemporary point of view, however, the possibility we have demonstrated to exist—that this theory of mind is not conceptually dependent on an extra-theoretical commitment to an error-theory of self-consciousness and is otherwise a theory of great explanatory potential—is an important one. The model continued to develop after Asaṅga and Vasubandhu, alongside the new accounts of Dignāga and Candrakīrti. The work of Sthiramati, Guṇaprabhā, and others represents the development of this account of mind.

The reconciliation of naturalism with the existence of a first-person perspective is the first work of a theory of self. The views of ourselves as corporeal beings and as 'presences of self to self' seem to pull in different directions. Immanuel Kant recognized the tension and sought to resolve it this way:

> I may further assume that the substance which in relation to our outer sense possesses extension is in itself the possessor of thoughts, and that these thoughts can by means of its own inner sense be consciously represented. In this way, what in one relation is entitled corporeal would in another relation be at the same time a thinking being, whose thoughts we cannot intuit, though we can indeed intuit their signs in the appearance. Accordingly, the very same being which, as outer appearance, is extended, is (in itself) internally a subject, and is not composite, but is simple and thinks. (*Critique*, A359–60.)

We stand in two relations to ourselves, one of which is as to a corporeal being and the other as to a subject of experience. P. F. Strawson says that we should think of ourselves as specimens of 'a type of entity such that both predicates ascribing states of consciousness and predicates ascribing corporeal characteristics, a physical situation etc. are equally applicable to an individual entity of that type' (1963: 100), and he identifies this as the concept of a person. Strawson is famously dismissive of what he called the '"no-ownership" or "no-subject" doctrine of the self' (1963: 95), according to which it is denied that that states of consciousness are ascribed to *any* subject, a doctrine which implies that our concept of a person is 'wrong or confused' (1963: 94). Strawson, however, notices that in its rejection of the concept of a corporeal person as the owner of states of consciousness, the no-ownership doctrine takes a fundamentally Cartesian view about the nature of ownership, and indeed, that it can be described as a form of dualism, a 'dualism of one subject—the body—and one non-subject' (1963: 98), and he suggests that 'both the Cartesian and the no-ownership theorists are profoundly wrong in holding, as each must, that there are two uses of "I", in one of which it denotes something which it does not denote in the other' (1963: 98). Strawson sought a middle ground with his theory of persons, but Strawsonian persons are not selves. My view is that Vasubandhu's new doctrine of mineness-markers and repository-consciousness closely resembles a very plausible account of *self*. Conceived of as a self, the underwritten stream of mineness-markers is neither Cartesian, nor Humean, nor Strawsonian (and neither Hindu, nor Buddhist, nor Cārvāka). Moreover, and unlike many accounts of the self, it is properly individuated, not subject to Attenuation, this because of its role in drawing on a particular repository of *de se* information. I believe that in some form it is among the most promising theoretical proposals for a naturalist theory of the immersed self to emerge from analysis developed within the Indian debate.

The reason for the plausibility of the theory is clear. The Buddhist aim is not merely to reject some given historical theory of self in the Indian discussion, but to diagnose what they take to be a deep mistake in our primitive conceptual scheme.[18] It is incumbent upon them, therefore, to provide an accurate descriptive metaphysics of self. As Bhikkhu Bodhi has put it: 'While it is true that the "no-self" doctrine excludes Upaniṣadic ideas about the self, the purpose for which the Buddha expounded it was not to negate any specific theory of the self but to correct the universal human proclivity to seek a substantial basis of personal identity amidst the five aggregates. It this were not the case, the teaching of "no-self", like the Buddha's rejection of sacrifice, would hardly have any relevance outside the narrow context of ancient Brahminism' (Bodhi 1997: 293). The descriptive metaphysics of self ought therefore to be separable from the error-theory, for it is not merely as a piece of anti-brahminical

[18] Witnessing the fact of death, the problem the Buddha confronted was not only the moral problem of the existence of suffering but also the metaphysical problem of explaining how it is possible for a first-person perspective to cease to be.

or anti-hard-naturalist polemic but a contribution to the description of the human mind.

I will next discuss a development that took place in Buddhism in the sixth century, and subsequently had wide repercussions in the Indian discussion of self, namely the introduction of a new and rival analysis of self-consciousness, the doctrine that mental states are reflexively self-aware. The Abhidharma interpreters of the early Vasubandhu, as well as the Nyāya followers of Vātsyāyana and the Vaiśeṣika followers of Praśastapāda, were all fiercely opposed to this new doctrine, and I believe with good reason. For, as I will argue, any theory of self based on the new doctrine is either severely attenuated or else unable to solve the conceptual problem of other minds, unable, that is, to explain how one can represent the mind of another within one's own or conceive that there can be a plurality of minds.

9

Reflexivism

Reflexivism is the thesis that self-consciousness consists in conscious mental occurrences being reflexively conscious of themselves.[1] Several Buddhist thinkers from the sixth century onwards sought to find in the doctrine new foundations for an account of subjectivity. Dignāga (480–540 CE), living in the famous Buddhist university of Nālanda, proposes an account of subjectivity with several ingredients. He acknowledges that we have conscious awareness of the items in our own mental lives, and he further claims that each such item has a 'subject-aspect' (*svābhāsa*) as well as an 'object-aspect' (*viṣayābhāsa*). Finally, and additionally, he claims that every mental occurrence is reflexively conscious of itself (*svasaṃvedana*). Detailed arguments for this theory are available in the Yogācāra school of Indian Buddhism.[2] I will examine the original formulation, the form it took in the work of Dignāga himself rather than in later Indian or Tibetan revision, for it is in this formulation that the theory is proposed as a response to earlier Buddhist thought and serves as a precursor to reaction from non-Buddhist thinkers.

Dignāga is responding to the ideas of Vasubandhu and Asaṅga. His new theory arises out of what a Buddhist might perceive as a problem in theirs. Their theory, although distinct from the model which posits an inner sense-organ (*antar-karaṇa*), is still built around the understanding of perceptual experience. When one item in the stream consciously attends to another, they said, it must have a base or anchor (*āśraya*), just as does the attention to what one sees, hears, touches, smells, or tastes; not, however a microstate of

[1] A closely related but distinct thesis is that a mental state is conscious just in case it reflexively represents itself (the 'self-representational theory of consciousness'); see Kriegel and Williford (2006).

[2] There has been considerable recent interest in this theory: Ganeri (1995); P. Williams (1998); Yao (2005); Arnold (2005); Garfield (2006); Dreyfus and Thompson (2007: 102–4); MacKenzie (2007, 2008); Thompson (2011); Kellner (2011); Coseru (2012: Ch. 8).

the body on which it supervenes, but rather another item in the stream itself. They therefore postulate the existence of a new sort of item, mineness-markers, flowing along with the rest, said to draw on information in the repository-consciousness and to imbue conscious experience with a sense of ownership. The trouble with that theory, from a Buddhist perspective, is that the account is too much like that of a self, not indeed an eternal soul, but certainly similar to a more minimal conception of self such as that of a sense of ownership imminent in experience (Zahavi 2005a: 125). Indeed, all that seems to differentiate it from a minimal self is the prior stipulation that an error is involved in so regarding it. The same might also be said, and perhaps with greater conviction, about the respository-consciousness, which seems to converge with a mental files conception of self (Peacocke 2010).

Dignāga goes to the philosophical heart of the matter. As soon as one postulates a base for experience distinct from the experience itself, whatever it may be, nothing can block its subsequent identification with self, its identification, in other words, with the *place* of experience, a site of experiential ownership. The only way to defend a No Place View, therefore, is to base each item within the stream of experience *in itself*. That is the fundamental point of transition from an Abhidharma to a Yogācāra View. (Nāgārjuna diagnoses the problem differently: he thinks that as soon as one allows the idea that experience has a base at all, the game is lost. That stronger claim leads immediately to the Mādhyamika View, that there is neither base nor place.)

The later Buddhist Ratnakīrti will argue that a purely reflexivist theory of self-consciousness cannot solve the *conceptual* problem of other minds (see Chapter 11).[3] In this chapter I will consider less severe difficulties with reflexivism, as well as the resources available to reflexivism to negotiate them.

Dignāga's defence of reflexivism is an early formulation of the argument that higher-order theories of consciousness are regressive. Several philosophers in the European phenomenological tradition have offered the same argument,[4] and Brentano, at least, drew inspiration from a suggestive

[3] The problem of explaining how it is that one is capable of forming a conception of a mental state as being someone else's: see Avrimides (2001: 135, 224).

[4] Notably Husserl, Sartre, and Brentano. See Brentano (1874: 121–30). For further references: Caston (2002: 791–2); Zahavi (2005a: 24–7); Thompson (2011).

passage in Aristotle.[5] It seemed self-evident to the philosophers of early modern Europe that one is aware of all the happenings in one's mind,[6] but it is a further claim that this entails the reflexivity of each individual mental state. Descartes and Arnaud are explicit reflexivists.[7] Following Rosenthal, let us call the thesis that conscious states necessarily involve self-awareness the Transitivity Principle, understood as the claim that 'a mental state's being conscious involves one's being conscious of that state in a suitable way' (Rosenthal 2000: 265; cf. 2005). A fully developed defence of the Transitivity Principle is provided by Janzen (2008). Janzen identifies four arguments in its favour, two historical and two new. The historical arguments are Sartre's *reductio*, that 'if one's consciousness of something were not a consciousness of itself, then it would be a consciousness ignorant of itself, an unconscious consciousness, which is absurd' (Janzen 2008: 74, citing Sartre 1956: p. lii), and Dignāga's memory argument (Janzen 2008: 75). The two new arguments Janzen proposes are a 'symmetry argument', which affirms that there is a symmetry between one's awareness of one's experience and one's awareness of an external object, specifically that there is something that physical objects or states of consciousness are like to a subject just in case the subject is aware of them (2008: 76–8), and an 'argument from spontaneous reportability', that 'in order to spontaneously report on a conscious experience, one must, in one way or another, be (or have been) aware of it' (2008: 80). Janzen's two new arguments share a certain structural likeness with Dignāga's memory argument. Having established the Transitivity Principle, supplementary argumentation is required to the effect that its truth is compatible only with reflexivism (the 'one-state' model of

[5] 'Further, if the perception of seeing is a different [perception], either this will proceed to infinity or some [perception] will be of itself; so that we ought to posit this in the first instance' (*On the Soul* 3.2, 425b15–17; trans. Sorabji 2006: 206–7). 'Philoponus' criticizes Aristotle and introduces a new theory of an 'attentive part' (*prosektikon*) in the rational soul (Sorabji 2006: 253–4), a move which strikes me as analogous to the Nyāya appeal to unconscious mechanisms; I discuss this further in Ch. 13. It is unclear, however, that Aristotle is referring to a regress of *activities* and not rather of *faculties*. For a denial that there is in fact a regress of faculties: Vātsyāyana (1997, *infra* 2.1.20).

[6] 'To imprint anything on the mind without the mind's perceiving it seems to me hardly intelligible . . . It is impossible for any one to perceive, without perceiving that he does perceive. When we hear, smell, taste, feel, meditate, or will anything, we know that we do so' (Locke 1975: 1.2.5, 2.27.9). 'For since all actions and sensations of the mind are known to us by consciousness, they must necessarily appear in every particular what they are, and be what they appear' (Hume 1978: 190).

[7] Descartes AT 7.559; see below. On Arnaud, see Caston (2002: 792 n. 86) for references. Dignāga's transformation of Buddhist philosophy of mind in a 'Cartesian' direction is, I will suggest in subsequent chapters, retrogressive.

self-consciousness), and not with higher-orderism, the theory that a mental state is conscious if it is the object of another, distinct, mental state (Rosenthal 1986). This is the purpose of the regress argument, as formulated by Dignāga and Brentano.

In sixth-century India the idea that mental states are reflexively self-aware was far from a mainstream opinion, with some version of higher-order theory of consciousness more widely affirmed, sometimes along with a doctrine that there is an 'inner sense' (*antaḥ-kāraṇa*) by which we perceive that we perceive, but also often without that unfortunate and dispensable idea. I will show in Chapter 13 that the Nyāya-Vaiśeṣika notion of *manas* is not that of an inner sense but rather a concept of an unconscious selector-comparator mechanism. Dignāga presents reflexivism as an alternative to the doctrine of an inner sense faculty. Later Buddhists like Dharmakīrti extend and develop the discussion, not necessarily in ways Dignāga would have agreed with.[8] Ironically, perhaps, several non-Buddhist philosophers also borrow the idea of a reflexivist understanding of the non-conceptual *de se* and transform it into constitutive conceptions of self.[9]

Aspects of Content

Dignāga claims that every experience has two distinct 'apparent aspects' (*ābhāsa*; cf. *ākāra*), an object-aspect (*viṣayābhāsa*) and a subject-aspect (*svābhāsa*):

Every cognition is produced with a twofold appearance, namely that of itself [as subject] (*svābhāsa*) and that of the object (*viṣayābhāsa*).[10]

[8] Dharmakīrti's endorsement of reflexivity is clear in the *Nyāya-bindu*: *sarva-citta-caittānām ātma-saṃvedanam* 'Every thought-element is reflexively aware of itself' (Dharmakīrti 1985: 1.10). See further Dreyfus (1997: 400–1). Dharmakīrti, however, seems to conflate two distinct concepts in his use of the term *svasaṃvedana*: following Dignāga, as a primitive non-objectual source of a sense of ownership (i.e. the implicit *de se*); but also as a cognition's immediate presentation to itself of its intentional content (i.e. the transparency of content). The second concept is in reference to the grounds of one's access to the contents of one's own mental states. We might see in Dharmakīrti's move a subtle response to the threat of Attenuation faced by Dignāga-type reflexivist theories.

[9] In particular, Prabhākara, Prabhācandra, and Rāmakaṇṭha. Śaiva Siddhānta has an Attenuated Phenomenal or Pure Consciousness View, in which the self consists in infallible reflexively self-aware consciousness; see Watson (2006).

[10] Auto-commentary below PS 1.9a (Hattori 1968; Dignāga 2005). All translations are from Hattori. See also Kellner (2010) for a study of the text in the light of new sources for the original as well as Jinendrabuddhi's commentary (Jinendrabuddhi 2005).

The claim that mental states have an object-aspect is to be understood as a commitment to the intentionality of the mental. It is part of Dignāga's larger philosophical commitment that the object-aspect of a mental state is not an external object. For him, *being-of-a-blue* is an intrinsic characteristic of a thought about something blue, part of what individuates it, independently of whether there is something blue suitably related to the thought or not. In perception, the object-aspect is something like a presented sensible quality. After Dignāga, Dharmakīrti will develop these ideas into a sophisticated theory of sentience (see Chapter 10).

The subject-aspect is an aspect of a state's content distinct from its outward-facing object-directed content. Dignāga claims that the subject-aspect is required by the possibility of our having a perspective on our own mental lives (on which, compare the discussion in the previous chapter):

> 1.11ab That cognition has two aspects is [known] from the difference between the cognition of the object and the cognition of that [cognition].

The cognition which cognises the object, a thing of colour, etc., has [a twofold appearance, namely,] the appearance of the object and the appearance of itself [as subject]. But the cognition which cognises this cognition of the object has [on the one hand] the appearance of that cognition which is in conformity with the object and [on the other hand] the appearance of itself. Otherwise, if the cognition of the object had only the aspect of the object, or if it had only the aspect of itself, then the cognition of cognition would be indistinguishable from the cognition of the object.

It is in order to able to distinguish thinking about thinking from mere thinking, according to Dignāga, that every mental state must have a subject-aspect, the aspect under which it appears from a first-person perspective, as opposed to a first-person stance (i.e. when it is observed rather than inhabited). The subject-aspect of experience is whatever it is in virtue of which attending to one's experience does not collapse into attending to the world as presented in that experience. Dignāga offers no substantive account of what this feature of experience is, and neither need he for the purposes of his larger argument. It is unlikely that he would agree to an identification of the subject-aspect simply with the 'what it feels like to have it' of the experience, that is to say with phenomenal character as a component of content separable from intentional content.[11] A better suggestion would be

[11] The thesis that the subject-aspect of conscious experience is identifiable with the phenomenal character of the experience is defended independently of Dignāga in Janzen (2008).

that the subject-aspect is, more specifically, related to the phenomenology of intentionality: what it is like to be in a state with a specific intentional content.[12] I am doubtful, though, that Dignāga's subject-aspect has anything to do with phenomenal character, the purported what-it-is-likeness of experience. I suggest that it is better described with the help of the idea of a mode of presentation as a constituent of intentional content: the subject-aspect is an intentional mental state's mode of presentation of its own object-directed intentionality. Given that a mode of presentation is itself a constituent of intentional content, the full intentionality of the state will therefore consist in both the object-aspect and the subject-aspect. A further claim now is that a mental state has a mode of presentation of its own full intentional content, itself a constituent of the state's intentional content. The obvious regress on intentional content can be averted, but only if what makes the further claim true is that the subject-aspect is a mode of presentation of itself as well as a mode of presentation of object-directed intentionality. If a representational state represents that it is representational, and if this too is something it represents, then it can only be that the representation of representation is reflexive self-representation. So, finally, one is led to the conclusion that the subject-aspect of an intentional state is a self-presenting mode of presentation of object-aspect intentionality.[13]

First-Person Access to the Subjectivity of One's Past Experience

Dignāga's aspects theory is expressly designed to enable a distinction between remembering a past event and remembering *experiencing* that event:

[12] See Horgan and Tienson (2002).

[13] The thesis that the subject-aspect is itself constituted by reflexive self-awareness, whether or not in Dignāga, is apparently endorsed more explicitly by the later Buddhist Śāntarakṣita: see P. Williams (1998). On the idea of self-presenting modes of presentation, see Horgan, Tienson, and Graham (2006: 54–7). They, however, identify a self-presentation with phenomenal character, as I think Dignāga would not. There are considerable affinities between Dignāga's view and that of Kriegel (2009), according to which 'conscious states have qualitative character in virtue of representing environmental features and subjective character in virtue or representing themselves' (2009: 2). Kriegal knew of Dignāga's dual-aspect theory and reflexivism through Ganeri 1995.

[That cognition has two aspects follows]

1.11c later also from [the fact of] memory—

This [expression] 'later also from [the fact of] memory' refers back to 'cognition has two aspects'. Some time after [we have perceived a certain object], there occurs [in our mind] the memory of our cognition as well as the memory of the object. So it stands that cognition is of two aspects.

It is possible to remember a past event without remembering *experiencing* that event.[14] This is the first premise ('P_1') in the argument for reflexivism. Dignāga's idea is that when one does in fact remember experiencing an event, the object-aspect of one's memory must be something other than remembering the event itself, for otherwise the distinction would collapse. What the posit of a subject-aspect does is to enable an explanation of one's ability to remember not just the world as it was in the past, but more particularly one's own occupation of a first-person stance in the past. To recall the subject-aspect of one's past experience is to remember oneself experiencing the event.

The argument for reflexivism will also exploit a more mundane fact about remembering:

[Reflexive] self-awareness is also [thus established]. Why?

1.11d. Because memory is never of that which has not been experienced.

It is unheard of to have a memory of something without having experienced [it before]. For instance, the memory of a thing of colour, etc. [does not arise unless the thing of colour or the like has been experienced].

That memory requires past experience might seem to be a tautology, but in fact the thesis needs to be stated with care. I cannot remember an event which occurred before I was born; however, I can remember *that* it occurred, if I have learned this fact in the past. What memory of a past event demands is not that one has directly witnessed that event for oneself, but that one has, at some prior time, come to think that it occurred. Malcolm (1977: 25):

[14] Thus Malcolm (1977: 24): 'As a matter of contingent fact, one does not always remember one's perception of a past event that one remembers.' Later Tibetan exegesis misrepresents Dignāga's argument at this point, formulating it as 'arguing that we cannot make sense of the memory of a past event without remembering it as *experienced*, and hence without having experienced it as *experienced*' (Garfield 2006: 222). Dignāga claims or need claim only that one *can* remember past experiencings, not that one *must*.

The logical grammar of 'remember' requires that if I remember *x* then previously I witnessed, learned about, or (in a broad sense) experienced *x*.

One can either read Dignāga as having this broad sense of 'experience' in mind or take it that he is concerned only with the subclass of memory, memories based on actual past experience. The second premise in Dignāga's argument ('P_2') is that if S remembers an event *x* then S has previously experienced *x*.

If one can remember one's own past experience, and the memory of something requires one to have cognized it (in the broad or narrow sense), then it follows that someone who does so must have cognized that past experience. Does it remain a possibility that the past experiencing which one now remembers was cognized by a distinct higher-order thought, and not by that very past experience itself? Dignāga argues by *reductio*: higher-orderism leads to a vicious infinite regress. If we are to be in a position to evaluate Dignāga's argument for reflexivism, we will need to reconstruct the regress with some care.

Before doing so, however, let me stress that the new theory of twin aspects has a philosophical merit which is independent of the subsidiary role it plays in the proof, and perhaps a far more significant one. The theory affords an account of the distinction between occupying a first-person stance and merely having a first-person perspective. The point is that the idea of a subject-aspect has a place in the explanation of what it is to own a thought. What makes a thought one's own is no mere matter of its occurrence in a certain causal chain rather than another, any more for Dignāga than for Vasubandhu. It has to do with the accessibility of the thought's subject-aspect, and this replaces Vasubandhu's claim that it has to do, rather, with the occurrence of a phenomenal marker of mineness, an additional item in the stream. As we will see several times in later chapters, problems of binding cannot be solved simply by positing extra items, and an advantage of Dignāga's representational theory is that it does not do so. The idea is instead that subjectivity is to be explained at the level of intentionality, and in particular in the exchange whereby the subject-aspect of one moment of thought—which is, to recall, the thought's representation to itself of its outward-directed intentionality—is transformed into the object-aspect of a later moment, so that instead of merely having a world in view, one has in addition oneself in view, a view on one's subjective past. This view is itself subjective: the subjectivity of one's view of oneself is encoded in the fact that the moment of thought that takes as its object-aspect the subject-aspect of an earlier moment has a subject-aspect of its own. Again, what this actually means is that thinking represents to itself that it itself is the intentional object of thinking. Dignāga replaces Vasubandhu's mental files theory of subjectivity with a self-representational theory of subjectivity, though without any implication that subjectivity is thereby naturalized.

Having a first-person perspective is thus a matter of accessing the subject-aspect of one's own thought, and Dignāga has just argued that one can do this even with respect to one's thought in the past. Occupying a first-person stance, by contrast, is a matter of being reflexively self-aware of the subject-aspect of one's thought, and this is something that can take place only in the present. Dignāga is a presentist about the first-person *stance*: it ceases at each moment and is recreated anew; it is always tensed to the present. What one can achieve is a view on one's past mental life; one can have a first-person *perspective* on the subjectivity of one's past.[15]

The Reflexivity of the First-Person Stance

The force of the regress argument can now better be appreciated. It is that the possibility of a first-person perspective on one's subjective past requires there to be a first-person stance consisting in reflexivity. Dignāga:

> Some may hold that cognition also, like a thing of colour, etc., is cognised by means of a separate cognition. This is not true because
>
> 1.12a-b1. If a cognition were cognised by a separate cognition, there would be an infinite regress—
>
> An infinite regress would result if a cognition were to be cognised by a separate cognition. Why?
>
> 1.12b2. Because there is a memory of this [separate cognition] too.

[15] An account of first-person access to the subjectivity of one's past experience is implied by Kierkegaard's use of the term 'contemporaneity' (*samtidighed*). Kierkegaard, however, seems not to draw the distinction Dignāga wants to between having one's subjectivity in view and occupying a first-person stance, and this leads him to understand the phenomenon in terms of a co-identity of past and present first person stances. Dignāga's theory is also useful in interpreting and clarifying Husserl's notion of retention.

It must be admitted that this cognition by which the [previous] cognition is cognised is [also] later remembered. So, if it should be that this [separate] cognition is experienced by a third cognition [so that it may be recollected], there would be an infinite regress.

In order to remember any event (*e*, say), I must previously have experienced that event. Call the previous experience e'. Suppose that e' is *distinct* from *e*. Then an infinite regress threatens. It threatens when we ask whether I also remember e'. If I do, then an iteration on the above argument proves there to exist some further experience (e''), my experience of my experience of *e*, and so on *ad infinitum*.

The argument is clearly enthymematic, and we need to identify the suppressed assumption. Dignāga claims that the experience of the experience is also remembered. One construal is that it is in principle possible to remember any past experience, in which case the missing premise (call it 'P_3*') is: If S experiences an event *x* then S can subsequently remember *x*. In combination with P_1, P_2, and a denial of reflexivism, there would now be a genuine regress. Getting a regress does not, however, require a principle as strong as P_3*. A weaker principle (call it 'P_3') will also do: If S experiences *x* at time t_1 then S can subsequently remember *x* for some time $t_2 > t_1$. What this states is that I can remember events experienced for at least some time after experiencing them, even if I forget them later. P_3 is the converse of P_2, which states that if S remembers an event *x* at t_2 then S experienced *x* at some time t_1 where $t_2 > t_1$. One need not suppose that Dignāga himself took P_3* to be in play as the background assumption needed to make the infinite regress argument go through, and in what follows I will assume only the weaker P_3.

With P_1, P_2, and P_3 in place, higher-orderism leads to a vicious infinite regress. Let me spell it out exactly. Suppose that at time t_1 an experience $e(x)$ of some event *x* occurs. By P_1 augmented by P_3, there could occur at some time $t_2 > t_1$ a memory $m(e)$ of that experience. Since such a memory is possible, then, by P_2, there must have occurred, at some time t_3 in the interval between t_1 and t_2, an experience $e'(e)$ of *e*. By hypothesis, $e' \neq e$, so $t_3 > t_1$ (it can't be before, since e' is an experience of *e*). Then, again by P_1 augmented by P_3, a memory $m'(e')$ of e' could happen at some time t_4 later than t_3, and by P_2, there must therefore have occurred an experience $e''(e')$ at some time t_5 between t_3 and t_4. By hypothesis, $e'' \neq e'$, so $t_5 > t_3$. And so on *ad infinitum*. The combined action of P_1, as augmented by P_3, and P_2 serves to generate an infinite sequence of temporally distinct experiences, each one having the previous one as its object-aspect.

Dignāga argues, surely correctly, that such a scenario is impossible, that the regress is genuinely vicious. It cannot be the case that subsequent to any ordinary experience there follows an infinite cascade of distinct higher-order thoughts:

> 1.12cd. [Further] in such a case, there could be no motion [of cognition] from one object to another. But actually such [a movement of cognition] is accepted. Therefore, reflexive self-awareness must be admitted.

Dignāga is surely right to claim that it is impossible to have an infinite number of distinct thoughts in a finite period of time. Subsequent to any experience of one object, there will therefore follow an infinitely long avalanche of temporally distinct higher-order mental events: the mind will be occupied for ever, and will never be able to 'move' on to some new experience of a different object.[16] The way out is to suppose that each experience is reflexively aware of itself (i.e. that $e' = e$). Dignāga's regress argument for reflexivism thus brings to the fore a deep conceptual link between memory and self-consciousness, centrally revolving around what is involved in being able to have a first-person perspective on one's past mental life. The brilliance of Dignāga's argument consists in the idea that the possibility of having a first-person *perspective* on one's own mental past requires that a first-person *stance* consists in being in the present moment reflexively self-aware.

Provisional Objections

There are several points at which the argument for reflexivism might seem to fail. It does not, however, fail where the Mādhyamika Buddhists Candrakīrti and Śāntideva claim it does, and, following them, Tibetan interpreters.[17] What Candrakīrti and Śāntideva claim is that the

[16] See also Dharmakīrti (1989: 513–14).

[17] Candrakīrti, *Madhyamakāvatāra* 6.72–8; Śāntideva, *Bodhicāryāvatāra* 9.17–25. For the Tibetan re-working, see P. Williams (1998).

argument rests on the false premise that the memory of a past event *necessitates* remembering experiencing it; but as my reconstruction above makes clear, the argument need depend on nothing stronger than that it is *possible* to remember past experiencings.[18]

A more telling objection pays closer careful attention to what the argument actually proves. Dignāga has shown at best only that at some point in the imagined chain of 'higher order' mental states, mental states must start to be reflexive, but he has not proved that ordinary experiences are. I might be in pain without noticing that I am in pain, but I perhaps cannot notice that I am in pain without noticing that I have noticed this. A restricted reflexivist thesis therefore claims only that experiences of a certain sort are reflexive, without claiming that every experience is so. Though considerably weaker than the unrestricted version Dignāga takes himself to have proven, this restricted version is still substantive. A restricted version of reflexivism is, I argued at the end of Chapter 4, also entailed by the most plausible form of emergentism.[19] The thesis so weakened would clearly not be acceptable to those Buddhists who espouse reflexivism, or more generally to those who make reflexivity the distinctive characteristic of subjective consciousness. On the other hand, there is a distinct theoretical attraction to the weakened view, in that it permits a new explanation of thought insertion: a thought from which one is alienated, it might be proposed, is one to whose subject-content one has access but which does not present itself reflexively. Indeed, it will be suggested by one of Dignāga's followers that this is the difference between a telepath's awareness of one's thought and one's own self-awareness.[20] And indeed, one might well describe someone suffering from thought insertion, with first-person access to thoughts they do not recognize as their own, as viewing their own subjective experience as if telepathically. The explanation of thought insertion in terms of a contrast between awareness of the subject-aspect and reflexive self-awareness thus seems to me to be a very promising one; but it requires abandoning reflexivism as a general theory of subjectivity.

[18] See n. 14 above. My point is confirmed by Kellner (2010: 213).

[19] Lehrer (1996) defends a corresponding weakening for self-presentation theories of consciousness; cf. Kriegel and Williford (2006). It might be construed as implying a disjunctivist analysis of self-consciousness, according to which what it is for a state to be self-conscious is different for different sorts of state.

[20] Dharmakīrti PV 3. 455–7; see Moriyama (2010).

A second source of hesitation is that although remembering a past external event requires a previous experience of the event, to put one 'in touch' with the event, so to speak, remembering a past *experience* might be thought not to require any comparable additional sense of being 'put in touch'. Dignāga appeals to two features of remembering, that remembering a past event requires a past experience of that event, and that it is possible to remember past experiences. The first principle gains its credibility from the thought that the past experience establishes a cognitive and epistemic contact with the event, that we cannot *remember* an event unless there has been a flow of information from it to us. The demand for a past experience is a demand for a link between the event and the present memory. In the case when the event is one of one's own experiences, however, one might think that no such *additional* linkage is needed. My past experiences, unlike other past events, are already causally available to my present memory: there is no work for a further experience to do. O'Shaughnessy makes a related point when he argues that sight is an avenue for knowledge of external events because it is mediated by the causally related event of noticing one's visual sensations, but that in the case of knowledge of one's own present experiences there is no analogous third event, so that the 'unlikeness to the perceptual situation shows there was here [in knowledge of one's own present experiences] no experienced *avenue* of knowledge' (O'Shaughnessy 2002: 106). Other philosophers have made similar points about the difference between self-knowledge and ordinary empirical knowledge (see also Chapter 12).[21] The argument against Dignāga is that the ongoing occupancy of a first-person stance is not after all analogous to the ongoing perception of an object, because the idea of tracking, of maintaining an informational link, is otiose: there is no clear sense in which ongoing first-person thought involves keeping track of oneself, and this because it is hard to see what it might mean to say that one has lost track of oneself. This argument then is directed as much against the twin aspects theory of subjectivity as it is against reflexivism. Representation always involves the possibility of misrepresentation, and so the theory permits as a possibility that the later moment which takes as its object-aspect the subject-aspect of an earlier moment might have got things wrong; but to what actual phenomenon could such an alleged possibility correspond?

[21] The argument in this paragraph is also damaging to Janzen's symmetry argument.

A third sort of objection is to be found in the work of the so-called Heidelberg school, such as that of Henrich, and reconstructed thoroughly by Zahavi (1999). The allegation is that the doctrine is viciously circular, the idea being that self-reflexion cannot turn an awareness which is not already self-aware into one which is.[22] A potential response is to claim that reflexivism bears upon a pre-cognitive level of self-consciousness that is presupposed by any conscious thought, that is, to distinguish between 'pre-reflective' and 'reflective' reflexive self-awareness (Zahavi 1999: 14–37). This distinction is indeed available in Dignāga's theory of self-consciousness: pre-reflective self-awareness consists in an outward-directed thought's having a subject-aspect, while reflective self-awareness consists in a thought having as its object-aspect the subject-aspect of a thought. As I mentioned before, it is unclear whether Dignāga admits the subject-aspect to be itself reflexive, although some of his later followers seem to.

Reflexivism is criticized by Nyāya and Vaiśeṣika theorists.[23] The general form of their argument is that Dignāga's picture of the mind suffers from a failing shared with Cartesian theories of mind, namely the idea that everything that happens in the mind is transparent to it. Arnaud, author of the fourth set of objections to Descartes's *Meditations*, already says:

> The author lays it down as certain that there can be nothing in him, in so far as he is a thinking thing, of which he is not aware, but it seems to me that this is false .... The mind of an infant in its mother's womb has the power of thought, but is not aware of it. And there are countless similar examples, which I will pass over. (Descartes AT 214; 1984: ii. 150)

Descartes's reply is to the point:

> I do not doubt that the mind begins to think as soon as it is implanted in the body of an infant, and that it is immediately aware of its thoughts, *even though it does not remember this afterwards* because the impressions of these thoughts do not remain in the memory. (Descartes AT 246; 1984: ii. 171, my italics)

Reflexivism does seem threatened by empirical cognitive scientific work on unconscious mental activity, by animal and infantile thought, and by sub-doxastic states and tacit knowledge.[24] Descartes's claim that infants simply

[22] See also Caston (2002: 792–4).

[23] For discussion, see Matilal (1986: 153–60). See also Chs. 13 and 15 below.

[24] For an attempt to defend the argument against this line of objection, see Janzen (2008: 110–29).

forget seems ad hoc, although there is something right in the intuition that there are limits to which an adult can retrieve a memory of occupying the first-person stance of an infant. I will claim in later chapters that the best explanation of the phenomenology of conscious experience and the emotions is by way of the postulation of unconscious psychological mechanisms.

The idea that reflexivity is a distinctive mark of the mental, and indeed a mark because of which the mental is irreducible to the physical, has exercised a considerable pull on philosophers (Chapter 2). Is reflexivism incompatible with hard naturalism? Descartes rejects the suggestion:

> My critic says that to enable a substance to be superior to matter and wholly spiritual (and he insists on using the term 'mind' only in this restricted sense), it is not sufficient for it to think: it is further required that it should think that it is thinking, by means of a reflexive act, or that it should have awareness of its own thought.
>
> This is as deluded as our bricklayer's saying that a person who is skilled in architecture must employ a reflexive act to ponder on the fact that he has this skill before he can be an architect. It may in fact be that all architects frequently reflect on the fact that they have this skill, or at least are capable of so reflecting. But it is obvious that an architect does not need to perform this reflexive act in order to be an architect. And equally, this kind of pondering or reflecting is not required in order for a thinking substance to be superior to matter. The initial thought by means of which we become aware of something does not differ from the second thought by means of which we become aware of it, any more than this second thought differs from the third thought by means of which we become aware that we were aware that we were aware. And if it is conceded that a corporeal thing has the first kind of thought, then there is not the slightest reason to deny that it can have the second. (Descartes AT 7.559; 1984: ii. 382)

Descartes is atypical in seeing no difficulty in the idea that a corporeal thing, if capable of thinking at all, would be just as capable of reflexive self-awareness. Dignāga does not seem to take it that embracing reflexivism *per se* is in conflict with espousing a materialist philosophy of mind, although Yogācāra Buddhists after him do so, and indeed veer rapidly into idealism. Ismael (2007) proposes a reflexive self-model theory with similarities to that of Dignāga, but one in which representations are sustained and supported by subpersonal information-theoretic and neurological mechanisms of cognition (a type of underpinning to which Nyāya philosophers attach great significance; see Chapter 13). This shows that one can have a reflexivist account of the immersed self but without Dignāga's concomitant error-theory. The main consideration standing in the way of adopting this attractive proposal is that, as I will demonstrate in greater detail in Chapter 11, reflexive accounts of self are Attenuated (cf. Millgram 2011; Ismael herself seems to acknowledge as much in her assertion that 'any subject of a reflexive act is a self', Ismael 2011: 782).

The strongest argument against reflexivism is none of the ones I have just discussed. Rather it is that it leads either to an Attenuated account of subjectivity (an account in which the question 'Which one is me?' can receive no answer) or else to the conceptual problem of other minds. Before developing this line of criticism further in Chapter 11, I will discuss the development and transformation of certain aspects of Dignāga's thought in the work of his reinterpreter, Dharmakīrti. Dharmakīrti will eventually argue that all first-person self-ascriptions of psychological predicates, expressed in statements such as 'I am in pain', involve a mistake. I want to examine his theory of sentience carefully because I believe that his argument against the epistemological legitimacy of the first-person stance rests on very deep assumptions about the nature of experience, ones I want to bring into sharper view.

10

Sentience

Sensation and Thought

The thesis that purely sensory experience has a distinctive sort of content has much to recommend it, but any philosopher who endorses it must eventually attempt to bridge the gap it opens between sensory and cognitive (or between non-conceptual and conceptual) content.[1] The Buddhist notion of 'exclusion' (*apoha*) or 'exclusion of what is other' (*anyāpoha*) serves here as a functional term for whatever additional explanatory resource is needed to bridge the gap.[2] The explanation might proceed either by working up from sensory experience or else by working down from conceptual content. Dignāga made the concept of exclusion central to any Buddhist theory of content, and I have elsewhere considered his top-down approach with the aid of trope-theoretic analysis (Ganeri 2001: 104–14). One of the innovations of Dharmakīrti (*c.*600–60) is to use the notion in pursuit, rather, of a bottom-up strategy, and it is this strategy that I want to explore here. I begin by examining relevant work in the philosophy of perception, so as to clarify whether and where a notion of exclusion might be operative in an account of the relation between perceptual and conceptual content, before arguing that Dharmakīrti's account should be understood as a version of the

[1] 'The central idea behind the theory of nonconceptual mental content is that some mental states can represent the world even though the bearer of those mental states does not possess the concepts required to specify their content' (Bermúdez 2003). Buddhists (but not Naiyāyikas) apparently endorse an Autonomy Thesis about non-conceptual (*nirvikalpaka*) content. The Autonomy Thesis asserts that a creature 'can be in states of nonconceptual content despite not possessing any concepts at all' (ibid.; cf. Peacocke 1994).

[2] Dignāga, *Pramāṇa-samuccaya* 5.25c–38 (Pinde 2009); Dharmakīrti, *svavṛtti* on *Pramāṇa-vārttika* 1.68–75 (Dharmakīrti 1960).

so-called 'relational theory' of sentience, and so, in particular, not as a sense-data theory.

'Bridging the gap' means, more accurately, showing how perceptual experience can supply normative constraints on belief and judgement—how it is that belief and judgement are accountable to and constrained by experience (see Millar 1991). It need not imply any commitment to a stronger thesis—call it the 'Construction Thesis'—that concepts can be constructed or built out of non-conceptual contents. It seems that the most that can be constructed out of non-conceptual contents are what I will call 'proto-concepts', mental constructions that share some but not all of the attributes possessed by concepts, but which are easily mistaken for fully fledged concepts, not least by cognizers themselves. This point will be of particular significance when the concept in question is the concept of *self*. We will be better able to understand the Buddhist claim that this concept involves an error, as well as to situate Buddhist theory more carefully in relation to Humean bundle theory.

The thesis with which I began has long been associated with sense-data theory, but that theory's commitment to the claim that the immediate objects of perceptual experience are disembodied and immaterial sensory elements (elements which, moreover, actually have the properties experience ascribes to ordinary things) has proved more mystifying than illuminating. The work I will refer to claims instead that what sensory experiences present are spatially located instances of phenomenal qualities. The twitches and itches, chirps and cheeps, flickers and flashes that comprise the manifest image are represented in sensory experience as a twitch here, an itch there, a flash in the distance, a cheep just off to the left, and so on. This claim has been most fully defended by Austen Clark in his *A Theory of Sentience* (Clark 2000), but his formulation, as he himself notes, is substantially in agreement with Christopher Peacocke's influential work on non-conceptual 'scenario content' (Peacocke 1992a, 1992b, 2001). Indeed, there are explicit acknowledgements of Buddhist theory in Clark's work (although no suggestion that he is familiar with the ideas of Dharmakīrti).

Let me note at the outset that Clark sees bridging the gap between sensation and thought as an important ambition of the theory:

> [W]orking upwards from sensory capacities, and downwards from subject and predicate in logic and grammar, we meet at feature-placing. The representation of features in space is arguably the most sophisticated of sensory capacities. From my point of view, looking up from the muck and goo of the simplest sentience, such spatial representation is a complex and sophisticated achievement. Yet here it is sitting just below the least sophisticated of linguistic capacities, those sufficient for a feature-placing language. And if we can make that one tiny step, sensation and thought can at last commune. They can share contents. (Clark 2000: 151)

I will notice three places where a notion of exclusion enters the theory of sentience. One is in the construction of *quality space* and the associated relational account of qualities; a second has to do with the *partition* of phenomenal appearance into qualitative features and their apparent locations; the third is at the *point of transition* from feature-placing to full object perception and reference.

Quality Space: The Structure of Phenomenal Appearance

Stimuli—particular occasions of transducer irritation—cause sensations, and to those sensations are ascribed two sorts of properties: the properties they represent things as having, and the properties in virtue of which they so represent things. A red sense-impression is not itself red, but there is some property it has because of which it is a sensation presenting red. The term 'qualia' blurs this distinction: qualia are thought to be properties represented by one's sensory experiences, and yet also to be properties of the sensory experiences themselves. We might rather label the two sorts of property 'content-explaining' and 'phenomenal'. Phenomenal properties are those that characterize how things appear: if the apple looks red, then red is a phenomenal property of the sensation. Content-explaining properties are those properties of sensations in virtue of which things appear the way they do. Confusion arises because often our only way to refer to a sensation presenting red is as I have just done: the phenomenal properties of sensations are used to name their content-explaining ones. In this chapter, I am interested primarily in the content of sensory experience, and I will use the terms 'quality' and 'qualia'—as in, 'the quality red'—to refer to the *phenomenal* properties of a sensation.[3]

Any catalogue of the contents of sensory experience in a given sense-modality must include a description of the qualities that are represented, and it has long been known to psychologists of perception that there is no simple correlation between the stimulus that produces a sensory experience and the quality (= phenomenal property) that the sensory experience presents. In the case of vision, for example, there are several different combinations of wavelengths that will all produce a sensation of any particular hue. Perceiving subjects have, moreover, discrimination thresholds below which distinct stimuli are perceived as presenting the same quality. And again, it is possible for the same stimulus to present different qualities to different perceivers.

If there is no correspondence between stimuli and presented qualities, how should the qualities that those stimuli present be defined? Clark argues that the relations of matching, discriminability, and relative similarity are used to construct what he calls a 'quality space', an 'ordering of the qualities presented by a sensory modality' (2000: 1; see also his 1993). Parameterized, in the case of vision, by hue, brightness, and saturation, the quality space places two qualities near to each other if perceivers tend to find instances of them similar, further away to the degree their instances are perceived as different. Thus:

> To the question 'What are the occupants of quality space?' the natural answer is 'qualities', and what these considerations show is that while we might be able to *label* a point in quality space with some stimulus specification—some class of stimuli which happened to present that quality—we cannot *identify* the quality with that class. A finite class of occasions might help to pick out the quality, but it cannot be used to define the identity of that quality. So from the very beginning, the relations of matching, discriminability and relative similarity among classes of stimuli are used to order something other than those stimuli themselves. Discriminations among stimuli serve to order the qualities that the stimuli present. (Clark 2000: 6)

This ordering is what generalizes across subjects: even if two people see the same light source as having a different colour, they will concur in placing that colour between others presented by different stimuli. Even if the sea

[3] The distinction between phenomenal and content-explaining properties might be thought to offer a further way to understand Dignāga's identification of an object-aspect and a subject-aspect in experience (see Ch. 9). I prefer, however, a representational construal of the distinction.

looks 'blue' to me and 'red' to you, we might agree that it has the same hue as the sky and a different one from the sun.

A quality space is like a structural description of a skeleton, which maps the invariant relationships between the various bones, even though in actuality no two skeletons have bones of the same shapes or size. The occupants of quality space are defined, not in terms of stimuli or class of stimuli, but through a 'structure description':

> [I]f we are to define a term [for a quality], we cannot mention any stimuli. We can mention only the structural properties that give the quale its place in the quality space. 'Orange' cannot be defined as 'the colour of ripe oranges' or in any similar way, no matter how sophisticated. It can only be defined as something like 'the colour midway between red and yellow, and more similar to either than to turquoise'. The terms 'red', 'yellow', and 'turquoise' would all receive similar analyses.[4]

Here, then is a first place where a notion of exclusion is employed in the description of phenomenal appearance. Phenomenal properties are defined by their relational position within an order rather than in terms of the stimuli that cause them to be presented. Paradigmatic stimulus instances cannot play any role in the definition of such terms, because of the problems of paradigm existence and contingency: if 'orange' is defined to be the colour of *this* ripe fruit, then *this* ripe fruit must exist for anything to look orange; and it is no longer a contingent matter that this fruit is indeed orange in colour. But neither conclusion is true.

Finally, there has to be a corresponding ordering among the properties of the internal states themselves (the 'content-explaining' properties) in virtue of which this ordering among phenomenal properties obtains: for vision, perhaps this lies in the functioning of so-called opponent processes. These provide the neurophysiological basis of the quality space. In that sense, the ordering is an inherited part of our natural endowment. Finding one colour more similar to a second than a third is not a matter of convention or social practice: it is built into the processes of vision.

The thesis that there is no correspondence between stimulus and presented quality in sensation is one that Dharmakīrti seems explicitly to

[4] Clark (2000: 16). In the appendix, Clark shows how this is done by defining a Ramsey sentence for the whole structure and assigning quality terms their Ramsey correlates.

endorse. A distinctive element in Dharmakīrti's theory of perception is the invocation of two sorts of phenomenal 'image' (*ākāra*). One sort, the image presented by particular sensory impressions, is itself said to be particular, the other is said to be general or universal. Scholars have noted that there is in Dharmakīrti a lack of congruence between the phenomenal content of a sensation, i.e. the first sort of 'image', and its cause (Dreyfus 1997: 85–6). While the cause consists in the stimulus produced by a multitude of external particles, sensation presents a single image:

Due to a relation with other things particles that are different than their own previous moments arise. In that sense, they are said to be aggregated (*saṃcita*), and as such they are said to be a condition for the production of awareness. Moreover, the distinctive quality that particles obtain does not occur without the other particles with which they are in proximity. Hence, since awareness does not have any necessary relation to a single particle, awareness is said to have a universal as its object.[5]

And what is the contradiction if many things that have the special characteristic [of producing awareness] when aggregated are not the cause of awareness individually, as is the case with the senses and such? And except for something being the cause, there is nothing else that could constitute that thing's being the apprehended object. That is, the apprehended object of an awareness is said to be that in the image of which awareness arises.[6]

On these passages, Dunne comments, '[T]he singularity of the perceptual image is not congruent to (i.e. has not isomorphic correspondence with) the singularity of its physical causes. Instead, the singularity of the image *correlates with* a singularity of causal function: multiple external causes are producing a single effect, the image' (2004: 108). When Dharmakīrti describes this image as a universal, he is referring to his own theory of generality, which is that all generality is a work of exclusion among particulars. I believe that he is therefore very close to articulating a version of the relational theory of sentience, that presented phenomenal qualities are defined not by way of paradigmatic external stimuli but rather by relations of exclusion that hold between them. Dharmakīrti endorses the thesis with which I began: perception has a content; this content is something other than the perception itself, but is not an ordinary physical object or part of

[5] PV 3.195–6; trans. Dunne (2004: 396).
[6] PV 3.223–4; trans. Dunne (2004: 411).

one. The content consists of a particular (*svalakṣaṇa*) and an image (*ākāra*). The content is non-conceptual (*nirvikalpaka*) in the sense that it is not describable in terms of concepts and language available to the perceivers themselves; it is, Dharmakīrti says, ineffable.[7]

Location and Binding

Phenomenal quality is not the only dimension of variation in the content of sensory experience: 'There is more to sentience than sensory qualities' (Clark 2000: 1). Even by the standards of a creature that had no higher cognitive abilities than sentience alone, one would be radically impoverished if there were nothing more to sentience than this:

> Consider a humble animal whose consciousness stops at sentience. One imagines its mental life to consist of nothing but a flux of sensory qualities. In a widely repeated and ancient image, its stream of mental processes is filled by variegated qualia, which over time pop up, bob along, combine, recombine, and ultimately sink back down into the muck. A mental life of pure sensation would be nothing but a stream, flux, a flow of such stuff. . . . But this picture, ancient and widely repeated as it is, radically underestimates the sophistication needed by even the simplest animal. An animal whose mental life is a pure flux of qualities . . . could not distinguish matte red next to glossy green from matte green next to glossy red . . . [The ability to do this] marks a significant threshold in the complexity of one's psychological organization. To pass it one needs somehow to focus the attribution of qualities, so that one can distinguish a scene containing a red square from one containing something that is red and something else that is square. (Clark 2000: 79)

The 'ancient image' is certainly a Buddhist one, familiar from early sources such as the Nikāya and the *Milinda-pañhā*. The problem here referred to is a version of what Frank Jackson (1977) called the 'Many Properties' problem, a problem about the way features get to be bound or integrated. A creature with only the capacities to discriminate red from green and matte from gloss could not distinguish between the two scenarios: both represent the same conjunction of qualities. Unless a sentient creature could solve this problem, it would also not be able to distinguish a single chirp from two simultaneous

[7] Dharmakīrti, *svavṛtti* on 3.1–2.

and qualitatively identical chirps coming from different locations. In fact, of course, the capacity to do this falls well below the capacity to employ concepts and language.

It might seem that the problem could be solved by the introduction of spatial qualia (also known as 'local signs'), but Clark shows why that cannot work in a series of helpful metaphors:

> Merely adding more qualities will not help: they will be lost in the flux with all the others. In a similar way, the ancient image of a thing as a bundle of such qualities—concretions settling out of the flux—*smuggles* in more organization than one might suppose. If the qualities are sticks, we need some distinct principle by which to bundle the sticks together. A piece of string serves admirably, but notice that it serves a rather different function than that served by additional sticks. Tossing in more sticks leaves one just as disorganised as before; they will soon be bobbing down the stream, undifferentiated from all the rest. Even special sticks, labelled 'spatial qualia', are soon lost.... We require some distinct principle by which to create bundles. Lacking string, the simplest way to count our things—our piles or bundles—is by location. Here is one bundle, and there is another... I suggest that the threshold of the Many Properties problem is the point at which we add to the flux of sensory qualities a distinct capacity for sensory reference. (Clark 2000: 79)

The argument here is that all but the simplest sentient creatures (perhaps a creature with only olfactory sensory abilities) do more than merely *enjoy* qualia. They must also have a distinct capacity to *place* those qualia: hear a sound as coming from a certain direction and at a certain distance. Places become objects of what Treisman and Gelade call 'focal attention': 'Any features which are present in the same central fixation of attention are combined to form a single object. Thus focal attention provides the "glue" which integrates the initially separable features into unitary objects' (1980: 98). The conclusion drawn is that any schema describing the contents of sensory experience must be partitioned into two dimensions of variation: variation in location, and variation in the qualities at those locations. It is important to this proposal that places are themselves able to function as loci of focal attention, and not only the objects that may or may not be located at those places. Referring to the experimental results of Michael Posner on the spatial cuing of attention, Clark argues that '[f]eature-placing can indicate or pick out a place by spatial coordinates derived from the operation of the sensory system itself; it does not need some object to glom onto—some object to which to attach its referential force' (2004a: 457).

Clark asserts that this pair of capacities is strongly akin to the capacities ascribed by P. F. Strawson to the user of a feature-placing language. A feature-placing language does not have resources for reference or predication; it exists below the level of the subject-predicate distinction. What it does have are resources to identify places and to locate features: thus the sentences in such a language are of the form 'Red here' or 'Raining now'. Speakers of such a language can judge 'Cow here' and 'Cow here again', but they cannot distinguish the case where this is true because of two cows and the case involving the same cow a second time. That is, they do not yet have the capacity to reidentify enduring particulars, the capacity fundamental to reference and so to predication. According to the feature-placing hypothesis, sensory experience analogously requires the capacity to identify phenomenal properties in quality space, and also the capacity to place those qualities at locations on or near the body of the sentient creature (locations with respect to which the sentient creature can stand in an ongoing information link). This latter capacity is what Clark slightly misleadingly calls the capacity for sensory reference. Singling out places is rather a proto-referential analogue to reference, and placing features there is a proto-predicative analogue to predication, in a feature-placing language.

Clark is right to be critical of the 'ancient image' of qualia in flux: one cannot solve the binding problem just by adding more items into the stream. Dharmakīrti's theory of sentience is much more sophisticated than this ancient Buddhist one, however. In particular, I think it is clear that he considers sensory content to have precisely the two dimensions of variation Clark identifies, location and quality. Dharmakīrti says that a sensory image is presented as determined in place and time.[8] His interpreter Dharmottara is even more explicit that a triple of image, place, and time constitutes the phenomenal content of perception.[9] The analysis is also attributed to Dharmakīrti by the Kashmiri Śaiva philosopher of language, Abhinavagupta.[10] Sensory experience presents images at spatio-temporal places. Even if they

[8] *svavṛtti* on PV 1.35; cf. *Hetubindu* 26,12–13.

[9] As is Mokṣākaragupta: *deśa-kāla-ākāra-niyataḥ puraḥ prakāśamānaḥ* (Mokṣākaragupta 2004: 21,10–11).

[10] Abhinavagupta (1986: i. 86,4–8 (on 1.2.1–2).

lack spatial *extension*, it does not follow that presented images are not spatially located at all.[11]

In the idea of feature-placing we have a second point at which the notion of exclusion (*apoha*) is involved in the description of sensory experience. Qualities belong at the level of generality, places at the level of particulars. One reason for this is that to a single place can be attributed many qualities, but a given quality has at most just one place (this is, indeed, a further argument against spatial qualities: they are not qualities). But P. F. Strawson points to another, yet more telling, asymmetry. According to him, the asymmetry between particulars and general characteristics has at its source the fact that, while both supply principles for the 'collection' of other particulars and general characteristics, the nature of the respective principles they supply is different. As Strawson puts it, there is

> a certain asymmetry which particulars and general characteristics of particulars have relative to each other, in respect, as I put it, of the possession of incompatibility ranges and involvement ranges. General characters typically have such ranges in relation to particulars, particulars cannot have them in relation to general characters. For every general character there is another general character such that no particular can exemplify them both at once; but for no particular is there another particular such that there is no general character they can both exemplify. Again, for many a general character there is another general character such that any particular which exemplifies the first must exemplify the second or vice versa; but there is no pair of particulars so related that every general character the first exemplifies must be exemplified by the second or vice versa. (1974b: 126)

The incompatibility range of a general characteristic is the group of other general characteristics which cannot also be exemplified by a particular which exemplifies it. Thus, if green is in the incompatibility range of red, then no place can be both red and also green. On the other hand, particulars do not have such incompatibility ranges: if a particular exemplifies a given general characteristic, that does not tell against any other particular doing so as well. Similarly with involvement ranges: scarlet is in the involvement range of red, because any particular that exemplifies scarlet must also exemplify red. Again, there is no analogue for particulars. These asymmetries are the reason we must distinguish the linguistic devices of identifying

[11] On the spatiality of Dharmakīrti's particulars: Keyt (1980); Dreyfus (1997: 85–6); Dunne (2004: 98–112).

reference and predication, 'such linguistic and other devices as will enable us both to classify or describe in general terms and to indicate to what particular cases our classifications or descriptions are being applied' (Strawson 1966: 47).

It is in the asymmetry between qualities and their apparent spatial locations that another application of the notion of exclusion is available. The idea behind the thought that the former are general and the latter particular, and that the former are 'located in' the latter, is that the former alone have incompatibility ranges: that is, for each quality, there are other qualities whose exemplification at a place is excluded by its own. If the dimensions of variation in phenomenal appearance were not so partitioned into two factors, one proto-referential, the other bearing the hallmarks of generality, then no amount of logical manipulation of the qualia could get us above the level of a mere flux of unrestituted sensory elements. In all this there are strong resonances with the Buddhist theory of exclusion (*apoha*), which is indeed used to generate hierarchies of generality by way of incompatibility ranges (see Ganeri 2001: Ch. 4). There are more specific resonances with Dharmakīrti. The following passage is typical:

> Those mentally experienced objects are apprehended as 'the same' by virtue of that universal because they appear in terms of an exclusion from some other things. But a particular is not what is apprehended as the same because it does not appear to a conceptual awareness. Those conceptual appearances appear as nondifferent in that they are excluded from some things, but they may also appear as nondifferent in that they possess exclusions from other things. Therefore, although those appearances are not real in and of themselves, conceptual cognition presents them as if they were; and one thus forms conventions for universals and co-referentiality even though the object of these conventions is false.[12]

Quasi-Objects

Feature-placing by itself is not enough for the introduction of objects. For that, we need sortal concepts, concepts that provided identity conditions for the things that fall under them. Clark argues that what feature-placing *is*

[12] 1.73; trans. Dunne (2004: 244).

enough for is to locate, count, and keep track of things, and those abilities permit the introduction of quasi-objectual entities, entities that lack the robust identity conditions of objective particulars, but can easily be mistaken as such. He attributes this idea explicitly to the Buddhists:

> [F]eature-placing can give us the wherewithal to locate, track and count some putative entities, such as the waves on the ocean as they come crashing onto the beach. But waves are still quite a way away from being individuals or 'objective particulars'. Consider: Two waves can fuse; one wave can split into two; 'a' wave has entirely different parts at different times; and if all those parts are arranged in just the same way at a different time, it is a purely verbal question whether we have the same wave again, or a different one that is qualitatively identical. Waves are often mentioned by Buddhist thinkers who want to point to something that appears to be an object but is not. In this I think they are right. (Clark 2004a: 465)

These entities appear to be objects but are not. The reason is that it is a constitutive part of the idea of a physical object that it can change its location. With feature-placing capabilities alone, including an ability to bind features together in focal attention, sensory content can be made to reach up as far as the cognition of quasi-objectual entities that can be counted, located, and tracked, but not reidentified as the same again as they undergo movement in the visual field. And it is a mistake, albeit one that is easy enough to make, to regard those entities as objective particulars.

The review so far presents us with a way to understand the jointly coordinated roles of what are labelled in Buddhism embodied reacting (*rūpa*), labelling (*saṃjñā*), and conscious attending (*vijñāna*). There is no definite mention in Clark's analysis of affective appraising (*vedanā*) and dispositional readying (*saṃskāra*): I will have more to say about these in Chapter 14. The question now is the relation between sentience and thought. We have here one place where a mistake involved in object-directed thought is to be located: a quasi-objective particular, without full criteria of identity, is *mistakenly* treated as if it were an object. It is fundamental to the Buddhist account of self-consciousness that the very same mistake is involved in *I*-thoughts, thoughts in whose content the subject features. Here too, the suggestion might be, something quasi-objectual, a streaming flow of phenomenal qualia which are either associated with the sense of 'mine' afforded by Vasubandhu's mineness-markers or themselves reflexively self-presenting, is mistaken for a subject with robust identity conditions.

Let us call the content of cognitions about quasi-objects 'proto-concepts'. Proto-concepts seemingly are constructible from non-conceptual sensory content, but there remains a gap between them and fully fledged concepts. I mentioned that it is distinctive of Dharmakīrti's theory that he acknowledges two sorts of image (*ākāra*), the particular image which is a phenomenal quality, and a general image. The general image is a close cousin of the notion of a proto-concept, something that represents a quasi-objectual entity but lacks full identity conditions: Buddhists use the example of the apparently circular whirling firebrand. This marks the transition from sensation to a primitive sort of typed perception, a sort that does not yet involve or presuppose any linguistic abilities or the related ability to combine, apply, and work with concepts (the ability to combine concepts into larger conceptual complexes being partly definitive of what a concept is, and of what it is to possess one).

A creature can solve the Many Properties problem if it has the capacity to discriminate between matte red next to glossy green and matte green next to glossy red. It might still not have the ability to perceive physical objects. If what we have said so far is correct, the further step is the same as the move up from a feature-placing language to a language of individual reference and predication. This step involves a new ability, the capacity to discriminate between red thing here and red thing there, on the one hand, and red thing here and *same* red thing there, on the other. For that, one needs sortal concepts and the associated ability to discriminate between distinct items of the same sort. Here again, the notion of exclusion has a role, for the relevant ability might be redescribed as an ability to distinguish between what an object is identical to and what is excluded from or other than the object. The idea of what is 'other than *x*' and the idea of what is 'identical to *x*' are complementary to one another. Notice that this role for exclusion is different from either of the preceding two, for it obtains between individual objects and not occupants of quality space. If what we mean by 'conceptual thought' is the employment of the full intentional machinery of reference and predication, then possession of this further ability is the criterion that distinguishes thinkers from the merely sentient.

I suggest, in fact, that at this third level the notion of exclusion has an even more important role: it can function as a semantic device for converting a sortal into a feature term. 'That which is non-water-pot' is a term that spreads its reference over many things of various sorts; it possesses no criterion of identity of its own. So its negation cannot have one either. In that sense, it is like 'gold' or 'red' in marking only the presence of a feature. A double negation transforms the subject-predicate sentence 'This is a pot' into the feature-placing 'No absence of pot here'. The capacities required of someone who understands this second sentence fall short of an ability to reidentify particulars. The semantic device of double negation serves to excise the sortality from a sortal concept: what remains is a feature-placing construct, a proto-concept. When Buddhists present a theory of meaning with the help of this device, saying for example that the meaning of the word 'cow' is that which is not non-cow (see Chakrabarti *et al.* 2011), the intention is thus to have articulated a conception of language as that which mediates between the proto-conceptual and full concept possession.

Does Object Perception Involve an Error?

Dharmakīrti's acknowledgement of the phenomenon of sensory error indicates that he admits that sensation is intentional. Possibilities for misplacing a quality at a location open up if sensory content has a feature-placing structure. These are, Dharmakīrti allows but Dignāga does not, genuinely *perceptual* errors. They are 'nonconceptual errors' (*bhrānti*: Coseru 2012; Dunne 2004: 88, 130; cf. Clark 2000: 191–7).

Perhaps the most distinctive aspect of Dharmakīrti's theory comes in at this point.[13] He claims that making the transition from sensation to object perception also involves an error. Specifically, the error involved is one that rests on what he calls a 'judgement of sameness' (*eka-pratyavamarśa-jñāna*).[14] It is because of this judgement that a proto-object, something that has the same status as a wave or a whirling firebrand, is erroneously considered to be

[13] Dharmakīrti, *svavṛtti* on 1.68–75; 3 *passim*. See Dreyfus (1997: 217–32); Dunne (2004: 84–144, 159–61); Katsura (1993); Tillemans (1995, 1999).

[14] Dunne (2004: 158–69): 'Dharmakīrti appeals to the notion of a "judgment of sameness" (*ekapratyavamarśajñāna*). On this argument, the claim that all the entities in question have the same effect rests ultimately on the fact that they eventually produce a second-order cognition—a judgment—in which the individuals in question are identified as the same type of entity. All the entities we call "blue", for example, produce perceptual images that, when the proper conditions are in place, will lead to the judgment, "This is blue." ... [I]t is "by their nature" (*svabhāvena, prakṛtyā*) all entities that we indirectly call a "water-jug" have the same effects. For the *apoha*-theory, perhaps the most important "same effect" that each of the entities in question produces is the aforementioned "judgment of sameness" (*eka-pratyavamarśa-jñāna*).'

an object with robust identity conditions. The perception of a single continuous circle of fire, in the illusion of the firebrand, is, according to this hypothesis, due to a judgement, one which obscures phenomenal content and misrepresents it as fully objectual:

> Real things are themselves different, but in conceptual cognition they appear as if nondifferent in that they appear in some single form. Those things appear that way in that their differentiation is obscured by an obscurative cognition which obscures the form of something else with its own form. That obscurative cognition, although based on those different real things, has the cognitive aspect of a single object.[15]

> The nature of things is such that although they are different, by their nature some of them are restricted to the accomplishment of the same telos (*artha*) such as inducing the same judgement (*eka-pratyavamarśa-jñāna*) or producing an awareness of an object.[16]

> Furthermore, all of these and other such conventions are erroneous (*vikalpa*) in that they are constructed through the imprints left by experiences of particulars.[17]

Although a judgement, the error occurs as an almost automatic reflex, one of which the judger is barely aware. It is a deeply ingrained habitual tendency (*vāsanā*), rather than an explicit act of deliberation. Is there anything in the relational theory of sentience corresponding to this idea? Yes:

> A consequence of this account is that qualitative character is a relational affair. Qualitative properties seem to be intrinsic properties, but they are not . . . Perhaps it is part of our ordinary conceptual framework that qualia are intrinsic. And perhaps that part is a portion of our folk inheritance that we must renounce. Empirical inquiry suggests that the facts of qualitative character have at root a relational form. (Clark 2000: 19)

This is the same error to which Buddhaghosa refers, in a passage I quoted in Chapter 7. Again,

> I take the experiments of Wallach and Gilchrist (and also now of Whittle) to be quite revealing. They strongly suggest that our intuitions that chromatic qualities are intrinsic qualities are just wrong. (Clark 2004b: 566)

15 1.68–9; trans. Dunne (2004: 339).

16 *svavṛtti* on 1.75; trans. Dunne (2004: 347). Cf. 3.29–30.

17 1.73; trans. Dunne (2004: 244).

In Wallach's experiment, a projector is used to project a circle of light onto a screen, while a second projects an encircling ring. Wallach found that the apparent brightness of the central circle can be altered without adjusting the first projector, simply by changing the brightness of the annulus: the brighter it is, the darker the centre appears. What seems to be an intrinsic property, the brightness of the central disk, is in fact a *relation* between two levels of luminance. It is indeed an 'unconscious error', a false bit of our folk inheritance, that leads us to think of the visual qualities (hue, saturation, brightness) as intrinsic monadic properties of the things they purport to qualify. That we are inclined to view the deliverances of our senses as ascribing intrinsic properties to external things, rather than as involving properties whose relational character is something for which the structure of our visual apparatus is responsible, is, quite possibly, an error we are naturally selected to make.

A final element of Dharmakīrti's theory that seems especially amenable to a relational interpretation is his thesis that only particulars have causal efficacy (*arthakriyā*), while constructed generalities lack it.[18] Here again, this is what a relational account does say. If that account is correct, then it is a mistake to try and define qualities in terms of their causal functional roles, whether long-arm roles that 'reach out into the world of things' or short-arm roles that are 'purely internal' (Block 1997). The reason is that the basic relations that define the structure of quality space are not causal ones.

> Rather than accept a theory that requires us to specify some particular 'causal niche' that is always and only occupied by sensations of orange, we should abandon the theory. There is no 'causal niche' filled characteristically and uniquely by sensations of orange. But a relational structure can be built up using relations other than 'causes'... [I]f our goal is to describe qualitative character, the root relations will be those of qualitative similarity. (Clark 2000: 18)

What defines orange is its falling between yellow and red, and so on—its patterns of exclusion. Likewise, the 'constructed universals' of Dharmakīrti's system are defined by formal relations and not causal ones: unlike the particulars, they do not have functional roles. Once again, paradigmatic particulars have no role in the definition of quality terms.

[18] PV 3.1–3; *svavṛtti* on 1.170–1.

Dharmakīrti's introduction of 'images' (*ākāra*) into his theory of perception is a response to the objection that a purely exclusionary account of sensory content of the sort proposed by Dignāga does not get the phenomenology right. We might compare this point with an objection that has been pressed against Clark's attempt to give a relational account of qualia:

> Sensory qualities have an 'absolute value' as well as a relative one; a determinate identity over and above their set of similarity relations . . . [I]t isn't pure difference alone that is presented by border regions. We don't just say this is *different from that*, but we describe the difference in terms of a quality—our visual system says 'redder here than there.' But what's *being redder*? (Levine 2004: 546–8)

> [S]ince the same difference can occur anywhere in the colour map, this leaves it mysterious why a certain pattern should look brown-and-orange rather than turquoise-and-olive (assuming that the differences within these pairs are the same.) (Matthen 2004: 517)

Clark's response is that a relational account will associate each quality term with a unique definite description as long as the relational structure is asymmetric and so non-invertible (Clark 2004b: 569); but that does not seem to speak to the objection, the force of which is that sensory experience presents qualities as having a positive value, so that a purely relational account is inadequate to the phenomenology of appearance. Contemporary work in the philosophy of perception is divided over whether the best way to proceed is broadly Fregean—that is, to introduce ways of perceiving or *manners of presentation* of sensory contents—or broadly Russellian—that is, to introduce further, more finely grained, sensory properties. Post-Dharmakīrti Buddhist discussion over the status of the 'image' can be interpreted as exploring similar and other possibilities (see Patil 2003; McCrea and Patil 2010).

To bridge the gap between sensation and thought, we must work up from the 'muck and goo' of basic sentience, and also down from the sophisticated world of identifying reference and predication. I have tried to show that there are various ways in which a notion of exclusion does indeed have a role to play in these two movements. Going up, by providing a relational account of the sensory features and an explanation of that in which the generality of features consists. Moving down, by converting sortals into feature terms. Feature-placing is then the middle ground where sensation and thought meet, in the formation of proto-concepts.

And if, as it seems, Dharmakīrti's theory of perception can attribute to sensory content greater richness than a sense-data analysis does, then his theory helps us to see how it is possible for sense-experience normatively to constrain the content of belief.

I-Thoughts and Quasi-Subjects

All Buddhist philosophers, of whatever particular persuasion, claim that *I*-thought involves an error. I have now identified two putative sources of error in object perception. One is the mistake involved when one takes what is in fact only a quasi-object (an entity without determinate individuation criteria, such as a wave) as if it were the sort of object that falls under a sortal concept and so can be reidentified as the same again. The second candidate is the sort of mistake that is involved when one treats what is in fact relational as if it were intrinsic.

This second sort of mistake, which the relational theory of sentience says we are prone to make about qualia, is illustrated by the concentric rings experiments of Wallach and Gilchrist. As applied to self-conscious first-person judgements, judgements in whose content the subject features, a Buddhist thinker might claim that such states mistake what is in fact a relational ingredient in the content of a self-conscious state for something intrinsic. Perhaps something along the lines of this second move is the strategy adopted by Nāgārjuna when he denies that anything has an 'own-nature' (*svabhāva*).

Alternatively, a Buddhist philosopher might seek to base their thesis that a mistake is involved in states of self-consciousness in the idea that *I*-thought mistakes what is in fact a wave-like flow of subjective awareness as if it were the consciousness of a single, continuous entity. All there really is to the flow of subjectivity is that each mental happening is reflexively self-aware. This strategy is clearly visible in the work of the Yogācāra philosophers Dignāga and Dharmakīrti, both of whom argue in defence of reflexivism, understood not just as the thesis that every mental state is reflexively self-aware, but as implying the further proposition that *this is all there is* to self-consciousness, so that any more substantive thesis about what is involved in thinking about oneself as oneself must involve an error. The leading idea is that there is a type of self-consciousness whose proto-conceptual content is beneath the level of subject-object content. No self features in self-consciousness as a constituent of content. What there is are *quasi-subjects*, the analogues of the quasi-objects I described above, formed by a binding of the subject-aspect of experience (*svābhāsa*) through reflexive self-awareness (*svasaṃvedana*). A distinctive sort of mistake is involved when such subjective contents are transformed by the cognizer into self-conscious states attributing psychological properties to oneself, *I*-thoughts. If we apply my suggestion about the sortality-excising semantic role of double negation to the first person, the idea would be that the word 'I' or 'self' be paraphrased as 'No non-I here' or 'No non-self here', where the paraphrases introduce only quasi-subjects. There is here certainly an original and important explanation of the intentional structure of self-conscious experience. Dharmakīrti refers to it in the course of an explanation of the distinction between one's own present awareness of one's mental states and that of a telepath's perception of them, thereby agreeing with Dignāga in seeing it as a constitutive theory of the distinction between a first-person stance and a perspective on one's mental life.[19] Dignāga and Dharmakīrti provide error-theories of what I earlier called the immersed self: there is no immersed self, but only legitimate subjectivity erroneously interpreted as such.

Concomitant with a denial of genuine subjects of consciousness, and motivated by an exactly analogous set of considerations, is the denial that there is genuine perception of an external world, and a well-documented though perhaps over-emphasized strain of subjective idealism runs through the work of Dharmakīrti and his successors. But neither an error-theory about the immersed self nor the error-theory about our attempts to form an objective conception of the world is mandated by a relational account of phenomenal content. I do not think that either one should be allowed to diminish the significance of Dharmakīrti as a philosopher. As I noted at the end of the last chapter, one might have a reflexivist theory of the immersed self without the associated error theory; so too one might hope to build such a theory on the basis of a relational account of sentience. Dharmakīrti's achievement is in making clear exactly what work a concept of self has to do. The fact that there is this further work to be done does not show that an

[19] PV 3. 455–7; see Moriyama (2010).

'error' is involved in first-person thought; nor indeed can it be right to describe it as an 'error' at all if it is not one from which human experience can be cured without the loss of its humanity.

The question which Buddhist successors to Dharmakīrti will ask is an excellent one. It is in effect the question whether there is anything which can solve the Many Properties problem for self-consciousness: does reflexivity explain the binding of self-presentations and so the ability to think about the distinction between one's own and other minds. These are urgent questions about phenomenal self-representation for No Place Views, ones to which I turn in Chapter 11. In later chapters of this book I will argue that rather than agree with Dharmakīrti that an error must be involved in object perception and self-conception, we can locate what is needed for there to be genuine subjects and an objective conception of the world; but that what is needed is to be found in ideas not available from within a purely Dharmakīrtian framework (see especially Chapter 15). In the course of showing this I will in effect reject the reductionism[20] implicit in the very idea of 'building up from below' that is at the heart of Dharmakīrti's bottom-up approach to the philosophy of mind.

[20] What Dunne (2004) describes as his 'foundationalism'.

11

Other Minds

Let us suppose that there are no selves, but that there are flows of reflexively self-aware moments of consciousness. There are memories of past moments in the flow, and perhaps anticipations of future moments as well. Something goes wrong, however, when a thought of the form 'I am happy' or 'I am in pain' occurs, that is, when there is a move up to first-person present-tense ascriptions of psychological states. What goes wrong is that such self-ascriptions imply that there is some determinate criterion for individuating flows of subjectivity when in fact there is none. The key insight was that reflexivity provides a principle by which to 'tie' together the subject-aspects of experiences in the content of self-conscious states. This is an analogue, for self-consciousness, of the role performed for Dharmakīrti by presented spatial location in solving the binding problem, presented spatial location being what ties together the object-aspects in intentional experience. Reflexivity is the source of presented present-tense 'quasi-subjects', just as feature-placing is of presented quasi-objects. Just as it is an illusion to think that one can keep track of waves in such a way as to give a determinate answer to the question 'Is this another wave or the same wave as before?', so the implication is that it is a mistake to think that when presented with a new occurrence of reflexive self-awareness there is any determined answer to the question 'Is this another, or is it me again?'

What does this imply for one's ability to form a conception of *others?* If one cannot form such a conception, then how can one cultivate compassion? Dharmakīrti is well enough aware of the dangers to have written a text arguing that one's conception of another can be grounded in an act of reason, namely a sort of argument from analogy.[1] One forms a conception of another as a flow of moments of consciousness, of which one is not

[1] Dharmakīrti (1997); cf. Kumārila, *Ātmavāda* 145a–d.

oneself conscious, but which one infers to exist as the best explanation of the physical movements of another body. In a remarkable development, however, the eleventh-century Buddhist thinkers Jñānaśrīmitra and Ratnakīrti reject this idea, and Ratnakīrti goes on to argue in detail that the Buddhist must accept that it is impossible to form a conception of another's mental life (Ratnakīrti 1957). Insofar as it takes Yogācāra Buddhist theory of mind to its logical conclusion, Ratnakīrti's work represents the clearest possible statement of the challenge that this theory confronts.

In what follows, I will summarize the contents and the main argument, and follow the summary with a new translation of Ratnakīrti's *The Refutation of Other Streams of Consciousness*. I have undertaken a new translation because I feel that the older translations miss the point of the text. What I will try to do is to bring out the fact that the work is not about 'the problem of other minds' as understood in traditional Western philosophy, which is a problem for epistemology—how can I *know* that other minds exist? Rather, it engages with a much deeper difficulty, the problem of whether one can form any conception of another's mental life at all (what has sometimes been called the 'conceptual problem' of other minds).[2] The importance of Ratnakīrti's text has not been fully appreciated among contemporary scholars, and this is partly a fault of the text itself. For the first half, in which Ratnakīrti sets out to dismantle Dharmakīrti's proof, is very densely argued. One gets to the real interest of the text only towards the end. Many scholars have perhaps thought that all Ratnakīrti is doing is 'refuting' Dharmakīrti's inference, and have not been aware that the 'refutation' to which Ratnakīrti refers is of the very possibility of forming a conception of another mind. After the translation, I will consider a way to take the discussion about self-consciousness further.

An Overview of the Argument

Ratnakīrti summarizes Dharmakīrti's argument that I can form an inferential understanding of other minds (TEXT 2). I know in my own case that my

[2] Avrimides (2001: 135, 224). Cf. Gallagher and Zahavi (2008: 184): 'If my self-experience is, in the primary instance, of a purely mental nature, i.e. if my body does not figure essentially in my self-ascription of (some) psychological states, while my ascription of mental states to others are based solely on their bodily behaviour, what, then, should guarantee the ascription of the same type of states to others? How would we ever come to be in possession of a truly general concept of mind that is equally applicable to different subjects?'

physical behaviour and use of language are consequent upon my being in certain sorts of mental state, such as wanting to do or say something. There is, therefore, a 'covariance in agreement and difference' (*anvaya-vyatireka*; cf. Chapter 3) between being in such mental states and behaviour. If I witness some such piece of behaviour, and am able to be aware that I have not willed or desired it myself, then I can infer that there is a willing or desiring that is not mine.

Ratnakīrti denies that the covariance on which the inference rests is, or even could be, established to hold. In order to establish that covariance, one would have to be able to perceive the desires and volitions of others, so as to confirm that they are correlated with those witnessed items of behaviour (TEXT 3). Ratnakīrti says that the argument is faced with a dilemma from which it cannot escape: either the fact that one perceives those desires and volitions makes them, after all, one's own, or else one cannot perceive them as belonging to another, and the inference is fallacious (TEXT 4).

Ratnakīrti's most important contribution comes next (TEXT 5). There is no way, he argues, to draw a boundary (*avadhi*) between distinct psychophysical streams and therefore no prospect of individuating minds. The argument is that thoughts do not identify themselves specifically as 'belonging to me' or 'belonging to you'—nothing in the content or internal form (aspect, image) of a thought, even if reflexively self-aware, tags it to one mind rather than another. One important implication of Ratnakīrti's argument is that a merely causal relation (for instance, Parfit's relation R) is insufficient to individuate distinct psychophysical streams. But Ratnakīrti's argument also bears upon the strategy for individuating minds that Dignāga appeals to, that what makes a past thought mine is that I uniquely can remember experiencing it. Ratnakīrti, it seems, places a more stringent demand on the concept of appropriation: in order to appropriate a thought to oneself, the thought must identify itself as belonging to one, and not to somebody else. An item of the mind, whether it be a belief or an emotion, is not really mine unless something in its internal form or content identifies itself discriminately as mine and not another's, an identification that cannot consist merely in its being self-reflexively aware of itself.

Why this more stringent requirement on self-appropriation? Perhaps because it is not enough to make my thoughts mine that I think of them as 'mine': we all do that. I must think of my thoughts in some way that uniquely presents them, as my unique possession and branded in some way that uniquely identifies them as mine. And if I am to be able to think of my thoughts as so branded, then the imprimatur must be internally accessible and not merely a function of causal connectedness. Without this, one has no conception of the distinction between one's own thought and that of another.[3]

A worry is raised concerning the omniscience of the Buddha (TEXT 9). If it is necessary to produce an argument in order to establish whether there are other minds or not, then it would seem that the Buddha's own words leave the matter open, and that might imply that he himself did not know. Ratnakīrti maintains, however, that the Buddha knew that there were no other minds, and therefore there was nothing he did not know. Presumably, we explain the apparent acknowledgement of other minds that the production of discourses and sermons implies as an instance of the 'oblique' character of the Buddha's teaching—the aim is to reduce suffering wherever it might occur in the great mass of undivided cognition that is the totality of experience.

If there is no manifest boundary between one mind and another, there is no division of the totality of the mental into distinct psychophysical streams. Ratnakīrti worries with good reason that this brings the Buddhist theory of mind dangerously close to that of the Upaniṣadic and Vedāntic 'soul-theory' (*ātmavāda*), in which there is only one mind, *brahman*, and no real difference between apparently distinct minds (TEXT 10). The only difference now is that the Vedāntic theory regards consciousness as like a single background hum, whereas on the Buddhist theory there is a sequence of discrete momentary consciousness events.

Reflexivism seemed preferable to the mineness-markers of Asaṅga and Vasubandhu insofar as they are too much like a self, that the No Place View collapses into a Minimal Ownership View. Now, however, the full implications of the rejection of their theory have been laid bare. While the earlier thinkers had at least good prospects of being able to draw a distinction between the experiences in the stream which are marked as one's own and those which are marked as another's (and so, for example, to be able to explain the existence of thought insertion), the reflexivist theory is left

[3] If no *concept* of other minds is possible, then neither is the strategy of arguing that belief in other minds while literally false is a convenient fiction; so an appeal to the notorious but philosophically slippery doctrine of 'two truths' will be of no avail against the argument.

without any comparable resource. It is, in the terminology of Chapter 2, an Attenuated theory, and the anxiety which Ratnakīrti voices at the end of his text, that the Yogācāra version of the No Place View effectively collapses into a Pure Consciousness View, is an expression of that very fact.

The Refutation of Other Streams of Consciousness

TEXT 1: *Statement of the Purpose of the Text*

Now this [treatise] is begun in order to determine the existence or non-existence of other streams of consciousness (*santāna*), in the light of the proof of the non-duality of all entities such as blue and yellow from awareness of one's mental representations (as with dreams and hallucinations), once the reality of all material things has been discounted by arguments such as that from the inseparability in awareness of thought and its objects.

TEXT 2: *Dharmakīrti's Argument*

[Dharmakīrti's position] Some say: The existence of other streams is known by inference. Given that there is observation of the phenomena (*ābhāsa*) of language and behaviour immediately after volition (*icchācitta*), and given that they are not observed in the absence of volition, it is known in one's own case that there is a cause-effect relation between the appearance of actions and volition: the relation consisting in the positive and negative concomitances (*anvaya-vyatireka*) established by cognition and non-cognition (*upalambha-anupalambha*). When one observes some separate phenomenon of language and behaviour and there is no awareness of volition in one's own mind, [some other] volition is inferred as its cause. So, another mind is established [by inference].

TEXT 3: *The Argument Refuted*

[Refutation of the inference, by constructive dilemma] Now this is examined. Is the volition that is being established as the cause of the phenomena of language and behaviour something perceptible by the inferrer or is it volition as such, [something] which is independent of the properties of visibility and invisibility?

[First alternative refuted] If we take the first alternative: At the time of inference of volition, given that it is perceptible by the inferrer, what scope is there for an inference of it? Its presence has been excluded by the perception called 'non-observation': as one says: 'non-cognition conveys absence'. And if volition is directly known at the time of inference, what is the point in inference?

Objection: In that case, a person seeing smoke in a mountain-thicket who simultaneously knows the causal relation between fire and smoke would not also infer the fire, since the presence of fire has been excluded by non-observation, and where there is perception, inference is fruitless.

Reply: There is no difficulty here with [the method of proof by] non-observation of the [in principle] perceptible, because the fire, though too far away at the time of inference, is capable of being seen [so we can't say that if it were there, we would see it, as proofs by non-observation require.] And the thesis that non-observation of what is [in principle] imperceptible proves absence is a contradiction [because, if it is imperceptible, non-observation proves nothing.] But in the case of an act of volition, [it cannot be said] that it is too far away. Volition is not spatially inaccessible, for it is observable by the inferrer to whom it is related.

[Second alternative refuted] Now the second alternative: Volition as such, independent of the properties of visibility and invisibility and common to one's own and other streams of consciousness, is understood to be the cause of the phenomena of behaviour and language. By what method of proof is that known? Noticing the absence of the phenomena of language and behaviour in the absence of volition as such, we want to discover their causal connection. It is not possible to understand either by reflexive awareness or by any other means the absence of volition as such as common to one's own and other streams of personality. There is knowledge of the causal relationship between smoke as such and fire as such, albeit inaccessible in space and time, when the inferrer, knowing by sensory perception the absence [of fire] prior to the origin of smoke [no smoke without fire], establishes the necessary causal relation (*tad-utpatti*) between the two and supposes of the conjectural fire as such, inaccessible in space and time, that 'were it present where and when smoke occurs, it would be perceived by me'. But the pervasion (*vyāpti*) does not include fires (e.g. that of digestion) that are by nature inaccessible (*svabhāva-viprakṛṣṭa*), whose absence the inferrer can never know. So, as for volition common to one's own and other streams of personality, if we could imagine that 'were it present it would be perceived by me', then we could comprehend its being a cause by means of a negative proof. But this argument fails if volition as such is inaccessible by nature. And it is not the case that another mind is remote in time since it exists in the present. We treat as remote in time what is past and future. Nor is it spatially remote. Where there is a white shell, one reflexively knows one's own thought having the appearance as a white form. One does not know a thought in another stream of experience appearing in the form of yellow at the same place. So how can this constitute spatial inaccessibility?

Objection: Volition as such is not by nature inaccessible because it is revealed by self-awareness as such. When one fire is seen by a particular sensory perception, another fire is not seen by the same perception. Just as it is established that fire as such is visible by visual perception as such, so volition as such common to one's own and other streams of experience is perceptible by self-awareness as such.

Reply: Is it not the case that what you mean by 'as such' (*mātra*) is intentional human sensory cognition, without any specific connection or lack of connection to a particular inferrer, as long as the possibility of visibility is not ruled out? But in that case, even gremlins would be visible. Nothing would be by nature perceptually inaccessible because even a gremlin is perceptible by some *yogin* or by another gremlin of the same kind. Hence, the expression 'as such' only has the force of abstracting from specific subjective features of a cognition, while retaining a connection with the inferrer. Dharmottara has said: 'The definition of perception takes account of some individual perceiver.'

Thus the condition for perceptibility is—'were a pot present at this place or time, it would certainly be perceived: it would be an object of my objective visual awareness'. But what is not possible is the formulation in relation to another mind: 'were another mind present, it would certainly be an object of my self-awareness'.

[Can we say that volition as such is after all perceptible?] Let us suppose that volition as such is perceptible when we grasp the causal relation. Then at the time of inference also, having supposed its perceptibility, given that there is proof of absence by means of non-observation, how can the inference get off the ground, since the thesis-statement (*pakṣa*) [this is a case of intention] has been blocked by perception? It makes no difference if volition is sometimes radically inaccessible and sometimes not. Hence, given the impossibility of supposing perceptibility of volition as such common to one's own and other streams of experience, how may one infer the proof of causality using an argument where the effect (action) is the logical reason (*hetu*) because one does not know that the absence of action is invariably connected with the absence of will, even if there is non-cognition of (volition) prior to the production of action.

A particular volition occurring in one's own stream is not perceptible by the inferrer. Moreover, as has been stated already, how can there be inference when the probandum has been ruled out by the non-cognition of the perceptible?

TEXT 4: *Summary*

So if [Alternative 1] what is to be inferred is a particular volition belonging to one's own stream, the inference is trumped by a perception; if [Alternative 2] what is to be inferred is volition as such common to one's own and other streams, then if [2a] it is known to be absence at the time when the causal connection is established by means of a non-observation as such not specifying whether it is perceptible, there is the very same defect in the thesis. But if [2b] it is not known, then the inference from behaviour etc. is based on a bogus reason, [namely having] doubtful negative correlation.

TEXT 5: *Refutation of Other Streams*

Since there is no proof of other streams of consciousnesss, and no disproof is found either, some people say, 'just let there be doubt on this point'. They should attend to the disproof that is about to be stated.

[A. There is a difference]. If there were another stream, there would, of necessity, be a difference between it and one's own stream. Otherwise, between one's own manifest stream and what is considered as the other stream, there would be no difference. But neither can one say that there is an identity between them. It follows that the other stream, unable to be either identical or different from one's own stream, is [absolutely] non-existent in the same way as is the hare's horn and the universal [and so incapable of being a relatum of either relation]. So how can there be a state of indecision?

[B. The difference has to be manifest, because it is what individuates streams]. Let it be, then, that there certainly is a difference between one's own stream in relation to another stream. This difference certainly should be manifest when one's own stream is manifest, as it is the very being (*svabhāva*) of a stream. How otherwise could it be settled that the difference between one's own and another stream is what constitutes their very being, even if there is a superimposition of contradictory properties marked by matter and consciousness [i.e. the Advaita theory].

[C. The difference is not manifest]. But this difference is not manifested. For if the differences were thought to be manifest, the other stream would incontrovertibly be manifest too, as its boundary. One should remember here everything said [by Jñānaśrīmitra] in his *Pravacana-pradīpa-śrī-sākāra-saṃgraha*, such as the following:

> 'If one thinks that the very being of one's own mind (*cetas*) is to be different from this [other mind], it should appear along with a boundary; otherwise, it is not cognized in itself.'
>
> 'There isn't even the shadow of a difference [between one's own and another mind represented in one's own]—so from what is it [one's own mind] different?'[4]

Just as when only one's own stream of experiences is manifest, difference from a non-manifest hare's horn does not appear, so likewise difference from a non-manifest other stream does not appear. Not even the slightest difference appears between one's own and another stream, just as there is none between one's own mind and a hare's horn. In the case of one's own experience, the hare's horn and another mind are on a par. It is not the case that either difference or non-difference

[4] Jñānaśrīmitra (1959).

appears in relation to the hare's horn, and similarly it is not possible to establish that difference appears in relation to another stream.

Just as a discrete object is established by removing the absences of similar and dissimilar things, in the same way it is right to say that there is representation of difference as distinct from representations of absences of similar and dissimilar things. But experience is not like that. If you insist that difference appears, that is just a manner of speaking. On this point the Bhāṣyakāra's (i.e. Prajñākaragupta's) comprehensive argument in the *Bheda-pratibhāṣa-dūṣaṇa* is to be understood.

TEXT 6: *External objects and other minds*

And even if there is no representation of difference, awareness of difference is to be admitted because we feel compassion for other minds, then how is the non-existence of physical objects proved?

It is possible to introduce a problem here also: if you say, 'external objects do not appear to anyone, but one stream of experiences appears to another, so there is no doubt about physical objects', we reply that all of this is problematic because it is also possible to say, 'one stream does not necessarily appear to another' and 'perhaps it does not exist' and 'it does not appear'. Moreover, even if physical objects do not appear to anyone, still how can the person subscribing to the theory that there is representation of difference prove their non-existence? This trivial point must be stressed here! And there is no defect in our argument. Hence, given that we are all idealists agreeing about the status of physical objects, how can you say that there are other streams of consciousness?

TEXT 7: *The reality of causation*

Moreover, the person who accepts that there is representation of difference between two minds cannot deny the reality of the causal relation. If a prior awareness grasps both its difference from a later awareness and its own priority, even without any representation of a boundary, and a later awareness grasps its difference from its predecessor as well as its own subsequent nature, as in the case of awareness of other streams, then the cause-effect relation is manifest and is comprehended, like any experienced form, as obtaining between earlier and later cognitions. So how in your opinion can Dharmakīrti's statement that the causal relation is a conventional construct be significant?

Moreover, how can you, who accept the apprehension of difference and do not question the existence of other streams of consciousness, escape from an opponent who asserts that mental content is void of perception grasping difference and adduces the reason 'illuminating' to prove that the sphere of experiences is uniform?

But you might say: by what means of knowledge is the non-existence of other streams of consciousness proved? Not in the first place by perception, whose object is positive realities, since it lacks the capacity to prove negatives. Nor by inference which is restricted to proving the possibly visible and which is incapable of proving the non-existence of another mind which is trans-empirical.

We reply: If there were another stream of experience, it would be a determinate entity from which one's own mind is different. Were it non-different from one's own stream, there would just be the other stream. When something that is being cognized does not appear as having a certain form, it is not appropriately treated as real in that form - as we do not treat a blue object in the same way as a yellow one. When one's own mind is being cognized, it is not apprehended as different in form from another stream of experiences [so it cannot be practically treated as such]. This inference is a case of 'the non-observation of an X' (*svabhāva-anupalabdhi*), independent of considerations of perceptibility, for the refutation of difference [from another mind] as belonging to the nature of one's own mind.

The reason here is not unestablished, because where there is representation of difference, there is representation of a boundary. But where there is no representation of a boundary, it is established that there is no representation of difference—as in the case of the absence of representation of difference from the hare's horn.

TEXT 8: *Summary*

Given that difference between one's own mind and another stream of consciousness has been rejected and given the self-evident impossibility of their identity, this proof establishes the indeterminability as different or non-different [of another mind from one's own].

How can doubt be entertained regarding other streams of consciousness on the grounds of absence of a disproof, considering that they are void of substantial reality like universals?

This little work has been written only to remind people of the topics dealt with in the learned works.

TEXT 9: *The problem of the Buddha's omniscience*

Moreover, you accept that there is an everyday problem about other streams of consciousness. What does the Buddha say? If he is in doubt, how is he omniscient? He never affirmed that there are other streams. So how can we say that he is omniscient? We have already considered the inference about other streams. Even if another mind were known by inference, this would not merit the ascription of omniscience. If the Buddha knows other minds by perception, there is a subject-object relation between his mind and other minds, and there is an acceptance of mind-independent objects by the back door. How can the theory escape these objections?

TEXT 10: *Conclusion*

According to our theory it is certain that other minds do not exist and the defect that the Buddha's omniscience is destroyed is absent. Insofar as our comments operate for the resolution of doubt concerning the existence of other minds on the part of those subject to the misconception belonging to the conventional outlook that there is apprehension of difference, we do not contradict ourselves. It is not in fact our opinion that there is never a problem concerning other streams of consciousness. But this treatise is offered at the level of ultimate truth. Because this argument for the non-existence of other streams of consciousness is of the same kind as the proof of non-duality of awareness, self-contradiction or its removal are not on the same level. The obfuscatory nature of the Vedānta doctrine has been exposed by the Bhāṣyakāra [Prajñākaragupta] simply by the proof that all form is internal to awareness. He says so in his commentary on Dharmakīrti's verse: 'The nature of perception is awareness of itself and not of anything else' [*Pramāṇavārttika, Pratyakṣapariccheda* 326].

If you say that belief in the self follows, we reply 'no' because there is awareness of the diversity of forms as internal to consciousness. What was not noticed by the Bhāṣyakāra is that the Vedānta doctrines, albeit superficially attractive, are a load of hateful rubbish: every apparently plausible hypothesis stemming from their books belongs to the conventional outlook because they taught on the assumption of the existence of other minds. So it leads to total confusion.

The Refutation of Other Streams is [hereby] completed.

Reflexivism Entails Conceptual Solipsism

Buddhists seek a naturalism that steers a middle course between a supernaturalist commitment to souls (Cartesian purely psychological individuals), on the one hand, and on the other Animalism, which, in taking the reference of 'I' to be the biological human being, is felt to leave insufficient scope for soteriology. The question before us is whether this pair of commitments has left them able to explain the structure of the representation of self in consciousness.

For one Buddhist thinker, Ratnakīrti, an inability to explain how *others* appear in one's own consciousness is the inevitable consequence of a reflexivist theory of mind. One way to make Ratnakīrti's point vivid would be to imagine that every individual reflexive experience is laid out in a single array, and that some way to partition this domain of experience is presented. If someone were then to ask the question 'Which partition am I?', there would, it seems, be no non-arbitrary answer. One has foresworn answering that question by referring to anything functioning as the *owner* of all and only one's own mental states, and one has also disavowed any answer that appeals to the individual human animal upon whose physical states all and only one's own mental states supervene. Reflexivist representational theories seem to lack any means by which to answer the question 'Which one am I?' Each experience comes, as it were, with a little mirror in which it can regard itself and its reflections of itself; but within these halls of mirrors there is nothing to reflect apart from nested images of the mirrors themselves (see also Ismael 2007, 2011). Ratnakīrti has argued that the Yogācāra theory does not meet this condition, since reflexively self-aware moments of experience do not supply materials either for the conception of a boundary between one's own experiences and those of another or for its phenomenal presentation. If the conclusion were simply that there are no selves, then a reflexivist might be happy to go with the flow of the argument. The problem, however, is much deeper: it is whether a mind constructed in accordance according to reflexivist principles would actually be able to sustain first-person phenomena (whether or not those phenomena are subsequently catalogued as illusory, fictitious, or in some other way erroneous).

Castañeda's work on the logic of self-consciousness can help to achieve a sharper focus here. Castañeda has pointed out that indirect discourse makes use of constructions for reporting speech that would be expressed by the speaker in the first person. The phrase 'he himself' is a construction of this sort. A piece of indirect discourse like 'Devadatta thought that he would go to the market' is strictly ambiguous as between a report of Devadatta's thinking that *he himself* would go to the market and Devadatta's thinking, of some other person, that he—that other person—would go. Castañeda introduces a typographical convention, now widely adopted, to disambiguate the two readings, marking the pronoun with an asterix when the first use is in play: 'Devadatta thought that he* would go to the market.' Baker's 'strong first-person phenomena' consist in the ability to have thoughts which are expressible by way of this reflexive personal pronoun, and she extends the typographical convention to include uses of the first person:

Following Hector-Neri Castañeda, I'll put an asterix beside a pronoun to signal that it is an attribution of first-person reference. Call a sentence an ' "I*" sentence' if it is of this form: 'I *f* that I* . . . ' where '*f*' is replaced by a linguistic or psychological verb and 'I* . . . ' is replaced by a sentence containing a first-person reference . . . An 'I*' thought is one in which the thinker conceives of herself as herself*, without identifying herself by means of any third-person referential device, such as a name, description, or demonstrative. 'I' is not a name for myself: I can use any name competently and still be mistaken about whose name it is. But I am never mistaken about who is picked out by my competent uses of 'I.' If I entertain an 'I*' thought, I do not have to identify the person I am thinking about; nor can I mistakenly believe that I am thinking about someone else. The ability to entertain 'I*' thoughts—thoughts that attribute to oneself first-person reference in indirect discourse—is the ability to conceive of oneself as oneself* . . . In short, S can think of herself as herself* if and only if S can think of herself in a way naturally expressible in the grammatical first person as the bearer of first-person thoughts . . . An ability to conceive of oneself as oneself* in the sense just described is both necessary and sufficient for the strong grade of first-person phenomena. (Baker 1998: 330–1)

Baker observes that the ability to conceive of oneself as oneself* implies several other abilities:

If one can think of oneself as the bearer of first-person thoughts, then one has the concept of a subject of thought and can think of others as subjects of thought. If one can think of oneself as oneself*, then, in addition to having desires (say), one can reflect on one's desires *as one's own* . . . To be able to think of oneself as oneself is not just to have a perspective or subjective point of view—dogs have perspectives—but also to be able to think of one's perspective as one's own, and to think of others as having different subjective points of view from one's own. (Baker 1998: 330)

The conjectured argument against the reflexivist theory of mind can now be restated. It is that in depriving the subject of the conceptual resources for genuine first-person reference, the subject has also been deprived of two abilities that are constitutive of a first-person stance, the ability to conceive of one's experience as *one's own*, and the ability to conceive of *other subjects* of self-conscious experience.

Castañeda introduces a new idea, the idea of an '*I*-strand', further to understand the phenomenon. By an '*I*-strand' Castañeda has in mind any one of the contrasts that partly constitute self-consciousness, such as the contrast between *I* and *you*, or between *I* and *it*. He decomposes the phenomenological structure of self-consciousness into patterns of such *I*-strand contrasts, where an intermingling of *I*-strands 'yields a spiralic process of steady enrichment of one's concept of *I*':

> *I*-strands hinge on contrasts between what one is qua oneself and something one is not. Alternatively phrased, an *I*-strand is the polar negation of something intrinsically non-*I*. Thus an *I*-schema [a bundle of *I*-strands] is a complex of negativities. To gain the concept of *I* is to acquire the capacity to pick out immediately instances of one or more of these polar negations. This instantiation is of course confronted by thinking of oneself qua oneself... To think of oneself as oneself is to think of something intimated to be (felt, as it were) the opposite of each of such and such [non-*I*s]... To apprehend oneself in the content (...*I*...) is to apprehend a manifold of polar negations of the different non-*I*s as one fully unified manifold of *I*-strands... The empirical contents of episodes of self-consciousness fall, then, within one or more of the negativities composing the *I*-strands. (Castañeda 1999: 275–6)

On the basis of this range of *I*/non-*I* contrasts, Castañeda is able to construct a hierarchy of levels of consciousness, ranging from mere sentience, through object perception, to what he calls '*I*-owned content':

1. sensory content, conceptually inarticulated: (a) bodily; (b) worldly
2. *I*-less articulated content pertaining to: (a) external objects; (b) bodily content; (c) occurring mental acts
3. *I*-less focal consciousness, the core of which is a complex of perceptual judgments
4. *I*-owned content articulating the contrast between Self and Object
5. *I*-owned content articulating intentional agency
6. *I*-owned content articulating the contrast between Self and others
7. *I*-owned content articulating an interaction between Self and you as well as absent persons. (Castañeda 1999: 278)

Levels 1, 2, and 3 correspond to the feature-placing and object-invoking levels I described in Chapter 10. As for the content of *I*-owned experience, Castañeda describes it as involving a network of internal structural relations, in particular, the relations of co-consciousness, co-integration, meta-integration, and subjection (1999: 284). Dharmakīrti points out something which Castañeda does not notice, the possibility of consciousness involving constructed quasi-subjects (a level 3.5 between 3 and 4). Castañeda's primary ambition is to formulate a framework within which different sorts of pathological disturbance can be classified. Different interminglings lead to the emergence of a variety of types of self-presentation, from the solipsist to the deist to the mystic: 'Solipsists find the total world at large to be merely experiental content of the only accessible *I* [while] mystics raise themselves up to the status of partial *Is* within an all-encompassing one' (Castañeda 1999: 277). *I*-owned content is what is needed for the two abilities logically necessitated by an ability to conceive of oneself as oneself★.

Castañeda's analysis of the structure of self-consciousness, with its emphasis on contrastive exclusion and on levels of pre-conceptual and conceptual articulation, is clearly very much in the spirit of the Buddhist approach I have set out in earlier chapters. He is keen to stress, moreover, that for him the phenomenally presented *Is* 'are evanescent subjective particulars existing only within and during episodes of self-consciousness' (1999: 288). However, he takes it that the theory is flexible enough also to explain more enduring forms of self-presentation:

> No permanent *I* underlies the history of a person. There exist successions of ephemeral *Is*, some of which are interlocking, overlapping because specious presents are overlapping. As long as there is a continuous consciousness from time t to time t' there could be an encompassing *I* that endures from t to t'. Yet there need by no such *I*. It all depends on the degree of organization of the experience of each moment during the interval (t, t'), and on how much overlapping and integration by co-consciousness and meta-integration the successive experiences have. The crucial ontological point is that the *Is*, exactly like all other indexical individuals, are ephemeral and subjective. They exist in the present. They link the person who has the experiences with the objective world... An *I* is the creation of a process of a thinking episode that includes co-consciousness of the unity of the thinking and its contents (1999: 247).

Buddhist theorists do not countenance an idea of the 'specious present' or 'extended now' and will not admit even short-lived *Is*, which for Castañeda are the result of overlappings and interlockings within short but extended intervals of time.[5] Ratnakīrti's argument is thus that reflexivism is unable to

[5] The phrase 'specious present', due to E. R. Clay, was made popular by William James, who defined it as 'the time duration wherein one's perceptions are considered to be in the present', and as 'the short duration of which we are immediately aware' (James 1890: 609). James quotes Clay as saying that 'time, considered relatively to human apprehension, consists of four parts, viz. the obvious past, the specious present, the real present, and the future. Omitting the specious present, it consists of three nonentities—the past, the future, and their conterminous, the present'.

countentance *I*-strands as genuine tropes of experiential content, reflexive self-consciousness being something akin to the solipsistic *I*, an *I*-schema in which the contrast between self and other remains unarticulated within the content of a thinker's consciousness.

This result is in tension with the Yogācāra claim to give an account of the phenomenological structure of self-consciousness. The great attraction of the Yogācāra theory lies in its claim to give a phenomenologically adequate description of the mind without metaphysical commitment. That claim, though, is precisely what has now been brought into question. A theory that cannot explain the possibility of *I**-thought also cannot explain the phenomenology of ownership, the phenomenology of presented other subjects of experience, and the phenomenology of a presented external world. While there is an acknowledgement of the third point in the Yogācāra move towards idealism, as far as I am aware among Yogācāra Buddhist thinkers only Ratnakīrti appreciates the force of the second point.

That reflexivism entails conceptual solipsism is acknowledged in non-Yogācāra sources. The Kashmiri Śaiva philosophers Utpaladeva, Abhinavagupta, and Rāmakaṇṭha appropriate Buddhist Yogācāra reflexivism but transform it into a constitutive theory of immersed self: the immersed self just is that which consists of reflexive self-consciousness. Abhinavagupta states clearly that this view implies conceptual solipsism, an implication he however seems to welcome.[6] The reflexivist Phenomenal or Pure Consciousness View of Kashmiri Śaivism is, in my terminology, severely Attenuated.[7]

[6] 'Even another person's awareness is one's own self... Thus at the level of ultimate truth all knowers in the world are only one knower, and he alone exists' (*para-jñānam svātmā eva . . . viśvaḥ pramātṛvargaḥ paramārthataḥ ekaḥ pramātā, se eva ca asti* | Abhinavagupta 1938: i. 102).

[7] Williford (2011) discusses Attenuation in connection with Sartre's analysis of self as a stream of non-objectifying reflexive consciousness. He argues that Sartre's is neither a no-ownership account (ownership consisting in the self existing as a 'for-itself') nor a form of Cartesianism (the existence of an ego qua entity is denied), that Sartre provides a 'third way' between the competing Humean and Cartesian traditions. He makes Ratnakīrti's point when he says that streams are not individuated by 'any special, phenomenologically available individuators immanent in them'; for Sartre they are rather 'individuated by their very nature'. Williford's depiction of Sartre is a good description of what I have called the Phenomenal View.

The Composition of Self-Consciousness

Does the non-reflexivist theory of pre-Dignāga Buddhist thinkers fare better? The fundamental idea is that the basic structure of mind is one of sub-experiential processes in combination (Chapter 7). Rather than interpret the theory as bearing directly on the mind-body problem, one may instead construe it as issuing from a standpoint of 'phenomeno-logic', the standpoint from which what comes into view is the compositional structure of phenomenal experience and conscious intention. This perspective allows one to describe *presented* relations of regular succession between contents, but the method does not give one third-person access to genuine causal relations. The Buddhist theory of 'dependent origination' (*pratītya-samutpāda*) can also be interpreted in this light, not as a theory of causation but as a description of phenomenal regularities in *perceived* time. In terms of Husserl's distinction, within phenomenology, between transcendental phenomenology and phenomenological psychology (Husserl 1927), the description of the approach as 'phenomeno-logical' should be taken to mean seeing it as falling firmly but exclusively within phenomenological psychology.[8] Much contemporary research into Buddhist philosophy of mind has been conducted rather within a framework of naturalization, seeking a hard naturalist rapprochement with contemporary science.[9] The fundamental intuition driving this research is that ownership is not itself a natural relation, and that only a no-self theory is naturalistically respectable. I have argued that this is, ironically, a deeply Cartesian intuition, and not one which is shared by the philosophers of first-millenium India. I believe it is more correct to regard the theory rather as providing a compositional phenomenological psychology. An important virtue is that this approach allows for a partial alignment between Vasubandhu's earlier work in Abhidharma and his later Yogācāra writings.[10] The point is that the earlier compositional theory of

[8] I am happy to find Bodhi (1993: 4) expressing the same idea with a clear if implicit reference to Husserl: '[Abhidharma is] a "phenomenological psychology" [whose] primary concern is to understand the nature of experience, and thus the reality on which it focuses is conscious reality, the world as given in experience.' Yogācāra epistemology represents an incorporation of transcendental phenomenology, insofar as it begins to concern itself with the conditions for the possibility of knowledge.

[9] Varela et al. (1991); Wallace (2003, 2007); Siderits (2003); Thompson (2007); Flanagan (2011).

[10] There are other proposals. Coseru (2012) argues that the relation is captured by saying that Yogācāra epistemology is naturalized by Abhidharma psychology, while Arnold (2012) tries to read Yogācāra in a causal-reductionist framework.

intentionality (the doctrine of *skandha*), read phenomenologically and not as a contribution to the mind-body problem, is now available to his later work on the phenomenological structure of self-consciousness.

The notion of a mineness-marker (*manas*) is proposed by Asaṅga and Vasubandhu as an explanation of first-person phenomena. Mineness-markers are intertwined in a stream of experience, tokens of 'mineness' running through the flow of experience and generating a sense of ownership in the stream's conscious attention to its own constituents by drawing on information in a first-personal mental file, the repository consciousness (*ālaya-vijñāna*). Consider this revised schema for the structure of self-consciousness:

Self-consciousness has an internal, contentual cumulative hierarchical structure:

(1) conceptually unarticulated sensory consciousness
(2) egoless, or better, *I*-less, articulated consciousness of objects
(3) unowned consciousness of occurring mental episodes
(4) *I*-consciousness (Castañeda 1999: 245).

The theory under discussion fits this hierarchy rather well. Stage (1) is that of embodied reacting (*rūpa*), hedonic appraising (*vedanā*), labelling (*saṃjñā*) and constructing (*saṃskāra*); stage (2) is that of consciously attending to objects (*viṣaya-vijñāna*); stage (3) is that of consciously attending to items in the stream (*mano-vijñāna*); and stage (4) is *manas*, the mineness which anchors phenomenal self-presentation. The entire point of Vasubandhu's later theory is to provide an explanation of the move from (3) to (4), from one part of the stream attending to another part to what is properly called self-consciousness, the possession of a first-person stance (the move articulated in Dignga's theory in the distinction between attending to a past subject-aspect and being reflexively self-aware; Chapter 8). For Vasubandhu the inhabitation of a first-person stance consists in the way one's states access stored information about oneself. It will follow that the different sorts of contrast between mine and not mine which constitute the various types of *I*-strand owe their distinctness to different ways of accessing such information and the different sorts of information accessed. In a fully integrated psyche the whole of a mental life is potentially able to bear within every state, whether that state be an emotion, a belief, or an intention to act. That is what it is fully to inhabit a first-person stance.

Where does this leave the error-theory of self-consciousness? *I*-strands overlap and interlock because they are phenomenal 'nows' in the specious present, and they amalgamate according to 'structural relations that subordinate an experience to a subject, that is, through which an *I* is posited, or hypostatised' (Castañeda 1999: 247). These are the relations that define the moment of transition from mere consciousness of one's mental states to consciousness of them *as one's own*. For Castañeda the *I* is not robust: it is a 'presentational occurrent', a 'unique, ephemeral, and irreducible representation', something 'fleeting, lasting only as long as the presentation (the experience) lasts' (Castañeda 1999: 264). Overlapping and interlocking in the specious present, however, makes possible in non-pathological cases the 'subordination of an experience to a subject'. So now the issue can be restated in this way: the point at which Buddhist theory imports an error-theory is the point at which the structuring relations that are constitutive of the subordination of an experience to a subject are branded pathological (*kliṣṭa*). Central to the pathologicization of self is the refusal to access the concept of a phenomenologically extended 'now', to maintain a strict version of presentism. I believe that the integration of content across different sensory modalities is the key factor in the 'subordination' of experience to a subject, and that so far from being pathological it is essential to the unity of consciousness of human beings with normal psychologies. There is impressive empirical experimental data seeming to support this claim, including the so-called 'rubber hand illusion' (see Tsakiris 2010, 2011) and studies of the emergence of a sense of self in child development (Meltzoff 1990, 1993a, 1993b). Without pathologicization, what one has is an attractive analysis of what I earlier labelled the immersed self, the subject as presented in self-consciousness (somewhat akin to the one entertained in Peacocke 2014).

In earlier chapters of this book I began to explore the relationship between consciousness and embodiment. At the end of Chapter 6 I said that we needed a more differentiated description of the intentional and phenomenological structure of self-consciousness if we are to understand the demands imposed by embodiment on the possession of a first-person stance, and conversely the implications of such a possession for embodiment. My review of the Buddhist discussion over the course of the last five chapters has presented us with a good deal of the depth and diversity of description that was missing. What I will be arguing in the coming chapters, however, is that embodied unconscious mechanisms make available cross-modal identities, and these are what render intelligible the possibility of binding and the 'subjection' of experience to subjects. The emergence of both selves and an objective conception of the world has its basis here. That is to say, no theory of immersed selfhood, no matter how accurate to the phenomenology, can be adequate without an understanding of its relationship to what I call the 'underself'. I will also now commence my investigation into a third dimension of selfhood, one that has so far not made an appearance. This is the 'participant self', the idea of self grounded in the recognition that ownership has among its component strands a dimension that embeds it directly in the space of reasons.

PART IV

Participation and the First-Person Stance

12

The Mind-Body Problem

If facts about the ownership of a mental life are not to be relegated to the level of the merely phenomenal they give reasons to think that there are such things as selves. It is then a further issue whether exemplification in a self is sufficient to individuate a strongly first-personal mental life, or whether the question of individuation refers to another set of considerations, such as the relationship between a mental life and a physical body. The conception of self articulated by philosophers in Nyāya and Vaiśeṣika affirms the reality of selves but is neither Cartesian nor Animalist: the self they propose is neither metaphysically independent of the body nor identical with it. Human beings have a mental life that depends essentially for its existence and individuation on its being embodied; but the owner of that mental life, the self, is not the body: it is a distinct but dependent existence. My aim now is to add detail to such a view about the nature and role of the self. A range of considerations purport to tell against the idea that mental properties are properties of the body (this chapter), and they are supplemented by an explanatory model of the dependencies that nevertheless obtain between mental and physical states (Chapter 13). In the work of these philosophers there can also be found a powerful further analysis of the nature of emotions and their role in determining relations of common ownership (Chapter 14), and a sophisticated analysis of the unity of consciousness (Chapter 15). The distinctness between selves receives clarification in the early modern period, where it becomes central to a defence of individual autonomy (Chapter 16). In the Conclusion I will reaffirm that the notion of ownership in play is that of endorsement rather than causal agency. In terms of my earlier distinction between procedural, immersed, and participant selves, the discussion of 'self' in these next chapters is a defence of the reality of the participant self.

Minimal Physicalism: An Ownership View

In some of his writings about the mind-body problem, Jaegwon Kim envisages a possibility in the philosophy of mind, a position which combines a commitment to dualism with an endorsement of supervenience of the mental on the physical:

Consider the radical dual-substance Cartesians: they are likely to take exception to the reading I gave above of [weak and strong supervenience] in which persons, or human bodies or organisms, are taken to instantiate both physical and psychological characteristics; they will contend that these two classes of properties call for disjoint sets of exemplifiers, that is, material and mental substances . . . But, in spite of their dual-substance ontology, some of these Cartesians may be prepared to hold that what happens in the realm of souls is entirely dependent on what happens in the realm of bodies. We thus face the task of making sense of a supervenience relation involving two domains of individuals, something that could suit the needs of these improbable but not unintelligible Cartesians. (1988: 132)

Kim goes on to show exactly how to construct multiple-domain supervenience in terms of a 'coordinating relation' which associates individuals in the base domain with individuals in the supervening domain, before explaining why, in his opinion, the view is improbable:

Let us turn to the case in which the coordinating relation is one-one. Such may be what some dual-substance Cartesians might envisage for souls and human bodies: each human soul 'animates' one unique human body, and each living human body is animated by one unique soul. For them, [weak and strong multiple-domain supervenience] can provide useful vehicles for formulating doctrines of supervenience: the character of a soul supervenes on the physical nature of its body. I said earlier that a position of this sort is intelligible if not plausible. We now know, it might seem, how to be a physicalist—that is, recognise the primacy of the physical—and keep Cartesian souls, too. The position is at least logically consistent, and our multiple-domain supervenience (with a one-one R) displays its metaphysical structure. But does it have any plausibility at all? This is not the place to argue the merits of mind-body theories, but it seems evident that the usual simplicity considerations may strongly incline us against it, leading us to do away with a separate domain of souls altogether (that is, identifying them with their one-one correlated human bodies). This move does not lead to the elimination of mentality from the world; psychological properties would now be attributed to human bodies and other appropriate organisms. (1988: 144–5)

If simplicity considerations constitute one argument in favour of the view that mental and physical properties are both to be attributed to the human body, in another paper Kim seems to offer a different sort of consideration. He observes that supervenience is not itself a relation of metaphysical dependence but simply one of property covariation, and that in particular mind-body supervenience is not an explanatory theory. What a solution to the mind-body problem must offer is an *explanatory* account of the pattern of covariation between mental and physical characteristics which are described when we say that a supervenience relation holds between them. He then continues:

> Mind-body supervenience captures a commitment common to all approaches to the nature of mentality that are basically physicalistic. For it represents the idea that mentality is at bottom physically based, an idea that can be shared by many diverse positions on the mind-body problem, from reductive type physicalism at one extreme to dualistic emergentism and epiphenomenalism at the other. In contrast, mind-body supervenience is inconsistent with radical forms of dualism, e.g. Descartes' dualism, which allow the mental world to float freely, unconstrained by the physical domain. Thus, mind-body supervenience can serve as a useful dividing line: it defines a *minimal physicalism*.[1] Cartesian substance dualism pictures the world as consisting of two independent spheres, the mental and the material, each with its own distinctive defining properties (consciousness and spatial extendedness respectively). There are causal interactions across the domains, but entities in each domain, being 'substances', are ontologically independent of those of the other. What has replaced this picture of a dichotomised world is the familiar multilayered model that views the world as stratified into different 'levels', 'orders', or 'tiers,' organised in a hierarchical structure. (1998: 191)

Kim does not refer, in this passage, to the 'implausible but not unintelligible' view discussed before, but only to a Cartesianism in which mind and body are metaphysically independent substances. A second objection to that view might nevertheless be that although qualifying as a minimal physicalism, it can offer no *explanation* of the multiple-domain supervenience which it claims to obtain between mental and physical substances.

What Kim calls 'minimal physicalism' is in my terminology a supervenience-based version of the Ownership View, the view that questions of ownership and questions of dependence have to be kept apart. Were it

[1] The phrase 'minimal materialism' is used by Lewis (1983: 361) in the same sense.

not for the difficulties just noted, such a view might be thought to have several important advantages. First, unlike Cartesianism, there is no implication that the mind can survive uncorrelated to any physical body. The theory therefore escapes the charge of supernaturalism, directed against the hypothesis of purely immaterial thinking substances. Second, again unlike real Cartesianism, there is no special problem about the interaction between mental and the physical realms, even if it has no better answer to general problems about mental causation that afflict any supervenience-based variety of physicalism. The crucial mistake of Cartesianism consists in its failure to acknowledge that there can be *metaphysical dependences* between distinct domains of individuals. In separating matters of ownership from issues about dependence, this version of the Ownership View is, furthermore, at an advantage as compared with 'non-Cartesian' substance dualist accounts in which supervenience is abandoned (e.g. Lowe 2008).

A supervenience-based Ownership View faces two challenges. The first is to give reasons to prefer a world-view with distinct but dependent domains of individuals to a picture in which there are layers or tiers of properties, all possessed by one single domain of individuals, for example human bodies. It needs to justify its claim that mental properties are first-order properties of minds rather than higher-order physical properties (functionalism). It must also distinguish itself from any view which regards mental properties as first-order non-physical properties of physical entities (property dualism). Kim's claim that the theory is implausible rests, it seems, on the thought that a multiple-tiers world-view is one of greater metaphysical simplicity than a many-domains world-view: why posit selves when higher-order functional properties will do the job? But considerations about simplicity are *ceteris paribus*—they come into play only when the two theories between which one is choosing are otherwise equal. It is not the case that the simplest theory is always the best theory—other theoretical advantages can outweigh simplicity. So one way to meet this first challenge is by negative dialectic: to provide theoretical reasons in favour of the hypothesis that mental properties cannot be properties of any physical entity such as a body. I will spend the remainder of this chapter examining reasons of this sort.

The second, and more fundamental, challenge for this Ownership View is to give an explanatory account of the multiple-domain supervenience of the mental on the physical. This is the positive or constructive part of the challenge which the view must face, a challenge to which I shall return in the next chapter.

Supervenience Again

Versions of the view are presented in the work of several Nyāya and Vaiśeṣika thinkers, achieving considerable sophistication and subtlety. That this philosophy of mind is an Ownership View is evident from an important passage early in the *Nyāya-sūtra*, one which has formal resemblances with the opening statements of Bṛhaspati's *Cārvāka-sūtra*:

The characteristic marks of the self are pleasure and pain, desire and dread, cognition and will. The body is the base (*āśraya*) of actions, the senses and the objects (*artha*). The senses—of smell, taste, sight, touch and hearing—arise out of the material elements (*bhūtebhyaḥ*). The material elements are earth, water, fire, wind and æther. Smells, tastes, colours, tactiles and sounds, the qualities of earth and the other elements, are the 'objects'. (*Nyāya-sūtra* 1.1.10–14)

Desire, dread, pleasure, and pain are the familiar ancient quadrad of emotional states. Along with cognition and will (*prayatna*), they are properties characteristic of the mental. The body, on the other hand, is the base of the five senses themselves, physical actions, and of sensible qualities. Comparing this statement with the corresponding remarks of Bṛhaspati, we can observe a shared interest in the metaphysical relationship that body, senses, objects, and consciousness have to the material elements. However, whereas for Bṛhaspati the body, senses, and objects are *resultant* combinations of elements, and consciousness an *emergent* property of the body, here it is the senses which emerge from the material elements that constitute the body, while the self provides a distinct location for mental properties. The self is an individual subject of consciousness not identical to the body.[2] One other evident feature of the text is that, whereas Bṛhaspati spoke only of 'consciousness' (*caitanya*), without drawing any distinctions, we see here a much greater sensitivity to the various different types of psychological property.

A variety of arguments are offered in favour of the claim that mental properties are not properties of physical bodies, and I will examine them in

[2] *Nyāya-sūtra* 3.2.18–31.

detail in the next section. Before that I want to consider the evidence for this being a supervenience-based account. The most telling fact is what is said about the nature of disembodied existence. The firm claim is that disembodiment, although allowed as a formal possibility, would not sustain a capacity to instantiate any mental properties at all:

[Objector:] 'In the final state, disconnected from anything, even what is good will be taken away—what sensible person would want this final state, unconscious and cut off from all pleasure?' . . .

[Reply:] What sensible person would not want a final state cut off from all pain and unaware of any pain? (Vātsyāyana 1997: 6,17–18 and 8,1–2)

There is no good argument that a self without a body experiences enjoyment (*bhoga*). (Vātsyāyana 1997: 23,16-17)

Liberation consists only in the pure existence (*svarūpa-sthiti*) of the self, as characterised by its separation (*uccheda*) from the distinctive qualities (*viśeṣa-guṇa*) with which the self is normally associated. (Śrīdhara 1984: 287,15–16)

Descartes claimed that the self is an immaterial substance which is capable of conscious thinking whether or not it is embodied.[3] The Naiyāyika agrees that the self is an entity, in at least the sense that it is the exemplar of cognitive and affective properties (the 'distinctive qualities' of selves) as well as of properties also exemplified by non-mental physical objects ('general qualities' like spatiality, temporality, countability). Naiyāyikas do hold too that *something* can continue to exist in a discarnate state, but they add that in such a condition of disembodied existence, this *something* is incapable of conscious thought of any kind, either sentience or intellectual activity.[4] Having a body is a necessary condition for there to be a subject of experience and thought, even if it is not considered to be a necessary condition for the merely formal existence of some attenuated entity, the sort of entity about which Strawson said that 'at the limit of attenuation there is, from the point of view of his survival as an individual, no difference between the

[3] '[M]y essence consists solely in the fact that I am a thinking thing. It is true that I may have (or, to anticipate, that I certainly have) a body that is very closely joined to me. But nevertheless, on the one hand I have a clear and distinct idea of myself, in so far as I am simply a thinking, non-extended thing; and on the other I have a distinct idea of body, in so far as this is simply an extended, non-thinking thing. And accordingly, it is certain that I am really distinct from my body, and can exist without it.' (Descartes AT 78; 1984: ii. 54).

[4] Thus: *śarīrātmasaṃyogādivyāpāratve 'pi janyajñānamātre hetutayā* (Mahādeva 1930: 95: 'A connection between the self and the body . . . is the generic cause of all cognitions.)'

continuance of experience and its cessation' (P. F. Strawson 1963: 116). Without a body, there are no senses, and so no possibility in particular of perceptual experience.[5] Might it be the case that although this is true for perceptual experience, it is not true for higher-order intellectual activities? The idea is considered but rejected: discarnate existence is quite devoid of mind.[6]

What follows from the last paragraph is that the instantiation of mental properties *depends* on the instantiation of physical properties; it does not establish that there is *determination*, and so does not yet demonstrate supervenience (for the distinction, see Chapter 3). What it does do is to dramatize the difference between the view now being considered and a Cartesian View, in which the possibility of the soul's having a rich mental life even when disassociated from any body is a consequence of the contingency of the relationship between them.

A step in the direction of determination is to be seen in the claim that the nature of a creature's desires is conditioned by the biological kind to which it belongs: human beings have human desires, but elephants have elephant desires, and so on:

'Desire (*rāga*) is also determined by the particular biological kind' (*Vaiśeṣika-sūtra* 6.1.13). So, human beings desire rice, deers grass, camels brambles. The governing factor is that unseen moral principle which determines the biological kind to which one is born; the kind itself is just a medium. Again, pigeons desire grain, while buffalos dislike horses, dogs jackels, mongeese snakes. (Śaṃkara Miśra 1969: 356,8–357,2)

[Objection:] 'If the desires of a neonate are the result of remembering past experiences, then in the case where a self that occupied a human body in its past life is born into an elephant's body, the desires of the elephant cub would be for such things as are sought after by human beings.'

[5] A central tenet of O'Shaughnessy's theory of consciousness is that 'consciousness necessitates the possession of a perceptual attentive capacity;' that even if—as in the case of Prabhācandra's thought-experiment—it can exist temporarily deprived of occurrent perceptual experience, nevertheless 'consciousness entails the potential for events of the type "perceptual experience" ' (O'Shaughnessy 2002: 11–12).

[6] 'The view of some people, that cognition (*jñāna*) belongs to the self but pleasure, pain, desire, dread and will belong to the inner psychic system (*antaḥkaraṇa*)—this is now rejected' *puruṣadharmo jñānam antaḥkaraṇasya tv icchādveṣaprayatnasukhaduḥkhāni dharmā iti kasyacid darśanam–tat pratiṣidyate* | (Vātsyāyana 1997: 193,2–3, above 3.2.34). Cf. 3.2.18, 3.2.37.

[Reply:] The answer is that the character of the child's desires depend on the body he has at the time; and the desires in the elephant cub would be those in accordance with the experiences undergone by that self in a remote previous life when in an elephant's body. (Vācaspati 1997: 476,17–477,2, on *Nyāya-sūtra* 3.1.26; trans. Jha 1984: 1170, modified)

There is here an anticipation of the idea that motivates the 'embodied mind' thesis, that 'minds profoundly reflect the bodies in which they are contained' (Shapiro 2004: 167), specifically that phenomenal duplication is incompatible with differences in body-type. The Nyāya-Vaiśeṣika self is an embodied self.[7]

Further evidence in support of supervenience can be found in the commentaries that surround the *sūtras* quoted above. While it is the self which is the owner (*ādhāra*) of mental properties, *Nyāya-sūtra* 1.1.11 refers to the body as being the 'base' (*āśraya*) of action, the senses, and sensory qualities. Offering synonyms of 'base', Vātsyāyana says that the body is the 'residence' (*adhiṣṭhāna*) of pleasure, and in another place describes the body as providing a 'home' (*āyatana*) for the self, mind, pleasure, and pain.[8] He begins to articulate the dependence invoked by these expressions. The body is the base of actions in the sense that when one wills to obtain something that one desires, it is the body where an action occurs. It is the base of the senses in that it is 'that by the benefiting of which they are benefited, and by the harming of which they are harmed'.[9] This phrase is suggestive, and Uddyotakara explains it in a way that brings us very close to an idea of supervenience; he says that the idea is not that the relation of the body to the senses is that of container and what is contained (*paryanta*), but that the senses are affected, in a lawful manner, by injuries or benefits befalling the body. The senses are under the regulation (*anuvidhāna*) of the body.[10]

[7] A lack of body is reflected in the lack of any mind at all. My contention is that discarnate existence, with no potential for mentality, is not a *self* (I will discuss this point more fully in Ch. 16). I am pleased to discover a confirmation of my point in a 19th-century commentary on the *Vaiśeṣika-sūtra*. Candrakānta, remarking on VS 3.2.15–6 (also discussed in Ch. 16), affirms that selves are individuated by the mental qualities they instantiate and that in liberation there are no distinct selves. So there is no individual discarnate survival. Candrakānta (1991) under *Vaiśeṣika-sūtra* 3.2.15–16.

[8] *jīva-manaḥ-sukha-duḥkha-saṃvittyāyatana-bhūtaṃ śarīram* | (Vātsyāyana 1997: 206,1–2, under 3.2.52).

[9] *yasyānugraheṇānugṛhītāni upaghātena copahatāni svaviṣayeṣu sadhvasādhuṣu pravartante, sa eṣām āśrayaḥ taccharīram iti* | (Vātsyāyana 1997: 17,6-7, under 1.1.11).

[10] *na ca ghraṇādimanaḥparyantam indriyṃ śarīravṛtti* | *tasmād ayuktam indriyaāśrayaḥ śarīram iti* | *śarīrānu-vidhānam indriyāśrayatvaṃ brūmaḥ* | (Uddyotakara 1997: 65, 7–8, under 1.1.11).

Similarly, it is not that the body is the container of the sensibles, but that the senses could not perform their function without the body. Extending the argument to pleasure, pain, and other properties of the self, the point for Uddyotakara is that psychophysical regularities are lawful, even though they are relationships among entities of different types.[11]

Why Mental Properties are not Properties of the Body

Kim is right to say that the minimal physicalist will object to an analysis in which 'persons, or human bodies or organisms, are taken to instantiate both physical and psychological characteristics'. Our philosophers present several arguments against precisely this view. The purpose of these arguments is to show that a multiple-tiers world-view incurs substantial explanatory debts of its own, and that its apparent simplicity actually comes at a very high price. Vātsyāyana contextualizes the arguments by rehearsing the physicalist's use of what I have called the 'Covariance Argument': mental properties are properties of the body because they covary with variations in the body's physical state. Our text begins by pointing out that this is not conclusive, that covariance does not imply colocation: 'One can observe, in a single individual, both its own properties and the properties of other things. So there is a doubt' (*Nyāya-sūtra* 3.2.46). We might wish to say that we do observe mental properties *in* human bodies, and covarying with them, without making them properties *of* bodies. This is a point made very explicitly by Vātsyāyana in his discussion of the dependence of sense-perception on the material sensory faculties:

[*Objection*:] There is no thinking apart from material aggregates like the body. Why? 'Because there is restriction based on the objects.' The senses have restricted objects: colour is not perceived when sight is absent, and is perceived when sight is present. That which does not happen in the absence of something, but does

[11] Compare Koons and Bealer (2010: p. xviii): 'Physics admits lawful relationships among physical entities that are extraordinarily diverse in nature and, in turn, admits relations of causal influence and law-grounded explanation among these entities. Physics allows, moreover, that some of these lawful relationships are brute facts having no further explanation. If such relations are tolerated in physics, why not in psychophysics?'

happen when it is present, is understood to stand in such a relation to it. So we say that sight is the perceiver of colour, that sight perceives colours. It is the same with the sense of smell and the others. Since each sense perceives its very own sort of object, they themselves are aware; and also because the presence or absence of the sense is correlated to the presence or absence of the perception of the object. This being so, what is the point of another thinking [thing]?

[*Reply*:] This is not sound reasoning, because there is something unresolved. What is unresolved is this: Is the correlation between the presence or absence of the sense and the presence or absence of the perception of the object due to the fact that the sense perceives, or is it due to the fact that its role in perception is to assist in the perceiving? This [correlation] could be due to the fact that its role in perception is to assist in the perceiving. (Vātsyāyana 1997: 136,7-15, under 3.1.2)

In this passage, it is agreed that there is a covariation between the states of the senses and states of sensory awareness. The dispute is over whether we are entitled to infer something else, namely that the senses are themselves aware, and the point made is that this does not yet follow, for it could also be the case that the covariation obtains even though sensory awareness is a property of something else. So the Covariance Argument fails to establish a case conclusively in favour of the proposal that mental characteristics be treated as characteristics of the body, and with it the picture of the world as consisting in tiers or layers of progressively more sophisticated properties of the same base domain of entities.

Praśastapāda provides five sorts of consideration to demonstrate that the proposal that mental properties are non-derivative properties of the body must itself face several complex challenges.[12] The same five arguments can also be identified in Gautama (*Nyāya-sūtra* 3.2). I will call them the Unity, Spatial Parts, Persistence, Self-Knowledge, and Self-Reference arguments. The Unity Argument is a version of the type of argument which Kant nicknamed the 'Achilles of all dialectical arguments', that the unification of representations requires there to be a single unifier.[13] Kant's view is

[12] Praśastapāda (1994: 16 §79): *te ca na sarīrendriyaguṇāḥ. kasmāt?* (1) *ahaṃkāreṇaikavākyatābhāvāt* (2) *pradeśavṛttitvād* (3) *yāvaddravyabhāvitvād* (4) *bāhyendriyāpratyakṣatvāc ca.* (5) *tathā 'haṃśabdenāpi pṛthivyādiśabdavyatirekād iti.* His provision of these arguments supplements *Vaiśeṣika-sūtra* 10.1, where it is simply denied that mental properties are physical.

[13] 'This is the Achilles of all dialectical inferences in the pure doctrine of the soul. It is no mere sophistical play . . . but an inference which appears to withstand even the keenest scrutiny and the most scrupulously exact investigation' (*Critique* A351). Kant learned of the argument from Mendelssohn (Nielsen 2008; Sassen 2008), who in turn cites as his source Plotinus *Enneads* 4.7.6: 'And if one [sense-

apparently that although such arguments cannot demonstrate that the self is a simple, they are effective against materialist explanations of the unity of consciousness.[14] The Spatial Parts and Persistence arguments attempt to demonstrate that there are fundamental differences between mental and physical properties in their spatial and temporal modes of occurrence. The claim is not, contra Descartes, that extension is the mark of the physical; rather it is that the differences in spatio-temporal behaviour imply that mental and physical properties cannot be exemplified by the same sorts of thing. The Knowledge and and Self-Reference arguments appeal rather to asymmetries in the way that mental properties and physical properties are known about or referred to.

I will examine the Unity Argument in detail in Chapter 15, considered as a positive argument for the unity of the self. Here I will comment briefly on its use in a refutation of materialism. In the particular form in which it is presented in the *Nyāya-sūtra*, what is at stake is the unification of perceptions from different sense-modalities in a common judgement about an object (*Nyāya-sūtra* 3.1.1; cf. Vātsyāyana under 1.1.10). Vātsyāyana argues that an individual's ability to bind the contents of distinct perceptions, in judgements like 'What I am seeing I am also touching', is incompatible with those perceptions simply being physical properties of parts of the body. Praśastapāda uses a technical term drawn from Mīmāṃsā ritual hermeneutics: he says that there must be *ekavākyatā*, a unity of sentential assertion. The hermeneutical principle is that groups of contiguous expressions are to be interpreted according to the assumption that they make a single common statement. There is likewise a suggestion, both in Vātsyāyana and Kant, that sentential unity provides a suitable analogy.[15] The point of the Unity Argument is then that the ability to do this requires there to be a single

object] enters through the eyes, and another through the hearing organ, there must be some one place to which they both go' (Mijuskovic 1974; D. Henry 2008). I wonder, though, if its ultimate origin is *Kena Upaniṣad* 1d: 'And who is the "lord" that joins sight and hearing?'

[14] Allison (1989: 195): 'Kant's position seems to be that the unity of consciousness, which the rational psychologist (presumably Leibniz) uses erroneously to establish the positive metaphysical doctrine of the simplicity and hence incorruptibility of the soul, can be used legitimately to establish the weaker thesis of the impossibility of a materialist explanation of the conceptual activities of the mind.'

[15] 'For representations (for instance the single words of a verse), distributed among different things, never make up a whole thought (a verse), and it is therefore impossible that a thought should inhere in what is essentially composite' (*Critique* A 352). 'After listening to the temporal sequence of letters, recognising them as words and sentences, and knowing the rules of reference, one grasps the resultant many-object meaning, which no one sense can perceive' (Vātsyāyana 1997: 137,9–10).

place where the contents of diverse perceptions from different sensory faculties can be compared and combined, a place that is outside the whole sensory apparatus.[16] It is not yet clear why that single place should not itself be a part of the body, but what is clear is that simply ascribing mental properties to the body leaves much work undone.

I will briefly note two versions of the argument, construed as an argument against materialism, in non-Indian sources. Proclus gives the argument a new slant:

The whole of a divisible individual substance cannot be conjoined with the whole of itself because of the separateness of its parts, occupying distinct positions in space from one another. No body, then, is of such a nature as to reflect upon itself in such a way that the whole is reflected upon the whole.[17]

Proclus' version relates the argument directly to a key theme of this book, the question of what is involved in providing a naturalist account not of consciousness in general but specifically of first-person phenomena. Ibn Sīnā presents an argument with exemplary clarity in his *Kitāb al-Najāt*:

We sometimes say, 'When I perceived such-and-such, I became angry.' Since this is a true statement, it is one thing that perceived and then became angry. That one thing is either the human body or the human soul. If it is the human body, then it would either be the totality of its organs or some of its organs. But it cannot be the totality of its organs, for it does not include the hand or the foot. It also cannot be two different organs, one of which perceived and the other became angry. For then it would not really be one thing that perceived and then was angry. It is also not the case that one bodily organ—according to someone who makes such a statement—is the object of both perception and anger. Rather, the truth is that the statement 'I perceived and then became angry' means perhaps that something within us perceived and something within us became angry. But the intention of one who utters, 'I perceived and then became angry' is not that this occurs to two things within us, but rather that the very thing to which perception conveyed this concept then became angry. Therefore, either the [literal] meaning of the statement is false, or else the truth is that the one who perceived and was angry is one thing. But since this statement is obviously [literally] true, then the thing to which perception conveys its perceptible is the very thing that becomes angry. And since it has such a position, even if it is a body, it does not have this position insofar as it is a

[16] Something akin, perhaps, to Velleman's (2005) conception of self as a centre of narrative unity.

[17] *Elements of Theology*, 15.

body. Instead, it has it by virtue of having a faculty that makes it suitable for the combination of these two things. This faculty is not physical, and it must therefore be a soul.[18]

E. J. Lowe has formulated an argument that is virtually identical to Ibn Sina's. Indeed he claims that it is the strongest argument for distinguishing the self from the body. The premises of his version of the argument are: (1) 'I am the subject of all and only my own mental states', and (2) 'Neither my body as a whole nor any part of it could be the subject of all and only my own mental states.' The conclusion is: (3) 'I am not identical with my body nor with any part of it.' (Lowe 2008: 96).[19]

Praśastapāda's second argument has to do with the respective mereological reach of mental and physical properties. Praśastapāda says that mental properties are not physical properties because they 'occur at a place' (*pradeśavṛttitvād*) in the body. The idea seems to be that pleasures and pains have a felt spatial location within the body, whereas the defining qualities of a physical object, such as its having weight or colour, are distributive over its parts. This is at least how Śrīdhara explains Praśastapāda's enigmatic formulation of the argument:

Pleasure and pain occur at a place, as for example, 'There is pain in my head' or 'My feet feel good,' and are not therefore properties of the body or the sense faculties, for they lack their characteristic feature (*viśeṣa-guṇa*), which is to occur distributively. In other words, the reason that pleasure and pain are not characteristic properties of the body or the sense faculties is that they do not occur distributively (*avyāpya-vṛttitvāt*). The characteristic properties of body and sense faculties are seen to occur distributively; for example, having a colour. (Śrīdhara 1984: 85,1–5)

Uddyotakara cites as another example of a characteristic bodily property the property of being warm (1997: 412,15). The force of the argument might be put as follows. The inference from 'S has physical feature P' to 'Every part of S has P' is valid if P is a characteristic physical quality, such as colour, warmth (mass, extension, etc.). However, the inference from 'S has mental

[18] Khalidi (2005: 54–5); cf. Lagerlund (2008: 80).

[19] Lowe's argument in support of the key premise (2) rests on his affirmation of the principle that 'no entity can qualify as the subject of certain mental states if those mental states could exist in the absence of that entity', along with his claim that my mental states can persist even if some parts of my body, and *therefore* my body as a whole, cease to exist. That appears to be an echo of Jayanta's conception of the body, described in Ch. 5.

feature M' to 'Every part of S has M' is not valid—at best *only some* part or parts of S have M, such as the foot or the head, or else S has M without *any* part of S having M. Pains are limited to a single part of the body, while beliefs are properties of the whole person but not of any part; so mental features differ from those features which characterize matter.

Clearly, the argument rests on the implicit premise that if mental properties were physical then they would be the sorts of property which are characteristic of the physical. It seems not to rule out the possibility that the body has its mental properties in the same way it has 'non-characteristic' physical properties, for example, by being emergent properties of the physical system. Badrinath Shukla, a modern Nyāya paṇḍit, identifies exactly this loophole, and uses it to argue for a reformed Nyāya in which mental properties *are* properties of the body (Shukla 1984 [1991: 2–3]). He moves towards something akin to P. F. Strawson's concept of a person.[20] The difficulty with both proposals is to make sense of the idea that there are predicates—P-predicates—whose character is such that they have both first- and third-person ascriptive uses, a kind of predicate 'which is unambiguously and adequately ascribable both on the basis of observation of the subject of the predicate and not on this basis, i.e. independently of observation of the subject' (Strawson 1963: 108). I will argue that it is a certain conception of self, rather than the Strawsonian P-predicate, which is the bridge between first-person and third-person positions.

There is, however, another way to understand the Spatial Parts Argument. What is perhaps being claimed is that, while it is perfectly acceptable to speak of the spatial location of mental properties—and this is one aspect in which the view is clearly not a Cartesian one—the way in which mental properties are located spatially is quite different from the way that physical properties are. Locating a pleasant sensation in my foot is one thing; locating a mole there something else altogether. Mental properties have a felt spatial location by way of having a certain sort of phenomenological content, and not by way of being physically present in the felt location itself. The distinction between two modalities of property-possession is formulated in the thought that it is characteristic of mental states not to occur

[20] Indeed there may be have been an indirect influence, insofar as efforts were being made to bring traditional Sanskrit paṇḍits into conversation with Oxford philosophy at that time (the so-called *saṃvāda* project).

distributively, but characteristic of physical states to do so. On this interpretation, the argument would apply as equally to emergentism as to reductive physicalism.

Gautama too refers to 'distribution in the body' as the cause of distinction between the mental and the physical (*Nyāya-sūtra* 3.2.50: *śarīra-vyāptitvāt*). Vātsyāyana interprets this *sūtra* in a third way again. The argument, according to him, is that if mental properties were physical then they would distribute over every part of the body, and in that case, since every part is conscious, there would many conscious subjects within a single body:

> The body and each of its parts is pervaded by the possibility (*utpatti*) of mentality, and none is, therefore, without the possibility of mentality. So if the body has mentality, then the parts will too, and one will have to accept the presence of multiple mentalities. (1997: 205,6–9)

I will call this the *Many Cognizers* version of the Spatial Parts Argument, to distinguish it from the *Distribution* version as presented by Śrīdhara.[21] Vātsyāyana seems fond of this argument, mentioning it on at least three separate occasions:[22]

> In the view of the materialist, would not there be many cognisers in the same body, for the numerous material elements will all be characterised by the properties of cognition, desire, dread, and will? There is no reason in favour of this. (1997: 195,8–12, under 3.2.37)

Moreover, if every part of the body is itself a locus of conscious states then each such part would count as a subject of experience, contradicting the idea that there is a single embodied subject of experience (Uddyotakara 1997: 421,6–9).

Spatial Parts Arguments are available also in non-Indian sources. Plotinus (*Enneads* 4.2.1.2) provides a series of such arguments, of which it is has been said that 'so far as is known, no one had entertained such thoughts before' (Martin and Barresi 2006: 36).

If the way in which mental properties have a spatial location is different in kind from the way physical properties do, so too, it is claimed, is the way in

[21] Uddyotakara casts doubt on the validity of the distribution version of the Spatial Parts Argument (1997: 412,16–17), but Udayana suggests that Vātsyāyana regarded the interpretation of the *sūtra* as about distribution as obvious, and that he chooses for that reason to present a different argument.

[22] Under 1.1.10, 3.2.37, and 3.2.50.

which they are located in time. The *Persistence Argument* runs as follows. Praśastapāda distinguishes between properties that only cease to be exemplified when the object in which they occur is destroyed from properties which can cease to be exemplified even though the object continues to persist.[23] An object's physical properties are potentially of the first sort; for example, the only way an object might cease to have a colour is by ceasing to exist, even though the particular colour it has might change over time (cf. *Nyāya-sūtra* 3.2.47). Mental properties do not admit of this possibility: there is always a way to lose a mental property short of destroying its exemplar. If mental properties were properties of the body then a distinction could be drawn, one which is not in fact able to be drawn, between two manners in which they can cease to be. So mental and physical properties persist in exemplification in fundamentally different sorts of ways.

This argument might seem to beg the question against the mortality of the self: if the self were mortal, then mental properties would cease to be exemplified upon its destruction. A good point is made by Vātsyāyana, however, who observes that if consciousness were a property of the body, and one can switch between being conscious and not being conscious, then the explanation for the switching must itself be entirely in terms of the body.[24] There is, perhaps, the suggestion here of the idea that one's beliefs and other intentional mental states are subject to rational revision. One cannot explain *why* someone has changed their mind, why they no longer believe something that they formerly did, just by referring to changes in the physical states of their body.

Jayanta's argument against Animalism, which I described in some detail in Chapter 5, is a version of the Persistence Argument, but made with respect to the identity of the self and the body as opposed to the identity of mental and bodily properties. The continuing persistence of the corpse after death is cited by Praśastapāda as a further reason not to identify the self with the body (Praśastapāda 1994: 15, §77). Indeed, Dharmakīrti takes this and the Many Cognizers Argument to be the best arguments against physicalism (Dharmakīrti 1971–2: 2.49–55). Contemporary philosophers have sometimes presented a version of the corpse argument. So, Ernest

[23] Praśastapāda's term is *yāvad-dravya-bhāvin* (Praśastapāda 1994: 16, §79; 20, §114). Gautama uses the very similar *yāvad-śarīra-bhāvin* (*Nyāya-sūtra* 3.2.47).

[24] Vātsyāyana (1997: 204,1–5, under 3.2.47).

Sosa: 'One cannot be the very same thing as one's body. For one's body normally remains in existence when one passes away, and no one thing could concurrently pass away and remain in existence' (1987: 156).[25]

The *Self-Knowledge Argument* again attempts to demonstrate that mental properties are different in kind from physical properties. The leading premise in this argument is that our source of knowledge about our mental properties is quite different in kind from our sources of knowledge about any physical property. While Praśastapāda says only that mental states are not perceptible by the external senses (*bāhyendriyāpratyakṣatvāt*), Vātsyāyana is more informative, claiming that the point is that physical properties are all either empirically perceivable or else imperceptible, whereas self-knowledge requires no mediation and is introspectible (Vātsyāyana 1997: 206,7–9, under 3.2.53):

> The properties of the body are of two sorts: those which are perceivable by an external sense, such as colour; and those which are imperceptible, such as weight. Consciousness (*cetanā*), however, is of a different sort. It is not perceivable by an external sense, because it is aware of itself from within (*saṃvedya*). Nor is it imperceptible, because it is an object of inner attention (*manoviṣaya*). Therefore, it is not a property of the body.[26]

The argument might be reinforced by the point O'Shaughnessy makes when he observes that sight is an avenue for knowledge of external events because it is mediated by the causally related event of noticing one's visual sensations, whereas in the case of knowledge of one's own present experiences there is no analogous third event, so that the 'unlikeness to the perceptual situation shows there was here [in knowledge of one's own present experiences] no experienced avenue of knowledge' (O'Shaughnessy 2002: 106).

Variants of the Self-Knowledge Argument are formulated in other Indian sources. I appear to have 'access' to my own mental states which is quite different in kind to the access any external observer might have to them. But if mental states are physical states, then there is no explanation for such an asymmetry of access (or, at the least, the multiple-tier model is under a

[25] For responses, see Shoemaker (1999); Olson (2004).

[26] Vātsyāyana (1997: 206,7–9, under 3.2.53). Cf. Uddyotakara (1997: 412,4–6); Śrīdhara (1984: 85,10–13).

substantive obligation to provide one). Let me call this the *Privacy of Access* Argument:

The physical states of the body, like its colour and so on, are perceived by oneself and by others, but desires and such like are perceived by oneself alone. Therefore, there is a difference between them and body states. (Vācaspati 1980: 767, 6–7 under *Brahma-sūtra-bhāṣya* 3.3.54)

If [your body and your mind] are identical, then just as other people know clearly your body, why do they not also know your states of mind, such as your desires and dreads? One's state of mind is known by oneself alone, one's body by oneself and by others too. The two are thus distinct, in just the same way as are a stomach–pain and an actor. (Śāntarakṣita vv. 1908–9)

An actor, performing on the stage, is seen by many people in the audience, but a stomach pain is felt by oneself alone. Versions of the epistemological argument have been discussed extensively in the more contemporary literature on the identity theory of mind, and I will say more about them later in this chapter.

The fifth argument, *Self-Reference*, serves more to diffuse an objection. One of the leading arguments of the Cārvāka is to point out that the use of the first person is such as to admit the predication of physical attributes, as in, for example, the sentence 'I am bulky (*sthulo 'ham*).'[27] Sentences like these are a problem for a philosophical position which denies that the self is identical to the body and affirms that the use of 'I' is always to refer to the self (*Vaiśeṣika-sūtra* 3.2.9–14). The extremely gnomic *sūtras* 3.2.10–14 grapple with the problem of whether the word 'I' is used primarily to refer to a self as subject of physical attributes, as in 'I am moving' and only derivatively to refer to the self as subject of mental attributes, such as 'I am happy', or whether it is the other way round.[28] Praśastapāda's contribution is to insist that 'I' is not the same as any word which refers to a physical

[27] As recorded by Mādhavācārya, the argument runs as follows: 'Since in "I am fat," "I am thin," these attributes abide in the same subject, and since fatness and so on reside only in the body, it alone is the self and no other; and such phrases as "my body" are significant only metaphorically' (Mādhavācārya 1908: 5, trans. Cowell and Gough).

[28] 'If there are clear perceptions like "I am Devadatta," "I am Yajñadatta", [then "I" refers to the body]. The perception of body is clear due to imposition, in the expressions "Devadatta goes" and "Yajñadatta goes." The imposition, however, is to be doubted. The cognition of "I" is a perception of a distinctive entity, since the word applies to the self-reflective self (*pratyagātman*), and not to anything else. But we do not apprehend the particular cognitions of Devadatta and Yajñadatta in consequence of their different bodies' (*Vaiśeṣika-sūtra* 3.2.10–14; trans. Thakur 2003: 63–4).

object.[29] A standard Vaiśeṣika move here is to claim that its use in the problematic class of sentence to refer to the body is a modulated use, non-literal but derivative on its normal use. Śrīdhara:

Surely the word 'I' has as its referent the body, as can be seen in the sentence 'I am bulky'? No—there are uses like 'I know' and 'I remember', and we have denied that the body is the location of states of knowledge and memory. So [what we say instead is that] the use of 'I' with respect to the body is non-literal (*lakṣaṇā*), grounded in the relation 'being an assistant to the self' (*ātmopakārakatva*), just as it is declared of a servant, 'He is indeed me.' (Śrīdhara 1984: 86,3–8)

When I say 'I am bulky', I am saying metonymically that the body which stands in a uniquely assistive relationship to me is bulky; I am not ascribing a physical property directly to myself.[30] This is the converse of Vasubandhu's proposal (Chapter 8), that the use of 'I' to refer to a self is a metaphor (*upacāra*), and also different from Kumārila's claim that the use of the first-person in ascriptions of physical properties is simply mistaken.[31]

Śaṃkara Miśra, however, adds to the discussion with a very important comment:

Since our mere intuitions [about the use of the term 'I'] are a false witness, we need to go in search of a deciding factor. Conducting the search, we see that even someone whose eyes are shut (*nimīlita-akṣa*) thinks 'I...'; and so the word 'I' should be regarded as denoting something which is outside the field of the external senses and distinct from the body. If it were to denote the body, it would not do so without dependence on the eyes, and it could denote another body too. How then is it that there are statements such as 'I am happy, whether fat or thin,' where there is a co-location [of mental and physical attributes]? The reason is that it is possible for the body to feature as the delimitor of the attribute happy, in a manner analogous to when it is said 'This forest contains a lion's roar'. Upon the body is superimposed throughout a quality of *being I* (*ahaṃtva-mātra*), in just the same way one thinks that one's body is hot, heat being detected through the sense of touch. (Śaṃkara Miśra 1969: 257)

There are several important ideas here. First, there is an argument that 'I' does not literally denote the body, because it is possible to refer to oneself

[29] *ahaṃ-śabdenāpi pṛthivyādi-śabda-vyatirekāt* |

[30] Compare here Baker's distinction between non-derivative and derivative properties (Baker 2000).

[31] *guruḥ sthūlaḥ kṛśo vā 'ham iti dehe 'pi yā matiḥ* | *bhrāntiḥ sā*... || (Kumārila, *Ātmavāda* 127a–c; 'The cognition "I am sturdy, fat or thin", though referring to the body, is erroneous.').

in the absence of any acquaintance with one's body. This recalls the argument of Ibn Sīnā and Prabhācandra described in Chapter 2. Second, there is an argument that if it were to refer to a body then it might be used mistakenly to refer to someone else's body, and such a mistake is never made, a point that seems to anticipate the thought that the use of the first person is immune to certain sorts of error through misidentification. Third, an explanation is offered of the apparent co-application of mental and physical predicates, one which does not make the body a literal referent of the word 'I'. The alternative explanation is that the physical predicate delimits a region in space as the spatial location of the mental property, but in a way other than by giving the mental property a physical substrate. Fourth, a new idea is introduced: what is now claimed is that the body is the region throughout which I impose the quality of being I (*ahantva-mātra*), perhaps proprioceptively, and that this same body is then also ascribed physical attributes. To say this is, I believe, effectively to substitute a subjective account of immersion, of the sort sought by Buddhist theory, with a bodily account, grounding the idea of the immersed self in bodily ownership, a basic presentation of one's body to oneself as one's own. Immersion is accounted for exclusively in terms of the felt presence and spatiality of the body.[32]

Ownership and Exemplification

To summarize, there seem to be three general sorts of consideration provided in favour of the claim that mental properties are not properties of the physical body. First, mental and physical properties differ with respect to their distribution among the parts of the individual exemplifying them (*vyāpya-vṛttitva*) and with respect to their endurance linked to the continued existence of the individual (*yāvad-dravya-bhāvitva*). It is characteristic of mental properties to be properties of the whole person or else to be delimited by a single part of the body, and to be temporary intrinsics; on the other hand, the properties which are characteristic of matter, such as mass or temperature, saturate every part and are essential. Second, mental

[32] The idea finds an articulation in Merleau-Ponty's claim that subjects realize their ipseity in their embodied being-in-the world (Merleau-Ponty 1962: 408).

properties do not have the same epistemology as properties belonging to the body; there is something distinctive about self-knowledge, partly to do with its immediacy and partly to do with privacy of access. Third, mental properties have an intentionality the unification of which is incompatible with their being properties of the body. The claim is that these asymmetries are better explained under the hypothesis that mental properties are properties of an individual distinct from the body than by the apparently simpler hypothesis that they are themselves properties of the body. From this range of arguments, the strongest line of thought seems to me to be that there is something about the manner of exemplification or mode of occurrence of mental properties which is quite different in kind from that of any physical property. The arguments are all attempts to give voice to a single thought: that the relationships of inhabitation and endorsement that are implied by the idea of *owning* a mental state, and so of having a first-person stance, are fundamentally different in kind from any relation of physical exemplification.

We might usefully compare the spectrum of Nyāya-Vaiśeṣika arguments with those that have been put forward against the identity theory of mind, as it was popularized by Place, Feigl, and Smart. Smart himself, in his original paper, replied to a range of hypothetical objections. He considers in particular the Self-Knowledge Argument, the objection that 'any illiterate peasant can talk perfectly well about his after-images, or how things look or feel to him, or about his aches and pains, and yet he may know nothing whatever about neurophysiology' (1959: 146). Smart's response was in effect to point out that the identities in question are contingent, like the identity between Hesperus and Phosphorus, and therefore *a posteriori*. This was largely accepted as being a decisive repost, and this version of the Self-Knowledge Argument initially gained little favour. The subsequent discussion noticed two sorts of argument to which Smart had not offered any response. The first rests on violations of Leibniz' law by arguing that mental states and processes differ from physical states and processes with respect to their non-intensional and non-modal properties. The 'stubbornest objection' of this sort is the one presented by Malcolm in a syllogistic form that the Indians would approve of: 'It is not meaningful to assign spatial location to some kinds of mental phenomena, e.g. thoughts. Brain phenomena have spatial location. Thus, brain phenomena have a property that thoughts do not have. Therefore, thoughts are not identical with any brain phenomena'

(1963: 663). This is a different version of the Spatial Parts Argument, one which clearly bears the influence of Cartesianism. Nagel tries to diffuse the argument by claiming that what should be identified are not mental and physical processes and states, but rather a person's having those states (1965: 341), for the location of *the having of* a brain state is not the location of some part of the brain, but of the person:

> If the two sides of the identity are not a sensation and a brain process, but my *having* a certain sensation or thought and my body's *being* in a certain physical state, then they will both be going on in the same place—namely, wherever I (and my body) happen to be. It is important that the physical side of the identity is not a brain process, but rather my body's being in that state which may be specified as 'having the relevant process going on in its brain.' *That* state is not located in the brain; it has been located as precisely as it can be when we have been told the precise location of that of which it is a state—namely, my body. The same is true of my having a sensation: that is going on wherever I happen to be at the time, and its location cannot be specified more precisely than mine can. (That is, even if a pain is located in my right shin, I am *having* that pain in my office at the university.) (1965: 343)

Nagel sums up his idea as follows: 'The location of bodily sensations is a very different thing from the location of warts. It is a phenomenal location, and is best regarded as one feature of a psychological attribute possessed by the *whole* person rather than as the spatial location of an event going on in a part of him' (1965: 344). Nagel's suggestion that the identity theory can be saved if the identity is restated in terms of properties rather than processes. But we might understand the Spatial Parts Argument as directed precisely against such a reformulation. What that argument points out is that *the way in which* a person has a mental property is different from *the way in which* they have a physical property: one is saturative, the other isn't. Since the way in which something has a property is a property of that property, if the observation about saturation is correct, then there is again a violation of Leibniz's law.

The second sort of objection to gain purchase was via an appeal to first-person access and authority, a variant of the Self-Knowledge Argument. Baier asks what we should say of a case in which a neurophysiologist monitoring a subject contradicts the subject's report that they are in pain. He argues that 'being about something private is incompatible with being about something public' (1962: 59). Armstrong (1963) and Smart (1962) considered this to be a strong objection, although Nagel (1965: 345) claimed that since the argument is again epistemological, the context is an intensional one, so that there is, as before, no threat to the contingent identity. Lowe (1996: 6) defends a modal version of the argument, taken against the doctrine that the self is identifiable with the physical body: 'That *these* experiences are *my* experiences is arguably known to me as a necessary truth; but that these experiences are associated with this body, though perhaps known to me, does not seem to constitute a necessary truth.' This is indeed a further justification of the distinction I drew, in Chapter 1, between base and place.

Rather than any of these objections, however, it has been Putnam's 'multiple realisation' argument (Putnam 1967) and Kripke's work on the necessity of identity (Kripke 1982) which defined the shape of the debate about the identity theory. Self-Reference Arguments have begun to gain prominence in contemporary discussion, usually hinging on issues to do with the immunity of error due to misidentification in relation to the use of the first person (see Chapter 8). A whole battery of fresh arguments have gained ground, from Jackson's Knowledge Argument to Chalmers's Two-Dimensional Argument.[33] It is worth noting that although he defended a property dualism in his (1996), Chalmers has moved to a position more accommodating of substance dualism: 'I remain neutral on the issue myself, but I am certainly not opposed to substance dualism (construed as the existence of fundamental nonphysical individuals), and there are some considerations (including issues about the combination [Many Cognizers] problem and the unity of consciousness) that tend to favour it' (2010: 139). For Chalmers, then, versions of the Spatial Parts Argument and the Unity Argument carry the most weight in redressing the balance between a multiple-tiers view and a many-domains view.

The claim is that mental properties are not the sorts of things that can be non-derivative properties of a physical body. Their mode of occurrence is different from that of physical properties, as is their manner of aggregation, as is their epistemology, and as is their role in determining reference. The underlying idea is that it is of the nature of mental properties to be owned,

[33] They include the knowledge argument, the property dualism argument, the disembodiment argument, the two-dimensional argument, the certainty argument, the zombie argument, the absent qualia argument, the inverted spectrum argument, the explanatory gap argument, the anti-individualism argument, the self-consciousness argument, and the mental causation argument. See Chalmers (2010: 141–206); Koons and Bealer (eds.) (2010).

and that the body cannot provide them with a *place* of ownership, in the terminology of Chapter 1. With this much, supporters of the Ownership View have common ground with Cartesians. What distinguishes the Ownership View is a second claim of equal importance, that mental properties are metaphysically dependent on physical properties, that the body provides the base for mental properties, a thought which I have been articulating in terms of the obtaining of a supervenience relation. I have sought also to demonstrate that the view of Gautama, Vātsyāyana, Praśastapāda, and Śrīdhara is a supervenience-based Ownership View. Participation, the endorsement of a first-person stance, requires embodiment but is not reducible to a physical attribute. One's commitments, preferences, and motivations are expressed through the body; they are not properties of the body.

Whatever one may feel about the ultimate success of the arguments, I believe that they do enough to show that 'the usual simplicity considerations' are not decisive, and that a many-domain world-view is not as implausible as Kim would have us believe; indeed that it is more or less as plausible as the sort of multiple-tiers world-view he prefers. This phase in the argument is, as I said at the beginning of the chapter, one of negative dialectic, its function to level the playing field by showing that the apparent simplicity of the multiple-tiers view comes at a high price in terms of the debts of explanation it incurs. The challenge now is to provide a constructive and explanatory account of the multiple-domain supervenience, itself merely a relationship of property covariation. In the next chapter I will ask whether the philosophers whose theory we are examining have any such constructive proposal to offer.

13

Attention, Monitoring, and the Unconscious Mind

Free Will

Plato famously insists that the soul governs the body and can oppose its appetites, thereby rejecting the epiphenomenalism in the *harmonia* theory, which makes the self merely a 'tuning' of the elements in the body (*Phaedo* 92e4–93a7; cf. Caston 1997: 323 ff., Sorabji 2003). We seem to find a similar sentiment articulated in *Nyāya-sūtra* 3.2.38. Here, one of the reasons cited for not identifying the self with the body or any bodily state or process[1] is that they fall under its governance (*pāratantrya*). The commentator explains that what this means is that

> The body's material, the senses, and the unconscious mind are led to perform acts of holding on (*dāraṇa*), impelling (*preraṇa*) and ordering (*vyūha*), on the basis of [the self's] tryings (*prayatna*). If they were themselves conscious they would have been autonomous [in their ability to do these things]. (Vātsyāyana 1997: 196,11–12)

Nevertheless, it would be a mistake to read into this passage a libertarian doctrine of free will. A libertarian claims that acts of will, or volitions, are the causes of overt behavioural effects, but are not themselves caused. The Nyāya view about intentions to act,[2] however, is that they are the causal intermediary between desires or aversions, on the one hand, and behavioural acts of reaching out for or withdrawing from, on the other:

[1] The *sūtra* refers only to 'unconscious mind' (*manas*), but Vātsyāyana explicitly states that 'mind' is given just as an example, and it should be construed with reference to the matter of the body and the senses as well (Vātsyāyana 1997: 196,6).

[2] The term *prayatna*, 'that which is towards action', an impulse to act, an intention (to act), a trying, volition, an act of will, etc.

'Acts of reaching out and withdrawing are caused by a person's desires and aversions (3.2.34).' A person thinks that something will cause pain or that it will cause pleasure, and wants to acquire for himself sources of pleasure and avoid sources of pain. Reaching out is a particular sort of striving after, associated with someone who wants to acquire what causes pleasure, and withdrawing is an escaping, associated with someone who wants to avoid what causes pain. (Vātsyāyana 1997: 193,5-8)

Again, however, desire is caused by the perception of something which one recognizes and remembers to have caused pleasure in the past, while aversion is caused by the perception of something which one recognizes and remembers to have given pain. Pain, in turn, is caused by physical damage to the body:

Injuring the body as the base (*āśraya*) of its effects, and the senses as the agents for its perceiving things, takes the form of destroying or causing rupture, deformity, pain, or damage. The body is the home (*āyatana*) or residence (*adhiṣṭhāna*) or base (*āśraya*) of the effect [of injury], which is the experience of pain or pleasure. Injury pertains to the body as the base (*āśraya*) of such effects, and to the senses as the agents for its perceiving things, and not to the self. (Vātsyāyana 1997: 139,1-5)

So intentions or trying are within the provenance of psycho-physical causal law, and are not regarded as *starting points* of causal chains leading to behaviour. One does not take evasive action without trying to do so, and in that sense action is under the governance of intention; but one's trying to do so might itself be the causal result of damage occurring to one's body. More importantly still, there is in this description no hint of the idea that is central to Plato, that one's desires and aversions can be opposed by the will. Here, 'trying' is just the means by which those desires or aversions lead to action; i.e. conscious or unconscious intentions to act.

The context in which this discussion of the body's governance by the self occurs is also important. The point has been made that certain types of behavioural activity, especially seeking, grasping, and putting things into an order, are indicative of the existence of desires and aversions, an argument which is effectively a form of the argument for other minds (cf. *Vaiśeṣika-sūtra* 3.1.21). It is objected that non-sentient material things also exhibit behaviours of one sort or another; the reply is that the difference has to do with the existence of lawful regularities (*niyama*):

'Since desire and aversion have as their characteristic marks [the physical behaviours of reaching out and withdrawing], there is no denial of them in earthly and other material things.' However, since we see reaching out and withdrawing in objects like an axe, what discriminates between them is the presence or absence of lawful regulation. (*Nyāya-sūtra* 3.2.35-7)

Uddyotakara (1997: 403,10–14) explains this in the following way. There are certain sorts of law governing the behaviour of all material substances, such as the law that things which possess weight fall. If the activity of the body were not under the control of the will, but independent of it, then its behaviour would be subject only to law of that sort. But the laws which govern human action are not of that sort; they are instead of the form 'A person reaches out for something if they desire it.' The whole point of this discussion is therefore, to put it in modern terms, that one cannot explain human behaviour without attributing to human beings intentional mental states, while we can explain the behaviour of ordinary material objects without any such attribution. The laws governing human action are necessarily psycho-physical laws, and different from the laws governing things like rocks and stones (which are therefore not themselves conscious; the difficulty with panpsychism is that it cannot make this distinction between two sorts of law). No conclusion to the effect that selves are unmoved movers follows from this, nor do these passages in themselves give us reason to question the supervenience of mental properties on physical properties.[3]

In Praśastapāda, four distinct sorts of activity are made to fall under the common heading 'impulse towards action' (*prayatna*) (Praśastapāda 1994: 60, §§295–6): i) the automatic physiological impulse that a living body makes, such as inhaling and exhaling even when asleep; ii) the impulse involved when, without conscious intervention, there is sensory awareness of the surroundings—for example, one's first perceptions at the moment of waking up; iii) the impulse that leads one to acquire something one desires

[3] Contrast this with the Jaina philosopher Prabhācandra (1991: 349,12), who provides the following syllogism: 'Moreover, the lived body is superintended by that which wills, for the body is the base of actions which are regulated by desires, like a chariot' (*tathā jīvaccharīraṃ prayatnavatā 'dhiṣṭhitam icchānu-vidhāyakriyāśrayatvāt rathavat*). The analogy between the self-body and the charioteer-chariot relations is much more suggestive of a libertarian conception of free will. One reason for the Buddhist inversion of the analogy, arguing that a chariot can be broken without remainder into its constituents, is to subvert that conception. The same chariot analogy is available in *Kaṭha Upaniṣad* 3 and in the *Mahābhārata* 7.173.56ab (Northern Recension).

or avoid something one fears; and iv) the impulse, while conscious, to hold the body's posture. Vaiśeṣika 'impulse to act' thus includes much more than only conscious intention, the third of these four categories; in particular, it also includes homeostatic activities and what belongs to the category of 'subintentional action' (O'Shaughnessy 1980). Intentions are, Praśastapāda says, always caused by desire or aversion, and in turn are intermediary causes of acts which aim at getting what one desires or avoiding what one dreads. It is striking, however, that he does not offer any additional definition of act-oriented impulsion, and instead simply provides synonyms (*saṃrambha*; *utsāha*). Neither does Udayana, who characterizes it only as the opposite of passivity (*alasatva*) (Udayana 1971: 251,15). I suggest that what we have in Praśastapāda is a functional definition of impulsion in terms of its causal role: intention to act (conscious or unconscious) is that which fulfils the causal role specified, instigated by desire or aversion, and issuing in acts aimed at their satisfaction. This is sufficient to explain the distinctive place of acts of will within the cognitive architecture of an agent. The inclusion of acts of will within a single category that spans autonomic control of respiration, the sensory system, and control of body posture, makes it very apparent that they are not thought of as privileged *first* causes of action, but rather as the uncoerced consequence of one's commitments and wishes.

Autonomy

If volitions are produced by prior mental states like beliefs and desires, and are not themselves voluntary, then does it follow that the self as such is inactive? Yet Nyāya and Vaiśeṣika philosophers describe the self as the 'agent' (*kartṛ*) of one's actions. It is also described as the 'individual cause' (*samavāyi-kāraṇa*), meaning that it is that in which one's mental states inhere, the ground of ownership (I will say more about the concept of an individual cause in the next section). In order to clarify matters, it will be helpful to introduce the distinction between agent causation and event causation (see, for instance, Lowe 2008: 121). A sentence like 'Wanting some pizza, Devadatta picked up the telephone' attributes causation to the person Devadatta; that is what it means for Devadatta to be the *agent cause* of the action. The crucial question is whether agent causation is *sui generis*, or whether it is reducible to event causation. A putative reduction of agent causation to event causation might look like this:

> Agent A caused event *e* if and only if there was some event, *x*, such that *x* involved A and *x* caused *e*, where an event *x* involves an agent A just in case *x* consists in some change in one or more of the properties of A. (Lowe 2008: 123–4)

The Nyāya and Vaiśeṣika position is that it is indeed so reducible. To say that a self is an agent of an action just is to say that an event involving the self, such as its coming to instantiate a particular act of willing, is the event cause of that action, an action whose base, as we said in the previous chapter, is in the body. When a person moves about, there is an event involving the self, namely its intending the body to move.[4] The intuition behind the accusation that the Nyāya-Vaiśeṣika self is inactive rests on a *prior* assumption that activity requires agent causation to be irreducibly distinct from event causation.

The agency of the self consists in its being 'involved in'—by way of being the individual cause of—intentions in action. Its activity does not consist in its being itself the first cause of any event. To say that the self is the individual cause of one's intentions to act is to say that one owns the intention—or, borrowing a little metaphorical licence from P. F. Strawson, the intention is oneself.[5] Classical agent causalism is the doctrine that individual persons are irreducible causes of basic actions, acts such as a raising of the arm.[6] Classical volitionism is the doctrine that what causes

[4] This is a natural way to read the contentious *Vaiśeṣika-sūtra* 5.2.18: *kāyakarmaṇātmakarma vyākhyātam* 'The activity of the self is explained by the activity of the body.' I cannot agree with Bronkhorst (1994: 91) that the phrase *ātma-karman* 'activity of the self' can refer only to movement in space. For a clear distinction between two notions, Kumārila: *tasmād acalato 'pi syāc calane kartṛtā 'tmanaḥ* (*Ātmavāda* 87ab; 'the self can be the agent of moving even if it does not itself move').

[5] To repeat: 'Our desires and preferences are not, in general, something we just note in ourselves as alien presences. To a large extent they are we.' (P. F. Strawson 1992: 134).

[6] e.g., Taylor (1966); O'Connor (2000). Lowe summarizes the doctrine as follows: 'Classical agent causalists hold that an irreducibly distinct species of causation comes into play uniquely in the sphere of intentional agency, while event causation reigns elsewhere. According to the classical agent causalist, when an intelligent agent, A, intentionally performs a so-called "basic" action, such as raising his arm, A is literally the cause of a certain occurrence—in this case, a rising of his arm—in a distinctive sense in which no event is or could be its cause and in a way which never happens in the worlds of inanimate objects. In particular, the classical agent causalist will deny that A's causing the arm-rising consists in, or even in any way involves, the causation of the arm-rising by some action or event in which A participates or of which A is the subject. So, for example, it will be denied that the arm-rising is caused by a volition or act of will of A's, or by the onset of some combination of belief and desire attributable to A' (Lowe 2008: 162–3).

basic actions are free acts of will, not themselves caused or causally determined by antecedent events.[7] Clearly the Nyāya-Vaiśeṣika theory of action falls into neither category. The self is not an irreducible agent cause; and a trying to act (*prayatna*) is not itself an uncaused occurrence in the self. Donald Davidson has argued that what causes action is the onset of states of belief and desire, and therefore that reasons are causes (Davidson 1980). In his view, there are no such things as acts of willing. The Nyāya-Vaiśeṣika theory occupies a middle position between volitionism and a Davidsonian theory of action: there are acts of willing, which are the immediate causes of action; however these acts of willing are themselves caused by the onset of states of belief, desire, and aversion, together with the memory of past pleasures and pains.

One might wonder, nevertheless, what point there is in a commitment to volitions but not classical volitionism, or indeed to selves as individuals but not to classical agent causalism. I believe that the point is to have a theory which is intelligible from both a third-person and a first-person standpoint. From a standpoint grounded in the realm of law, the account reads like a Davidsonian theory of action: the onset of a desire causes an act of willing, which in turn causes an action to take place. In this description, there is no reference to mysterious first causes of action, like agent causation or volition. Yet fatalism was formulated among the hard naturalists as the thesis that desires and acts of will are causally inefficacious:

> There is no scope for action according to one's wishes. What is the use of efforts?'[8]

The claim here that it makes no difference to the causal flow what one wills or desires. So the Nyāya-Vaiśeṣika claim that they do cause actions is already a direct rejection of fatalism. When one moves to a standpoint grounded in the space of reasons, when one thinks in terms of the 'condition of our humanity' (P. F. Strawson 1985: 33), one can redescribe the same chain now as that of wanting something, deciding to get it, and getting up in order to do so. There is no automatic transition from the want to the action; the reference to a decision is ineliminable. The theory is not Davidsonian, because the claim is not that the same occurrence falls both under a

[7] e.g., Ginet (1990); Lowe (1996).
[8] Anon. fragment (fr. 6, R. Bhattacharya 2002c: 76).

description as a *happening* in the causal chain, and under a description as a *decision*. Rather, the thought is that the decision, a state of the self, supervenes on a happening, a state of the body, in accordance with an explanatory model of supervenience. The agency or activity of the self consists in its *owning* (being the 'individual cause' of) acts of will: moving my arm is something that I do. To own an intention is to inhabit and endorse it; the intention is me and this is what my freedom consists in.[9] The action of an autonomous agent is action on an uncoercively formed intention. That is compatible with there being subpersonal guidance mechanisms in the control of action. To put the matter another way, the underself does not pre-empt the participant self. Rather, its normal operant procedures are essential to the autonomy of agency: coerced action necessarily involves an external forcing of the underself.

Three Sorts of 'Cause': Efficient, Individual, and Feature

In early Nyāya philosophy of mind not only willings but all mental properties are asymmetrically covariant with physical properties, yet not themselves properties of the physical body. These philosophers develop a theory of causation in which there are three distinct sorts of 'cause', which are, however, more appropriately regarded as three types of metaphysical dependence.[10] I will suggest that within this model there are resources for an explanatory account of multiple-domain supervenience.

It is evident that the Indian use of the term 'cause' (*kāraṇa*) needs to be construed rather generously; indeed, a failure to do so has led to a lack of appreciation of the distinction between hard and liberal varieties of naturalism in Indian theory, as I demonstrated in the Historical Prelude. The three sorts of 'cause' in the theory now under discussion are:

[9] 'The transition from attribution to avowal is an expression of the person's rational freedom' (Moran 2001: 151).

[10] A similar point has been established in connection with Aristotle's four types of 'cause' (*aitia*); Stein (2011: 121); Hennig (2009). See also Ganeri (2007: 140–2) on the distinction between reasons and causes in the context of the ambiguity of the word *hetu*.

- Efficient, or 'instrumental', causation (*nimitta-kāraṇya*).
- Individual, or 'exemplifying', causation (*samavāyi-kāraṇya*).
- Feature, or 'non-exemplifying', causation (*asamavāyi-kāraṇya*).

Efficient or instrumental causation is the relation that obtains, for example, between the swinging of an axe and the felling of a tree. There is a disagreement about whether it is the axe itself or the swinging which is the instrumental cause.[11] If the latter, then the relation is essentially event causation, and the efficient cause is that event 'involving' an agent which causes the effect. If the former, then this same event is to be specified as one which 'involves' both agent and instrument. With this notion, we already have one putative explanatory model for multiple-domain supervenience: the instantiation of properties in the base domain event-causally explains the instantiation of properties in the supervening domain. The dependence involved is that of event-causal necessitation. This is, however, a diachronic relation, and therefore not adequate as a model of the synchronic relationship obtaining between the body's physical states and the self's mental states. A pain might be caused by tissue damage, but it is not caused (in the sense of efficient or instrumental causation) by the C-fibre firing on which it supervenes.[12]

I have mentioned individual 'causation' already in this chapter. It is a broad category of metaphysical dependence. One variety is the dependence of a whole on its parts, for example the pot on its neck, base, handles, and so on (for that reason, the whole is said by these philosophers to inhere in the parts). It includes too what is called 'material causation' (*upādāna*), such as the relation between a crown and the piece of gold that constitutes it, or between the pot and the whole piece of clay.[13] Another variety is the exemplification of a property in an individual object (a property inheres in or is exemplified by an object). Within this variety there is an important subvariety, the ownership of mental states by a subject: my having a headache is paraphrased as the state of affairs in which I am the individual cause—the owner—of the headache. The dependence involved in all cases is that of metaphysical inseparability (*ayutasiddhatva*): a whole cannot exist as separated from a set of parts, nor a pot from a constituting lump of clay; a

[11] For sources: Matilal (1985: 372–8); Ganeri (1999).

[12] Sosa (1987: 166); but cf. P. F. Strawson (1985: 64).

[13] Bhaduri (1947: 311), referring to Uddyotakara on *Nyāya-sūtra* 4.1.49.

property cannot exist as separated from its exemplars. Individual causation is a sort of existential dependence relation—it answers the question 'Of what?' (and as a special case, 'Whose?').[14]

The idea of an individual cause is not the same as that of an agent or substance cause, 'the causation of an event by an individual substance' (Lowe 2008: 159). An individual cause does not *produce* an event, but *provides* a quality or a composite with a metaphysical location. Generally:

Agent A is the individual cause of something x if and only if x inheres in A.

We can indeed paraphrase the reductive analysis of agent or substance causation given above in terms of a combination of instrumental and individual causation:

Agent A caused event e if and only if there was some event, x, such that x involved A and x is the instrumental cause of e, where e consists in some change in one or more of the properties of an object B, the individual cause of e.

So, for example, the potter, A, is the agent cause of the creation of a pot in so far as he utilizes his potter's stick to fashion a lump of clay, B. The instrumental cause is the fashioning, an event consisting in a change in the relational property between the potter, his stick, and the clay. Agent causation, therefore, is reducible to a combination of instrumental and individual causation.

According to the Constitution View, the self is constituted by the body, which is therefore the individual cause (specifically, the material cause) of the self. The constitution theory is a variety of Ownership View, but one which is a rival to the view encouraged by Nyāya. For it does not seem to make sense to say that the self is *made out of* the body, as a pot is made out of clay, and the relationship between a person and their body might be *analogous* to constitution, but cannot be at one with it.[15]

Can one say that the self is a quality or property of the body? That view was indeed mentioned by Prabhācandra as one of the three options for a materialist (see Chapter 3), and is perhaps consistent with the idea that the

[14] Parfit's analysis of adjectival dependence is closely related: Xs are adjectival on Ys only if Xs are essentially of or in Ys, and there could not be Xs without Ys, and an X of one Y could not have been an X of a different Y (Parfit 1999: 239).

[15] The most influential defence of a Constitution View is that of Baker (2000). For criticism of the Constitution View, specifically in the form defended by Baker, see Olson (2001); Sider (2002); McRea (2002); Lowe (2008: 168).

self is the form of the body, that is to say with Aristotelian holomorphism. This is again a version of Ownership View rival to that of Nyāya.

Even if it does not capture the relation between self and body, is the idea of individual causation of help in the explanation of the supervenience that holds between mental and physical properties? To say that mental properties are wholes which have physical properties as their parts is to take a step in the direction of a trope-theoretic analysis, for example the view that a mental occurrence is a trope-cluster of more basic physical tropes. Another possibility is that mental properties are properties of physical properties, which is a step in the direction of an idea that motivates functionalism, namely the idea that mental properties are *second-order* physical properties. Following Putnam, let us define a second-order property as follows:

F is a second-order property over D $=_{\text{def.}}$ F is the property of having some property P in D such that C(P), where C specifies a condition on members of D.

So, for example, if D is a domain of chemical properties, and C(P) is the condition 'when ingested, instances of P relieve pain', then the second-order property F is the property 'being an analgesic'. An instance of P is also an instance of F. When the condition C is specified in terms of causal relations, we call F a 'causal role' or a 'functional property'. This is so in our example, where different first-order chemical properties meet the same causal condition 'when ingested, blocks pain', and so the property which aspirin and ibuprofen share is a second-order functional property. P is said, in conventional parlance, to 'realize' F. So let us define a new property, this time a property of properties: the property of being an F-realizer. P has this property, for example. The trouble with this suggestion, as applied to the case in hand, is that it commits a category mistake. Being in pain is a property of me, not a property of my C-fibre firings. They have the property of *being pain*, not the property of *being in pain*. It is the self which is the individual cause of mental properties, and not any physical property of the body. This is a consideration which leads the Nyāya philosopher to reject a reductive physicalism such as functionalism, and instead to affirm the existence of selves as the bearers of first-order mental properties.

The third sort of 'causation' in our model is feature causation, or more accurately 'non-exemplificative' (*asamavāyi*) causation. Feature causation is perhaps the most distinctive conceptual contribution of Nyāya-Vaiśeṣika theory in this area. The nature of the dependence is illustrated (but only illustrated) by the relationship between the colours of the threads in a garment and the colour of the garment itself, an example which serves to emphasize that its first role is within an explanatory model of the determination relationship between macro- and micro-properties. Śrīdhara clearly distinguishes between a view that macro-properties are merely resultants, the product of aggregation,[16] and the view that they are irreducibly distinct from, but nevertheless dependent on and determined by, micro-properties:

> As the whole is brought into being (*ārabdha*) by its parts, so the colour in the whole ought be to brought into being by the colours in those parts. In the parts, however, the colour is not solely white, nor solely black, but black, white, green, and so on. But there is no general rule (*niyama*) to the effect that this colour is brought into being by one colour alone among them, and not by the others, for each of all of them is known from other cases to be able to contribute. Nor is it right to say that they cannot all bring anything about, since they are mutually contradictory; because coloured wholes are observed to exist, and colourless objects cannot be seen. Nor is it the case that the colours of the parts, of various shades, are accumulated (*samucchita*), and in that way comes about a perception of the whole. For it would be possible to imagine this in other cases too, and it would result in the elimination (*uccheda*) of the colour of the whole. So the colour of the whole is brought into being in a joint way (*sambhūyatā*). Being so brought about as naturally following on from (*anugama*) causes of different sorts, it should have black, white, green, and so on in its nature; so it is said to be 'mixed' (*citra*). (Śrīdhara 1977: 75–6)

A macro-property, then, is jointly produced by and follows on from the micro-properties, its nature determined by theirs; but it is not merely an aggregation of them.[17] The properties of a macro-entity are necessitated (with nomological force) by the properties of its parts, including presumably their structural and spatial relationships. There is a suggestion in this passage that feature causation might be compatible with the macro-micro determination relation described in later Cārvāka Emergentism (see Chapter 4).

[16] The view of Dharmakīrti, e.g. (1971–2: 3.194–224).

[17] Philoponus too uses the analogy between psychological properties and colours, arguing that a given colour supervenes on but is not the result of the blend. He says that the colour is not explained by the blend, this because a range of blends, rather than just one particular blend, underpins a given colour. Philoponus in *De Generatione et Corruptione* 169,1–172,25 (trans. Philoponus 1999: 73–7); see also Sorabji (2010: 33–4), Berryman (2002). This is an example of an interesting affinity between Philoponus and Praśastapāda (another is the theory of impetus).

Speaking of macro-properties and micro-properties is misleading insofar as it suggests a layered world-view, with stratified layers of properties belonging to a single domain of entities. In fact, in the doctrine of feature causation and 'mixtion-properties' (*citra-rūpa*) what we have is an alternative to the layered-world picture. The point of the account is to give a metaphysical picture that explains how properties of one individual or domain of individuals can be irreducibly supervenient on properties of another individual or domain of individuals (this remains the case even if the chosen example of colour is not judged successful). It gives us a picture in which there are metaphysically dependent *domains* of individual objects, as opposed to one in which there are *tiers* or layers of properties but only one object domain. Another example might be the way the temperature of a body is determined by the motions of its molecular constituents, where, in this example, the properties within each domain are of different types.

One important question is what constraints must be placed on the 'coordination' relation between the separate domains if feature causation is to be genuinely explanatory? Standard Nyāya-Vaiśeṣika doctrine is that it has to be inherence (*samavāya*), a strong relation of metaphysical inseparability. It is open to us, however, to make other proposals.[18] It is helpful to frame the discussion around whether or not to accept Sellars's 'Principle of Reducibility'. What the Principle asserts is that:

If an object is *in a strict sense* a system of objects, then every property of the object must consist in the fact that its constituents have such and such qualities and stand in such and such relations, or roughly, every property of a system of objects consists of properties of, and relations between, its constituents.[19]

The utility of the Principle is that it affords a criterion by which to decide when an object is strictly identical to a system of objects, and when it is merely correlated with such a system:

Telling us, as it does, that if an object is (as contrasted with *is correlated with*) a whole of parts, its having *P* consists in its parts having properties and standing in relations,

[18] So the notion of feature causation is flexible enough to include determination within a single domain or across several, and to include both reductive and non-reductive forms of determination.

[19] Sellars (1963: 27). See also Chapter 1.

it also tells us that if an object has a property which violates the principle, then in that context it is *correlated* with rather than *consists* of the 'parts.'[20]

Śrīdhara, rejecting the idea that the colour of a whole object is merely a resultant of the colours of the parts, is both acknowledging the Principle and affirming that the coloured object is only correlated with the system of parts rather than consisting of them—it is not a bare aggregate, like a heap. Buddhist argumentation against physicalism likewise endorses the Principle of Reducibility, using it to argue that if the self is identical to the body, then the body's physical constituents must have mental properties too—this is the Many Cognizers Argument described above.

The question is whether a proposal like Śrīdhara's can be put to work in an understanding of the relationship between the mental properties of the self and the physical properties of the body. Or, turning the question on its head, we might ask what the base (*āśraya*) relation must be, if it is to be the case that the physical properties of the body are feature causes of the mental properties of the self. The use of analogies notwithstanding, it remains as before an open possibility that psycho-physical relationships are the only relationships to exhibit the particular base relation in question.

Feature-causation is a type of macro-micro determination relation. It is the way in which the qualities of a macro-object are determined by the qualities of its micro-constituents. Its role in the definition of *base* is this: 'X is the base of experience' is true just in case each item of experience is feature-caused by some state of X. The thought that something supplies a 'place' of ownership to mental states is likewise technically expressed by saying that it is their 'individual cause'. A subject of experience is the individual cause of a mental state just in case they own that mental state. Its role in the definition of *place* is this: 'X is the place of an item of experience' is true just in case it is the *individual cause* of the experience. Applying these distinctions to the question of agency, the point of the suggestion made at the end of the last section is that it is compatible with the idea that the self is an agent qua owner ('individual cause') of acts of willing that those acts of willing should be supervenient upon ('feature caused' by) micro-physical properties of the body, specifically the control mechanisms of action-guidance.

[20] Sellars (1971: 411).

The Underself

Embedded within the expansive Nyāya-Vaiśeṣika ontology is a metaphysics of mind that embraces real individual selves that host a portfolio of specifically mental qualities—positive and negative affective states (pleasure and pain), true and false intentional cognitive states, attractive and aversive appetites (desire and dread), and willings or intentions to act. With the introduction of the notion of feature causation, we have the beginnings of a model to explain how the mental states of selves supervene on the physical states of bodies. Our philosophers add flesh to the bones of the account with a further claim: each self is asserted to have an accompanying but distinct 'unconscious mind' (*manas*),[21] responsible for a range of unconscious executive functions including the regulation of respiration and the relay of signals between the body and consciousness, and in general for the mediation of all aspects of the relationship between the body's sensory systems, memory stores, and the conscious states of the self. It is also instrumental in the self's awareness of its own states as sort of 'internal monitoring capacity'.[22] Its most fundamental and distinctive function is to be an unconscious comparator mechanism, comparing states of commitment and motivation, and providing feedback that manifests in the phenomenology of emotion and agency.[23] It has a role in the selective attention to sensory stimuli[24] and in the retrieval of information from dispositional memory (*bhāvanā*). The hypothesis of such a unconscious mechanism is a distinctive and indispensable explanatory element in the philosophy of mind I have been reconstructing.

The unconscious mind has a procedural role in vision:

[21] The same term *manas* is used here in yet another sense. Vasubandhu and the Nyāya-Vaiśeṣika philosophers are both keen to appropriate some of the connotations, especially that of internal monitoring and the grounding of a sense of ownership, but to distinguish themselves from an endorsement of an apperceptive inner sense-organ, the common meaning of the term *manas* among many other thinkers. Both new concepts of *manas* are surrogate notions of self, the first a theory of the *immersed presented self*, the second an operationalized theory of *underself* as a neurophysiological process.

[22] The phrase is due to Lycan (1997; cf. 1987, 1996). The idea is also in Armstrong (1968: 92–9). Others who have postulated subpersonal comparator mechanisms: Frith (1987, 1992); Campbell (1999); Reisenzein (2009).

[23] For evidence that affect and cognition are not subserved by separate and independent neural circuits, see R. Davidson (2003); Storbeck and Clore (2007).

[24] *Nyāya-sūtra* 1.1.16, 3.1.15–17, 3.2.19–31, 3.2.38, 3.2.56–9.

When an object is in physical contact with the sense-faculty, cognitions arise or do not arise in the self; this is why there is unconscious mind. (*Vaiśeṣika-sūtra* 3.2.1)

It is postulated as that which regulates whether one consciously notices something visually present to one.[25] The model is applicable not just to vision, but also to other cognitive processes: dreaming (9.23), memory (9.22), and importantly self-consciousness (9.11). The unconscious mind is also held to be involved in reasoning, language understanding, intuition and hypothesis-formation (Vātsyāyana 1997: 29,1–2; *supra* 1.1.16).[26]

Vātsyāyana links the unconscious mind with the formation of an objective conception of external objects. One has the ability to take in bits of information in any temporal order from a variety of sources, and then to reconstruct the information piece by piece so that one achieves a thought about a single object (Vātsyāyana 1997: 207,10-16; under 3.2.56). Likewise, one can listen to a sentence uttered word by word, or even a series of sentences, and then put them together into a single propositional content. The general nature of its role is further clarified by Śaṃkara Miśra: the feature cause of perceptual cognition is the 'contact' between the senses and unconscious mind.[27] Śaṃkara Miśra goes so far as to draw an analogy with the question of macro-qualities. For a single flavour is experienced from the 'mixtion' (*citra*) of the tastes of the various different ingredients combined in a dish of food; and in the same way, one perceives a single object though a 'mixtion' of tactile and visual sensations.[28] The idea, then, is that just as the temperature of a body is determined by and supervenes on the various motions of the particles which are so organized as to constitute it, so the visual perception of an object is determined by and supervenes on the interactions between the various sensory inputs which are organized by the structuring and coordinating function of unconscious mind. As I indicated before, it is possible to see this as compatible with the determination relation of later Cārvāka Emergentism.

As mentioned, unconscious mind is also assigned an important role in self-consciousness:

[25] *śrotrādyavyāpāre smṛtyutpatti-darśanāt bāhyendriyair agṛhīta-sukhādigrāhyāntarabhāvāc cāntaḥkaraṇam* | (Praśastapāda 1994: 17, §81).

[26] Lakoff and Johnson (1999: 12) introduce the term 'cognitive unconscious' to denote 'all unconscious mental operations concerned with conceptual systems, meaning, inference, and language'.

[27] Śaṃkara Miśra (1969: 234,3); cf. Bhaduri (1947: 295).

[28] Śaṃkara Miśra (1969: 234,7–11).

Within one's own self, self-consciousness is due to an interaction of a specific sort between self and mind.[29]

Vātsyāyana mentions self-knowledge of pleasure and pain (1997: 29,1–2; *supra* 1.1.16). One is not invariably conscious of oneself or one's own mental states.[30] When one is, the account implies that this is due to an element of recursion: the unconscious mind takes its own activity as the target of its attention. This is what it is, at a higher level, for the self to enter into the content of consciousness.[31]

The same idea has been proposed in more recent literature, with the suggestion that episodes of consciousness 'sit on top of an underlying hierarchy of physical-physiological mechanisms [where] each monitorial subsystem may be enlarged into a system that records the monitorial activity' (Castañeda 1999: 285). Unsurprisingly, things can go wrong when this system attempts to take the whole of itself—the cognizing subject as such—as a target of cognition. Metzinger claims that difficulties of this sort prove that 'no such things as selves exist in the world: nobody ever was or had a self. All that ever existed were conscious self-models that could not be recognised as models' (Metzinger 2003: 1). His analysis, however, admits of both an eliminativist interpretation, according to which belief in self is a mere artefact of an information-processing system, and a reductionist interpretation, according to which what the self is an information-processing system that has generated a phenomenal self-model (see Baker 2007: 12; Zahavi 2005a: 8; 2011: 324). Metzinger's reason for preferring an eliminativist interpretation of his own theory (2003: 396–7) is that he sees it as entailed by the observation that self-modelling systems misrepresent their own nature to themselves; he says that they involve a 'naïve-realistic self-misunderstanding' (2003: 332, 436–7, 564; 2011). This is just the argument Dharmakīrti employs in the context of the transition from the representation of quasi-objects and quasi-subjects to a conception of objects and subjects as fully objective with determinate identity conditions, and his analogous talk of an 'unconscious error' (Chapter 10). Both thinkers I believe are led to this position because of self-imposed limits on the

[29] *ātmany ātma-manasoḥ saṃyoga-viśeṣād ātmapratyakṣam* | (*Vaiśeṣika-sūtra* 9.11; Thakur 2003: 112).

[30] For a clear statement of this fundamentally anti-Cartesian commitment: Śaṃkara Miśra (1969: 481,1–2). For a discussion of unconscious emotion, see Ch.14.

[31] *ātmā pratyakṣaḥ sākṣātkāraviṣayo yatra jñāne tat tathā* | (Śaṃkara Miśra 1969: 581,1).

resources they believe can legitimately be drawn on in forming an objective conception; for Metzinger, the limitation is imposed by his wish to naturalize the first-person stance, and for Dharmakīrti, it is due to his desire to have a bottom-up or 'foundational' epistemology of content. I will show in Chapter 15 that in the absence of such self-imposed limitations, the resources for an objective conception of self and world are fully available.

The hypothesis that the unconscious mind has a dual role—a role in guiding attention to external stimuli and a role in self-monitoring—seems to have considerable explanatory power. In particular, it offers the potential for an explanation of what is known in psychiatry as *thought insertion*, the phenomenon in which subjects believe that thoughts not their own have intruded into their mental space. Thought insertion seems to call into question the immunity to error through misidentification in subject uses of the first person, for subjects fail correctly to identify themselves as the owner of their thought. The reason that the Nyāya-Vaiśeṣika model of unconscious mind can explain thought insertion while Cartesian models struggle is that it draws a distinction between two senses in which experiences are of or in a subject. The idea that a subject owns their experience is expressed in the technical vocabulary of individual causes: the subject is the individual cause of the experience. The different idea that the experience is individuated by the subject is expressed in the vocabulary of feature causes: the subject's physical states feature cause their mental states. Without this distinction, the possibility that a subject who has an experience can believe that they don't own it seems mysterious, because experience is always *someone's* experience, and whose can it be other than the person who owns it? So it seems from a Cartesian point of view that whenever an experience is internal to a subject it presents itself as owned by them.

The present theory identifies the equivocation in this formulation. What one should say, rather, is that an experience which is internal to a subject, in the sense that the subject's body is the feature cause of the experience, fails to present itself as owned by the subject, in the sense of having the subject as its individual cause. The Cartesian equivocation between 'being internal' and 'being owned' is hereby laid bare. The phenomenon of thought insertion can be coded in the present theory in terms of the unconscious mind mistakenly confusing its two roles, self-monitoring and attention to external sensory inputs. To put it in procedural vocabulary, the idea would be that the unconscious mind 'makes contact with' (or: tokens an efference copy of) one of one's thoughts and brings it to consciousness, but incorrectly marks it as having been sourced externally, not internally. So it appears to the conscious subject as something alien, as something from outside, even though it is their own.[32] Positing a single aspect of unconscious cognitive functioning responsible for two roles, one to do with self-knowledge and the other to do with attention to information from external sources, provides a theoretical framework that can make sense of what otherwise seems to be an inexplicable mistake.[33] Again, since the same mechanism is involved both in the guided control of action and in the presentation to the subject of the action as willed, a possible explanation for the instances of mismatch noticed by Libet might be developed, where ownership of an act of willing seems to lag behind unconscious processes of control.[34] Processes of comparison, selection and monitoring are the substrate in the 'cognitive unconscious' which ground the avowal or non-avowal of an intention, the ownership of an act of will, in just the same way as unconscious cross-modal comparisons are the substrate of our conscious experience of objects (Chapter 15) and subdoxastic comparisons are the substrate for normative emotional response (Chapter 14). The salient point in each case is that no judgement is involved: the comparisons take place at a level below that of judgement. That indeed is why, in a case of thought insertion, there is no sense of freedom but rather one of alien intrusion. In Chapter 1 I drew a contrast between the idea of a property being 'rooted' in

[32] Cf. Spence, who in criticizing Frith's agency model of thought insertion, conjectures that 'rather than comprising solely a failure to monitor conscious intentions (as in Frith's theory), does alien control actually involve an increased awareness of unconscious intentions, automatic programs that should remain outside awareness? Are these the "intentions" attributed to the "other" ' (Spence 2001: 170).

[33] A systemic account of attention in which the dual function I am highlighting is recognized is provided by O'Shaughnessy (2002: 291–2). Compare also the *prosektikon* postulated by 'Philoponus' in his commentary on Aristotle's *De Anima*: 'For there ought to be one thing apprehending all, since the human being is one. If *one* laid hold of these and *another* of those, it would be, as he [Aristotle *De Anima* 3.2, 426b17–21] himself says elsewhere, as if you perceived this and I that. It must then be one thing, and that is the attentive part (*prosektikon*). This attentive part roves over all powers, cognitive and vital . . . Besides, it is absurd that the same sense should know that it sees. For it must be by turning back on itself after having seen the colour that it gets to know that it sees. But if it turns on itself, it also has an activity which is separate, and what has a separate activity has a separate essence . . . For a thing's turning on itself is nothing other than its apprehending its own activities. So Aristotle does not speak rightly, but, as we said, it belongs to the attentive part of the soul to get to know the activities of the senses' ('Philoponus' in *De Anima* 3, 464,30–466,29; trans. Charlton, cited in Sorabji 2006: 253–4; cf. Caston 2002: 803).

[34] On the contrast between the conscious phenomenology of free will and unconscious initiation of 'voluntary' action, see Spence (1996); Libet (1999).

an individual and the idea of bare attribution. The hypothesis of unconscious mind is just the way to substantiate the thought that ownership involves the 'rooting' of mental properties in subjects.

I suggest that we do now have a constructive explanation of the multiple-domain supervenience between mind and body proposed in the last chapter. Conscious states of mind supervene on—that is to say, are 'feature caused' by—the physical states of an unconscious mechanism of comparison, selective attention, self-monitoring, information retrieval, and action-guidance. This metaphysical dependence discharges the requirement that the theory of mind be a 'minimal physicalism'. Yet ownership, and with it the occupancy of a first-person stance, is not thereby naturalized, because a subject's possession of a mental state only supervenes on but is not reduced to a condition of the unconscious mind (the distinction is marked by the appeal here to the idea of an 'individual cause'). It is open that the unity of a subject's mental life and the freedom of their will admit of non-causal explanation.[35] In the next three chapters I will begin to articulate the form that such an explanation might take. I will argue that such explanations are in play in the analysis of the nature of ownership as a matter of inhabitation and endorsement, and in a different way in the construction of a relation of common ownership between mental states. Subjects are doubly embedded in the space of reasons.

[35] 'Non-causal' meaning 'not efficient causal'; a broader concept of causality can span the breach between the realm of law and the space of reasons.

14

The Emotions

In this chapter I will argue that emotions have an indispensable role within the theory of mind being developed. They serve to define a relation of common ownership among the mental states—cognitive, agentive, and evaluative—of a single subject. They do this because they are non-cognitive signals of congruence or mismatch in the content of those states. As such they supervene on comparisons made at the subpersonal level. They are also calls to action, felt from within a first-person stance as demands. Emotions are a bridge between the participant self and the underself, and also between these two and the immersed self.

What Is an Emotion?

According to a theory first advanced in detail by Praśastapāda, the core attributes of an emotion are an appraisal, an inclination to action, and a capacity to be felt.[1] Pleasure, for example, is elicited by the appraisal of something as likeable or pleasant, is exhibited in an inclination to maintain a continuing relationship with the object, and is felt as agreeable or gratifying or favourable. Desire is elicited by the appraisal of something not at hand as potentially so, is exhibited in an inclination to create a relationship with it, and is felt as a 'calling out'. Anger is elicited by the appraisal of something as obstructive, exhibited in an inclination to sever the relationship with it by harming it, and felt as a burning or inflammation. An emotion is not merely a feeling, but there is something it feels like to have one. An emotion is identical neither to a judgement nor a perception nor a memory, nor to any other intentional mental state, although it has such states as antecedents.

[1] Praśastapāda (1994: 58–60, §§ 290–6).

Indeed, emotions do not themselves have intentional content, but they can become objects of intentional states.

From the time at least of the *Vaiśeṣika-sūtra* (first or second century CE), the emotions have been classified under four generic headings: pleasure (*sukha*), pain (*duḥkha*), desire (*icchā*), and dread (*dveṣa*). Each type of emotion is associated with a basic affect: favouring, hurting, yearning, and burning. The emotions are further identified by characteristic patterns of stimulus and reaction. Pleasure and pain arise, typically, as a result of sensory contact with a proximal object; but also in response to things remembered or anticipated. Desire and dread follow on from pleasure and pain, but also from memory. The reaction associated with pleasure and pain is one of inner surge, while the reaction associated with desire and dread is one pertaining to an urge to act. All four generic emotions have a distinctive evaluative dimension: pleasure-giving and desirable objects are evaluated as good, pain-causing or fearsome objects are evaluated as bad.[2]

In specifying an emotion, some object must be mentioned as the target of antecedent appraisal, but this object is not an intentional object for the emotion—the emotion is not 'about' that object. One may be angry *because* someone is being wilfully obstructive, and one's inclination to react by hitting out might be directed *at* that person or some other thing, but neither the 'because' nor the 'at' specifies an intentional object for the emotion. Vaiśeṣika philosophers claim that emotions are not forms of awareness (belief, judgement, perception, memory). That is to say, an emotion does not have an intentional object (*viṣaya*; *viṣayākāra*). It is true that pleasures are caused by something in the proximal environment, and that desires respond to a perceived lack of something; but in neither case is it correct to describe the target of the antecedent appraisal as an intentional object of the emotion. The core affects are changes in the state of conscious subjects, but not necessarily changes that the subject is conscious of.[3] One argument is that

[2] Cf. the Stoic classification is of all emotions into four generic ones: pleasure (*hēdonē*), distress (*lupē*), appetite (*epithumia*), and fear (*phobos*), the first pair directed at the present and the second at the future, the first in each pair involving an apparent good, the second an apparent evil (Sorabji 2002: 29). The division of emotions into pleasure, pain, desire, and dread is also endorsed by some modern psychologists, e.g. Berridge (1999).

[3] Cf. the comments of Vācaspati and Udayana under *Nyāya-sūtra* 1.1.4, well summarized by Matilal (1986: 295–8). See also Śaṃkara Miśra, commenting on *Vaiśeṣika-sūtra* 10.1.3–4 (Śaṃkara Miśra 1969: 522–4; trans. 1911: 328–9). The section *Vaiśeṣika-sūtra* 10.1.1–4 is the original source for the doctrine that emotions are non-cognitive.

emotions have different causal roles from states of awareness.[4] Another is that emotions structure the space around the subject hodologically, by attributing gerundival properties, while cognition simply identifies objects.[5] A third is that one can perform a thought-experiment in which one holds fixed the objects of awareness and varies the emotion. Udayana compares two individuals who listen to the same piece of music. One is a music-lover and finds the perception of the music agreeable; the other is a dispassionate sage, who is unaffected by the same perception.[6] A fourth argument is that there is a difference in the phenomenology between emotion and cognition.[7] A fifth argument is that emotions are not governed by the epistemic norms that bear upon belief and doubt: there is nothing in emotion corresponding to the balancing of evidence and weighing up of alternatives which is characteristic of judgement.[8]

If the above account is correct, then we shall need to distinguish three senses in which the term 'object' (*artha*) is used in reference to emotion. If used in the sense in which judgements have propositional objects and perceptions have intentional objects, I will translate it as 'content' (*artha-pravaṇa*). According to the present theory, emotions do not have content (cf. Udayana 1986: 385). If used in the sense in which desires have objects, that is things or states or events to which the desire is directed and upon which its satisfaction hinges, I will translate it as 'target' (*aprāpta*). Finally, if used in the sense in which hatred has something as its object, something against which one rages, I will call it the 'focus' (*apādāna*). Enmity has a focus: the to-be-avoided thing whose identification is constrained by recollection and pain.

A distinction can be drawn between what it is to *feel* an emotion and what it is to *notice* one. One way to make that distinction is in terms of the notions of 'world-directed' and 'self-directed' focus. To *feel* afraid is to find the world scary; it is expressed in sentences such as 'That dangerous thing is coming towards me.' To *notice* that one is afraid is expressed rather in

[4] See Matilal (1986: 295–8); Faddegon (1918: 403).

[5] Udayana (1967: 254–9); Matilal (1986: 301).

[6] Udayana (1967: 254–9); Matilal (1986: 301).

[7] Jayanta (1982–4: i.118); cf. Tuske (2011).

[8] Śaṃkara Miśra on *Vaiśeṣika-sūtra* 10.1.2 (Śaṃkara Miśra 1969: 522,2–8; trans. 1911: 327, cf. Thakur 2003: 117).

first-person present-tense ascriptions of a psychological state, such as 'I am afraid of this thing.' One notices that one is afraid because one feels afraid: self-knowledge—at least knowledge about one's own emotional states—is therefore a matter of attending to how the world presents itself. To see the world as fearsome *is* to know oneself afraid.

An emotion is also a state of 'action-readiness', a tendency towards action. The theory places emotions fundamentally within an account of goal-directed, motivated behaviour. Pleasure and pain are emotion types associated with the *end state* of action; they indicate, respectively that this is a state to be preserved and continued, or that this is a state to be relinquished. Desire and dread are emotion types associated with *goal-seeking*; they indicate respectively that something is a goal to be striven for, or that it is one to be shunned. So emotions reinforce or undermine goal seeking, and stabilize or destabilize end states. Notice the importance of gerundival descriptions in these specifications: emotions create a 'hodological space' around the perceiver, of objects to be sought or avoided, of paths for reaching what is desired and avoiding what is disliked.[9]

In every emotion, then, there is a core affect, a range of instigator conditions, and a spectrum of symptomatic effects. The range of instigator conditions can be quite heterogenous, and determines the range and identity of the types there are of that emotion. The symptomatic effects include the implications for behaviour and the physiological manifestations of the emotion (a reddening of the cheeks, for example, in the case of anger). An emotion is an attribute of the whole of one's being, one which happens as a result of one's engagement with things other than the emotion itself, and which expresses itself in feeling and in action dispositions. To understand the theory better, let us see how it is worked out in the case of one particular generic emotion: pleasure. An analogous description could then easily be drawn out for the generic emotion that forms much of the basis of Indian, especially Buddhist, soteriology, namely pain (*duḥkha*).[10]

[9] On the idea of a hodological space, see Lewin (1937); Lambie and Marcel (2002); Frijda (2007: 204–5).

[10] The first of the Buddha's four noble truths is 'Everything is pain' (*sarvaṃ duḥkham*). I take this to mean that there is an element of negative affect involved in the ownership of any mental state.

A Theory of Pleasure

Praśastapāda presents a worked-out theory of pleasure. Pleasure, he argues, can be felt and can be cognized, but is not itself either the feeling or the cognition. Rather, the characteristic of pleasure is a condition of agreeableness or favourableness (*anugraha*). It is a response to the presence of something marked as liked or desirable, something typically noticed in one's physical presence but which might also be remembered or anticipated. Pleasure, he says, is associated with the action of 'embracing', and it also manifests in physiological responses such as the eyes shining:

The mark (*lakṣaṇa*) of pleasure is agreeableness (*anugraha*). Pleasure is that which arises if something 'reached for' (*abhipreta*) like a garland, which is nearby, from a sense-object contact in attending to the thing liked (*iṣṭa-upalabdhi*), as well as, subject to the requirements of such things as ethical merit (*dharma*), from a connection between the unconscious mind and the self; it is the cause of a brightening of the eyes and that sort of thing, an embracing (*abhiṣvaṅga*), and an agreeableness (*anugraha* again).[11]

Several later philosophers contribute to the analysis. Vyomaśiva makes an excellent point when he observes that what causes pleasure is the object reached out for, and not the inner state itself.[12] In other words, this analysis discourages the view that pleasure is merely an introspectible inner episode. Rather, it is a change in psychological condition which comes into being when attending to something else. Śrīdhara correlatively observes that pleasure does not arise in someone whose attention is elsewhere or who is preoccupied, even if something pleasant is at hand. More importantly, he takes seriously the idea that pleasure is a kind of favour: one is in favour, things are going well, the world is being hospitable.[13] He explains that the second use of the word 'agreeable' or 'favourable' refers to a cognition (*saṃvedana*) of pleasure, distinct from the pleasure itself, and notes further that 'when a pleasure is generated, it produces a cognition of itself, and that is a favour to the self'. In addition, the pleasure produces a passion or attraction (*anurāga*) in the direction of the object responsible for the pleasure

[11] Praśastapāda (1994: 58, §290a).
[12] Vyomaśiva (1983: ii. 216, 9–12).
[13] Śrīdhara (1984: 259).

itself. The third philosopher to enrich the account is Udayana. It is symptomatic of pleasure, he says, that one continually wishes it to flow without interruption, and to be repeated again and again. This is the significance he gives to the term 'embracing'.[14]

A feature of the analysis is the provision it makes for there to be several types of pleasure. It provides for a distinction between sensory pleasures and nonsensory pleasures of the mind, as well as allowing there to be pleasures in directing one's attention towards the future or towards the past. The appraisal that precedes pleasure is not restricted to things in one's present environment: one can take pleasure now in remembering something good that happened in the past, or also in anticipating (*saṃkalpa*) something good yet to take place. The memory and anticipation are not of past or future pleasures, necessarily, but of past of future goods from which one derives pleasure now just as one does from a present good.

Udayana distinguishes four kinds of pleasure: sensual pleasure from objects (*vaiṣayika*), pleasures of the mind (*mānorathika*), pleasures belonging with repeated practice or training (*ābhyāsika*), and those associated with self-respect, such as achievement (*ābhimānika*).[15] Aesthetic pleasures are discussed, as well as the possibility of there being pleasure when dreaming.

Praśastapāda permits pleasures of a distinctive kind to sages:

> Pleasure is produced by memory, in the case of something that is in the past. It is produced by anticipation (*saṃkalpa*), in the case of something that is in the future. But the pleasure of the wise, who are without anticipation, desire or memory, is a result of their wisdom (*vidyā*), peace of mind (*śama*), contentment (*santoṣa*) and particular merit.[16]

Vyomaśiva and Śrīdhara offer different interpretations of the pleasant emotions available to a sage. Vyomaśiva says that they are: pleasure in that knowledge of the truth which derives from the study of philosophy, peace of mind in the sense of the eradication of passion and other disruptive emotion; contentment as a sense of satisfaction; and the pleasure of the sage's

[14] Udayana (1971: 248).

[15] Udayana (1967: 258, 710). Śaṃkara Miśra (1969: 523,2–3) too reports the same four sorts of pleasure, pertaining to objects, the mind, accomplishment, and habit ('*caturvidhaṃ hi sukhaṃ vaiṣayikaṃ mānorathikam ābhimānikam ābhyāsikaṃ ca*').

[16] Praśastapāda (1994: 58, §290b).

particular merit.[17] Śrīdhara says that they are: pleasures based on self-knowledge; peace of mind in the sense of control over the senses; contentment as not wanting anything except such as needed to sustain the body; and finally pleasure in excellence of merit, consisting in a withdrawing.[18]

The analysis also clarifies the relationship between pleasure and pain. They are in a sense opposed, but one is not merely the absence of the other.[19] Pleasure is a stable state, a state of acceptance and continuing interaction with something in one's environment. The felt lack of such things, of the pleasure they afford, shapes one's will to act in order to associate oneself with them. Pain is an unstable state, a state of interaction with things that is not to be endured and intolerable. The felt presence of such things, of the pain they cause, shapes one's will to act in order, not merely to dissociate oneself from them, but often to destroy them altogether. When there is a congruence with an object or state appraised as liked or desired, the feeling is one of gratification (*anugraha*) or favourableness (*anukūla*) and the emotion is called 'pleasure' (*sukha*). When with an object or state appraised as disliked, the feeling is one of hurting (*upaghāta*) or disfavourableness (*pratikūla*) and the emotion is called 'pain' (*duḥkha*).[20] Clearly the range of the term 'pain' is much wider than simple physical pain, but includes being depressed, distressed, dissatisfied, or unhappy, a lack of flourishing. Pleasure exhibits behaviourally in phenomena such as a brightening of the eyes, pain in being downcast (*dainya*). As well as being *indicative* of desire-satisfaction, pleasure and pain are *generative* of desires and hates. Śrīdhara emphasizes that pleasure is not merely the absence of pain, nor pain merely the absence of pleasure, for they give rise to two distinct sorts of motivation: 'I will avoid this' and 'I will seek this out'. For Vyomaśiva, on the other hand, the reason they are distinct is that the basic affects of favouring and hurting are irreducibly distinct.[21]

Pleasure and pain are asymmetrical in still another way: pleasures fade with sustained commerce, while pain continues. The pleasure derived from

[17] *vidyā-śama-santōṣa-dharma-viśeṣa-nimittam iti kāraṇopanyāsaḥ* | *vidyā tattvajñānaṃ tasmāt tattvajñāninām sukham* | *tathā śamo rāgādi-vināśaḥ, tasmāc ca śānta-manasāṃ sukham* | *santoṣo viṣayeṣv alam-pratyayaḥ, tasmāc ca sukham* | *keṣāñcad dharma-viśeṣāc ceti* | (Vyomaśiva 1983: ii. 216, 26–217,2).

[18] Śrīdhara (1984: 259).

[19] *Vaiśeṣika-sūtra* 10.1.

[20] Praśastapāda (1994: 59, §291). Cf. *Nyāya-sūtra* 1.1.21.

[21] Vyomaśiva (1983: ii. 216,17–18). For a review of contemporary discussion on this topic, see Frijda (2007: 86–8).

the continuing presence of something tends to diminish, but, at the same time, if it were no longer there, this would still be felt as a lack. So a will to act based on gaining sources of pleasure leads to 'craving' (*tṛṣṇā*), a state that demands to be maintained, not for the pleasure it affords but for the need it keeps at bay, a state of high dependency.[22]

The key elements in this analysis of pleasure, then, are as follows. First, pleasures are conditions marked as being favoured; second, this expresses itself in feelings of satisfaction; third, it exhibits in a disposition to act articulated in terms of an 'embracing', which has shades of reaching out, of holding or remaining, and of returning and repeating. That pleasures are non-cognitive mental states, and in particular, that they are neither perceptions nor judgements, is only implicit in Praśastapāda's text, Praśastapāda turning to a discussion of pleasure *after* discussing the varieties of cognition. That aspect of the theory is drawn rather from *Vaiśeṣika-sūtra* 10.1.1–3 and the commentaries on *Nyāya-sūtra* 1.1.4. A pleasure-response consists in one or more of three things: a physiological reaction, an affinity felt for the object whose presence led to the pleasure, and a conscious awareness of the pleasure itself.

Remarkably, in the last few years psychologists have begun to reach a view about pleasure with many similarities to the analysis presented here. Nico Frijda, summarizing the latest research, argues that the phenomenology of pleasure is not that of a felt inner state but rather what he calls a 'niceness gloss' applied to the object, and inciting the core responses of acceptance and commerce: 'Pleasantness is the demand character of things-to-be-dwelt-with or interactions-to-be-continued-with' (2007: 67). Central to acceptance is that the object is assimilated: 'The experience of pleasure is an expansive one. One stretches out' (2007: 68). The Vaiśeṣika claim that pleasure is associated with a wish to maintain commerce, and pain with a wish to break it, receives support in the study of Baumeister, Vohs, DeWall, and Zhang (2007). The importance of appraisal processes in emotion is confirmed by Scherer, Schorr, and Johnstone (2001). Finally, pleasures are classifiable according to the grounds for acceptance of the object, and Frijda distinguishes the following types: sensory pleasures, non-sensory likings (including especially due to past and future objects), pleasures of gain and relief, achievement and mastery pleasures, activity pleasures,

[22] *Nyāya-sūtra* 4.1.56, and Vātsyāyana's commentary.

social pleasures, and aesthetic pleasures (2007: 75). A common feature of many pleasures is that they indicate to a subject that some competence they possess is functioning well; pleasure is a sort of success signal, a monitor of adequate functioning.

Emotions and Agency

Emotions are felt motivational tendencies to form and sustain congruences with objects or states appraised as beneficial (*hita*), and to avoid or break congruences with objects or states appraised as harmful (*ahita*).[23] When the tendency is to sustain an appropriate congruence with an object or state appraised as liked, the feeling is one of gratification or favourableness and the emotion is called 'pleasure'. When an inappropriate congruence is sought to be broken (*amarṣa*) with an object or state appraised as disliked, the feeling is one of hurting or disfavourableness and the emotion is called 'pain'.[24] The motivational tendency to establish a new congruence with an object, under constraints shaped by memory and pleasure, is felt as a yearning (*prārthana*) and the emotion is one of 'desire' (*icchā*). Desire is defined as an unfulfilled longing for something one wants but does not have, a category that includes the anticipation (*saṃkalpa*) of a future pleasure.[25] The motivational tendency to avoid a congruence with an object, under constraints shaped by memory and pain, is felt as a blazing (*prajvalana*) and the emotion is one of 'emnity' or 'dread' (*dveṣa*).[26]

Desire and dread too exist in a variety of modalities. According to Praśastapāda the modalities of desire are: for sex (*kāma*; lust); for food (*abhilāṣa*; hunger); for repeated gratification (*rāga*; passion, compulsion); to act in relation to a distal goal (*saṃkalpa*; anticipation); for the eradication of others' pain (*kāruṇya*; compassion); for the relinquishing of what one perceives as failings (*vairāgya*; dispassion); to mislead others (*upadhā*; deceit); to keep something hidden inside (*bhāva*; discretion or repressed desires).[27]

[23] Praśastapāda (1994: 60, §296).

[24] Praśastapāda (1994: 58–9, §§290–1).

[25] *svārthaṃ parārthaṃ vā 'prāpta-prārthanecchā* | . . . | *kāmo 'bhilāṣo rāgaḥ saṃkalpaḥ kāruṇyaṃ vairāgyam upadhā bhāva ity evamādaya icchā-bhedāḥ* | (Praśastapāda 1994: 59, §292).

[26] Praśastapāda (1994: 60, §294).

[27] Praśastapāda (1994: 59, §293).

The modalities of hate are: anger (*krodha*), an agitation (*vikāra*; a state-change) in the body and the senses lasting only a short while; malice (*droha*), which is an unsignalled agitation ending in a lasting harm (*avakāra*); insult (*manyu*), which is a repression of the inability to harm back one by whom one has been harmed; envy (*akṣamā*), which is rage at the good qualities in another; indignation (*amarṣa*), which arises when one's own good qualities are held in contempt.[28]

What one desires is to establish the sorts of congruences that are beneficial, either to oneself or to another. Because they are beneficial, one desires them, and because one has desired them, they are pleasurable when they occur. To appraise something as *appropriately* desired is to appraise it as desired because beneficial. Pleasure, as we have seen, can also occur as a derivative response to the recollection of a past event and also to the anticipation or imagination (*saṃkalpa*) of a future one. Imagining that one has achieved one's goal is pleasurable, and so too is recalling some past accomplishment. In every case, however, pleasure is associated with goal accomplishment, the delivery of a desired outcome. Affect is indirectly motivational: from a desire for food to a desire to eat to a desire to taste. One comes to desire the affect for itself, when initially it was only an outcome-indicator.

An act of will or intention (*prayatna*) is responsible for motivated actions whose function is to get what is beneficial and give up what is harmful. When the will is directed towards acquiring things productive of benefit, it is shaped by one's needs, wants or desires (*icchā*); when directed towards surrendering things productive of harm, it is shaped by one's rages, irritations and tempers (*dveṣa*).[29] Wants are 'requests' (*prārthana*) for things one does not have, a request expressible as 'May this be mine'. Rages are inflammations directed against things that have caused us pain; they lead to a will to act expressible as 'I will destroy it'. Praśastapāda introduces a normative ethical dimension to the discussion, saying that when directed against agencies bent on disrupting the moral order, rages have merit (*dharma*), but as directed against those who protect and nourish it, they attract blame (*adharma*).

[28] Praśastapāda (1994: 60, §294). A slightly different list is given by Vātsyāyana under *Nyāya-sūtra* 4.1.3.
[29] Praśastapāda (1994: 60, §295).

Emotion and the Participant Self

To say that emotions are states of the self is, in the theory of mind developed in the previous two chapters, to say that they are *owned* by the subject and not merely occurrent mental events. I suggested at the end of the last chapter that the point of treating states of mind as owned by a self has to to with making available a noncausal explanation of the unity of the subject. According to the theory of emotion just presented, emotions do not have any intentional content, and are not even necessarily themselves the objects of conscious thought (the Transitivity Principle does not apply to them). They are non-cognitive states of the self, mediating a relationship between appraisal and will, between the belief that something good or bad is at hand and the act of obtaining or avoiding it. I mentioned that many pleasures serve to indicate to a subject that some competence they possess is functioning well, that pleasure or pain is a sort of success signal, the result of monitoring for adequate functioning. Can we then argue that the key role of emotions in the unity of the self consists in their being owned non-cognitive signals, so that, for example, pleasure is *my* signal to myself that an action I have performed has led successfully to the satisfaction of one of *my* desires? What this signal consists in is not just a feeling of agreeableness but also, more importantly, an 'embracing', a request or demand for continued commerce, and so to a further propensity to act.

The idea that emotions are non-cognitive signals has an important virtue: it integrates extremely well with the hypothesis that there is an unconscious selector comparator mechanism (*manas*). Many emotions, for example, can be regarded as indicators of match or mismatch between a subject's background and occurrent beliefs and desires. Delight is an indicator that a standing desire is now believed to be satisfied, and sorrow the indicator that a standing desire is believed to be unsatisfiable. These emotions are thus person-level expressions of a comparison, itself conducted at a subpersonal level, of the contents of one's beliefs and desires. In a similar vein, Reisenzein (2009) has argued for the existence of 'a mechanism that compares the newly acquired belief to the preexisting desires, looking for match and mismatch—a belief-desire comparator... and... a mechanism that compares the newly acquired belief to the preexisting beliefs for match versus mismatch—a belief-belief comparator' (2009: 11). He sees an analogy between the functioning of these mechanisms and that of sensory transduction: 'Instead of sensing the world, these "internal transducers" sense the state of the belief-desire-system and signal important states and state changes in this system as it deals with new information' (2009: 14). Reisenzein summarizes the theory as being that 'emotions are the nonpropositional signals of congruence and incongruence produced by the two basic, hard-wired comparator mechanisms that service the belief-desire system' (2009: 15). So, for example, surprise is an emotion signalling the situation in which a standing belief is overridden, a situation expressible as 'Certain (p, t) & Bel $(\neg p, t{-}1)$'.

This conjecture fits with several of the analyses our philosophers offer of emotions. They say that delight (*harṣa*) is the pleasure one has on fulfilling a longing for something desired, fear (*bhaya*) the distress when one is unable to rid oneself of the wish to flee in the presence of what will lead to something undesired, sorrow (*śoka*) the unfulfillable longing for something desired from which one is separated.[30] Simone Weil defines joy as the feeling of reality; in our model it is the non-cognitive sign that one believes one's beliefs to be true. What Reisenzein omits from his description, perhaps because it is too evident to need explicit mention, is an appreciation of the essential role the concept of self plays in this theory of emotions as outputs of unconscious comparator activity. The self is that single owner of the beliefs and desires among which comparisons are made: it is essential that the sure belief at t is a belief owned by the same subject as the negative belief at $t{-}1$ if an emotion is to serve as a signal, that is to say as evidence of an incongruence.

Attention should not be restricted only to the informational states (*jñāna*) of the subject, for we have seen that action-instigation (*prayatna*) is intrinsic to emotion. Śrīdhara tellingly describes the action-propensity involved in desire as 'I will seek this out' and in rage as 'I will destroy this', reinforcing the point that the desire and the ensuing will to act stand in a relation of common ownership (my emotions are not signals that someone else should act, or merely that there should be action: they are signals that *I* should act). Vātsyāyana therefore asserts that

[30] These definitions are provided by Uddyotakara in his comments on *Nyāya-sūtra* 3.1.18. The text reads: *abhipreta-viṣaya-prārthanāprāptau sukhānubhavo harṣaḥ* | *aniṣṭa-viṣaya-sādhana-sannipāte tajjihāsorhānā-śakyatā bhayam* | *iṣṭa-viṣaya-viyoge sati tatprāptyaśakya-prārthanā śokaḥ* | (1997: 344, 9–11).

On coming across the kind of object already known to be the cause of pleasure, one is motivated to attain objects of the same kind, and such a motivation is not possible without an identical subject that perceives various objects and recognises them.[31]

Ownership is related to an idea of inhabitation (one occupies a first-person stance as a participant within, not as a witness of, a mental life); and to say that an emotion is an owned state of a subject is to say that the subject feels its action-request as a demand, not merely as a force. That is why our philosophers are right to say that desire presents itself as an 'I will seek this out' and anger as an 'I will destroy this'. Emotions as noncognitive signs of match and mismatch are thus also a consequence of unconscious belief-will and desire-will comparisons. One might will one's arm to rise but see that someone is restraining it, an incongruence signalled in frustration if no malicious intent is ascribed, and in anger if it is. Rage is a sign that one wills the destruction of something one believes has caused one harm. Emotions are also evidence to a subject of their moral evaluations of proposed courses of action or of past behaviour. In Praśastapāda's theory this finds expression in the role he gives to *dharma* and *adharma* in his theory of pleasure and pain. The desire for something appraised as immoral or unworthy is signalled by feelings of disgust or self-loathing.

The theory that emotions are non-cognitive signals of value is to be distinguished from the idea that they are *judgements* of value and importance (Nussbaum 2001; Sorabji 2002), and also from the idea that they are *perceptions* of value and importance (at least in Praśastapāda's cognitive analysis of perception; a theory of sentience such as that of Dignāga or Dharmakīrti might have different implications). The theories agree in assigning to the emotions an indispensable role in a subject's rational and evaluative architecture. Yet just as I will argue in Chapter 15 that cross-modal identities are not themselves judgements, but issue from unconscious processes of comparison, so too here I believe that an emotion which issues from an unconscious belief-belief comparison does not itself consist in a pair of judgements. The theory here has more affinity with Korsgaard's (2009) 'constitutional model', according to which reason, the passions, and agency are in an inner balance; she contrasts this with a Platonic 'combat model', in which a conflict between reason and the passions precedes action.

[31] Vātsyāyana (1997: 16,8–11); commenting on *Nyāya-sūtra* 1.1.10.

It follows from the analysis that pain has a utility and instrumental value of its own. It is to be eradicated, not because it is painful, but because of the incongruence its occurrence signals, and indeed the elimination of the incongruence is the right way to eliminate the pain, and not merely by suppressing the pain itself. Insofar as Indian soteriology praises the eradication of pain, it is attaching value to a mental life of coherence and consistency. I believe however that Nyāya and Vaiśeṣika philosophers are right when they say that the possibility of pain is integral to any mental life, because there is always the possibility that mismatches and incongruences will arise, and that a state entirely free from even the possibility of pain will be a condition of complete insentience, rather than one of ideal rationality. I have already said that I do not regard such a condition as in any meaningful sense the survival of an individual. In a real human life the value of the generic emotion of pain in any of its species consists in the indication it provides that something is amiss. The theory here disagrees with the Davidsonian hypothesis that rationality is a constitutive ideal for the mental, as it does with the Rawlsian conjecture that fairness is a constitutive ideal of justice; what it claims instead is that lapses in rationality are signs that a mental wrong needs righting, as lapses in fairness are indicators of an injustice in need of resolving.

What this theory of emotion does recommend is that the idea of the unity of an individual subject's mental life, the role of the emotions as indicators of the occurrence of binding or lack of binding at cognitive and agentive levels, and the idea of unconscious mechanisms engaged in activities of monitoring and comparison, are interrelated. The unity of the self and the posit of an unconscious comparator mechanism are what make it intelligible that one's experiences, judgements, motivations, intentions, values, and emotions can bear upon each other, that is, exercise rational demands on each other (why, for instance, a belief-belief mismatch is signalled by surprise and motivates revision of at least one of the beliefs). Emotions constitute evidence, and beliefs justify action, only when standing in a relation of common ownership. To the occupant of a first-person stance, an emotion is a demand: to act so as either to maintain a congruence or resolve a mismatch. Ownership is endorsement, and emotions are the presence within a participant stance of coherence or conflict among the various things endorsed. Two states stand in a relation of common ownership only if they are constituent endorsements in a single first-person stance (I will say more about this in Chapter 16). The relation of common ownership between states of cognition, evaluation, and motivation is the relation which obtains when the contents of the states bear upon each other in such a way that comparisons for congruence or mismatch are signalled by a core affect and exhibit in action. And for a state to be owned is therefore precisely for it to engage the whole of one's being through its potential to make normative demands on any other owned state (including, for example, the way perception normatively constrains belief): this is what gives substance to the ideas of inhabitation, participation, and endorsement that attributions of ownership imply. This too is what it means to describe a mental state as 'rooted' in the self, an entanglement of reasons and justifications underpinned by the procedural holism of a single comparing, monitoring, selecting subroutine.[32] Ownership entails embodiment because some of these demands can be satisfied only in action. Emotions are what integrate the participant self with the underself, and they do so through their implications for action.

I noted in the last chapter that malfunctions of attention and monitoring provide the subpersonal substrate for pathologies like thought insertion; here too one will expect that malfunctions of congruence and comparison will be associated with pathologies of emotion, and so, as a consequence of what I said in the last paragraph, with pathologies of identity and self.

The proposal is that items of mind exhibit rational demands only in the context of a subject. The argument for there being subjects of consciousness is that the conviction that perceptions, volitions, beliefs, desires, values, pleasures, and pains bear rationally on one another in signalled congruence and conflict requires that they stand in a relationship of common ownership and thereby are jointly constitutive of a single first-person stance. Our philosophers develop this thought in two ways: through an argument first presented at *Nyāya-sūtra* 3.1.1, that identity of content across sensory modalities requires a unitary subject, and through an argument first presented at *Vaiśeṣika-sūtra* 3.2.16, that the distinctness of distinct mental lives requires there to be distinct unitary subjects. I mean to evaluate these two arguments in the final two chapters of the book.

[32] 'The same function which gives unity to the various representations in a judgement also gives unity to the various representations in an intuition' (Kant, *Critique* A79/B104–5).

15

Unity

Milinda: Is there, Nāgasena, such a thing as the self?
Nāgasena: What is this 'self', O King?
Milinda: The living principle within, which sees colours through the eye, hears sounds through the ear, experiences tastes through the tongue, smells odours through the nose, feels touch through the body, and discerns things through the mind – just as we, sitting here in the palace, can look out of any window out of which we wish to look, the east window or the west, or the north or the south.[1]

One can observe that, after seeing an object with the eyes, one remembers how it tastes and salivates. So, like a spectator who is looking through more than one round window, it is known that there is a single perceiver for both sight and taste.[2]

And who is the 'lord' that joins sight and hearing?[3]

Nyāya philosophers claim that a proof of the reality of selves is constructible from the manifest ability of a conscious subject to integrate the deliverances of the various sense-modalities. 'Because of touch and sight', gnomically asserts *Nyāya-sūtra* 3.1.1, meaning that because through touch and sight the self-same object is perceived, and perceived *as the same*, there must be a single, unitary perceiver. In this chapter I will explore the possibilities for a philosophical defence of realism built around the idea that the self is that in virtue of which an integration (*pratisandhāna*; 'bringing together') of the

[1] *Milinda-pañhā* 2.3.6. The text contains answers provided by the Buddhist monk Nāgasena to questions put to him by the Indo-Greek king Menander I (r. 155–130 BCE).

[2] Praśastapāda (1994: 15,15–16,2, §78).

[3] *Kena Upaniṣad* 1d. Compare Plotinus *Enneads* 4.7.6: 'And if one [sense-object] enters through the eyes, and another through the hearing organ, there must be some one place to which they both go.' This is the passage Mendelssohn cites, in his misleadingly titled *Phaedon*, as his source for the argument Kant would later dub the 'Achilles of all dialectical inferences'. Nielsen (2008); Mijuskovic (1974).

deliverances of the senses is possible.[4] This is a version of what, in Chapter 12, I called the Unity Argument. Standing in a relation of common ownership is what makes possible the integration of the contents of perceptions in distinct sensory modalities.

Lennon and Stainton (2008) provide a general survey of this type of argument. In their terminology, what is being proposed here is a version of the *Narrow Achilles*, which argues from premise P1: There is a unification of representations, and premise P2: Only a unified substance can unify representations, to the Conclusion: The human mind is a unified substance (2008: 5). Different Nyāya formulations interpret P1 as a thesis about the unification of sensory contents from distinct sensory modalities, and as a thesis about the unification of representations across time, but also sometimes as about the unification of information from the various sources of knowledge, and as about the unification of aspects of an object into a representation of a single object. Vātsyāyana:

> After seeing the colour, one smells the scent; or, after smelling the scent, one sees the colour. So a single subject of consciousness recognises perceptions which might be about anything and whose temporal sequence is not rule-governed. And through this recognition the presentations of many objects in perception, inference, testimony, doubt and insight belong to an agent. After hearing the treatises which are about all manner of things, one comprehends things that are not heard. After listening to the temporal sequence of letters, recognising them as words and sentences, and knowing the rules of reference, one grasps the resultant many-object meaning, which no one sense can perceive. (Vātsyāyana 1997: 137,6-11; under 3.1.3)

What Lennon and Stainton call the *Broad Achilles* defends a stronger conclusion, that the human mind must also be immaterial and immortal. I believe that we should resist any such extension, and will argue that to the extent that Nyāya and Vaiśeṣika thinkers succumb to it, they are mistaken to do so (see also Chapter 16). The soundness of a Unity Argument does not depend on drawing these further consequences. Natural selves are unitary entities which endure for finite periods of time and,

[4] Gautama, *Nyāya-sūtra* 3.1.1, and the commentaries on this text by Vātsyāyana, Uddyotakara, and Vācaspati; Udayana (1986: 710–19, 752), along with the commentaries by Śaṃkara Miśra and Raghunātha Śiromaṇi. Modern discussions: Matilal (1994: 289); A. Chakrabarti (1992: 103–17).

because consciousness necessitates a potential to perceive, are metaphysically dependent on physical bodies: they are neither 'immaterial' (i.e. metaphysically independent of matter) nor 'immortal' (i.e. eternal, permanent). Insofar as Nyāya and Vaiśeṣika thinkers are willing to entertain the Broad Achilles, they make themselves hostages to fortune and easy prey to Buddhist and Cārvāka criticism. They also confuse what is otherwise an attractively naturalistic account of the mind with extraneous anti-naturalistic elements. I will show in the next chapter that early modern thinkers better distinguished issues about the Narrow and Broad versions of the argument which the earlier philosophers conflate.[5]

The Self as Genuine Subject

The leading idea is that the capacity to think of one's perceptions as cross-modally unified is incompatible with an aggregative model of the mind of the sort explored in several earlier chapters of this book. The Unity Argument purports to demonstrate that the self is a genuine individual. To be an individual is here stipulated to be the common locus of many properties (*jāti*) and/or property-tropes (*guṇa*). The claim is that the self is the single subject of many psychological properties—perceptions, beliefs, desires, dreads, intentions, pleasures, and pains. So the self is not what I earlier called a 'quasi-object' (Chapter 10), like a wave, without determinate identity conditions. Neither is the self to be thought of merely as an aggregate: it is not something of the same type as heaps and bundles.

When Parfit originally defined Reductionism, he did so in terms of a commitment to what he called the 'impersonal description' thesis, the claim that 'though persons exist, we could give a *complete* description of reality without claiming that persons exist' (Parfit 1984: 212, 225–6). Later, partly in response to arguments in Campbell (1994) and Cassam (1997a), he distanced Reductionism from this thesis (Parfit 1999). The idea behind

[5] A transitional step from the Narrow to the Broad Achilles involves the idea that unity requires simplicity. I will separate the question of unity from the question of simplicity. An individual can be a unity and still have an internal structure. In Iamblichus' description of the self is a dynamic unity of 'proceeding out', 'remaining', and 'returning', for instance, the self is a unity but not a *simple* unity (Steel 1978: 57). In the theory I propose, likewise, the self is a unity of participation, immersion, and coordination.

the impersonal description thesis is that talk of persons is redundant, in the sense that any fact described by mentioning a person could also be described without mentioning any person. Nyāya philosophers capture the intended distinction in a different way. They point to two readings of the logical form of third person perceptual ascriptions: 'He is looking at the apple with his eyes,' 'He is touching the apple with his right hand.' Appealing to the idea of deep case or thematic role (*kāraka*), the perceiver is encoded here as agent or affector, the apple as patient or thing affected, and the sense-organ as instrument or means of which the affecting takes place. What is observed is that the thematic relation between agent and instrument is ambiguous at the level of logical form, because it can represent either an adjectival or a collective relation (in the terminology of Chapter 1). Vātsyāyana:

> Is the self a mere assemblage of body, outer and inner sense-organs, thoughts and feelings, or is it something else? Why is there such a doubt? It is because both ways of using words are attested. A 'way of using words' is a reference to the relation between the agent and the instrument of the action. This reference is of two kinds: [first,] as between a part and a totality, as in 'A tree stays up with the help of its roots', or 'A house is supported by its pillars'. There is also a reference to a relation as between one thing and something else, as in 'One chops with an axe', or 'One sees with the help of a lamp.' In our case, there are usages like 'One sees with one's eyes', 'One thinks with one's mind', 'One ponders with one's intellect', 'One feels pain or pleasure due to one's body.' In these cases it is unclear whether the use is as between a part and the totality which is the assemblage of body and so on, or as between one thing and another different thing. (Vātsyāyana 1997: 697–701)

The question then is whether third-person perceptual ascriptions ought to be construed as having the underlying form of an ascription of one thing (a property or trope) to something else (an object), or as describing the relation between a totality and one of its constituents. The point is that there is both an 'is' of predication and an 'is' of composition. A realist claims that the surface grammatical form of these sentences is an accurate guide to their underlying logical form, while the rival theory accepts that the surface form ascribes a property to a subject, but argues that the underlying relation is collective. The sentences, let us say, have a *subject-free* underlying form (which is *not* to say that there can be a complete description of reality which does not mention subjects).

I will consider what is required of someone who has the capacity to think of their perceptions in distinct modalities as having the same object. That is, what does it take to find intelligible a judgement of the form 'That which I felt through touch I am looking at with my eyes?'[6] I will argue that one can make sense of such judgements only if one thinks of both oneself and the objects of perception as loci of many properties.[7] The capacity in question is one which requires the possession of a first-person stance.[8] So what the argument aims to demonstrate is that a first-person stance, the ability to conceive of oneself as oneself, requires that one conceive of oneself as an individual, a genuine subject. Correlatively I will argue that the subject-free paraphrase of the linguistic forms that describe these capacities actually presupposes the truth of the adjectival construal.

Cross-Temporal Identities

One formulation of the Unity Argument begins with the platitude that I cannot recollect your experiences, and I cannot recognize an object you have seen. According to this version, what needs to be explained is one's capacity, having once seen an object, to reidentify that same object by touch alone, making the argument turn on the role of memory (*smṛti*) and recognition (*pratyabhijñā*).[9] The argument in this form is said to turn on the principle that one cannot remember the contents of another's past experience. One ought not object to the argument by denying the principle on which it rests, because even a Buddhist will agree that there is a constitutive link between memory, reidentification and personal identity (see Chapter 9).

[6] *yaṃ cāspākṣaṃ sparśanena, taṃ cakṣuṣā paśyāmīti* | (Vātsyāyana 1997: 135,15).

[7] This is in agreement with experiments in developmental psychology showing that an infant's cross-modal capacities are essentially implicated in their development of a sense of self (Meltzoff 1990, 1993a, 1993b).

[8] 'If one can think of oneself as the bearer of first person thoughts, then one has the concept of a subject of thought and can think of others as subjects of thought. If one can think of oneself as oneself*, then, in addition to having desires (say), one can reflect on one's desires *as one's own*' (Baker 1998: 330).

[9] Vātsyāyana (1997: 135,15). This formulation is especially popular with non-Nyāya philosophers; e.g. Prabhācandra: 'Those who have not had prior experiences of the results following from what is desired or undesired would not, in a lawful manner, wish to seek or avoid them. That to which the prior experience is ascribed, it is the self, a distinct existence' (Prabhācandra 1991: 3478, 1–3).

On this formulation the Unity Argument seems at first to be invalid. Why shouldn't one be able to identify a currently touched object with an object about which one has memories implanted in one of another's perceptions of it? The point is that the implanted memory will not in general be derived from a single isolated past visual experience, but from a whole series of such experiences, in which the object is seen from a number of different points of view, as located on a table, as adjacent to other objects, and so on. Touching the object now, one perceives both the shape of the object and the spatial relations in which it stands with other objects, and recognizes them as the same as those of the object presented to one in one's implanted memories. One's capacity to identify the now perceived object with the object represented in memory does not *require* one to have been the source of those memories.

Against this, however, it might be urged that what is at stake is one's capacity to discriminate between the object now touched and a qualitatively identical duplicate. Imagine that the object currently being held has a clone, that someone has seen the clone, and that a memory derived from their experience is implanted. The moral of such an example might be that in order to be able to reidentify an object now touched with one previously seen, one's memory must represent one as having charted a path through space, in such a way that it offers one reasons for believing that it is the same object that was earlier seen and is now touched. The mere recollection of an object with the same shape as the one now being touched (and as standing in the same spatial relations with other objects) does not itself supply one with such a reason.

A more severe difficulty is rather that memory is too deeply implicated to be treated as if it were an isolable and unproblematic notion in terms of which reidentification and the identity of self over time can be explained. What is required is a common explanation of all three. For, as P. F. Strawson said about memory and experience, 'From whatever obscure levels they emerge they emerge together' (Strawson 1966: 112). Memory is already too thick a phenomenon to be used without the risk of begging the question as the premise in a Unity Argument.

Binding

According to a standard interpretation, the claim is that if the self is what compares and combines perceptions it cannot be merely a collection of those perceptions. The unity of self is what solves the binding problem. To this Buddhists typically rejoin that the self might be a collection of perceptions *and* of judgements of identity (which they call 'automatic judgements'). It is important to see that this rejoinder fails. Bostock, commenting on a famous passage in Plato that seems to envisage something like the version of the argument now being discussed,[10] says that

If it is the mind that makes judgements about its perceptions, and in particular comparisons between them, then they must all be perceptions of one and the same mind ... [I]t will not do simply to reform the theory by saying that the mind is a collection, not only of perception, but also of judgements, and no doubt other things too ... Mere collections do not seem to provide for the kind of unity that Socrates is pointing to .... it is difficult to say how this unity is accounted for if the 'one thing' in question is taken to be merely the collection of all the things which, as we say, 'it' does. (Bostock 1988: 153)

Clark, with the Buddhist rejoinder explicitly in mind, makes the same point:

Merely adding more qualities will not help: they will be lost in the flux with all the others. In a similar way, the ancient image of a thing as a bundle of such qualities – concretions settling out of the flux – *smuggles in* more organization than one might suppose. If the qualities are sticks, we need some distinct principle by which to bundle the sticks together. A piece of string serves admirably, but notice that it serves a rather different function than that served by additional sticks. Tossing in more sticks leaves one just as disorganised as before; they will soon be bobbing down the stream, undifferentiated from all the rest. (Clark 2000: 79)

The original Nyāya formulation seems to make a similar argument:

[The self is a unity] because a single object is grasped by touch and sight. [If you say] 'no, for there is restriction [of each sense] to its proper object', [we reply] this is not a refutation, because the existence of the self follows too from that very restriction. (*Nyāya-sūtra* 3.1.1–3)

The claim is that the unity of the self follows even if the senses are restricted to their proper sensibilia, rather than, as in the cross-modal version, one and

[10] 'It would surely be strange if we had several senses sitting in us, as if in a wooden horse, and it wasn't the case that all those things converged on some one kind of thing, a mind or whatever one ought to call it: something with which we perceive all the perceived things by means of the senses, as if by means of instruments' (*Theaetetus* 184d1–5).

the same object is presented in different sensory modalities. Yet although the standard Buddhist response fails, the idea that the unity of the self is what is required to solve the binding problem is indeed a mistaken one. The unity of consciousness is modelled on the unity possessed by a set of properties when they all share a common location. And yet the appearance of an explanation is an illusion: the integration in the *content* of a collection of perceptions is not accounted for by the idea that the perceptions as *vehicles* have a common location. The binding version of the argument exhibits the kind of fallacy labelled by Millikan 'content externalising' (Millikan 1991): it projects properties of the vehicle of thought onto its content.[11]

The Nyāya argument is framed in terms of sight and touch, and it seems right that sight and touch are to be distinguished from the other senses in that they both present such spatial properties of the objects as position and shape, which are properties in virtue of which one can be said to be perceiving the object itself rather than its sensory properties.[12] So the weight of the Nyāya argument falls on cross-modality rather than binding. Although a version of the binding argument is considered, it is not a good way of capturing the force of the argument at *Nyāya-sūtra* 3.1.1.

Tracking

Let us next consider a version of the argument based on the idea of temporal tracking. This version claims that an adequate account of the role of the self must be able to make out the distinction between *tracking* an object over time and *recognizing* it as the same at different times. That distinction is one between separating or not separating the information reaching the self from an object via the senses. However, if the self is nothing but a causally

[11] Compare: 'Nothing, indeed, can be represented that is simpler than that which is represented through the concept of a mere something. But the simplicity of the representation of a subject is not *eo ipso* knowledge of the simplicity of the subject itself.' (Kant, *Critique* A 355). My reconstruction below will not be vulnerable to the objection which Kant presses against the 'Achilles of rational psychology'.

[12] The Nyāya view is that it is a requirement on object perception that one can apprehend the object's shape. Śrīdhara clearly states that 'grasping a single object in both sight and touch is explained by assuming that it has a specific shape'. Halbfass (1992: 104), commenting on this, concludes that 'we are not dealing with an underlying substrate, but with shape as the common datum of tactual and visual perception.' This does not follow: the point is rather that we perceive objects in sight and touch because sight and touch inform us about the physical boundaries of the object.

interconnected sequence of bundles of mental and physical events, then the information from a single object is necessarily separated:

> There can be no [integration] in the case of a mere thought-series, each thought having a fixed object, *as in the case of different bodies*. . . . The phrase 'as in the case of different bodies' is to be explained thus. Just as even for the no-self theorist, a thought-series where each thought has a fixed object but is in a different body is not integrated, so too the objects of [the thoughts of] a single body ought not be integrated, as there is no difference [between the two cases]. (Vātsyāyana 1997: 16,7; 16,16–20)

The thought is that one who keeps track of an object in time does not separate the information he or she receives from the object at different times. Someone who *recognizes* an object as the same as one previously encountered does so by assimilating the contents of two dossiers or mental files, one containing information derived from one's current perceptions, the other containing information from one's past perceptions. The problem for the Reductionist is that it has become a substantive matter as to whether the current mental file contains information from the same object as the earlier one; that is, an act of judgement is implicit in the identification. So the critical distinction—between *tracking* an object over time and *recognizing* an object as the same at different times—collapses.

If one is tempted by that model of the sense-faculties which likens them to channels of information, distinct conduits through which distinct sorts of sensory information from the object flows, then unification and organization of the information must be viewed as a substantive work of judgement. In Chapter 10 I described Dharmakīrti's sophisticated version of this picture. The point I made there was that something about his picture made it impossible for him to see genuine object perception as other than resting on a mistake, and we are now able to see what that is. It is a mistake to think that when I am holding an object in my hands and simultaneously looking at it, I am *judging* that *this* is the same as *that*, the first perceptual demonstrative being grounded in touch, the second in sight. It is certainly not the case that the cross-modal identity is like the identity between Hesperus and Phosphorus, known *a posteriori* by means of an empirical inquiry in conjunction with background hypotheses and reasoning. Campbell points out that a subject simultaneously looking at and touching an object need make no conscious division between his or her visual and tactual input, the cognitive skills in question belonging rather to a subpersonal level, part of the cognitive substrate that makes a conceptual life possible (Campbell 1989: 283). We may also note that there are distinctive kinds of cross-modal *illusion*, and this supports the suggestion that cross-modal identities exhibit the kind of 'belief-independence' described by Evans (1982: 123). Ventriloquism affords an example—one *hears* the ventriloquist's voice as coming from the direction where one *sees* the puppet (cf. Ayers 1991: i. 187). Another example comes from experiments where the subject's visual field is inverted—here, since everything within the visual field is initially seen as inverted, the subject's frame of reference must come from outside the *visual* field, for example from *proprioceptive* information about the orientation of one's body.

If this is on the right lines, then the model of the senses as channels of information and the conception of the self as that which compares and combines their deliverances in judgements come to seem like twin elements in a philosophical error. If cross-modal identities are *perceived*, not *judged*, then there is no work of comparison and combination for the self to do. These points lend still further credence to the theory of mind developed in the last three chapters, in which an unconscious comparator mechanism (the 'underself') is responsible for the synthesis of sensory data from different sources into conscious object perception.

I nevertheless do not believe that the version of the Unity Argument based on temporal tracking is sound. The reason is simply that even if there is no separation of information but just a single file for each object, many people can consult the same file. The same file of information can be available to successive moments of experience (compare the idea of a repository-consciousness; Chapter 8). Dharmakīrti is wrong to think that object perception involves an error, mistakenly locating the formation of a thought about a single object in a 'judgement of sameness', a judgement which, he rightly points out, could never be empirically justified (see Chapter 10). Might he nevertheless be right that self-consciousness presents at best only quasi-subjects? In the next section I will argue not.

The Conception of Oneself as Oneself

I will now consider what is required of someone who has the capacity to think of their perceptions in different modalities as perceptions of one and the same object. The conclusion of the argument is that one cannot think of one's perceptions in different modalities as having a common object unless one conceives of one's experience as being of an objective world, and that this in turn requires a conception of the numerical identity of that to which one's perceptions belong: cross-modality requires objectivity, and objectivity requires unity. Parfit believed that Reductionism is threatened by the Kantian argument that 'we could not have knowledge of the world about us unless we believe ourselves to be persons, with an awareness of our identity over time' (Parfit 1984: 225). It is not clear that he ought to have been worried: there is no straightforward conflict between the argument that a conception of an objective world requires a conception of oneself as the numerically identical subject of one's experiences and the Reductionist thesis that, from an external standpoint, it is possible to analyse the continued existence of a person in terms that do not presuppose the identity of the person over time. For this reason, what this version of the argument does is to refute not Reductionism about the self directly as a metaphysical hypothesis but rather the Reductionist's account of the first-person stance. At the end of this chapter I will give a supplementary argument demonstrating that it is a peculiarity of the concept of self that the way one must conceive of oneself as being is also the way one is.

Kant argued that it is not possible to have a conception of an objective world without thinking of that world as spatial, and of oneself as located within it and following a spatio-temporal route through it. A standard interpretation of his argument runs as follows. A self-conscious subject is one who is in a position to think of their experience as including perceptions of objects in what P. F. Strawson calls 'the weighty sense', that is, as being particular items which are capable of being perceived *and of existing unperceived* (Strawson 1966: 28). An idea due to Evans is that in order to make sense of the idea that one can perceive what can also exist unperceived, one must think of perception as having certain spatio-temporal *enabling conditions*, such that in order to perceive something one must be appropriately located—both spatially and temporally—with respect to it (Evans 1985: 261–2). One can then make sense of the fact that a perceivable object is not actually perceived by thinking that the enabling conditions for its perception are not satisfied. Grasping the idea that perception is subject to spatio-temporal enabling conditions requires that one think of perceiver and thing perceived as standing in a suitable spatio-temporal relation, and so of oneself as having a location in the world. Likewise, grasping the idea that a temporal sequence of perceptions are of one and the same object requires that one think of the thing perceived and the perceiver as standing in a more or less stable spatial relation over a period of time, and so of oneself as following a continuous path through space.

Now the conception of an object appealed to in the Unity Argument is not that of an object 'in the weighty sense', an object which is perceived but capable of existing unperceived. The Unity Argument begins with the idea that one's experience is such that one can think of it as including distinct perceptions of the same object at a single time. For one's experience to satisfy this condition, one has to be able to think of it as including perceptions of objects which are, let us say, 'plurally perceivable', capable of being perceived more than once at the same time. 'At the same time' refers here to the time of the object and not to the time of the perceptions: one has to be able to think of one's experience as including distinct perceptions of the same temporal slice of the object.

What is it to be able to make sense of the idea that one's perceptions are of objects which are plurally perceptible, and so to be able to think thoughts of the 'I touch what I see' type? The idea of an enabling condition is not what is required here, for the contrast is not between perceiving and not perceiving. What one needs is the ability to apply the distinction between thinking of one's perceptions as plural perceptions of the same temporal slice of the object, and thinking of them as being of different objects or of the same object at different times. That is, one must have a grasp of what might be called the *convergence conditions* for perception.

The Kantian strategy was to observe how someone who thinks of their perceptions as subject to enabling conditions must think of both the objects and the subject of perception as spatially located. There is a similar double requirement on one's possession of the concept of a convergence condition. Grasping the idea of one's distinct perceptions as being of the same temporal slice of a single object requires, it is claimed, that one thinks of both the objects and the subject of perception as unitary loci of multiple properties.

Consider first the requirement on objects. Thinking that a perception of something red and a perception of something firm are perceptions of a single object at a single time requires that one is able to think of the object as simultaneously both red and firm. Without a conception of objects as the unitary loci of many properties, one could not make sense of the idea that one has here plural perceptions of the state of a single object, and not that one's perceptions are of distinct objects or are of perceptions of distinct temporal slices of an object. So the capacity to think of the objects of one's perceptions as plurally perceivable requires that one thinks of them as individuals, the common loci of many properties. Vātsyāyana:

When one thinks 'that pot which I saw, I now touch' or 'That which I touched, I now see', one does not grasp an aggregate of atoms, and an aggregate of atoms not being grasped, what is grasped is nothing but a single thing. (Vātsyāyana 1997: 235,8–10 on *Nyāya-sūtra* 4.1.35–6)

Can one not reply that a bundle too can be thought of as having many properties? No, for we must keep in mind the distinction between thinking of one's perceptions as being *of* something and thinking of them as being *caused by* something. A bundle can be a common cause but not a common object of distinct perceptions. Thinking of a bundle in which one element is red and one element firm is not thinking of a single object simultaneously red and firm.

How robust is the concept of objectivity which the idea of plural perceptibility sustains? One might doubt whether it sustains a notion of objects 'out there', unless it can be shown that thinking of objects as plurally perceptible requires, in addition, that one is able to think of them as objects 'in the weighty sense', as both perceptible and capable of existing unperceived. Imagine someone who thinks of objects as plurally perceptible and who has the following sequence of perceptions: first, both touching and seeing an object; then just touching it; then again both touching and seeing it; and finally just seeing it. This person is able to think of the object as existing even when unseen, and as existing even when untouched. Can we now argue that if he can conceive of it as unseen and as untouched then he can conceive of it as both unseen and untouched? If so, then since the argument could run for any of the modalities, it will follow that he must be able to conceive of the object as unperceived altogether.

There is, of course, a logical gap between the claim that one can conceive of an object as existing independently of any one perception and the claim that one can conceive it as existing independently of every perception. Notice, however, that the concept of an object sustained by cross-modality is considerably more robust than the one to which Strawson refers in the hypothesis of a purely sense-datum experience, in which the objects of awareness are such that 'there was no distinction to be drawn between the order and arrangement of the objects and the order and arrangement of the subject's experiences or awareness of them' (Strawson 1966: 99). For a subject who is capable of thinking of the objects of experience as existing untouched or as existing unseen is certainly capable of applying the distinction between her experience and what her experience is of. And it is precisely the capacity to apply that distinction that possession of the concept of an objective world requires (cf. Strawson 1966: 73).

How must one conceive of *oneself* if one is to be able to make sense of the idea that perception has convergence conditions? One has to think of one's perceptions as integrable, as capable of converging on the very same object. In addition, one has to do this without, as it were, begging any substantive question about the identity of the object in the two perceptions. Thinking of one's perceptions in distinct modalities as having the same object is not a matter of thinking that some object a is being seen, and that some object b is being touched, and *judging* that $a = b$. Imagine looking at an object one is also holding and is a certain distance away. What is involved in the idea that it is the same object that is both seen and touched? As we have seen, it will not do to assimilate this to a case of the perceiver judging that that (visually presented) object is the same as that (tactilely presented) object. For there is no separation in the information one derives from an object simultaneously touched and seen, of the sort that could ground distinct demonstrative references to it, and so no question here of making an informative identity judgement. This is the point of the observation that the idea of perceptual integration is not a matter of an idea of recognition or reidentification,[13] and also of the idea that the two demonstratives have the same sense (Campbell 1989). An analogy with binocular vision is suggestive: seeing an object with both eyes does not involve any act of judgement that the object perceived by the left eye is identical to that perceived by the right eye.[14]

A further distinction, as already mentioned, is that between thinking of one's perceptions in distinct modalities as being *of* the same object, and thinking merely of them as being *caused* by the same object. What is it to take a perception as being of, rather than merely from, an object? It is, at the very least, to regard the perception as locating the spatial boundaries (shape

[13] Udayana (1986: 752).

[14] I borrow the analogy, but not its significance, from *Nyāya-sūtra* 3.1.7.

and size) of the object. It is for this reason that the Unity Argument is framed with reference to sight and touch, for it is only sight and touch that sustain the capacity to identify spatial boundaries.[15]

It has now to be shown that to think of one's perceptions in different modalities as capable of converging on a single object, one has to think of oneself as the single locus of those perceptions. The argument here turns on the idea of commensuration. If one did not think of oneself as a single subject of one's perceptions, then a substantive question about the position, shape, and size of the object would arise: namely, whether the position, shape, and size of the object as located by one's visual perception is that same as its position, shape and size as located by one's tactile perception. Suppose one takes oneself to have a visual perception of an apple and a tactual perception of an apple. The thought that one is seeing and touching the very same apple depends on the idea that the apple visually perceived has the same size and position as the apple perceived by touch. If the two perceptions had different subjects, then a substantive identity question would arise, namely, whether the *scale* and the *origin* of the spatial map employed in the location of the object in visual perception is the same as the scale and the origin of the spatial map employed in the location of the object in tactile perception. For the perceived size of the object is correlated to the scale, and the perceived location to the origin of the spatial map. We have seen, however, that the idea that one's perceptions are subject to cross-modal convergence conditions carries with it the idea that no substantive identity question of this sort arises. One does not think of oneself as having to *judge* that the apple seen is the same as the apple touched. The force of this argument is that one who thinks of their perceptions as cross-modally integrated must regard those perceptions as belonging to a *single* perceptual and reasoning system, one which draws upon a single way of representing objects' spatial properties.

If we are to think that it is the same object that is both seen and touched, then we must expect changes in one's visual representation of the place of the object to be correlated with changes in one's tactual representation of its place. As one stretches out one's arm, one expects the object to look further

[15] Campbell (1989: 289) notes that, unlike the other modalities, 'sight and touch both have the capacity to sustain, of themselves, our ordinary conceptions of enduring spatial things'. This is, of course, the reason for the Nyāya appeal to sight and touch in their version of the Unity Argument.

away. The thought that these perceptions are of the same object is linked to the thought that tactual and visual representations of the object's location vary synchronically. One can make sense of that expectation only if one thinks of the perceptions as all locating the object with respect to a single spatial map, and hence of all the perceptions as one's own.[16] The idea that one appeals to a backwards projection of the *egocentric* content of one's perception—that objects are represented as a certain distance away, to the left or the right, and so on—as a way of placing oneself on a spatial map, should not be confused with the thought that this is what grounds one's conception of oneself as spatially located. For it can at best ground a 'geometric' conception of oneself as occupying a point of view. This is all that is entailed too by Milinda's conception of the senses as being like so many windows opening out onto the world, with the self as an 'onlooker', a conception also found in Praśastapāda (1994: 15–16, §78).

The conclusion of this argument is that it is necessary for self-consciousness and for the possession of a first-person stance that one conceives of oneself as an individual. Others have argued for a stronger thesis: that one must conceive of oneself as a *physical* object. I do not believe that the stronger claim is defensible. The argument of Chapter 13 can be read as showing that one must indeed conceive of oneself as metaphysically dependent on a physical object, namely one's body; but the arguments in Chapters 5 and 12 are then to be read as demonstrating that it would be a mistake to conceive of oneself as identical to one's body.

What would it be to think of oneself as a physical object? In Cassam's view, it is to think of oneself as something which has the Lockean primary qualities, shape, place and solidity (Cassam 1997b). It is very hard to see, however, how any argument that purports to demonstrate that one must conceive of oneself as the bearer of primary qualities would not also be consistent with conceiving of oneself simply as only embodied. Such indeed is the force of several of the arguments in Chapter 6. Furthermore, my argument has been that to occupy a first-person stance one must think of

[16] Tsakiris (2010, 2011) reports empirical findings that subjects for whom a rubber hand is put in their visual field and stroked with a brush, while at the same time the subject's unseen actual hand is stroked as well, begin to identify the rubber hand as their own, as part of their own body. The illusion seems to confirm that cross-modal unity is crucial to the concept of self. Of particular relevance here is the discovery that the emergence of the illusion requires that the rubber and real hand are stroked in the same way and in sync.

oneself as an individual, and that is to think of oneself as the owner of mental properties; but the relationships of inhabitation, participation, and endorsement that explicate the idea of ownership bring with them nothing corresponding to Lockean primary qualities. Campbell more plausibly argues that to think of oneself as a physical object is rather to think of oneself as something which is internally causally connected and as having the capacity to function as the common cause of many phenomena (Campbell 1997). Cassam objects that causal structure alone will not sustain a conception of the self as a physical *object*, rather than as an 'object' of a more attenuated type (a process, for example). Causal structure alone does not discriminate between objects and quasi-objects; this is indeed the reason Dharmakīrti claims that to conceive of oneself as an object is a mistake, and the reason that more is required than Dharmakīrti allows. Campbell's answer is to introduce the idea of a 'categorical ground' of causal capacities:

> [Y]our grasp of the identity of the self is knowledge of its place in a network of causal-explanatory relations; sameness of the self over time is the categorical ground which explains the internal causal connectedness of the self over time. (Campbell 1997: 662–3)

In other words, one conceives of oneself as internally causally connected only because one conceives of oneself as identical over time. Yet it is unclear why this should be true: why one should not conceive of oneself merely as a quasi-object, without determinate identity conditions? Dharmakīrti would say that the move Campbell recommends is precisely the 'unconscious error' of mistaking what is only a quasi-object for a genuine one. There is, then, in neither Cassam nor Campbell, grounds for thinking that a conclusion stronger than the one I have drawn is available.

Oneself and One's Conception of Oneself

In the last section, I considered what is involved in the capacity to understand self-ascriptions of the form 'I touch what I see', and I argued that one must conceive of both the objects and the subject of perception as individuals, the location of many properties. Might it nevertheless be the case that, although my ability to occupy a first-person stance entails that

I must conceive of myself as an individual (a genuine subject and not a quasi-subject), I might be in error? Perhaps the Buddhist or the Reductionist description is metaphysically correct, its correctness demonstrable from a third-person perspective, but not a description one could ever come to conceive of as applying to oneself in the first person. A Buddhist would most certainly not welcome this eventuality, because it would imply that Buddhist therapy for self-delusion is doomed to failure: the error would be one from which no amount of reflection and no mental exercise could free one.[17] I do not believe that such a scenario is a coherent possibility; indeed I believe that it is a peculiarity of the concept of self that any way one must conceive of oneself as being is also a way one is.

I will develop an idea from Raghunātha, an early modern reformer whose innovative views about the self I will describe in more detail in Chapter 16. Raghunātha says:

> The combining awareness 'I am now touching the pot I saw' proves that the earlier and later perceptions have the same subject, as it would not be possible if the subjects are different. . . . For the thought 'I Maitra am now touching the pot I Caitra saw' is not a possible one. (Raghunātha 1986: 756)

The idea is that there is a connection between the possibility of unifying self-ascription and the fact that the self to whom the perceptions are ascribed is numerically identical. The suggestion is that whatever it is that fixes the content of first-person thoughts does so in such a way that two tokens of the word 'I', as they occur in an expression of the combining judgement, cannot fail to co-refer, and that this co-reference is what ensures the identity of the subject. As we have seen, a Reductionist is not committed to denying that one can have thoughts which are genuinely first-personal and self-ascriptive: what he or she is committed to is denying that it is necessary to ascribe those thoughts to a thinker. That is, the claim is that there is a level of description in which 'the subject of experiences is mentioned only in the *content* of the thought' (Parfit 1984: 225–6). The redescription of 'Caitra thinks: I touch what I see' might be something like 'The thought: I touch what I see, occurs as part of this aggregate of psychological and physical events.'

[17] Buddhists of a more esoteric bent might actually welcome the eventuality if it implies that we should give up conceiving and instead embrace emptiness.

Raghunātha's claim is that such redescriptions are not genuinely reductive. They are not genuinely reductive because the redescription itself depends on an implicit reference to subjects. To show this, I will give an argument based, not from the token-reflexive rule for the first-person (Campbell 1994: 162–3), but on its anaphoric behaviour spanning intensional operators. Consider the following pair of inferences:

[A] *I* touch the pot that I see.
∴ *I* touch the pot.

and

[B] I touch the pot that *I* see.
∴ *I* see the pot.

Such inferences are part of what Evans calls the 'functional characterization' of *I*-thoughts, inferences whose validity is partly constitutive of the possession of the concept (Evans 1982: 262; Cassam 1997a: 188–9). Clearly, these inferences are valid only when the tokens of the first person co-refer, and so when the same person is the subject of both perceptions. It would not be valid to infer from 'I touch the pot that I see', thought by Caitra, to 'I touch the pot', thought by Maitra. Neither would it be valid to infer from 'I touch the pot that I see', thought by Caitra, to 'I see the pot', thought by Maitra. This is the force of Raghunātha's observation.

The problem for a Reductionist of any persuasion is how to retain those patterns of validity without mentioning genuine subjects (as the referents of names or of the first-person pronoun). In the redescription, inference [A] becomes:

It is thought by this aggregate: I touch the pot that I see.
∴ It is thought by this aggregate: I touch the pot.

The argument against the Reductionist now is this. If the only thing that makes this inference valid is that the aggregate is identified as the reference of a token of the first person, then the re-description is not genuinely subject-free, for the concept of a subject is itself being used to demarcate aggregates.

What then is it that fixes the content of the ascribed thought, and in particular the reference of the first person? My suggestion is that it is the existence of an anaphoric rule spanning the intensional context. It is surely just the anaphoric rule that a token of 'I', when embedded in a speech or propositional attitude report, refers to the subject of the report. If one reports Caitra's utterance by saying 'Caitra said: I am F', the first person refers to Caitra and not to the reporter. Just this rule is the rule governing uses of the first person which occur *within* speech reports. The rule is explicitly formulated by a follower of Raghunātha, Gadādhara (Gadādhara [Bhaṭṭācārya] 1927: 112–20; cf. Ganeri 1999: 235–44). His point is that the word 'I' does not always take wide scope—in contexts that are weakly quotational, instead of forcing a pronominal substitution, there is instead a reference-shift from the utterer to the subject. The rule for the free use of the first person, the usual token-reflexive rule, is suspended in weakly quotational contexts. Applying the anaphoric rule here, in the redescription 'It is thought by this aggregate: I see the pot,' the aggregate is denoted only anaphorically, as co-referent with the first person. Nothing short of relativization to subjects will get the content-specifications of, and so the inferential relations between, self-ascriptive thoughts right. Hindi echoes Sanskrit in permitting coreference of the first person pronoun with a superordinate speaker in reported speech contexts, rather than forcing deictic reference to the utterer (Zanon 2012). The feature is found in Amharic, and is common to languages with logophoric pronouns such as Ewe, Manambu, and Ainu (Hagège 1974; Tamura 2000; Giorgi 2009: 190, n.7).

Notice that in this phase of the argument, nothing depends on the embedded predicate—the integration of visual and tactile content bears only on the role of the first person *within* belief contexts. So the structure of the argument is: if the role of the first person is substantival within belief contexts, and if, by virtue of the anaphoric rule, its role within and without belief contexts is the same, then its role outside belief contexts must be substantival also. The anaphoric rule for the first person is what we need to span vehicle and content. This rule is what licenses the argument from a fact about the content of self-conception to a fact about the self, without any mere conflation of properties of the content with properties of the vehicle. Anaphoric relations are the bridge between the substantival conceptual role of the first person and its use as a referring expression. They are the guarantee that the subject of weak and strong first-person phenomena coincide, that when one conceives of oneself as oneself, conceiver and conceived are one and the same, that 'I' and 'I*' co-refer in a sentence like 'I wonder whether I* should go out'.

I have distinguished three versions of the argument from cross-modality. According to the first version of the argument, what needs to be explained is one's capacity, having once seen an object, to reidentify that same object by touch alone. According to the second, what needs to be explained is one's capacity to identify an object touched as the same as an object simultaneously seen. According to the third version of the argument, what needs to be explained is one's capacity to think of one's perceptions in different modalities as perceptions of one and the same object. The first version appeals to an *explanans* insufficiently distinct from the *explanandum*. The second version falsely assumes a model of the senses as effecting a division in the input of sensory information. The third version establishes that one must conceive of oneself as the unitary owner of one's experiences if one is capable of cross-modal self-ascription within a first-person perspective. These are arguments for unity; none of them sustains any conclusion about simplicity, immateriality, or eternality.

The ability to integrate distinct individual experiences brings with it, in addition, several other abilities. One is the ability to conceive of the world objectively, that is as existing perceived but also possibly as unperceived. Another is the ability to conceive of one's own experience as converging upon a single subject of experience, and so to conceive of oneself as an individual entity. That is to say, one conceives of one's experience, no longer according to an aggregative model, but rather in terms of a conception in which there are subjects of experience who enjoy mental lives. Finally, one now has the ability to think of oneself as oneself*, that is, to achieve a strong first-person perspective with respect to one's own existence. The availability of such a perspective does not come out of reflexive self-awareness; rather, it is only when one's experience assumes the form of that of a genuinely objective world, that is to say, is fully intentional, that the conceptual skills implied by the Unity Argument can come into play.

Unity arguments are where the inter-relatedness of the procedural, participant, and immersed self is most fully expressed; or, to put it another way, where participation, immersion, and coordination find joint articulation in the idea of self. Nothing in this argument supports a further claim to the effect that the self is permanent or eternal, or metaphysically independent of the physical body. Our reconstruction of the Unity Argument makes it apparent that it is a Narrow, not a Broad, Achilles. What I will show in the next chapter is that the conception of self as the embodied common owner of multiple mental properties also serves to ground a conception of selves distinct from one's own. There is no conceptual problem of other minds.

16

The Distinctness of Selves

Many Selves

There is a multiplicity of distinct selves. An account of how they are distinct, one from another, is a way to address the threat that afflicts Cartesian conceptions of self, that in the limit 'there is absolutely nothing left to distinguish any Cartesian "I" from any other, and it is impossible to see any more what would be subtracted from the universe by the removal of *me*' (B. Williams 1973a: 42). *Vaiśeṣika-sūtra* 3.2.15–7 is the earliest source to address the question. One view is presented first, that there is but one self:

Self is one because there is no distinction in the production of pleasure, pain and cognition.[1]

The very next *sūtra*, however, asserts that selves are many, and this indeed is the standard Vaiśeṣika position, that the occurrence of mental states is 'restricted' by or to particular selves:

Selves are many because of restriction.[2]

The apparent conflict between these two statements raises an obvious problem for the commentators. Some take the first to be the statement of an opponent view, to which the second is the answer; others argue that the first refers to a divine self (*īśvara*), and the second to human selves (*jīva*). Vyomaśiva is unique: he finds in the second statement an anticipation of a Sequential View about self, and in the first an affirmation of the unity of the individual self within a single body:

[1] *sukha-duḥkha-jñāna-niṣpattyaviśeṣād aikātmyam* | (trans. Thakur 2003: 65, slightly modified).

[2] *nānā vyavasthātaḥ* | (Thakur 2003: 65, modified).

The Buddhists think that the many moments of consciousness (*vijñāna*) that exist in a single body constitute [each of them] a 'self'. In order to deny such an assertion, [it is said that] for each body there is one [self] not many.[3]

Accepting that there are indeed many selves, Praśastapāda's important move is to say that individual selves fall under a generic kind, selfhood (*ātmatva*).[4] This is, as Śrīdhara says, what guarantees selves have identity conditions; but he then immediately raises a serious difficulty, that the identity conditions of selves cannot be at all similar to those of ordinary physical objects:

The reality of a perceptible entity is concomitant with an awareness of its shape, but a self does not have any shape through an awareness of which its reality is affirmed. Failing to apprehend any concomitant property, the reality of self is undermined. So, when there is no proof which demonstrates even its existence, what is the point of worrying about its qualities? (Śrīdhara 1977: 138)

Praśastapāda's proposal, developing the idea of 'restriction' in the *sūtra*, is that selves are individuated by their unique mental lives, the particular sets of pleasures, pains, desires, dreads, and willings that they host, creating a single space of reasons in which contents bear rationally on each other, that idea being, as I showed in Chapter 14, what enables a definition of common ownership.[5] In keeping with the classical tradition, Praśastapāda also holds, however, that there is a possibility of survival after 'liberation' (*mukti*) from all embodiment, which—since embodiment is a requisite for having a mental life—must necessarily be survival in an insentient condition. His second proposal, then, is that for each self there is a distinct 'differentiator' (*viśeṣa*), a non-repeatable individual difference, a haecceity in something like the sense of Scotus, that is to say, a primitive non-qualitative thisness. He imports this notion from Vaiśeṣika atomic theory, where individual differentiators are invoked to provide individuating conditions for partless, and so shapeless, atoms.[6] He does remark that differentiators supply a condition for individuation 'in the case of liberated selves and minds,

[3] *tathā hy ekasmin śarīre 'nekaṃ vijñānam ātmeti śākyā manyante* | *tatpratiṣedhārthaṃ pratiśarīram eko nānekah* | (Vyomaśiva 1983: i. 155, 9–11).

[4] *ātmatvābhisambandhād ātmā* | (Praśastapāda 1994: 14, §76).

[5] *sukhaduḥkhecchādveṣaprayatnaiś ca guṇair guṇy anumīyate* | (Praśastapāda 1994: 16, §79). Curiously, cognition (*jñāna*) is not mentioned here, nor mental dispositions (*bhāvanā*).

[6] *anteṣu bhavā antyāḥ svāśrayaviśeṣakatvād viśeṣaḥ. vināśārambharahiteṣu nityadravyeṣv aṇvākāśakāladigātmamanaḥsu pratidravyam ekaikaśo vartamānā atyantavyāvṛttibuddhihetavaḥ* | (Praśastapāda 1994: 84, §369).

because no other condition exists',[7] seeming to allow the other account when it is embodied human selves that are being discussed.

Praśastapāda's second answer might usefully be compared with that of Plotinus, and following him Porphyry, who says that what differentiates discarnate souls in the intelligible world is 'mere difference' (*heterotês*).[8] The role in Vaiśeṣika of individual differentiators is important evidence that theirs is not a metaphysics which countenances 'bare particulars', substrata underlying properties and responsible for the individuation of otherwise indiscriminable objects—if atoms and selves were bare particulars, then individual differentiators would be superfluous.

Rootedness: Against Bare Particularism and Mere Difference

The first early modern philosopher, Raghunātha Śiromaṇi (*c.*1560–1640) begins his *Inquiry into The True Nature of Things* with an astonishing statement:

> Among these matters [to be discussed], God is not something distinct from space and time, since there is no proof to the contrary. For wherever particular effects arise, these arise simply from God by his being combined with particular causes.[9]

This identification of space and time with God, or of God with space and time, is startling enough, the second sentence stating that God as delimited by a specific time and place is the cause of any given happening, or equivalently that effects are spatio-temporally located occurrences. Yet it is only further into the work that the truly provocative dimension to Raghunātha's position is made clear:

[7] *muktātmamanaḥsu cānyanimittāsambhavād* . . . (Praśastapāda 1994: 84, §370).

[8] Plotinus 6.9 [9] 8 (29–32); see Sorabji 2005: iii. 370–1. I discuss similarities between Praśastapāda and the Neoplatonists on the individuation of selves in Ganeri (2007: 209–12). For a modern defence of the idea that persons have individual essences: Chisholm (1976: 29).

[9] *tatra dikkālau neśvarād atiricyete mānābhāvāt | tattan-nimitta-viśeṣa-samavadhāna-vaśād īśvarād eva tattat-kārya-viśeṣāṇām upapatteḥ* | (Raghunātha 1915: 1,3–3,1; trans. Potter 1957: 23, revised).

The kind selfhood, insofar as it is the limitor of the individual-causality of pleasure and so on, is not of God.[10]

The individual ownership of psychological properties is the reason there is a plurality of individual selves, falling under a common kind, rather than a single amorphous consciousness, which Advaita Vedānta thinkers identify both with self (*ātman*) and with *brahman*. The 'individual cause' of an attribute is, as we have seen, the particular to which the attribute belongs, and the property of being the individual cause of mental states, that is to say their bearer, is constrained by the particular's exemplification of the kind selfhood. In other words, it is because an individual falls under the kind selfhood that it is able to 'restrict' the instantiation of mental attributes. Connell's distinction (Connell 1988: 90) between two ways in which something can be thought to have a property is helpful in distinguishing Raghunātha's point from a substratum theory. While substrata or bare particulars exemplify properties by way of a simple attributional tie, real individuals are constituted by capacities and potentialities which serve as the grounds for the properties they instantiate; Connell therefore speaks of the property being 'rooted in' the individual. Raghunātha's definition gestures towards the capacities that underlie ownership and because of which experiences are 'rooted in' subjects, as opposed to the idea of mere 'differentiation' (*viśeṣa*) that seems to be endorsed by Praśastapāda.

Raghunātha denies that such considerations apply to God, and indeed that God does not fall under the kind selfhood. In saying this, he is breaking with the classical thinkers, who had argued that God must be a self because no other sort of entity has psychological properties, and God has the property of thinking (*buddhi*) (Vātsyāyana 1997: 228,6). This argument from elimination was not entirely free from difficulty, even for the ancients, because they took it that thinking, like all other psychological attributes, requires embodiment. One solution, albeit an ad hoc one, was to say that God's psychological attributes are different in kind from human mental properties, and in particular, that his thoughts are not transient (Uddyotakara 1997: 432–3). For Raghunātha, it is preferable to admit a new type of entity into one's ontology than to get into all of the ancient

[10] *sukhādi-samavāyi-kāraṇatāvacchedakatvena siddham ātmatvaṃ jātir neśvara iti* | (1915: 44,2–45,1; trans. Potter 1957: 55, revised).

contortions. In doing so, he is strongly affirming that the concept self is a concept whose domain of application is with respect to human beings; that is, that selves are natural entities.

Kṛṣṇadāsa nicely summarizes the debate about whether God falls under the kind or not:

> The kind selfhood is established as that which delimits the individual causality pertaining to pleasure, pain and so on. This kind does include God as well, although pleasure, pain and so on do not arise in him since their causes, like the unseen residue of past acts (*adṛṣṭa*), are absent. That is because the hypothetical principle that an eternal substance must produce whatever effects it is *capable* of producing—this principle is unwarranted. Other philosophers say that there is no evidence in favour of the thesis that the kind does include God. It is also said, however, that it does not follow that God is a tenth sort of substance, because the principle of classification is 'being the bearer of cognition'.[11]

Although God does not actually suffer pain or enjoy pleasure, nor even perhaps aversion, he has the capacity to do so, and that is enough to make him count as a self (the commentators do not take the 'and so on' to cover desire, will, and thought, all of which seem allowed to God). Raghunātha's alternative solution is mentioned, that God does not fall into the kind *self* at all, but is instead a different sort of individual altogether. Finally, a fix preferred by some early modern philosophers is noted, that we restrict the criterion for selfhood to thought or cognition alone. This last suggestion permits God to enjoy dispassionate reflection, but on the other hand will preclude selfhood to any creature capable only of feeling and motivation but not of conscious thought. The real significance of Raghunātha's idea might best be captured by saying that the idea of a God's-eye view is not that of an involved, participant view, and so not that of a first-person stance, but represents the fiction of an immersed self existing independently of a procedural or a participant self.

Raghunātha rejects the view that selves have uniquely individuating differentiators. Indeed, he rejects the whole idea that there are such things. His rejection of the category is quite different in kind from that of some

[11] *ātmatvajātistu sukhaduḥkhādisamavāyikāraṇatāvacchedakatayā sidhyati | īsvare 'pi sā jātir astyeva aḍṛṣṭādir ūpakāraṇābhāvān na sukhaduḥkhādyupapattiḥ nityasya svarūpayogyasya phalāvaśyambhāvaniyama ityasyāprayojakatvāt | pare tu īśvare sājātir nāstyeva pramāṇābhāvāt na ca daśamadravyatvāpattiḥ jñānavattvena vibhajanād ityāhuḥ* | (Kṛṣṇadāsa 1923: 381–4).

philosophers who come after him, for whom 'rejecting' a category means showing how its members can be included in (*antarbhāva*) some other more basic category. Raghudeva says, in his commentary on the *Inquiry*, that 'the meaning of the statement "differentiator is not another category" is that it is not a [sort of] being different from the five beginning with substance'.[12] He thus offers a reductionist, not an eliminativist, reading of Raghunātha's thesis. He does not specify how the reduction should go, but presumably in the case of atoms, it will make use of the qualities of spatial and temporal separation of one from another, or the quality of contact between atoms and regions in space and time.

What then is Raghunātha's view about discarnate survival? He does not say explicitly. Against the general consensus that the condition entails insentience, one of his followers, Rāmabhadra, will argue that it is in a state of 'bliss' (*ānanda*) or permanent happiness, thereby seeming provocatively to entertain a Pure Consciousness View.[13] Presumably, however, he will still face a difficulty unless he thinks that the bliss in question varies in quality from one liberated entity to another. I doubt, however, if this is Raghunātha's view. Philosophers in the Vaiśeṣika tradition mostly do not agree with Advaita Vedānta that there is an identity between individual and divine self, either actual or strived for, and they explain those Vedic passages which seem to countenance such an identity as encouraging us to engage in an imaginative exercise with therapeutic value.[14] What such exercises help us towards is not identification with *brahman*, but rather to reflect on the consequences of a state of discarnate existence (actual or imagined), such a state being one in which one is free from all the emotional and cognitive turmoil associated with embodiment. The idea of discarnate existence might perhaps also be best read as a therapeutic imaginative exercise rather than as involving the admission of a genuine metaphysical possibility (one can perhaps imagine being in such a state even if it is not a possible state to be in; see Chapter 2). In the nineteenth century Candrakānta will recommend that once liberated the distinction between selves is dissolved, thereby

[12] *viśeṣo 'pi na padārthāntaram iti | na dravyādipañcabhinno bhāva ityarthaḥ |* (Raghudeva 1915: 30,21–2).

[13] *Mokṣa-vāda* (MS Poona 460, 20b–21b; quoted and discussed by P. K. Sen 2003: pp. lxxv–lxxviii). Sen notes that Rāmabhadra's view about liberation resembles that of Advaita Vedānta, and suggests that he was the reason later Naiyāyikas went to some lengths to analyse the nature of the liberated state (*mokṣa*), a topic that would not normally have attracted their attention.

[14] Kṛṣṇadāsa (1923: 399).

preserving individuation by embodied mental life and rejecting altogether the doctrine of brute individual difference.[15] This is to agree with the point I have made, that any imagined state of discarnate existence is not the existence of a *self*. This also seems to me to be the implication of Raghunātha's declaration that selfhood is the limitor of the individual-causality of mental states.

Jayarāma, a century and a half after Raghunātha, agrees that we should focus on embodied selves (Jayarāma [Nyāyapañcānana] 1985: 443; the Sanskrit term he uses is *jīva*). Why think of such selves as falling into a distinct basic kind, rather than as being identical with the biological body or reducible to psychological streams of experience? Jayarāma's answer is that the level at which one formulates psychological generalizations is one that brings in its own domain of individuals. To get the correlations right—between an occurrence of *this* pain and the occurrence of *that* wish to flee—we have to be able to ascribe the pain and the wish to the same 'place'; and that means we need a domain of 'places' which can serve as the locations ('individual causes') of these distinctive types of lawful correlation. The existence of diachronic nomological regularities among mental states are what sustain distinctive identity conditions for selves. The resultant identity conditions for selves are not the same as the identity conditions of bodies (cf. Chapter 5), nor are they the same as the identity conditions of streams of experience (cf. Chapter 15). In saying all this Jayarāma comes close to articulating the emergentist idea that higher domains or levels constitute 'special sciences' (see Chapter 3).

Not every kind is a real kind (*jāti*); some are simply the product of nominal classification (*upādhi*). The kind *beast*, for instance, does not correspond to anything in the natural world, but simply includes any animal with certain characteristics that humans happen to find vulgar. Why should the kind *self* be any different? Jayarāma, following the usual Nyāya practice, takes it that for something to be a genuine kind it must play a fundamental role in generalizations. The generalizations relevant to the mind are such as those which relate pleasure and pain to desire and dread, and relatedly to the origin of perception and memory. Jayarāma concludes that if *self* is a true kind, then this must be so because selfhood delimits that in which the whole range of generated mental states occur. He suggests that the use of the term

[15] Candrakānta (1991). Indeed he interprets VS 3.2.15–16 as an affirmation of this thought.

'self' in application to God is by way of metonymic extension from its correct literal meaning, an extension based on the fact that God is the possessor of eternal knowledge. This is an echo of the earlier discussion about the two uses of 'I' (see Chapter 12).

The fact that the identity conditions of selves are distinct from those of animal bodies or streams of experience does not entail that selves persist indefinitely. While it may be coherent to suppose that a single self might persist in several bodies sequentially, or to cease to persist before the body does, there is no reason to think that it can persist in the absence of any body whatever, or indeed in the absence of any stream of experience. There thus seems to be a tension between the early modern emphasis on grounding the identity of selves in the generalizations applying to mental states, and an inherited commitment to the doctrine that selves are eternal or permanent (*nitya*). As we have seen, that inherited commitment brings with it a host of difficulties. Combined with a naturalistic commitment to the idea that mental states supervene on physical states, the doctrine implies that when a self eventually ceases to be embodied, it loses any mental life at all; and then the distinct identity of different selves can be ensured only with the doctrine that each self has an individual 'differentiator' (*viśeṣa*), a unique non-qualitative property (for there is, to repeat, no suggestion that selves are bare particulars). Without the doctrine that selves are eternal, the further claim that they have individual differentiators becomes otiose. To say this is, in effect, to reclassify selves: instead of belonging in the category of simple and otherwise indiscernible entities for which a theory of ultimate individuation in terms of haecceities is required, they should be seen as belonging with ordinary composite entities, individuated according to standard non-ultimate criteria (on this distinction, see Moreland 1998: 254). To deny that selves are eternal does not imply that they are momentary: an object can endure through an interval of time and yet nevertheless have a finite lifespan. There is no reason to accept the false choice between momentariness (*anityatā*; 'impermanence') and eternality (*nityatā*; 'permanence'). What remains is the fundamental idea that the criteria for the individuation of selves is *sui generis*. Unlike fundamental scientific laws, these criteria constitutively involve evidential considerations (*pramāṇa*), especially reason-giving (*anumāna*), and also considerations of responsibility and duty (*dharma*). That is to say, the criteria according to which selves are individuated are firmly locatable within the standpoint of a liberal naturalism.

It is worth observing that the two inherited doctrines mentioned above are passed over virtually in silence in all the early modern discussions of the nature of the self. The reason, I have suggested, is that selfhood begins to be thought of as more similar to a biological or artefact kind than to a fundamental physical kind, so that there is no longer any need for a special theory of ultimate individuation.[16] The theory of self is, in the language of the emergentists, a 'special science'. Such a theory of self is at the very heart of an early modern revolution in the concept of the individual. Able to serve as the foundation for a politically liberal conception of the autonomous individual,[17] it was at the centre of controversy with less secular visions of humanity in early modern India. Mahādeva Puṇatāṃkara's 'Examination of Selfhood as a Basic Kind' (*Ātmatva-jāti-vicāra*) is the most important intervention into what was a pivotal philosophical debate in seventeenth-century Vārāṇasi, one which had wider political ramifications in early modern South Asia.[18]

First-Person Realism

The unsustainable doctrine that selves are eternal has its origins in a failure by earlier thinkers to see how their discovery of a description of the individual subject as a rational, perceiving, emotive, and agentive being is a description of a different order from the description of the physical world

[16] As a chair can be made of metal or wood, but must be such as to sustain a person's weight, so a self can supervene on different sorts of body, but must be such as to sustain commitments, preferences, and intentions.

[17] Thus Christman and Anderson (2005: 9) argue that autonomy rests on a preservation of the idea of ownership: 'The respect that individuals claim for their preferences, commitments, goals, projects, desires, aspirations, and so on is ultimately to be grounded in their being the person's own. It is because those preferences, commitments, and so on are a person's own that disregarding them amounts to disregarding him or her qua that distinctive individual. By contrast, disregarding preferences, commitments, and so on that are the product of coercion or deception does not seem to involve a violation in the same sense, raising the vexing issue of what makes some preferences, commitments, and so on "one's own," and others not.' The grounding of autonomy in a concept of self is explored in further detail in Ekstrom (2005); Christman (2009).

[18] I am editing and translating the text from manuscripts preserved by the Nepalese-German Manuscript Cataloguing Project (MGMCP) at the Nepal Research Centre.

and its six categories of types of existence.[19] The elision leads swiftly to thinking of natural selves on the model of Vaiśeṣika material indivisibles, whose simplicity (lack of parts)—according to criteria of persistence appropriate for material entities—entails that they are eternal, and so to move from a Narrow to a Broad Achilles, thereby falling into what I earlier called Payāsi's Trap. The revolution which Raghunātha instigates in the sixteenth century begins with his recognition that the source of the limitations of classical metaphysics are its reductionist proclivities, and his consequent appreciation that realism must provide different kinds of account for different kinds of individual.[20] First-Person Realism, realism about selves, cannot be reduced to realism about physical objects. The refusal to include God in the kind *self* is an affirmation that selves are natural—as opposed to supernatural—entities, specifically that embodiment is essential to membership of the kind.

In a more contemporary idiom, the conception of self I find derivable from various strands in Nyāya and Vaiśeṣika discussion is something as follows. The question 'Just what is a self?', insofar as it implicitly calls for a reduction of selves to some other kind of thing ('Into which of our familiar categories are you saying that selves fall?), must be answered by robustly denying that the reality of selves requires that they are reducible to anything else.[21] First-Person Realism affirms that first-person discourse is a realist discourse but denies that it is reducible to any non-normative realist discourse. Our concept of self is that of a place for the ownership of commitments, intentions, and preferences; that of something which persists even in deep dreamless sleep and other states of catatonia or non-consciousness in virtue of continuing dispositions of endorsement[22] whose categorical base is the unconscious mind; that in virtue of which a being can occupy a first-person stance.[23] To call the self an 'entity' is just to say that it is

[19] See Chs. 13 and 14, and for further discussion of the 'flatness' of early Vaiśeṣika metaphysics, Ganeri (2011: 201).

[20] See Ganeri (2011: 163–220, esp. 179–80, 201), specifically in connection with the non-reductive realism of Raghunātha.

[21] Whence the 'definition' (*lakṣaṇa*) of self as that which falls under the kind selfhood.

[22] On the impressed cognitive dispositions (*bhāvanā*): Praśastapāda (1994: 62, §305). This grounding of commitments, preferences, and values in a categorical base is how the theory avoids the radical discontinuity of endorsement that is a feature of Sartrean theories of ownership.

[23] Just as, in the standard Nyāya analogy, a chef continues to be a chef even when not actually cooking, but could hardly count as one if in principle unable to cook.

something which is capable of having states and properties, but is not a state or property (or a bundle of states and properties) itself, that there is some answer to the question 'Is this me again?', and to insist that the use of the word 'I' is one of genuine reference. This view agrees with Baker that in a supervenient emergentism 'a full account of reality would include the supervenient base together with the emergent items . . . If the first-person perspective is emergent, then it belongs in a full account of reality' (Baker 2011: 170 n. 2).

The concept *self* is the concept of something necessarily embodied, something whose existence is made sense of by the idea of unconscious mechanisms of comparison, monitoring, and information-retrieval, the states of which its states supervene on and indeed emerge from, mechanisms the character of which is determined by the very fact that they support the emergence of consciousness, underwrite the phenomenology of mineness, and explain the congruences and mismatches responsible for emotion and common ownership. To be conscious (in the intransitive sense) is to be occupying in the present moment a first-person stance, and since this implies the capacity of any one of one's owned states to engage the whole of one's being through its potential to make normative demands on any other—and so for that state to be 'rooted' in the self—it entails that the single comparing, monitoring, selecting subroutine which is the unconscious mind or underself is in a state of characteristic activity, distinct from the more modularized state it is in when one is not conscious. The self is embodied because to own a mental state (that is to say, to inhabit and endorse it) is to be responsive in principle to its demands for action: that is why a discarnate state of being cannot be one in which there are any owned states of mind (that is to say, it is a state for which the ideas of involvement and participation are idle).

Unlike selves, immaterial spiritual substances seem as good a candidate as one could wish for of the kind of supernatural entity a naturalist attitude disavows. They make possible the idea that mental lives can persist independently of physical realization, and in doing so they violate the completeness of physics. Not only is it a mystery how immaterial spiritual entities could interact with the physical world, but, as Kim has pointed out, it is also a mystery how they could be causes at all. According to his diagnosis, the fundamental problem with the Cartesian picture is that the non-spatiality of

Cartesian souls precludes their participation in causal relations (he calls this the 'pairing problem'; Kim 2001). Lacking in spatial location, there is nothing to pair particular souls with particular effects: if two souls simultaneously acquire or lose a certain property, there is no way, even in principle, to decide which of the two is the cause of some subsequent event. The fundamental difficulty with the Cartesian picture is thus not the problem of interaction between the mental and the physical, but the problem of Cartesian minds being causes at all, even between themselves. What is important to notice here is that Cartesianism is *not* a form of First-Person Realism. This is because, first, as Kim's pairing argument demonstrates, statements about the causal relations between distinct Cartesian selves are not determinately either true or false. Nor, second, are statements concerning their identity, difference, addition, or subtraction, determinately true or false: 'There is absolutely nothing left to distinguish any Cartesian "I" from any other, and it is impossible to see any more what would be subtracted from the universe by the removal of *me*' (B. Williams 1973a: 42). No conception of self that falls to the Attenuation problem can exemplify a version of First-Person Realism.

McDowell says that we should 'see thinking and knowing as belonging to our mode of living, even though we conceive them as phenomena that can come into view only within a *sui generis* space of reasons' (McDowell 2004: 95). From the perspective of First-Person Realism there is something right and something wrong in this remark. What comes into view within the space of reasons is not just thinking and knowing, but thinking and knowing as essentially owned by thinkers and knowers. That one has ownership of one's experience is deeply connected to our sense of freedom and tied to our ideas of autonomy, responsibility, and justice (consider the use of the word in talk about 'taking ownership of' a project or task). When Strawson says that liberal naturalism involves itself with a 'condition of our humanity', he has in mind natural attitudes which rest on this idea of ownership, such as the sense of resentment because one has not received one's due from others ('reactive' attitudes: P. F. Strawson 1974c; cf. Bilgrami 2006). So what comes into view is thinking and knowing as states of mind owned by individual subjects. The trouble with McDowell's description is not that any hint of a lingering Cartesianism remains, but rather that in its strident wish to distance itself from Cartesianism, it has become too Animalist (cf. McDowell 2009). The claim that 'thinking and knowing belong to our mode of living' does not do sufficient justice to the thought that they belong to us, to real individual subjects of experience. To put the thought another way, it is the defining feature of a first-person position that one occupies and endorses one's states of mind and is not merely a spectator of them, and so it is from this stance alone that the relationships definitive of liberal naturalism, the *pulls* of reasons and the *demands* to act, come into view, the correlatives of non-causal relationships of ownership and common ownership. McDowell correctly insists that 'the fact that we are knowers and thinkers does not reveal us as strangely bifurcated, with a foothold in the animal kingdom—surely part of nature—and a mysterious separate involvement in an extranatural realm of rational connections' (McDowell 2004: 95). What blocks the possibility of bifurcation in the theory under discussion is the very nature of ownership as a relationship simultaneously responsive to normative demands and necessitating physical embodiment. Mental states must be anchored to the world because their common ownership is indicated by demands for action and because their ownership implies the possibility of perceptual experience. So the individuation of subjects through a relationship of common ownership entails individuation by bodies.

My own preference is for a conception of self according to which the self is more than a neurophysiological process but less than an entity capable of discarnate existence, that it is a unity of immersion, participation, and coordination; a unity but not a simplicity. A very unique philosopher from another tradition who proposes to think of human selves as middling in status is the Syrian philosopher Iamblichus (245–326 CE). In the report of Priscian:

> According to Iamblichus, the particular self embraces both characteristics equally, both permanency and change, so that in this way its intermediate position is preserved; for, while higher beings are stable, mortal ones are completely changeable. The particular self, however, as middle, is undivided, yet it is multiplied together with mundane beings; it does not only remain permanent, but also changes because it lives through so many divisible lives. And it changes not only in its habits, but also in its *ousia*.[24]

Like all Neoplatonists, Iamblichus thinks that the self aspires ultimately to free itself from the body. Early Nyāya-Vaiśeṣika philosophers agree,

[24] Priscian, *Metaphrasis* 32,13–18 (trans. Steel 1978: 57). Cf. 'Simplicius', *De Anima* 6,7–13; 89, 33–90, 25; 240,33–241, 26.

although I have argued that for them what exists as thus 'liberated' (*mukta*) is no longer describable as a self, since it lacks any mental life at all. Indeed, these philosophers also endorse a distinct notion of liberated freedom within life (*jīvan-mukti*). It is said that 'someone with true insight, *while he still lives*, is freed from delights and troubles'[25]—so the freedom aimed for is not some higher theological state but the condition of a living being.

I think that a move in either direction—of radical separation from, or excessive identification with, the body—involves a sort of alienation, a loss in one's ability to negotiate the asymmetry between the first-person and the third-person stances. I would identify the 'higher beings' with the myth that the self is pure immersion (a phenomenological hall of mirrors), the 'mortal ones' with the myth that the self is a mere underself (nothing more than a physically realized self-monitoring database), and the ones in the middle, we human beings, with the idea of a unity of immersion, participation, and coordination. I would thus agree in spirit with Iamblichus when he also says that a self is a unity of proceeding out, returning, and remaining (Steel 1978: 57). This recognition that the self is a unity of three factors is not in conflict with realism about selves, for instead of a naïve realism one can hold to what Dummett has called 'sophisticated realism' (1991: 324), in which realism is understood as a commitment to genuine singular reference, in this case the genuine reference of the first person, in a manner that is compatible with the compositionality of the object of reference.[26] Indeed, I have elsewhere argued that the recognition that realism and compositionalism are not incompatible is what freed early modern thinkers after Raghunātha from the ancient oscillation between the two (Ganeri 2011: 180); so Buddhist demonstration that an entity is composite in no way impugns its claim to be real. The endorsement of such a view carries with it no implication that participation and immersion, constitutive elements in the unity of the self, are themselves reducible to physical processes, still less does it carry any commitment to Reductionism, the view that the self is reducible to a psycho-physical stream. It merely affirms that the claim that the self is a unity of immersion, participation and coordination is consistent with realism about self.

[25] *jīvanneva hi vidvān saṃharṣāyāsābhyāṃ vipramucyate*; quoted by Uddyotakara (1997: 22,3).

[26] 'If it is his rejection of the principle of bivalence that marks the reductionist's divergence from realism, then the realist may continue to be a realist, despite espousing even a full-blooded reductionism, as long as he continues to adhere to the principle of bivalence' (1991: 327–8).

Conclusion: A Theory of Self

The aim of this book has been to reclaim the self as a naturalistically respectable item, with a legitimate role in the explanation of subjectivity as the occupant of a genuine first-person stance. A natural self is metaphysically dependent on the body from which its states emerge and upon which they supervene, and it survives no longer than the body does; but it does not have the same identity conditions as the body, and neither are the mental states of the self reducible to physical states of the body. For a body to have a self is for it to have the capacity to assume a first-person stance, a fact which I have seen as being closely associated with the idea that mental states are owned and not merely occurrent. For a self to have a body is for it to have capacities for agency and sentience, activities which are criterial to a relation of common ownership as delimited by normative emotional response. Both consciousness and self-consciousness have a composite phenomenal and intentional structure, one which in non-pathological psychologies requires there to be genuine subjects of consciousness and not merely quasi-subjects. An essential role is played by unconscious and embodied mechanisms of attention, comparison, monitoring, and information retrieval in explaining the unity of the self as a single immersed and participatory subject, as well as in mediating the dependence of consciousness on the physical. The resulting theory is a version of what I have described as the Ownership View of self, in which first-person stances are individuated by relationships that necessitate embodiment.

In the course of my defence of this view I have rejected both error-theoretic and reflexivist theories of self-consciousness, and I have argued against Animalist, Reductionist, and Cartesian accounts of the self. In this analysis, furthermore, selves are neither naturalizable in favour of neural architectures nor capable of discarnate existence; the theory of self is a normative special science in a liberal naturalism. My view is that the self is a unity but not a simple unity, that it is metaphysically dependent on there being physical objects and properties, and that it is of finite temporal span, a little less than that of the body. In denying simplicity, I am drawing inspiration from Buddhist discussion of the compositionality of first-person phenomena, especially that of Vasubandhu; in denying immateriality, I borrow from Cārvāka theory of emergence, and especially from Bhaṭṭa Udbhaṭa; in denying eternality, I am in disagreement with first-millennium Nyāya-Vaiśeṣika, but find indications of support in Raghunātha Śiromaṇi, the first modern thinker.

I said in Chapter 1 that I see the development of this conception as embedded in a distinctive sort of research programme into the self, one which takes the form of a dialogue between Ownership Views and No Place Views. I will therefore now recast the discussion in a more explicitly dialectical form. I will argue that the debate can be seen as being driven by two competing conceptions of ownership, at work, at least implicitly, in the thought of opposing thinkers. That is why I believe that there is after all no genuine incompatibility: Buddhist dismissal of ownership understood as involving causal agency is compatible with Nyāya-Vaiśeṣika analysis of ownership in terms of endorsement. Indeed, in the account as summarized above, we can distinguish three legitimate notions of ownership, and they justify us in speaking of three dimensions to selfhood: the immersed phenomenal self as a genuine subject in self-consciousness; the underself as an unconscious mechanism of comparison and attention; and the participant self as the engaged occupant of a first-person stance.

No-Self: Ownership as Agency. The Buddhist View is that there is no self. Vasubandhu provides a powerful analysis of the phenomenology of ownership (see Chapter 8), but combines it with the claim that appearances are deceptive. The phenomenal mineness of a mental state, the *appearance* of ownership that comes with it and the correlative *sense* of self, is strongly associated with its rootedness in deep strata of the psyche, in its informational links with the repository-consciousness. Yet for Vasubandhu there are no real ownership relations, and no real selves. The most plausible way to make sense of this position is to take it that what it recommends is an analysis of real ownership in terms of causal agency. The idea goes back to Vasubandhu's interpretation of the Buddha's celebrated declaration that it is a fundamental mistake ever to identify oneself with any of the mental happenings in one's mind.[1] The mistake in question, for Vasubandhu, is thinking that these happenings are things that one *does*, that one is the agent of. One does not first form an intention to think a thought, and then think it, as one might be said to form an intention to raise one's arm in advance of raising it. The idea that there is a 'thinker' in this sense is an illusion, one which is indeed the result of falling into Payāsi's Trap.

The point at issue can be clarified by examining a particular recent theory about the psychopathology known as thought insertion, a theory which has been accused of falling into a similar trap and for similar reasons. A symptom typical of schizophrenia, thought insertion is the occurrence in a subject's mind of a thought they describe as not one of their own but an intrusion or insertion. Some patient reports frequently cited in the literature are:

'Thoughts come into my head like "Kill God." It's just like my mind working, but it isn't. They come from this chap, Chris. They are his thoughts.'

'I look at the window and I think that the garden looks nice and the grass looks cool, but the thoughts of Eamonn Andrews come into my mind. There are no other thoughts there, only his . . . He treats my mind like a screen and flashes thoughts onto it like you flash a picture.'

'I have never read nor heard them; they come unasked; I do not dare to think I am the source but I am happy to know of them without thinking them. They come at a moment like a gift and I do not dare to impart them as if they were my own.'

'One evening the thought was given to me electrically that I should murder Lissi.'[2]

Thought insertion is thus different from pathologies in which a subject feels that their own thoughts are being manipulated or controlled by external forces. In thought insertion patients disown the thought altogether, and indeed in several of these cases they attribute it explicitly to someone else.

One influential approach to the problem of thought insertion sees an explanation as resting on the idea of ownership as casual agency. Whereas a subject who thinks that their thoughts are being influenced will still maintain that it is they who are *doing* the thinking, in the case of a thought

[1] 'Therefore, monks, all embodied reacting, hedonic appraising, labelling, constructing and conscious attending whatsoever, whether past, present or future, whether gross or subtle, inferior or refined, far or near, should be seen by means of clear understanding as it really is, as "this is not mine, I am not this, this is not my self" (cited Gethin 1998: 137; trans. modified for terminological consistency).

[2] Fernández 2010: 67–8.

insertion, the subject believes that someone else has done the thinking for them. A model has been developed by Feinberg and Frith on the basis of an analogy with disorders of passivity in motor control, from which they develop a picture of thought insertion in which what malfunctions are postulated motor processes involved in the activity of thinking, leading to a mismatch between introspective access and one's sense of agency (Feinberg 1978; Frith 1987). The theory about motor control is that an efference copy of an intention to move is sent to a subpersonal comparator site, which compares it with reafference feedback of body posture. If there is a match, then the subject has a sense of agency, otherwise not. The suggestion is that the same model can be applied to thinking, considered as being itself a sort of motor process: an efferent copy of my intention to think a thought is sent to a comparator site and compared against feedback from self-monitoring of my actual thoughts. When there is a mismatch, I do not have a sense of agency in connection with the thought concerned—it has the phenomenology of an alien presence. Thus Frith (1987: 639): 'The classic . . . symptom of a "made" volitional act [alien control] corresponds particularly closely to an inability to monitor the intention to act . . . The experience of thoughts being initiated without any apparent intention to have them would be described by the patient as thought insertion.'

This model clearly shares a common assumption with the model of ownership I believe to be in the background of the original Buddhist denial of self. It has been argued, moreover, that Frith's analysis does not capture what is distinctive of thought insertion, because it will not distinguish between cases of thought insertion and cases of non-paranoid thoughts that seem just to come into our minds, apparently spontaneously (Spence 1996; Campbell 2002; Bortolotti and Broome 2009: 208). More importantly, it has also been argued that a model of thinking which claims that normal thinking is preceded by an intention to think, so that thinking is an action performed in a manner parallel to bodily movement, cannot be correct and indeed is paradoxical. Thus Spence: 'Frith's theory of the defective internal monitor, failing to monitor willed intentions . . . contains a number of problems, not least of which is the proposal that the subject may be performing "actions", which are preceded by "intentions to act" of which he or she is unaware. Using Frith's own definition of action as necessitating prior intention, a paradox is revealed: These schizophrenic acts are volitional "acts" because they are preceded by (conscious) willed intentions.

These intentions are conscious. Yet, the patient is (hypothesized to be) unaware of this (conscious) intention to act.'[3] These arguments against the model of Feinberg and Frith are powerful, and support the Buddhist denial that there is any such thing as ownership in the sense of causal agency with respect to one's own thinking, or that there is anyone 'doing' the thinking. If the only model of ownership available were a casual agency model, then the conclusion that there are no selves might indeed be a legitimate one to draw, and this indeed is what leads to a natural scientific suspicion of self.

A different reaction to the argument, however, is to say that other notions of ownership are available. One possibility is that there is genuine immersed ownership, and so legitimate conceptions of a phenomenal self distinct from any idea of the causal agent doing the thinking. Indeed, Vasubandhu's analysis of the phenomenal structure of self-consciousness and Dignāga's reflexivist self-model theory actually provide non-agentive analyses of the notion of an immersed sense of ownership, and I have argued that both are consistent with the rejection of the error-theory they are associated with.[4] While Buddhists may also deny the phenomenal self,[5] the historical response of Kashmiri Śaivism and Prābhākara Mīmāṃsā was to develop a constructive conception of self as an phenomenal self.

A different possibility is to argue in favour of the legitimacy of a non-phenomenological notion of ownership, and so for a constructive conception of self other than as a phenomenal self. This is the route historically chosen by Nyāya and Vaiśeṣika philosophers and Bhāṭṭa Mīṃāṃsā. Nyāya-Vaiśeṣika thinkers restrict the role of immersion to that of bodily ownership,

[3] Spence (2001: 167). The argument is also pressed in Stephens and Graham (2000). Further criticisms of Frith's theory are in Gallagher (2004). The difficulties in the idea that thinking is a motor process do not undermine the importance of the idea that there are subpersonal comparator mechanisms; what the criticism shows is rather that that idea has been misapplied.

[4] As I noted in Ch. 9, Dignāga's theory of subjectivity offers materials for a good alternative way to explain thought insertion, according to which an alien thought is one in which there is access to the subject-aspect but no reflexivity (the person's access to their own thought is that of a telepath). This requires two departures from Dignāga, first in making reflexivity constitutive of a robust notion of ownership, and second in rejecting reflexivism as a *general* theory of subjectivity. This quasi-Dignāgan theory is a phenomenological account of thought insertion, an alternative to both Frith's agency account and Moran's endorsement analysis. I believe that it has merits too over Gallagher's (2004) neurophenomenological explanation.

[5] As I mentioned before, acknowledging the phenomenological presentation of the immersed self and also claiming it to be an illusion is a position that is in danger of falling into incoherence (unlike the Humean view that no such self is presented). Dreyfus (2011) presents a careful Buddhist-inspired argument for the irreality of the immersed self. More often it is simply assumed that the immersed self must have attributes it need not have, such as presenting an unchanging bare particular.

the phenomenal self for them at best a body map. It is open to a Buddhist also to deny the non-phenomenal self (and I mentioned in Chapter 1 that this strikes me as a plausible way to read the earliest Buddhist writings, as contrasted with the 'phenomenological turn' that Buddhism would subsequently take), but the arguments in favour of such a self are untouched by the criticism of causal agency and immersion.

Self: Ownership as Endorsement. Nyāya-Vaiśeṣika thinkers defend a liberal naturalist and non-phenomenological conception of what it is to say that someone owns their own mental states. What drives this philosophy is the idea that the use of reason is determinative in whether to acknowledge a thought as one's own. Vātsyāyana's view is that we are all too easily persuaded that motivations, desires, and ideas are ours when in reality they have nothing to do with us, a mistake of taking to be myself what is not myself.[6] Not to regard a thought as 'mine' is to refuse to allow it to carry any evidential weight in my mental life. This is not a consideration about agency, since one can consistently accept that one is the producer of an attitude or emotion but still think that one should dissociate oneself from it in the sense intended, and one can likewise give weight to attitudes which one does not have any sense of agency with respect to, for example simple perceptions. Given that the methods we need to bring about this dissociation are said at the outset to be evidence-based and rational (*Nyāya-sūtra* 1.1.1), it is clear that the notion of ownership in play here is one of endorsement and commitment. Disowning a thought is breaking a commitment, specifically an entitlement to use that thought in the justification of one's beliefs or actions; likewise, if I disown a particular feeling of hurt or anger, I break any reason or right to act on it. Endorsing a belief is committing oneself to its being true, and so to resolving the question of whether it is one's own by referring to the very facts that determine if it is true or not (which is why, in *Nyāya-sūtra* 4.2.1–9, it is claimed that competence in the ways of gaining knowledge of the external world is the route to gaining self-knowledge).[7]

[6] *kiṃ punas tanmithyājñānam iti anātmanyātmagrahaḥ | ahamasmīti moho 'haṃkāra iti |* (1997: 258,10–1; *supra* 4.2.1). This states that taking something to be oneself (*ahaṃkāra*) is liable to error, not that it is always erroneous.

[7] Compare Evans (1982: 225): 'In making a self-ascription of belief, one's eyes are, so to speak, or occasionally literally, directed outward—upon the world. If someone asks me "Do you think there is

Recent studies of thought insertion do recognize that there are several different elements within the notion of ownership of one's thoughts. Among the constituent ideas motivating ascriptions of ownership, at least the following have been identified:

- to have one's body as the neural substrate of the thought (*physical base*)
- to locate a thought within one's personal spatial boundaries (*spatiality*)
- to be able to access the content of the thought directly and first-personally (*introspective access*)
- to ascribe the thought to oneself (*self-ascription*)
- to be the one who generates or authors the thought (*agency*)
- to endorse the content of the thought (*authority*).[8]

Moran develops an account based on the idea that the failure of ownership in play has to do with endorsement. He distinguishes attributional self-knowledge from avowal, where attributional self-knowledge involves 'the alienated, opaque attribution of attitudes to oneself' (2001: 106), as if one is merely a witness to one's mental life, while avowal characterizes what I have been describing as the genuine occupancy of a first-person stance:

> The person might be *told* of her feeling of betrayal, and she may not doubt this. But without her capacity to endorse or withhold endorsement from that attitude, and without the exercise of that capacity making a difference to what she feels, this information may as well be about some other person, or about the voices in her head. From within a purely attributional awareness of herself, she is no more in a position to *speak for* her feelings than she was before, for she admits no authority over them. It is because her awareness of her sense of betrayal is detached from her sense of the reasons, if any, supporting it that she cannot become aware of it by reflecting on that very person, the one by whom she feels betrayed. The rationality of her response requires that she be in a position to *avow* her attitude towards him, and not just describe or report it, however accurately, for it is only from the position of avowal that she is necessarily acknowledging facts about *him* as internally relevant to that attitude (say, as justifying or undermining it). (Moran 2001: 93)

going to be a third world war?," I must attend, in answering him, to precisely the same outward phenomena as I would attend to if I were answering the question "Will there be a third world war?" '

[8] Modified from Bortolotti and Broome (2008: 211). The sense of ownership which is grounded in the activity of the underself is missing from this list.

When it is a matter of the thoughts that are one's own (in the sense now under discussion), one is not a mere bystander; the very activity of reflecting and deliberating requires endorsing one's attitudes, and Moran echoes Strawson when he says that 'the transition from attribution to avowal is an expression of the person's rational freedom' (2001: 151). This is the underlying significance of the connection made between ownership and autonomy in *Nyāya-sūtra* 3.2.38 (see Chapter 13). What is missing in cases of thought insertion, Moran proposes, is the avowal of the thought.[9] For a state to be owned is just for it to engage the whole of one's being through its potential to make normative demands on any other owned state:[10] this is what gives substance to the ideas of inhabitation and endorsement that attributions of ownership imply, and underscore what I earlier described as the 'rootedness' of states of mind.[11] Neither thought insertions nor alienated desires are endorsed; and there is also a less demanding concept of ownership, one according to which mental states are owned simply insofar as their content is accessed in subpersonal processes of comparison and monitoring. That is why it is not paradoxical to say of someone that they are alienated from their 'own' thoughts.

I have observed two other places where an idea of endorsement is prominent in Nyāya-Vaiśeṣika philosophy of self. It is visible in the analysis of emotion. Emotions are not judgements, but they nevertheless exhibit in normative demands on action, and are instigated by appraisals. They are metarepresentational signs of congruence or conflict. The emotion of betrayal would be seen as elicited by a mismatch between a standing expectation and an occurrent belief, its contractive affect exhibited in an inclination to action targeted at the betrayer, not least in the formation of a new attitude concerning them. Endorsement implies embodiment, because

[9] Moran's suggestion receives further elaboration in Hoerl (2001); Bortolotti and Broome (2009); Fernández (2010). This use of the term 'endorsement' is due to Frankfurt, who uses it in his account of a notion of identification (Frankfurt 1977), identification requiring 'acceptance' but perhaps not always 'positive evaluation' (see his replies to the discussion in Buss and Overton 2002).

[10] This is the point of the Spatial Parts Argument discussed in Ch. 12.

[11] On Frankfurtian identification as a mode of ownership: 'The decision determines what the person really wants by making the desire on which he decides fully his own. To this extent the person, in making a decision by which he identifies with a desire, constitutes himself. The pertinent desire is no longer in any way external to him. It is not a desire that he "has" merely as a subject in whose history it happens to occur, as a person may "have" an involuntary spasm that happens to occur in the history of his body' (Frankfurt 1988: 170). Cf. Moran (2002: 214): 'As I understand it, in the activity of "identification" someone determines what shall be part of him as a person.'

one could not feel the force of such an emotion and be unable, even if only in principle, to respond to its demands. Endorsement is what makes the difference between inhabiting an emotion and merely observing it within oneself.[12] The idea of endorsement is visible too in the discussion of the unity of consciousness. A being capable of a first-person stance is entitled to assertions that trade on the truth of cross-temporal and cross-modal identities with respect to its own self-ascribed experience. The argument that thoughts of the type 'This object I am touching is the same as the object I am seeing' require unity establishes that ownership is what creates a single normative space in which the contents of one's attitudes, emotions, and intentions bear rationally upon each other. Having a first-person stance implies the ability to conceive of oneself as oneself and so the ability to conceive of one's thoughts as one's own. I have argued that this requires that one must conceive of oneself as an embodied individual. The self is a necessarily embodied place for endorsements, what the individual pulls and demands implicit in each and every 'mine' lay claim to and because of which they pull together or pull apart.

Among our resolutions, evaluations, and emotions, there are some from which we do want to distance ourselves. We achieve this by making them into objects of consciousness, and thereby 'not self', opening them to the deliberative question 'Shall I make them mine?' (cf. Vātsyāyana 1997: 258,10–1 above *Nyāya-sūtra* 4.2.1, cited above). A tension between naturalism and the first-person stance arises only when it is imagined that this distancing can be achieved with respect to the whole of our mental life at once. For then it begins to seem that one must either imagine that there is a pure or formal self standing behind all awareness, or else that it is possible to become impersonal, without a first-person stance at all. The compatibility between naturalism and the first-person stance ceases to seem mysterious when one abandons the idea that one becomes estranged from the entirety of one's conscious life. Distancing oneself from one attitude always pre-

[12] Again Moran (2002: 210): 'It is because their normative structures are so manifestly different from a judgment's requirement of justification . . . that it is worth exploring how [pleasures] can nonetheless be seen as normative responses of this person, in a way that explains why pleasure (like love and caring, and unlike a sensation) is subject to identification and failure to identify, and are thus the expression of the active nature of the person. We can . . . preserve this crucial aspect in which pleasures, like loves and cares, are aspects of the whole person's engagement with the world, without "rationalizing" or "intellectualizing" them.'

supposes the avowal of others. One might indeed argue that it would be better to adopt the stance of merely witnessing one's anger or betrayal rather than inhabiting it; but my point is that one can assume a spectatorial stance with regard to some of one's states only if one is occupying a stance of endorsement with respect to others.

It is for all these reasons there is no room for a no-ownership theory of self when ownership is understood to consist in endorsement. A consequence is that the debate over whether subjectivity requires an phenomenal self is effectively finessed: one who takes endorsement to be the central idea in the notion of ownership will regard that debate as irrelevant to the question of the reality of the self.[13] Ownership (the question of 'place') is now understood in terms of participation and endorsement, and so as implying the *occupation* of a first-person stance and not merely the *witnessing* of a set of attitudes and emotions within oneself; and individuation (the question of 'base') is understood in terms of a common ownership relation obtaining between clusters of commitments, resolutions, and intentions, circumscribed by normative emotional response and implying agency and sentience and so embodiment. This too is what it means to describe a mental state as 'rooted' in the self, an entanglement of reasons and justifications underpinned by the procedural holism of a single comparing, monitoring, and selecting unconscious mind. The very fact that thought is something owned, something 'mine' and not mere stimulus or construct of causal response, already implies involvement in the space of reasons; to put the point in more Kantian terms, spontaneity is a condition for the possibility of avowal. It is from a liberal naturalist standpoint that the self which occupies a first-person stance comes into view, and this is compatible with the claim that no entity exists that might be visible from the perspective of a scientific naturalism, such as an agentive motor of thinking. Buddhists are right to deny the existence of any such thing.

[13] The debate about whether subjectivity requires an phenomenal self is the theme of Siderits, Thompson, and Zahavi (2011), the favoured no-self analysis of immersion seeming there to be reflexivism. The debate is described as being over whether an egological or non-egological analysis of subjectivity is correct. However, each distinct idea about ownership sustains its own notion of subjectivity, and, moreover, the phrase 'egological' does not specify what the role of an ego is meant to be. My present point is that the arguments against a non-egological theory of immersion are orthogonal to the discussion of participation.

In terms of our imaginary genealogy, what is fundamental to the paradigm shift instigated by the philosophy of early Buddhism is the simultaneous replacement of hard naturalisms and anti-naturalisms with a liberal naturalism. In a single stroke, Buddhism counters two conceptions of self at once: the Pure Consciousness Views of the Vedic and Upaniṣadic schools, and the Animalism of early materialists. It counters them through a critique of the concept of ownership on which they all depend, and substitutes three No Place Views and a Flame View—the views respectively of the four major Buddhist schools, Abhidharma, Yogācāra/Sautrāntika, Madhyamaka, and Vātsiputrīya. What this also does, however, is to make thinkable previously unimagined conceptions of self, the Ownership, Phenomenal, and Tornado views, adopted respectively by Nyāya-Vaiśeṣika, Kashmiri Śaiva, and late Cārvāka philosophers. Historically it would be a decluttered version of the Nyāya-Vaiśeṣika Ownership View that would gain prominence in early modern India, perhaps because of the distinctive support it affords to an increasingly secular conception of individual autonomous agency. This new theory distances itself both from scientistic conceptions of ownership, such as those of the early materialists, and from Vedic and Upaniṣadic Pure Consciousness theories of immersion: it too is a 'middle way'. Instead of denying the facticity of ownership altogether, however, it substitutes a new participatory analysis based on the idea of endorsement. That move is an instance of a general pattern in the history of ideas, where if some phenomenon is discovered not to have a characteristic it has been conceived to have, the options are either to deny the reality of the phenomenon (thereby granting the correctness of the original conception) or to offer a new conception of the phenomenon in which it does not have that characteristic: a pattern of intellectual progress in which critique is the engine of conceptual change.

My own view is that in a full account of human subjectivity, three distinct dimensions in the concept of self are equally in play, corresponding to three dimensions in the notion of ownership. There is an *underself*, the subpersonal monitoring of the mental states, autonomous or alienated, that one embodies, 'ownership' here implying a relation of unconscious access to the content of one's states of mind.[14] There is an immersed self, the element of first-person presentation in the content of consciousness, 'ownership' now referring to a phenomenologically present sense of mineness. Finally, there is a *participant self*, the inhabitation of a first-person stance, 'ownership' involving the relations of involvement, participation, and endorsement. Without an underself, one would have no mental life at all, and with only an underself, one's existence would be nothing more than that of a self-monitoring database. With an immersed but no participant self, one's desires and commitments would be as if that of a virtual avatar or simulacrum, experienced 'from the inside' but without any normative pull or demand.[15] With a participant but no immersed self, one would be as if afflicted by a disorder in which one's occupation of a first-person stance is devoid of phenomenal substance, and while one is not alienated from one's commitments and desires, they do not feel alive to one. Fully first-personal subjective consciousness is at once *grounded* (in 'friction' with the world and subject to its constraint), *lived* (in experiential openness and presence to the world), and *engaged* (with the pulls and demands of emotion and intention on the world). Therefore, a self is a unity of coordination, immersion, and participation. Where my proposal differs from that of any classical author, Buddhist or Nyāya, is in attaching equal significance to immersion and participation, and indeed in seeing the interplay between them (mediated by and grounded in unconscious mechanisms) as constitutive of self.

The philosopher Amiel seems to have managed temporarily to achieve both forms of dissonance by practising psychological exercises on himself. Of immersion without participation, he says,

I find myself regarding existence as though from beyond the tomb, from another world; all is strange to me; I am, as it were, outside my own body and individuality; I am depersonalized, detached, cut adrift. Is this madness? No. Madness means the impossibility of recovering one's normal balance after the mind has thus played

[14] A variety of ideas about subpersonal comparison are discussed in Feinberg (1978); Frith (1987, 1992); Campbell (1999, 2002); Ismael (2007); Reisenzein (2009). I have not agreed with Frith's model of thought insertion, but do not for that reason discount the idea of subpersonal comparison itself, or the idea that it has a role to play in an explanation of alien thought. In the analysis I have preferred the features emphasized are procedural holism and the double role of attention, these being the characteristics needed for correlation with the 'rootedness' of mental properties and the possibility of alienation.

[15] This is, I think, the intuition underlying Weyl's criticism of Husserl; see Ch. 2.

truant among alien forms of being, and following Dante to invisible worlds. Madness means incapacity for self-judgement and self-control. Whereas it seems to me that my mental transformations are but philosophical experiences. (Amiel 1889: 352)

And of participation without immersion,

Is the living layer of consciousness super-imposed upon hundreds of dead layers? . . . My mind is the empty frame of a thousand vanished images. Sharpened by incessant training, it is all culture, but it has retained hardly anything in its meshes. It is without matter, and is only form . . . It is etherealized, algebraicized. Life has treated it as death treats other minds; it has already prepared it for a further metamorphosis. Since the age of sixteen onward I have been able to look at things with the eyes of a blind man recently operated upon—that is to say, I have been able to suppress in myself the results of the long education of sight. (Amiel 1889: 351)

When, a few days later, he has ceased to be in the grip of these 'philosophical experiences', he describes in vivid terms what it is for immersion and participation to come together as one: 'This afternoon I have had a walk in the sunshine, and have come back rejoicing . . . I was overwhelmed with sensations. I was surprised and grateful . . . Once more my eyes beheld the vast horizons, the soaring peaks, the blue lakes, the winding valleys . . . The scene left upon me an indefinable impression, which was neither hope, nor desire, nor regret, but rather a sense of emotion, of passionate impulse' (Amiel 1889: 353). And he associates his rediscovered and now keenly felt sense of engagement and presence with the theme with which I began, the 'ambiguity of it is characteristic of human nature, which is ambiguous because it is flesh becoming spirit, space changing into thought, the Finite looking dimly out upon the Infinite'; and their reconciliation in what he marvellously describes as 'intelligence working its way through love and pain' (Amiel 1889: 353), a fine depiction of alive involvement. In a normal human psychology immersion and participation do not come apart, and their unity is not so keenly felt. Indeed, in a normal human psychology it is not that there is a participant self and an immersed self in union, but that participation and immersion are mutually constitutive of each owned thought and every moment of mineness.That is what we learned from the discussion of the composition of consciousness in Chapters 7 and 8. There is but one self, artificially divided.

While their analysis of immersion solely in terms of bodily ownership seems to me to concede too much to the critique of subjective immersion, and although their description of unconscious procedure is often naÿvely corpuscular, and their claim that involvement is compatible with discarnate existence an unsupported extension of their own analysis, Nyāya-Vaiśeṣika philosophers have been careful to distinguish by name the three aspects of self I have identified: the first is *manas* ['*mind*'], one's unconscious mind or underself; the second *ahaṃtva* ['*I-ity*'], the presented subject-element in phenomenal consciousness, the immersed self;[16] and the third is *ātman* ['*self*'], one's engaged participant self. I have considered a range of Buddhist analyses of immersion: the phenomenal mineness theory of Vasubandhu; the reflexive self-representational account of Dignāga with its doctrine of the subject-aspect; and Dharmakrti's quasi-subject analysis of the content of subjective consciousness.[17] I have favoured supplementing bodily immersion with a subjective theory of the immersed self derived from Vasubandhu's analysis (but without his error-theory) as the only analysis able to permit grounding by unconscious mechanisms and to have the right phenomeno-logical structure to cohere with the participant self.[18] Most

[16] Cf. Śaṃkara Miśra (1969: 257), translated on p. 243 above.

[17] As I have mentioned, still another option is to advance a Pure Consciousness account of immersion, for example by claiming that it is a sort of 'witness' consciousness. Fasching (2011) recommends the proposal as a constitutive account of the immersed self, which he describes as a dimension of experiential 'presence'. Albahari (2006) combines the proposal with an endorsement of an error-theory about the witness-consciousness, leading to a quasi-Buddhist theoretical position. The problem faced by any theory of immersion based on a Pure Consciousness View is, however, that of Attenuation.

[18] This point also tells against no-self analyses of immersion: participation requires there to be a participant self, and the possibility of unity between participation and immersion therefore also requires there to be an immersed self. The process by which a self constitutes itself through unification of two distinct factors is considered by Kierkegaard (1989), who speaks of a relation which is the "synthesis of the infinite and the finite, of the temporal and the eternal, of freedom and necessity", where "the self is not the relation but the relation's relating to itself". Attempts to do so paying heed to one factor without the other are the source of that alienation which he terms "despair", for example, without necessity the self "exhausts itself in possibility, yet it never moves from where it is nor gets anywhere", whereas "the determinist's self cannot breathe because it is impossible to breathe necessity alone." This strongly echoes what I said on p.329 about pure immersion and pure participation. "The self," Kierkegaard goes on, is "the conscious synthesis of infinitude and finitude, which relates to itself", for "what is decisive with regard to the self is consciousness, that is to say, self-consciousness". We might read Dignāga (see Chapter 9) in this light, his object-aspect and subject-aspect isolating two factors, and *svasaṃvedana* their "relation's relating to itself". That is, we might read Dignāga not as proposing a straightforward reflexivism, his position reducing to a purely immersive theory only with the addition of further claims about the nature of mental content. The concept of a relation's relating to itself is what Nyāya philosophers investigate when they discuss the idea of a "self-linking relation" (*svarūpa-sambandha*): the capacity so to be related is internal to the relatum. Where I disagree with Kierkegaard is in his claim that synthesis is established from above; my view is that it is established from below, in the processes and mechanisms of the underself.

generally, the trouble with purely reflexivist analyses of immersion is that there is no way then to draw the distinction between immersion and participation: the best that can be done is to distinguish between simple access to the subject-aspect of a thought and reflexive self-awareness—but this is still a distinction *internal* to immersion. An analysis of participation requires that one step out from the phenomenological standpoint.

Strawson is right, therefore: 'Our desires and preferences are not, in general, something we just note in ourselves as alien presences. To a large extent they *are* we' (P. F. Strawson 1992: 134). My desires and preferences are me because in accepting them I acknowledge their demands as my own, an acknowledgement that roots the desires and preferences in my whole being in such a way that any other state that is also me is subject to revision in the light of them, and vice versa. They are me because their conflict or congruence with other of my states is what gives shape to my emotions as exhibited in inclinations to action and felt affect. They are me because in accepting them I make myself a participant in the commitments they incur, in the world as they represent it, both in its factual content and in the gerundival description of paths to be followed and goals to be shunned. They are me because I am aware of myself in them, an awareness that creates a range of me/not-me contrasts in such a way that the phenomenal presentation of the desire as my own consists in the call it makes on a body of information I have about myself, including my preferences, capabilities, and values. That is to say, they are me because my immersion in them consists in their rootedness in deep levels of my psyche, and not in the mere reflexivity of representation. They are me, in short, because I am engaged by them and alive to them. And this unity of immersion and participation might require a Herculean effort of ratiocination were it not for the fact that my desires and preferences are also me because beneath the ground-level of consciousness they are bound by subterranean roots to the rest of me, in unconscious procedures of comparison, monitoring, and feedback. So no effort is required, and no coercion: my desires and preferences are me because in respect of them, there is freedom. Finally, the reason there is a correlation between felt affect and the neural states on which my desires and preferences supervene is that they are me: supervenience is just a constraint on the dynamic system that is my neural base.

The self is a unity of immersion, participation, and coordination; the first-person stance is at once lived, engaged, and underwritten. The interplay between immersion and participation, mediated by and grounded in unconscious mechanisms, is constitutive of self. And all is in harmony with the idea of the natural.

Bibliography

Abhinavagupta (1938). *Īśvara-pratyabhijñā-vivṛti-vimarśinī*, ed. M. K. Shastri (Bombay: Kashmir Sanskrit Texts Series 90), 3 vols.

——(1986). *Īśvara-pratyabhijñā-vimarśinī of Abhinavagupta, on the Īśvara-pratyabhijñā of Utpaladeva*, ed. K. A. Subramania Iyer and K. C. Pandey (Delhi: Motilal Banarsidass).

Albahari, Miri (2006). *Analytical Buddhism: The Two-Tiered Illusion of Self* (Basingstoke: Palgrave Macmillan).

Alexander, Samuel (1920). *Space, Time, and Deity: The Gifford Lectures at Glasgow, 1916–1918* (London: Macmillan), 2 vols.

al-Faḍl, Abu (1873–1907). *The Āīn-i Akbarī*, trans. from Persian by H. Blochmann and H. S. Jarrett (Calcutta: Baptist Mission Press), 3 vols.

Allison, Henry E. (1989). 'Kant's Refutation of Materialism', *Monist* 79: 190–209.

——(2004). *Kant's Transcendental Idealism: An Interpretation and Defense* (New Haven and London: Yale University Press), rev. and enlarged edn.

Amiel, Henri Frédéric (1889). *Amiel's Journal*, trans. H. Ward (2nd edn., New York: A. L. Burt).

Anacker, Stefan (1984). *Seven Works of Vasubandhu, the Buddhist Psychological Doctor* (Delhi: Motilal Banarsidass).

Anscombe, G. E. M. (1975). 'The First Person', in Samuel Guttenplan (ed.), *Mind and Language* (Oxford: Clarendon Press), 45–65.

Armstrong, D. M. (1963). 'Is Introspective Knowledge Incorrigible?', *Philosophical Review* 72: 418–19.

——(1968). *A Materialist Theory of the Mind* (London: Routledge & Kegan Paul).

——(1978). *Universals and Scientific Realism* (Cambridge and New York: Cambridge University Press), 2 vols.

Arnold, Dan (2005). 'Is *svasaṃvitti* Transcendental?', *Asian Philosophy* 15/1: 77–111.

——(2010). 'Self-Awareness (*svasaṃvitti*) and Related Doctrines of Buddhists Following Dignāga', *Journal of Indian Philosophy* 38: 323–78.

——(2012). *Buddhas, Brains, and Believing: The Problem of Intentionality in Classical Buddhist and Cognitive-Scientific Philosophy of Mind* (New York: Columbia).

Avrimides, Anita (2001). *Other Minds* (London: Routledge).

Ayers, Michael (1991). *Locke* (London: Routledge, 1991), 2 vols.

Bacon, John (1995). *Universals and Property Instances: The Alphabet of Being* (Oxford: Blackwell).

Baier, Kurt (1962). 'Smart on Sensations', *Australasian Journal of Philosophy* 40/1: 57–68.

Baker, Lynne Rudder (1998). 'The First-Person Perspective: A Test For Naturalism', *American Philosophical Quarterly* 35/4: 327–48.

——(2000). *Persons and Bodies: A Constitution View* (Cambridge: Cambridge University Press).

——(2001). 'Materialism with a Human Face', in Corocan (2001: 159–82).

——(2007). 'Naturalism and the First-Person Perspective', in Georg Gasser (ed.), *How Successful is Naturalism?* (Frankfurt: Ontos-Verlag), 203–26.

——(2011). 'Does Naturalism Rest on a Mistake?', *American Philosophical Quarterly* 48/2: 161–73.

——(2013). *Naturalism and the First-Person Perspective* (New York: Oxford University Press).

Balcerowicz, Piotr (2005). 'Monks, Monarchs and Materialists', *Journal of Indian Philosophy* 33/5–6: 571–82.

Barrett, L., Niedenthal, P. M., and Winkielman, P. (eds.) (2005). *Emotions: Conscious and Unconscious* (Guilford: New York).

Basham, A. L. (1951). *History and Doctrines of the Ājīvikas: A Vanished Indian Religion* (London: Luzac & Co.).

Baumeister, R. F., Vohs, K. D., DeWall, C. N., and Zhang, L. (2007). 'How Emotion Shapes Behaviour: Feedback, Anticipation, and Reflection, Rather Than Direct Causation', *Personality and Social Psychology Review* 11: 167–203.

Beckermann, Ansgar, Flohr, Hans, and Kim, Jaegwon (eds.) (1992). *Emergence or Reduction?* (Hawthorne: de Gruyter).

Bedau, Mark (1997). 'Weak Emergence', *Philosophical Perspectives* 11: 375–99.

——(2008). 'Downward Causation and Autonomy in Weak Emergence', in Bedau and Humphreys (2008: 155–88).

——(2010). 'Weak Emergence and Context-Sensitive Reduction', in Timothy O'Connor and Antonella Corradini (eds.), *Emergence in Science and Philosophy* (London: Routledge), 46–63.

Bedau, Mark, and Humphreys, Paul (eds.) (2008). *Emergence: Contemporary Readings in Philosophy and Science* (Cambridge, Mass.: MIT Press).

Bell, John L. (2004). 'Hermann Weyl's Later Philosophical Views: His Divergence from Husserl', in Richard Feist (ed.), *Husserl and the Sciences* (Ottawa: University of Ottawa), 173–88.

Bergmann, Gustav (1967). *Realism* (Madison: University of Wisconsin Press).

Bermúdez, José Luis (1998). *The Paradox of Self-Consciousness* (Cambridge, Mass.: MIT Press).

——(2003). 'Nonconceptual Mental Content', in Edward N. Zalta (ed.), *The Stanford Encyclopedia of Philosophy* (Summer 2003 Edition), URL = <http://plato.stanford.edu/archives/sum2003/entries/content-nonconceptual/>.

——(2005). 'The Phenomenology of Bodily Awareness', in Smith and Thomasson (2005: 295–306).

Bermúdez, José Luis, Marcel, Anthony, and Eilan, Naomi (eds.) (1995). *The Body and the Self* (Cambridge, Mass.: MIT Press).

Berridge, K. C. (1999). 'Pleasure, Pain, Desire, and Dread: Hidden Core Processes of Emotion', in D. Kahneman, D. Diener, and N. Schwarz (eds.), *Foundations of Hedonic Psychology: Scientific Perspectives on Enjoyment and Suffering* (Sage: New York), 525–57.

Berridge, K. C., and Winkielman, P. (2003). 'What is an Unconscious Emotion? (The Case for Unconscious Liking)', *Cognition and Emotion* 17: 181–211.

Berryman, Sylvia (2002). 'The Sweetness of Honey: Philoponus against the Doctors on Supervening Qualities', in Cees Leijenhorst, Christoph Lüthy, and Johannes M. M. H. Thijssen (eds.), *The Dynamics of Aristotelian Natural Philosophy from Antiquity to the Seventeenth Century* (Leiden: Brill), 65–79.

Bhaduri, Sadananda (1947). *Studies in Nyāya-Vaiśeṣika Metaphysics* (Poona: Bhandarkar Oriental Research Institute).

Bhattacharya, Ananta Kumar (1958–9). 'Cārvāka darśana', *Darśana* 6 [1365 Bengali year]; trans. in D. P. Chattopadhyaya and M. Gangopadhyaya (1990: 452–73).

Bhattacharya, Ramkrishna (1997). 'Cārvāka/Lokāyata Philosophy: Perso-Arabic Sources', *Indo-Iranica* 50: 85–91.

——(1999a). 'Svabhāvavāda vis-à-vis Materialism: A Review in the Light of Some *Mahābhārata* Passages', *Ānvīkṣikī* (*Journal of the Department of Sanskrit*, Jadavpur University Calcutta) 18: 92–101.

——(1999b). 'Ajita Keśakambala: Nihilist or Materialist?', *Journal of the Asiatic Society* 41/1: 74–83.

——(2000). 'Perception and Inference in the Cārvāka Philosophy', *Journal of the Asiatic Society* 42/1–2: 29–38.

——(2001). 'Haribhadra's Views on Svabhāvavāda and the Lokāyata', *Jain Journal* 36/1: 46–52.

——(2002a). 'Cārvāka Fragments: A New Collection', *Journal of Indian Philosophy*, 30/6: 597–640. Repr. in Bhattacharya (2009).

——(2002b). 'Verses Relating to Svabhāvavāda: a Collection', *Sambodhi* 25: 75–90. Repr. in Bhattacharya (2009).

——(2002c). 'Jayantabhaṭṭa's Representation of the Cārvāka: a Critique', in Joachim Heidrich et al. (eds.), *Indian Culture: Continuity and Discontinuity: In Memory of Walter Ruben (1899–1982)* (Berlin: Trafo): 85–93. Repr. in Bhattacharya (2009).

——(2009). *Studies on the Cārvāka/Lokāyata* (Florence: Società Editrice Fiorentina).

Bhattacharya, Ramkrishna (2010a). 'Lokāyata Darśana and a Comparative Study with Greek Materialism', in Partha Ghose (ed.), *Materialism and Immaterialism in India and the West: Varying Vistas* (*History of Science, Philosophy and Culture in Indian Civilization*, vol. xii, pt. 5; Delhi: Centre for Studies in Civilizations), 21–34.

——(2010b). 'Commentators on the *Cārvākasūtra*: A Critical Survey', *Journal of Indian Philosophy* 38/4: 419–30.

Bilgrami, Akeel (2006). *Self-Knowledge and Resentment* (Boston: Harvard University Press).

Block, Ned (1997). 'Inverted Earth', in Ned Block, Owen Flanagan, and Güven Güzeldere (eds.), *The Nature of Consciousness: Philosophical Debates* (Cambridge, Mass.: MIT Press).

Bodhi, Bhikku (1993). *A Comprehensive Manual of Abhidharma* (Kandy: Buddhist Publication Society).

——(1997). 'Review of *How Buddhism Began*', *Journal of Buddhist Ethics* 4: 292–6.

——, ed. (2007). *A Comprehensive Manual of Abhidhamma. The Abhidhamma Saṅgaha of Ācariya Anuruddha*, Pali text originally edited and translated by Mahthera Nrada (Kandy: Buddhist Publication Society, 3rd ed.).

Bollée, Willem (2002). *The Story of Paesi (Paesi-kahāṇayaṃ). Soul and Body in Ancient India. A Dialogue on Materialism. Text, Translation, Notes and Glossary* (Wiesbaden: Harrassowitz Verlag).

Bongard-Levin, G. M. (1978). 'Āryabhaṭa and Lokāyatas', *Annals of the Bhandarkar Oriental Research Institute*, 58–9 (Diamond Jubilee Volume), 69–77.

Bortolotti, Lisa, and Broome, Matthew (2009). 'A Role for Ownership and Authorship in the Analysis of Thought Insertion', *Phenomenology and the Cognitive Sciences* 8: 205–24.

Bostock, David (1988). *Plato's Theaetetus* (Oxford: Clarendon Press, 1988).

Brentano, Franz C. (1874). *Psychologie vom empirischen Standpunkt* (Berlin: Duncker & Humblot).

Brewer, Bill (1995). 'Bodily Awareness and the Self', in Bermúdez and Eilan (1995: 291–310).

Broad, C. D. (1925). *The Mind and Its Place in Nature* (London: Routledge & Kegan Paul).

Bronkhorst, Johannes (1994). 'Studies in Bhartṛhari 5: Bhartṛhari and Vaiśeṣika', in Saroja Bhate and Johannes Bronkhorst (eds.), *Bhartṛhari, Philosopher and Grammarian* (Delhi: Motilal Banarsidass), 75–94.

——(2008). 'Udbhaṭa, a Grammarian and a Cārvāka', in Mrinal Kaul and Ashok Aklujkar (eds.), *Linguistic Traditions of Kashmir: Essays in Memory of Pandit Dinanath Yaksha* (New Delhi: D. K. Printworld), 281–99.

Buddhaghosa (1921). *The Expositor (Atthasālinī)*, trans. Pe Maung Tin (Pali Text Society: Distributed London: Routledge & Kegan).

——(1977). *Visuddhi-magga*, Swami Dwarikadas Shastri crit. edn. (Varanasi: Baudha Bharati, 1977). Trans. Bhikkhu Ñāṇamoli, *The Path of Purification* (Colombo: Semage, 1964).

Buss, Sarah, and Overton, Lee (eds.) (2002). *Contours of Agency: Essays on Themes from Harry Frankfurt* (Cambridge, Mass.: MIT Press).

Cakradhara (1982–4). *Granthibhaṅga*, in *Nyāyamañjarī with the Commentary Granthibhaṅga by Cakradhara*, ed. Gaurinath Shastri (Varanasi: Sampurnananda Sanskrit University, 1982), 3 vols.

Campbell, John (1989). 'Is Sense Transparent?', *Proceedings of the Aristotelian Society* 88: 273–92.

——(1994). *Past, Space, & Self* (Cambridge, Mass.: MIT Press).

——(1997). 'Reply to Cassam', *Philosophy and Phenomenological Research* 75/3: 660–4.

——(1999). 'Schizophrenia, The Space of Reasons, and Thinking as Motor Process', *Monist* 82/4: 610–25.

——(2002). 'The Ownership of Thoughts', *Philosophy, Psychiatry & Psychology* 9/1: 35–9.

——(2004). 'What is it to Know what "I" Refers to?', *Monist* 87/2: 206–18.

Candrakānta (1991 [1869]). *Vaiśeṣika-sūtra-bhāṣya* (Varanasi: Vyasa Publishers).

Candrakīrti (1960). *Prasannapadā*, in P. L. Vaidya (ed.), *Madhyamakaśāstra of Nāgārjuna with the Commentary Prasannapadā by Candrakīrti* (Buddhist Sanskrit Texts Series 10; Darbhanga: The Mithila Institute; 2nd edn. 1987).

Cardona, George (1967–8). '*Anvaya* and *vyatireka* in Indian Grammar', *Adyar Library Bulletin* 31–2: 313–52.

——(1981). 'On Reasoning from *anvaya* and *vyatireka* in Early Advaita', in D. Malvania and N. J. Shah (eds.), *Studies in Indian Philosophy* (Ahmedabad: L. D. Institute of Indology), 79–104.

Cassam, Quassim (1997a). *Self and World* (Oxford: Clarendon Press).

——(1997b). 'Subjects and Objects', *Philosophy and Phenomenological Research* 57/3: 643–8.

Castañeda, Hector-Neri (1999). *The Phenomeno-Logic of the I: Essays in Self-Consciousness*, ed. James G. Hart and Tomis Kapitan (Bloomington: Indiana University Press); Chapter 10 includes 'Self-Consciousness, I-Structure and Physiology' and 'The Reflexivity of Self-Consciousness: Sameness/Identity, Data for Artificial Intelligence in Philosophy of Mind', articles with overlapping content which are often cited separately.

Caston, Victor (1992). 'Aristotle and Supervenience', *Southern Journal of Philosophy* 31 (suppl.): 107–35.

——(1997). 'Epiphenomenalisms, Ancient and Modern', *Philosophical Review* 106/3: 309–63.

——(2001). 'Dicaearchus' Philosophy of Mind', in William W. Fortenbaugh and Echart Schütrumpf (eds.), *Dicaearchus of Messana: Text, Translation, and Discussion*, (New Brunswick, NJ: Transaction Publishers), 175–93.

Caston, Victor (2002). 'Aristotle on Consciousness', *Mind* 111: 751–815.

Chakrabarti, Arindam (1992). 'I Touch What I Saw', *Philosophy and Phenomenological Research* 52/1: 103–17.

——(2003). 'Perception, Apperception and Non-conceptual Content', in Amita Chatterjee (ed.), *Perspectives on Consciousness* (Delhi: Munshiram Manoharlal): 89–107.

——(2004). 'Is Nyāya Realist?', in Krishna, Daya (ed.), *Discussion and Debate in Indian Philosophy: Issues in Vedānta, Mīmāṃsā and Nyāya* (New Delhi: Indian Council of Philosophical Research).

Chakrabarti, Arindam, Siderits, Mark, and Tillemans, Tom (eds.) (2011). *Buddhist Semantics and Human Cognition* (New York: Columbia University Press).

Chakrabarti, Kisor (1996). *Classical Indian Philosophy of Mind: The Nyāya Dualist Tradition* (Albany, NY: SUNY Press).

Chalmers, David (1996). *The Conscious Mind: In Search of a Fundamental Theory* (New York: Oxford University Press).

——(2006). 'Strong and Weak Emergence', in Clayton and Davies (2006: 244–54).

——(2010). *The Character of Consciousness* (Oxford: Oxford University Press).

Chattopadhyaya, Debiprasad (1959). *Lokāyata: A Study in Ancient Indian Materialism* (New Delhi: People's Pub. House).

Chattopadhyaya, Debiprasad, and Gangopadhyaya, Mrinalkanti (eds.) (1990). *Cārvāka/Lokāyata: An Anthology of Source Materials and Some Recent Studies* (New Delhi: Indian Council of Philosophical Research in association with Ṛddhi-India, Calcutta).

Chau, Thich Thien (1999). *The Literature of the Personalists of Early Buddhism* (Delhi: Motilal Banarsidass).

Chisholm, Roderick (1976). *Person and Object: A Metaphysical Study* (La Salle, Ill.: Open Court Publishing Co.).

——(1979). 'Is There a Mind-Body Problem?', *Philosophical Exchange* 2: 25–34.

Christman, John (2009). *The Politics of Persons: Individual Autonomy and Socio-Historical Selves* (Cambridge: Cambridge University Press).

Christman, John, and Anderson, Joel (2005). 'Introduction', to John Christman and Joel Anderson (eds.), *Autonomy and the Challenges to Liberalism* (Cambridge: Cambridge University Press), 1–23.

Chrudzimski, Arkadiusz (2004). 'Two Concepts of Trope', *Grazer Philosophische Studen* 64: 137–55.

Clark, Austen (1993). *Sensory Qualities* (Oxford: Clarendon Press).

——(2000). *A Theory of Sentience* (Oxford: Clarendon Press).

——(2004a). 'Feature-Placing and Proto-Objects', *Philosophical Psychology* 17/4: 443–69.

——(2004b). 'Sensing, Objects and Awareness: Reply to Commentators', *Philosophical Psychology* 17/4: 553–79.

Clayton, Philip, and Davies, Paul (eds.) (2006). *The Re-Emergence of Emergence* (Oxford: Oxford University Press).

Colebrooke, H. T. (1837). *Miscellaneous Essays* (London: W. H. Allen), 2 vols.

Connell, Richard (1988). *Substance and Modern Science* (Notre Dame, Ind.: University of Notre Dame Press).

Corocan, Kevin ed. (2001). *Soul, Body, and Survival: Essays in the Metaphysics of Human Persons* (Ithaca, NY: Cornell University Press).

Coseru, Christian (2012). *Perceiving Reality: Consciousness, Intentionality, and Cognition in Buddhist Philosophy* (New York: Oxford University Press).

Coulson, Michael (1976). *Sanskrit: An Introduction to the Classical Language* (New York: Hodder and Stoughton).

Cowell, E. B. (1862). 'The Cārvāka System of Philosophy', *Journal of the Asiatic Society of Bengal* 31: 317–90.

Cox, Collett (1995). *Disputed Dharmas: Early Buddhist Theories on Existence. An Annotated Translation of the Section on Factors Dissociated from Thought from Saṅghabhadra's Nyāyānusāra* (Tokyo: The International Institute for Buddhist Studies).

Crane, Timothy (1999). 'The Significance of Emergence', in Carl Gillett and Barry Loewer (eds.), *Physicalism and Its Discontents* (Cambridge: Cambridge University Press, 1999), 207–24.

Dainton, Barry (2008). *The Phenomenal Self* (Oxford: Oxford University Press).

Damasio, A. R. (1999). *The Feeling of What Happens* (San Diego, Calif.: Harcourt).

Davidson, Donald (1980). *Essays on Actions and Events* (Oxford: Clarendon Press).

Davidson, Richard (2003). 'Seven Sins in the Study of Emotion: Correctives from Affective Neuroscience', *Brain and Cognition* 52: 129–32.

Davies, Paul (2006). 'The Physics of Downward Causation', in Clayton and Davies (2006: 35–51).

Davis, Jake and Thompson, Evan (2013). "From the Five Agreggates to Phenomenal Consciousness: Towards a Cross-Cultural Cognitive Science," in Steven Emmanuel ed., *A Companion to Buddhist Philosophy* (London: John Wiley and Sons), pp. 585–597.

De Caro, Mario (2010). 'Varieties of Naturalism', in Koons and Bealer (2010: 365–74).

Dennett, Daniel (1992). 'The Self as a Centre of Narrative Gravity', in F. Kessel, P. Cole, and D. Johnson (eds.), *Self and Consciousness: Multiple Perspectives* (Hillsdale, NJ: Erlbaum).

Descartes, René (1984). *The Philosophical Writings of Descartes*, ed. John Cottingham (Cambridge: Cambridge University Press), 2 vols.

Dharmakīrti (1960). *The Pramāṇavārttikam of Dharmakīrti: The First Chapter with the Autocommentary*, ed. Raniero Gnoli (Rome: Serie Orientale Roma 23).
——(1971–2). *Pramāṇa-vārttika-kārikā* (Sanskrit and Tibetan), Chapters 2, 3, 4', ed. Y. E. Miyasaka, *Acta Indologica* 2: 1–206.
——(1985). *Nyāya-bindu*, ed. Dwarika Das Shastri (Varanasi: Baudha Bharati). Translation: M. Gangopadhyaya, in his *Vinītadeva's Nyāyabindu-ṭīkā* (Calcutta: ISPP, 1971).
——(1989). *Pramāṇa-vārttika*, ed. P. C. Pandeya (Delhi: Motilal Banarsidass).
——(1997). *Santānantara-siddhi*. Tibetan text, edited, and restored into Sanskrit by J. S. Negi (Varanasi: Central Institute of Higher Tibetan Studies), and again by M. R. Chinchore (Varanasi: Central Institue of Higher Tibetan Studies). Translations: H. Kitagawa, 'A Refutation of Solipsism', *Journal of the Greater India Society* (Calcutta) 14/1 (1955): 55–73; Thomas Wood, *Mind Only: A Philosophical And Doctrinal Analysis of the Vijñānavāda* (Honolulu: University of Hawaii Press, 1991): 207–18.
Dignāga (2005). *Dignāga's Pramāṇa-samuccaya, Chapter 1: A Hypothetical Reconstruction of the Sanskrit Text*. ikga.oeaw.ac.at/Mat/dignaga_PS_1.pdf. Translation (from Tibetan): Hattori (1968).
Dretske, Fred (1988). *Explaining Behaviour: Reasons in a World of Causes* (Cambridge, Mass.: MIT Press).
Dreyfus, Georges (1997). *Recognizing Reality: Dharmakīrti's Philosophy and Its Tibetan Interpretations* (Albany, NY: SUNY Press).
——(2011). 'Self and Subjectivity: A Middle Way Approach', in Siderits, Thompson and Zahavi (2011: 114–56).
Dreyfus, Georges, and Thompson, Evan (2007). 'Asian Perspectives: Indian Theories of Mind', in Morris Moscovitch, Evan Thompson and Philip David Zelazo (eds.), *The Cambridge Handbook of Consciousness* (Cambridge: Cambridge University Press), 89–116.
Duerlinger, James (1993). 'Reductionist and Nonreductionist Theories of Persons in Indian Buddhist Philosophy', *Journal of Indian Philosophy* 21: 79–101.
——(2003). *Indian Buddhist Theories of Persons: Vasubandhu's 'Refutation of the Theory of Self'* (London: RoutledgeCurzon).
Dummett, Michael (1991). *The Logical Basis of Metaphysics* (Cambridge, Mass.: Harvard University Press).
——(1993). *Origins of Analytical Philosophy* (Cambridge, Mass.: Harvard University Press).
Dunne, John D. (2004). *Foundations of Dharmakīrti's Philosophy* (Boston: Wisdom Publications).

Dupré, Jon (2004). 'The Miracle of Monism', in Mario De Caro and David Macarthur (eds.), *Naturalism in Question* (Cambridge, Mass. and London: Harvard University Press).

Ekstrom, Laura Waddell (1999). 'Keynote Preferences and Autonomy', *Philosophy and Phenomenological Review* 59: 1057–63.

——(2005). 'Alienation, Autonomy, and the Self', *Midwest Studies in Philosophy* 29: 45–67.

Evans, Gareth (1982). *The Varieties of Reference* (Oxford: Clarendon Press).

——(1985). 'Molyneux's Question', in his *Collected Papers* (Oxford: Clarendon Press).

Faddegon, B. (1918). *The Vaiśeṣika System, Described with the Help of the Oldest Texts* (Amsterdam: Johannes Müller).

Fasching, Walter (2011). 'I Am of the Nature of Seeing: Phenomenological Reflections on the Indian Notion of a Witness-Consciousness', in Siderits, Thompson, and Zavahi (2011: 193–216).

Feigl, H. (1958). 'The "Mental" and the "Physical"', in H. Feigl, M. Sriven, and G. Maxwell (eds.), *Concepts, Theories and the Mind-Body Problem* (Minneapolis: Minnesota Studies in the Philosophy of Science), vol. ii.

Feinberg, Irwin (1978). 'Efference Copy and Corollary Discharge: Implications for Thinking and Its Disorders', *Schizophrenia Bulletin* 4: 636–40.

Fernández, Jordi (2010). 'Thought Insertion and Self-Knowledge', *Mind & Language* 25/1: 66–88.

Field, Hartry (1989). *Realism, Mathematics and Modality* (Oxford: Blackwell).

Fink, Hans (2008). 'Three Sorts of Naturalism', in Jakob Lindgaard (ed.), *John McDowell: Experience, Norm, and Nature* (Oxford: Blackwell Publishing), 52–71.

Fodor, J. A. (1983). *The Modularity of Mind: An Essay on Faculty Psychology* (Cambridge, Mass.: MIT Press).

Frankfurt, Harry (1977). 'Identification and Externality', in Amelie Rorty (ed.), *The Identities of Persons* (Berkeley and Los Angeles: University of California Press). Reprinted in Frankfurt (1988: 58–68).

——(1988). *The Importance of What We Care About: Philosophical Essays* (Cambridge: Cambridge University Press).

Frauwallner, Erich (1973). *History of Indian Philosophy* (Salzburg: Otto Muller Verlag), 2 vols.; trans. V. M. Bedekar. Reprinted (New Delhi: Motilal Banarsidass).

Frijda, Nico H. (2007). *The Laws of Emotion* (London: Lawrence Erlbaum Associates).

Frith, C. D. (1987). 'The Positive and Negative Symptoms of Schizophrenia Reflect Impairment in the Perception and Initiation of Action', *Psychological Medicine* 19: 359–63.

——(1992). *The Cognitive Neuropsychology of Schizophrenia* (Hove: Lawrence Erlbaum).

Gadādhara Bhaṭṭācārya (1927). *Śaktivāda*, ed. G. D. Sastri (Benares: Kashi Sanskrit Series).

Gallagher, Shaun (2004). 'Neurocognitive Models of Schizophrenia: A Neurophenomenological Critique', *Psychopathology* 37: 8–19.

——(2005). *How the Body Shapes the Mind* (New York: Oxford University Press).

——(ed.) (2011). *The Oxford Handbook of the Self* (Oxford: Oxford University Press).

Gallagher, Shaun, and Zahavi, Dan (2008). *The Phenomenological Mind* (London: Routledge).

Galloway, Brian (1978). '*Vijñāna, saṃjñā* and *manas*', *Middle Way* 53/2: 72–5.

——(1980). 'A Yogācāra Analysis of the Mind, Based on the *vijñāna* Section of Vasubandhu's *Pañca-skandhaka-prakaraṇa* with Guṇaprabhā's Commentary', *Journal of the International Association for Buddhist Studies* 3/2: 7–20.

Ganeri, Jonardon (1995). 'Self-Intimation, Memory and Personal Identity', read to the Sussex Philosophy Society, Nov. 1995, and subsequently published in the *Journal of Indian Philosophy* 27 (1999): 469–83.

——(1999). *Semantic Powers: Meaning and the Means of Knowing in Classical Indian Philosophy* (Oxford: Clarendon Press). Rev. 2nd edn.: *Artha* (Delhi: Oxford University Press, 2011).

——(2001). *Philosophy in Classical India: The Proper Work of Reason* (London: Routledge).

——(2007). *The Concealed Art of the Soul: Theories of Self and Practices of Truth in Indian Ethics and Epistemology* (Oxford: Clarendon Press). 2nd edn in paperback, 2012.

——(2011). *The Lost Age of Reason: Philosophy in Early Modern India 1450–1700* (Oxford: Clarendon Press).

——(2016). *Attention and Consciousness: Buddhaghosa's Theravāda Philosophy of Mind.*

Garfield, Jay (2006). 'The Conventional Status of Reflexive Awareness: What's at Stake in the Tibetan Debate?' *Philosophy East and West* 56: 201–28.

Gautama (1997). *Nyāya-sūtra*, in Anantalal Thakur (ed.), *Gautamīya-nyāya-darśana with Bhāṣya of Vātsyāyana* (Delhi: Indian Council of Philosophical Research). See also *Nyāya-darśanam*, ed. Taranatha Nyaya-Taraktirtha and Amarendramohan Tarkatirtha (New Delhi: Munshiram Manoharlal Publishers, 1985). Translation: Mrinalkanti Gangopadhyaya, *Gautama's Nyāya-sūtra with Vātsyāyana's Commentary* (Calcutta: Indian Studies, 1982).

Gethin, Rupert (1986). "The Five *khandhas*: Their Treatment in the Nikāyas and Early Abhidhamma," *Journal of Indian Philosophy* 14.1: 35–53.

——(1998). *The Foundations of Buddhism* (Oxford: Oxford University Press).

Gillett, Carl (2006). 'Samuel Alexander's Emergentism: Or, Higher Causation for Physicalists', *Synthese* 153/2: 261–96.

Ginet, Carl (1990). *On Action* (Cambridge: Cambridge University Press).

Giorgi, Alessandra (2009). *About the Speaker: Towards a Syntax of Indexicality* (Oxford: Oxford University Press).

Gokhale, Pradeep P. (1993). 'The Cārvāka Theory of *Pramāṇas*: A Restatement', *Philosophy East and West*, 43/4: 675–82.

Gold, Jonathan (2011). 'Vasubandhu', in Edward N. Zalta (ed.), *The Stanford Encyclopedia of Philosophy* (Summer 2011 Edition), URL = <http://plato.stanford.edu/archives/sum2011/entries/vasubandhu/>.

Gubeljic, Mischa et al. (2000). 'Nature and Second Nature in McDowell's *Mind* and *World*', in Marcus Willaschek (ed.), *John McDowell: Reason and Nature* (Münster: Lit Verglag): 41–9.

Guṇaratna (1969). *Tarka-rahasya-dīpikā, a Commentary on Haribhadra Sūri's Ṣaḍ-darśana-samuccaya*, ed. M. K. Jain (Calcutta: Bharatiya Jnanapitha Publications). Partial translation in Chattopadhyaya and Gangopadhyaya (1990: 266–98).

Hagège, Claude (1974). "Les pronoms logophoriques," *Bulletin de la Société de Linguistique de Paris* 69: 287–310.

Halbfass, Wilhelm (1992). *On Being and What There Is: Classical Vaiśeṣika and the History of Indian Ontology* (Albany, NY: SUNY Press).

——(1997). 'On Happiness', in J. Mohanty and P. Bilimoria (eds.), *Relativism, Suffering, and Beyond: Essays in Memory of Bimal K. Matilal* (Delhi: Oxford University Press).

Halbig, Christoph (2008). 'Varieties of Nature in Hegel and McDowell', in Jakob Lindgaard (ed.), *John McDowell: Experience, Norm, and Nature* (Oxford: Blackwell Publishing), 72–91.

Hale, Bob (1979). 'Strawson, Geach and Dummett on Singular Terms and Predicates', *Synthese* 42: 275–95.

——(1996). 'Singular Terms (1)', in Matthia Schirn (ed.), *Frege: Importance and Legacy* (Berlin: Wlater de Gruyter), 438–57.

Hampshire, Stuart (1975). *Freedom of the Individual* (Princeton: Princeton University Press).

Harvey, Peter (1995). *The Selfless Mind: Personality, Consciousness and Nirvāṇa in Early Buddhism* (London: RoutledgeCurzon).

Haskar, William (1999). *The Emergent Self* (Ithaca, NY: Cornell University Press).

——(2001). 'Persons as Emergent Substances', in Corocan (2001: 107–19).

——(2010). 'Persons and the Unity of Consciousness', in Robert C. Koons and George Bealer (eds.), *The Waning of Materialism* (Oxford: Oxford University Press), 175–90.

Hattori, Masaaki (1968). *Dignāga, on Perception* (Cambridge, Mass.: Harvard University Press).

Hayes, Richard (1988). *Dignāga on the Interpretation of Signs* (Dordrecht: Kluwer Academic Publishers).

Heil, John (1992). *The Nature of True Minds* (Cambridge: Cambridge University Press).

Hennig, B. (2009). 'The Four Causes', *Journal of Philosophy* 106: 137–60.

Henry, Aaron, and Thompson, Evan (2011). 'Witnessing from Here: Self-Awareness from a Bodily versus Embodied Perspective', in Gallagher (2011).

Henry, Devin (2008). 'The Neoplatonic Achilles', in Lennon and Stainton (2008: 59–74).

Henry, Michel (1975). *Philosophy and Phenomenology of the Body*, trans. G. Etzkorn (The Hague: Martinus Nijhoff).

Hirakawa, Akira, et al. (1973). 'Introduction', in Akira Hirakawa (ed.), in collaboration with Shunei Hirai, So Takahashi, Noriaki Hakamaya, and Giei Yoshizu, *Index to the Abhidharmakośabhāṣya (Pr. Pradhan edn.), pt. I* (Tokyo: Daizō Shuppan Kabushikikaisha), pp. i–xxxxiv.

Hoerl, Christoph (2001). 'On Thought Insertion', *Philosophy, Psychiatry, and Psychology* 8: 189–200.

Hoernle, A. F. R. (1956–60). 'Ājīvikas', in J. Hastings, J. A. Selbie, and L. H. Gray (eds.), *Encyclopaedia of Indian Religion and Ethics* (Edinburgh: T. & T. Clark), vol. i.

Horgan, Terry, and Tienson, John (2002). 'The Intentionality of Phenomenology and the Phenomenology of Intentionality', in D. Chalmers (ed.), *Philosophy of Mind: Classical and Contemporary Readings* (Oxford: Oxford University Press), 520–33.

Horgan, Terry, Tienson, John, and Graham, George (2006). 'Internal-World Skepticism and the Self-Presentational Nature of Phenomenal Consciousness', in Kriegel and Williford (2006: 41–61).

Hume, David (1978). *A Treatise of Human Nature*, ed. L. A. Selby-Bigge and P. H. Nidditch (Oxford: Clarendon Press).

Humphreys, Paul (1996). 'Aspects of Emergence', *Philosophical Topics* 24/1: 53–70.

——(1997a). 'How Properties Emerge', *Philosophy of Science* 64: 1–17.

——(1997b). 'Emergence, Not Supervenience', *Philosophy of Science* 64: 337–45.

——(2000). 'Extending Ourselves', in Martin Carrier, Gerald Massey, and Laura Ruetsche (eds.), *Science at Century's End* (Pittsburgh: University of Pittsburgh Press): 13–32.

Husserl, Edmund (1927). 'Phenomenology', Draft D of an article for the *Encyclopædia Britannica*, trans. Richard Palmer, *Journal of the British Society for Phenomenology* 2 (1971): 77–90.

——(1984). *Einleitung in die Logik und Erkenntnistheorie. Vorlesungen 1906/07* (Dordrecht: Marinus Nijhoff).

Ismael, Jenann T. (2007). *The Situated Self* (New York: Oxford University Press).

——(2011). 'Responses', *Philosophy and Phenomenological Research* 82: 780–7.

Jackson, Frank (1977). *Perception: A Representative Theory* (Cambridge: Cambridge University Press).

Jacobi, Hermann trans. (1895). *Jaina Sūtras, pt. II* (Sacred Books of the East, vol. xlv; Oxford: Clarendon Press).

Jagadīśa Tarkālaṃkāra (1924). *Sūktī, a commentary on Praśastapāda's Padārthadharmasaṃgraha*, ed. M. M. Gopinath Kaviraj and Panditraj Bhundhiraj Shastri (Chowkhamba Sanskrit Series 61; Benares: Vidya Vilas Press). Repr. (1983).

James, William (1890). *The Principles of Psychology* (New York: H. Holt & co.), 2 vols.

Janzen, Greg (2008). *The Reflexive Nature of Consciousness* (Amsterdam: John Benjamins Publishing Co.).

Jayanta Bhaṭṭa (1982–4). *Nyāya-mañjarī with the Commentary Granthibhaṅga by Cakradhara*, ed. Gaurinath Shastri (Varanasi: Sampurnananda Sanskrit University), 3 vols.

Jayarāma Nyāyapañcānana (1985 [1659]). *Garland of Categories (Padārtha-mālā), with Laugākṣī Bhāskara's Prakāśa*, ed. N. Srinivasan (Sarasvati Mahal Library, series no. 217; Tanjore).

Jayarāśi (1940). *Tattvopaplava-siṃha*, ed. Sukhlalji Samghavi and Rasiklal Parikh (Gaewkwad Oriental Series 87; Baroda: Oriental Institute).

Jayatilleke, Kulatissa Nanda (1963). *Early Buddhist Theory of Knowledge* (London: G. Allen & Unwin).

Jeannerod, M., and Pacherie, E. (2004). 'Agency, Simulation and Self-Identification', *Mind and Language* 19: 113–46.

Jha, Ganganatha (1984). *The Nyāya-sūtras of Gautama* (Delhi: Motilal Banarsidass).

Jinendrabuddhi (2005). *Viśālāmalavatī Pramāṇa-samuccaya-ṭīkā, ch. 1*, ed. Ernst Steinkellner and Helmut Krasser (Vienna: Austrian Academy of Sciences Press).

Jñānaśrīmitra (1959). *Sākāra-saṃgraha-sūtra*, in *Jñānaśrīmitra-nibandhāvali*, ed. Anantalal Thakur (Patna: KP Research Institute), 515–78.

Johansson, Rune E. A. (1979). *The Dynamic Psychology of Early Buddhism* (London: Curzon).

Kahneman, D. (1999). 'Objective Happiness', in D. Kahneman, D. Diener, and N. Schwarz (eds.), *Foundations of Hedonic Psychology: Scientific Perspectives on Enjoyment and Suffering* (Sage: New York), 3–25.

Kamalaśīla (1968). *Tattva-saṅgraha-pañjikā*, ed. Swami Dwarikadas Shastri (Varanasi: Bauddhabharati).

Kaṇāda (1961). *Vaiśeṣika-sūtra, with the Commentary of Candrānanda*, ed. Muni Sri Jambuvijaya (Gaekwad's Oriental Series 136; Baroda: Oriental Institute).

Kant, Immanuel (2003). *Critique of Pure Reason*, trans. Norman Kemp Smith (Palgrave Macmillan).

Kapstein, Matthew (2001). *Reason's Traces: Identity and Interpretation in Indian & Tibetan Buddhist Thought* (Boston: Wisdom Publications).

Karmo, Toomas (1977). 'Disturbances', *Analysis* 37: 147–8.

Karunadasa, Yakupitiyage (2010). *The Theravāda Abhidhamma: Its Inquiry into the Nature of Conditioned Reality* (Hong Kong: Centre of Buddhist Studies, The University of Hong Kong).

Katsura, Shoryu (1979). 'The *apoha* Theory of Dignāga', *Journal of Indian and Buddhist Studies* 28/1: 16–20.

——(1993). 'On Perceptual Judgement', in N. K. Wagle and F. Watanabe (eds.), *Studies in Buddhism in Honour of A. K. Warder* (Toronto: University of Toronto Press), 66–75.

Kaviraja, Gopinatha (1990). 'Lokyata and the Doctrine of *svabhāva*', *Sarasvati Bhavana Studies* 2: 93–111; repr. in Chattopadhyaya and Gangopadhyaya (1990: 441–51).

Kellner, Birgit (2010). 'Self-Awareness (*svasaṃvedana*) in Dignāga's *Pramāṇasamuccaya* and *-vṛtti*: A Close Reading', *Journal of Indian Philosophy* 38: 203–31.

——(2011). 'Self-awareness (*svasaṃvedana*) and Infinite Regresses: A Comparison of Arguments by Dignāga and Dharmakīrti', *Journal of Indian Philosophy* 39: 411–26.

Keyt, C. M. (1980). 'Dharmakīrti's Concept of the *Svalakṣaṇa*'. PhD Dissertation, University of Washington.

Khalidi, Muhammad Ali (2005). *Medieval Islamic Philosophical Writings* (Cambridge: Cambridge University Press).

Kierkegaard, Søren (1989). *The Sickness Unto Death*, trans. Alastair Hannay (London: Penguin).

Kim, Jaegwon (1988). 'Supervenience for Multiple Domains', *Philosophical Topics* 16: 129–50.

——(1993). *Supervenience and Mind* (Cambridge: Cambridge University Press).

——(1998). *Mind in a Physical World: An Essay on the Mind-Body Problem and Mental Causation* (Cambridge, Mass.: MIT Press).

——(1999). 'Making Sense of Emergence', *Philosophical Studies* 95: 3–36; repr. in Bedau and Humphreys (2008: 127–54).

——(2001). 'Lonely Souls: Causality and Substance Dualism', in Corocan (2001: 30–43).

——(2005). *Physicalism, or Something Near Enough* (Princeton: Princeton University Press).

——(2006a). 'Emergence: Core Ideas and Issues', *Synthese* 151/3: 547–59.

——(2006b). 'Being Realistic about Emergence', in Clayton and Davies (2006): 189–202.

Klong chen pa (1968). *The Treasury of Wish-fulfillment (Yid bzhin mdzod)*, in Dodrup Chen Rinpoche (ed.), *The Seven Treasuries* (Gangtok: National Library of Bhutan).

Koons, Robert, and Bealer, George (2010). 'Introduction', in Koons and Bealer (eds.) (2010: pp. ix–xxxi).

Koons, Robert, and Bealer, George (eds.) (2010). *The Waning of Materialism* (Oxford: Oxford University Press).

Korsgaard, Christine (2009). *Self-Constitution: Agency, Identity and Integrity* (Oxford: Oxford University Press).

Kramer, Jowita (2008). 'On Sthiramati's *Pañca-skandhaka-vibhāṣā*: a Preliminary Survey', *Nagoya Studies in Indian Culture and Buddhism: Saṃbhāṣā* 27: 149–72.

——(2013). "Notes on the *rūpa* Section of the *Pañcaskhandakavibhāṣā*," China Tibetology 2: 86–99.

Kriegel, Uriah (2009). *Subjective Consciousness* (Oxford: Oxford University Press).

Kriegel, Uriah, and Williford, Kenneth (eds.) (2006). *Self-Representational Approaches to Consciousness* (Cambridge, Mass.: MIT Press).

Kripke, Saul (1982). *Naming* and *Necessity* (Cambridge, Mass.: Harvard University Press).

Kṛṣṇadāsa (1923). *Necklace of Verses (Kārikāvalī) aka. Divisions of Language (Bhāṣā-pariccheda), with the Pearl-necklace of Principles about Reason (Nyāya-siddhānta-muktāvalī)*, ed. S. R. Shastri (Madras: Sri Balamanorama Press). The text is often erroneously ascribed to Viśvanātha.

Krueger, Joel (2011). 'The Who and the How of Experience', in Siderits, Tillemans, and Zahavi (2011: 27–55).

Kulkarni, V. M. (1968). 'Svabhāva-vāda (Naturalism): A Study', in *Sri Mahavira Jaina Vidyalaya Suvarna Mahotsava Grantha*, ed. A. M. Upadhye et al. (Bombay: Sri Mahavira Jain Vidyalaya), 10–20.

Kumārila (1929). *Ślokavārttika*, ed. K. Sambasiva Sastri, in *The Mīmāṃsa-ślokavārttika with the commentary Kāśikā of Sucaritamiśra* (Trivandrum Sanskrit Series No. 90; Trivandrum).

Lagerlund, Henrik (2008). 'The Neoplatonic Achilles', in Lennon and Stainton (2008: 59–74).

Lakoff, George, and Johnson, Mark (1999). *Philosophy in the Flesh: The Embodied Mind and Its Challenge to Western Thought* (New York: Basic Books).

Lambie, J. and Marcel, A. (2002). 'Consciousness and Experience: A Theoretical Framework', *Psychological Review* 109: 219–59.

Lehrer, K. (1996). 'Consciousness', in A. Schramm (ed.), *Philosophie in Osterreich* (Vienna: Verlag Holder-Pichler-Tempsky).

Lennon, Thomas M., and Stainton, Robert J. (eds.) (2008). *The Achilles of Rational Psychology* (Berlin: Springer).

Levine, Joseph (2004). 'Thoughts on Sensory Representation: A Commentary on Austen Clark's *A Theory of Sentience*', *Philosophical Psychology* 17/4: 541–51.

Lewes, George Henry (1875). *Problems of Life and Mind* (London: Kegan Paul).

Lewin, K. (1937). *Towards a Dynamic Theory of Personality* (New York: McGraw-Hill).
Lewis, David (1983). 'New Work for a Theory of Universals', *Australasian Journal of Philosophy* 61/4: 343–77.
——(1986). *Philosophical Papers* (Oxford: Oxford University Press).
——(1998). *Papers in Philosophical Logic* (Cambridge: Cambridge University Press).
Libet, Benjamin (1999). 'Do We Have Free Will?', *Journal of Consciousness Studies* 6: 47–57.
Locke, John (1975). *An Essay Concerning Human Understanding*, ed. Peter H. Nidditch (Oxford: Oxford University Press).
Loewer, Barry (1996). 'Humean Supervenience', *Philosophical Topics* 24/1: 101–28.
Lowe, E. J. (1996). *Subjects of Experience* (Cambridge: Cambridge University Press.)
——(2001). 'Identity, Composition, and the Self', in Corocan (2001: 139–58).
——(2008). *Personal Agency: The Metaphysics of Mind and Action* (Clarendon Press: Oxford University Press).
Lusthaus, Dan (2002). *Buddhist Phenomenology: A Philosophical Investigation of Yogācāra Buddhism and the Ch'eng Wei-shih lun* (London: Routledge).
Lycan, William G. (1987). Consciousness (Cambridge, Mass.: MIT Press).
——(1996). *Consciousness and Experience* (Cambridge, Mass.: MIT Press).
——(1997). 'Consciousness as Internal Monitoring', in Ned Block, Owen Flanagan, and Güven Güzeldere (eds.), *The Nature of Consciousness: Philosophical Debates* (Cambridge, Mass.: MIT Press), 755–71.
McCrea, Lawrence, and Patil, Parimal (2010). *Buddhist Philosophy of Language in India: Jñānaśrīmitra on Exclusion* (New York: Columbia Univesity Press).
Macdonald, Cynthia (1989). *Mind-Body Identity Theories* (London: Routledge).
Macdonald, Cynthia, and Macdonald, Graham (2010). 'Emergence and Downward Causation', in Cynthia Macdonald and Graham Macdonald (eds.), *Emergence in Mind* (Oxford: Oxford University Press), 139–68.
McDowell, John H. (1996). *Mind and World* (2nd edn., Cambridge, Mass.: Harvard University Press).
——(1998). 'Two Sorts of Naturalism', in his *Mind, Value, and Reality* (Cambridge, Mass.: Harvard University Press), 167–97.
——(2004). 'Naturalism in the Philosophy of Mind', in Mario De Caro and David Macarthur (eds.), *Naturalism in Question* (Cambridge, Mass.: Harvard University Press), 91–105.
——(2008). 'Responses', in Jakob Lindgaard (ed.), *John McDowell: Experience, Norm, and Nature* (Oxford: Blackwell Publishing, 2008), 200–67.
——(2009). 'Referring to Oneself', in his *The Engaged Intellect* (Cambridge, Mass.: Harvard University Press), 186–203.

MacKenzie, Matthew D. (2007). 'The Illumination of Consciousness: Approaches to Self-Awareness in the Indian and Western Traditions', *Philosophy East and West* 57/1: 40–62.

——(2008). 'Self-Awareness Without a Self: Buddhism and the Reflexivity of Awareness', *Asian Philosophy* 18/3: 245–66.

McLaughlin, Brian (1992). 'The Rise and Fall of British Emergentism', in Beckerman, Flohr, and Kim eds. 1992; repr. in Bedau and Humphreys (2008: 19–60).

——(1995). 'Varieties of Supervenience', *Supervenience: New Essays*, ed. Elias E. Savellos (Cambridge: Needham Heights).

——(1997). 'Emergence and Supervenience', *Intellectica* 25; repr. in Bedau and Humphreys (2008: 81–98).

McRea, Michael (2002). 'Lynne Baker on Material Constitution', *Philosophy and Phenomenological Research* 64/3: 607–14.

Mādhavācārya (1908). *The Sarva-darśana-saṃgraha*, trans. E. B. Cowell and A. E. Gough (London: Kegan, Paul, Trench, Trübner & Co.), 3rd edn.

Mādhavadeva Bhaṭṭa (1903–4). *The Essence of Reason (Nyāya-sāra)*, ed. Nagesvara Pant Dharmadhikari, in *The Pandit*, NS 25: 455 and 26: 97, pages also sequentially numbered 1–246; repr. (Benares: Medical Hall Press 1905).

Mahādeva Puṇatāmakara (1930). *Precious Jewel of Reason (Nyāya-kaustubha), Pratyakṣa-khaṇḍa*, ed. Umesh Mishra (Saraswati Bhavana Texts 33/1; Benares: Vidya Mandir Press).

Malcolm, Norman (1963). 'Scientific Materialism and the Identity Theory', *Journal of Philosophy* 60: 662–3; repr. in *Dialogue* 3 (1964): 124–5.

——(1977). *Memory* (Ithaca, NY: Cornell University Press).

Marcel, Gabriel (1949). *Being and Having* (Westminster: Dacre Press).

Marr, David (1982). *Vision: A Computational Investigation into the Human Representation and Processing of Visual Information* (New York: W. H. Freeman & co.)

Martin, C. B. (1980). 'Substance Substantiated', *Australasian Journal of Philosophy* 58: 3–10.

Martin, Raymond (2008). 'Review' of Sorabji (2006), *Mind* 117: 223–8.

Martin, Raymond, and Barresi, John (2006). *The Rise and Fall of Soul and Self: An Intellectual History of Personal Identity* (New York: Columbia University Press).

Matilal, Bimal Krishna (1986). *Perception: An Essay on Classical Indian Theories of Knowledge* (Oxford: Clarendon Press).

——(1985). *Logic, Language and Reality: An Introduction to Indian Philosophical Thought* (Delhi: Motilal Banarsidass).

——(1987). 'Cārvāka', in Mircea Eliade (ed.), *Encyclopedia of Religion* (New York: Macmillan Pub. Co.); repr. (2nd edn. 2005), iii. 1446–7.

Matilal, Bimal Krishna (1994). 'The Perception of Self in Indian Tradition', in Roger T. Ames et al. (eds.), *Self as Person in Asian Theory and Practice* (Albany, NY: SUNY Press).

Matthen, Mohan (2004). 'Features, Places and Things: Reflections on Austen Clark's Theory of Sentience', *Philosophical Psychology* 17/4: 497–518.

Meltzoff, Andrew (1990). 'Foundations for Developing a Concept of Self', in Dante Cicchetti and Marjorie Beeghly (eds.), *The Self in Transition* (Chicago: University of Chicago Press).

——(1993a). 'The Role of Imitation in Understanding Persons and Developing a Theory of Mind', in Simon Baron-Cohen, Helen Tager-Flusberg, and Donald Cohen (eds.), *Understanding Other Minds: Perspectives from Autism* (Oxford: Oxford University Press).

——(1993b). 'Molyneux's Babies: Cross-modal Perception, Imitation, and the Mind of the Preverbal Infant', in Naomi Eilan, Rosaleen McCarthy, and Bill Brewer (eds.), *Spatial Representation: Problems in Philosophy and Psychology* (Oxford: Blackwell).

Merleau-Ponty, M. (1962). *Phenomenology of Perception*, trans. C. Smith (London: Routledge).

——(1964). *Signs*, trans. R. C. McCleary (Evanston, Ill.: Northwestern University Press).

Metzinger, Thomas (2003). *Being No-one: The Self-Model Theory of Subjectivity* (Cambridge, Mass.: MIT Press).

——(2009). *The Ego Tunnel: The Science of the Mind and the Myth of the Self* (New York: Basic Books).

——(2011). 'The No-Self Alternative', in Gallagher (2011).

Mijuskovic, B. L. (1974). *Achilles of Rationalist Arguments* (Berlin: Springer).

Mill, John Stuart (1843). *A System of Logic, Ratiocinative and Inductive* (London: John W. Parker), 2 vols.

Millar, Alan (1991). *Reason and Experience* (Oxford: Clarendon Press).

Millgram, Elijah (2011). 'Ismael's Anscolmbian and Dennettian Selves', *Philosophy and Phenomenological Research* 82: 759–62.

Millikan, Ruth Garrett (1991). 'Perceptual Content and Fregean Myth', *Mind* 100/1: 1–21.

Mipham, Ju (2004). *Speech of Delight: Mipham's Commentary on Śāntarakṣita's 'Ornament of the Middle Way'*, trans. Thomas Doctor (Ithaca, NY: Snow Lion Publications, 2004).

Mishra, Umesha (1936). *Conception of Matter According to Nyāya-Vaiśeṣika* (Allahabad: Self-published).

Mohanty, J. N. (1992). *Reason and Tradition in Indian Thought* (Oxford: Clarendon Press, 1992).

Mokṣākaragupta (2004). *Tarka-bhāṣā* (in Sanskrit and Tibetan), ed. Lobsang Norbu Shastri (Varanasi: Central Institute of Higher Tibetan Studies). Translation: *Tarka-bhāṣā: An Introduction to Buddhist Philosophy*, trans. Yuichi Kajiyama (Kyoto: Memoirs of the Faculty of Letters, 1966).

Moran, Richard (2001). *Authority and Estrangement: An Essay on Self-Knowledge* (Princeton: Princeton University Press).

——(2002). 'Frankfurt on Identification: Ambiguities of Activity in Mental Life', in Buss and Overton (2002: 189–217).

Moreland, J. P. (1998). 'Theories of Individuation: A Reconsideration of Bare Particulars', *Pacific Philosophical Quarterly* 79: 251–63.

Morgan, C. Lloyd (1923). *Emergent Evolution* (London: Williams and Norgate).

Moriyama, Shinya (2010). 'On Self-Awareness in the Sautrāntika Epistemology', *Journal of Indian Philosophy* 38: 261–77.

Muir, J. (1862). 'Verses from the *Sarva-darśana-sangraha*, the *Vishnu Purāna*, and the *Rāmāyana*, illustrating the tenets of the Chārvākas, or Indian Materialists, with some Remarks on Freedom of Speculation in Ancient India', *Journal of the Royal Asiatic Society of Great Britain and Ireland* 19: 299–314 [Read to the Society on Saturday, 14 Dec. 1861].

Mullins, Simon, and Spence, Sean (2003). 'Re-examining Thought Insertion: Semi-Structured Literature Review and Conceptual Analysis', *British Journal of Psychiatry* 182: 293–8.

Nagel, Thomas (1965). 'Physicalism', *Philosophical Review* 74/3: 339–56.

——(1974). 'What Is It Like to Be a Bat?', *Philosophical Review* 83: 435–50.

——(1979). *Mortal Questions* (Cambridge: Cambridge University Press).

Ñāṇamoli, Bhikkhu (1976). *The Path of Purification: Visuddhimagga* (Berkeley: Shambhala Publications).

Nielsen (2008). 'Did Plato Articulate the Achilles Argument?', in Lennon and Stainton (2008: 19–42).

Nolan, D., Restall, G., and West, C. (2005). 'Moral Fictionalism versus the Rest', *Australasian Journal of Philosophy* 83: 307–30.

Noordhof, Paul (2010). 'Emergent Causation and Property Causation', in Cynthia Macdonald and Graham Macdonald (eds.), *Emergence in Mind* (Oxford: Oxford University Press, 2010), 69–99.

Nussbaum, Martha (2001). *Upheavals of Thought: The Intelligence of Emotions* (Cambridge: Cambridge University Press).

O'Connor, Timothy (1994). 'Emergent Properties', *American Philosophical Quarterly* 31: 91–104.

——(2000). *Persons and Causes: The Metaphysics of Free Will* (Oxford: Oxford University Press).

O'Connor, Timothy, and Churchill, John Ross (2010). 'Is Non-reductive Physicalism Viable within a Causal Powers Metaphysic?', in Cynthia Macdonald and Graham Macdonald (eds.), *Emergence in Mind* (Oxford: Oxford University Press, 2010), 43–60.

O'Connor, Timothy, and Wong, Hong Yu (2005). 'The Metaphysics of Emergence', *Noûs* 39: 658–78.

Olivelle, Patrick (1998). *The Early Upaniṣads: An Annotated Text and Translation* (New York: Oxford University Press).

Olson, Eric (2001). 'Review of Persons and Bodies: A Constitution View', *Mind* 110: 427–30.

——(2004). 'Animalism and the Corpse Problem', *Australasian Journal of Philosophy* 82/2: 265–74.

O'Shaughnessy (1980). *The Will: A Dual Aspect Theory* (Cambridge: Cambridge University Press) (2nd edn. 2008).

——(2002). *Consciousness and the World* (Oxford: Oxford University Press).

Overgaard, Morten (2004). 'On the Naturalizing of Phenomenology', *Phenomenology and the Cognitive Sciences* 3: 365–79.

Papineau, David (1993). *Philosophical Naturalism* (Oxford: Blackwells).

——(2009). 'Naturalism', *The Stanford Encyclopedia of Philosophy* (Spring 2009 Edition), Edward N. Zalta ed., URL = <http://plato.stanford.edu/archives/spr2009/entries/naturalism/>.

Parfit, Derek (1984). *Reasons and Persons* (Oxford: Clarendon Press).

——(1999). 'Experiences, Subjects, and Conceptual Schemes', *Philosophical Topics* 26: 217–70.

Parsons, Terence (1991). 'Tropes and Supervenience', *Philosophy and Phenomenological Research* 51: 629–32.

Patil, Parimal (2003). 'On What It Is That Buddhists Think About: *apoha* in the *Ratnakīrti-Nibandhāvali*', *Journal of Indian Philosophy* 31: 229–56.

Peacocke, Christopher (1992a). 'Scenarios, Concepts, and Perception', in Tim Crane (ed.), *The Contents of Experience: Essays on Perception* (Cambridge: Cambridge University Press).

——(1992b). *A Study of Concepts* (Cambridge, Mass.: MIT Press).

——(1994). 'Nonconceptual Content: Kinds, Rationales and Relations', *Mind and Language* 9: 419–29.

——(2001). 'Does Perception Have a Nonconceptual Content?' *Journal of Philosophy* 98: 239–64.

——(2010). 'Self-Consciousness', *Revue métaphysique et de morale* (special issue: *Le Moi, The Self, Le Soi*, ed. B. Longuenesse) 68: 521–51.

——(2014). *The Mirror of the World: Subjects, Consciousness, and Self-Consciousness* (Oxford: Oxford University Press.)

Penelhum, Terence (2000). *Themes in Hume: The Self, The Will, Religion* (Oxford: Clarendon Press).

Perry, John (1998). 'Myself and I', in Marcelo Stamm (ed.), *Philosophie in Synthetisher Absicht* (Stuttgart: Klett-Cotta), 83–103.

Philoponus (1999). *On Aristotle On Coming-to-Be and Perishing 1.6–2.4*, trans. C. J. F. Williams (London: Duckworth).

Pinde, Ole Holten (2009). *Dignāga's Philosophy of Language: Dignāga on anyāpoha: Pramāṇasamuccaya V: Text, Translation, and Annotation*. PhD Thesis, University of Vienna.

Place, U. T. (1956). 'Is Consciousness a Brain Process', *British Journal of Psychology* 47: 44–50.

Potter, Karl H. (1957). *Inquiry into the Truth about Things (Padārtha-tattva-nirūpaṇa)*, trans. Raghunātha Śiromaṇi (Harvard Yenching Institute Studies, 17; Cambridge, Mass.: Harvard University Press).

——(1999). *Encyclopedia of Indian Philosophies*, viii. *Buddhist Philosophy from 100 to 350 AD* (Delhi: Motilal Banarsidass Publishers).

——(2003). *Encyclopedia of Indian Philosophies*, ix. *Buddhist Philosophy from 350 to 600 AD* (Delhi: Motilal Banarsidass Publishers).

Prabhācandra (1990). *Prameya-kamala-mārtaṇḍa*, ed. Nyaya Shastri Mahendrakumar (3rd edn., Delhi: Sri Satguru Publications).

——(1991). *Nyāya-kumuda-candra*, ed. Nyaya Shastri Mahendrakumar, 2 vols. (2nd edn. Delhi: Sri Satguru Publications).

Praśastapāda (1994). *Praśastapāda-bhāṣya* [aka *Padārtha-dharma-saṃgraha*], in Johannes Bronkhorst and Yves Ramseier, *Word Index to the Praśastapāda-bhāṣya* (Delhi: Motilal Banarsidass).

Priestley, Leonard (1999). *Pudgalavāda Buddhism: The Reality of the Indeterminate Self* (Toronto: Centre for South Asian Studies).

Priscianus Lydus (1886a). *Solutiones eorum de quibus dubitavit Chosroes Persarum rex*, ed. I. Bywater, in *Supplementum Aristotelicum* i/2 (Berlin: George Reimer), 39–104.

——(1886b). *Metaphrasis in Theophrastum*, ed. I. Bywater, in *Supplementum Aristotelicum* i/2 (Berlin: George Reimer), 1–37. Translation: Pamela Huby, *On Theophrastus on Sense-Perception* (London: Duckworth, 1997).

Proclus (1963). *The Elements of Theology*, trans., introd., and com. E. R. Dodds (Oxford: Clarendon Press).

Pseudo-Nāgārjuna (1994). *Le Traité de la Grande Vertu de Sagesse de Nāgārjuna (Mahā-prajñā-pāramitā-śāstra)*, trans. from the Chinese by Étienne Lamotte (Louvain: Bibliothéque du Muséon, 1944), vol. ii.

Putnam, Hilary (1967). 'The Nature of Mental States', in W. H. Capitan and D. D. Merril (eds.), *Art, Mind, and Religion* (Pittsburgh: Pittsburgh University Press.) Repr. in David M. Rosenthal (ed.), *Materialism and the Mind-Body Problem* (Englewood Cliffs, NJ: Prentice-Hall, 1971).

Quine, W. V. (1969). 'Epistemology Naturalized', in *Ontology, Relativity, and Other Essays* (New York: Columbia University Press), 69–90.

——(1981). *Theories and Things* (Cambridge, Mass: Harvard University Press).

Raghudeva [Nyāyālaṃkāra Bhaṭṭācārya] (1915). *Exegesis of the Inquiry (Padārtha-tattva-nirūpaṇa-vyākhyā)*, in Raghunātha (1915).

Raghunātha Śiromaṇi (1915). *Inquiry into the Truth about Things (Padārtha-tattva-nirūpaṇa)*, ed. V. P. Dvivedi (Varanasi).

——(1986). *Ātma-tattva-viveka-dīdhiti*, in Udayana (1986).

Rāmatīrtha (1911). *Vidvamanorañjanī*, in *The Vedānta-sāra of Sadānanda together with the commentaries of Nṛsiṃhāsarasvatī and Rāmatīrtha*, ed. G. A. Jacob (Bombay: Tukaram Jayaji).

Ratnakīrti (1957). *Santānāntara-dūṣaṇa*, in Anantalal Thakur (ed.), *Ratnakīrti-nibandhāvalī* (Patna: KP Research Institute): 138–42.

Reat, N. R. (1987). "Some Fundamental Concepts of Buddhist Psychology," *Religion* 17: 15–28.

Recanati, François (2004). *Literal Meaning* (Cambridge: Cambridge University Press).

——(2007). *Perspectival Thought: A Plea for Moderate Relativism* (Oxford: Oxford University Press).

Reisenzein, Rainer (2009). 'Emotions as Metarepresentational States of Mind: Naturalizing the Belief-Desire Theory of Emotion', *Cognitive Systems Research* 10: 6–20.

Riepe, Dale (1961). *The Naturalistic Tradition in Indian Thought* (Seattle: University of Washington Press).

Robb, David (1997). 'The Properties of Mental Causation', *Philosophical Quarterly*, 47: 178–94.

Ronkin, Noa (2005). *Early Buddhist Metaphysics: The Making of a Philosophical Tradition* (London: Routledge).

Rosenthal, David (1986). 'Two Concepts of Consciousness', *Philosophical Studies* 49: 329–59.

——(2000). 'Consciousness and Metacognition', in D. Sperber (ed.), *Metarepresentation* (New York: Oxford University Press), 203–14.

——(2005). *Consciousness and Mind* (Oxford: Clarendon Press).

Roy J.-M., Petitot, J., Varela, F. J., and Pachoud, B. (1999). 'Beyond the Gap: An Introduction to Naturalizing Phenomenology', in J. Petitot, F. J. Varela, B. Pachoud, and J.-M. Roy (eds.), *Naturalizing Phenomenology: Issues in Contemporary Phenomenology and Cognitive Science* (Stanford: Stanford University Press).

Rueger, Alexander (2000a). 'Physical Emergence, Diachronic and Synchronic', *Synthese* 124: 297–322.

——(2000b). 'Robust Supervenience and Emergence', *Philosophy of Science* 67: 466–89.

Ryle, Gilbert (1949). *The Concept of Mind* (London: Hutchinson's University Library).

Saṃghabhadra (1999). *Nyāyānusāra*, trans. Collette Cox in Karl Potter (1999: 650–715).

Śaṅkara (1917). *The Brahma-sūtra-bhāṣya with the Commentaries Bhāmatī, Kalpatarū and Parīmāla*, ed. N. A.K. Sastri and V. L. Sastri Pansikar (Bombay: Nirmaya Sagar Press).

Śaṅkara Miśra (1969). *Vaiśeṣika-sūtra-upaskāra*, ed. Dundhiraja Sastri (Kashi Sanskrit Series 195; Varanasi: Chowkhamba Sanskrit Series Office). Trans: *The Vaiśeṣika Sūtras of Kaṇāda, with the Commentary of Śaṅkara Miśra*, trans. Nandalal Sinha (Allahabad: The Panini Office, Bhuvaneswari Asrama, 1911).

Sartre, Jean-Paul (1956). *Being and Nothingness*, trans. H. E. Barnes (New York: Philosophical Library). Translation of *L'Être et le néant* (Paris: Tel Gallimard, 1943).

——(1957). *The Transcendence of the Ego: An Existentialist Theory of Consciousness* (New York: Noonday Press).

Sassen, Brigitte (2008). 'Kant and Mendelssohn on the Implications of the "I Think" ', in Lennon and Stainton (2008: 215–34).

Scherer, K. R., Schorr, A., and Johnstone, T. (2001). *Appraisal Processes in Emotion: Theory, Methods, Research* (Oxford: Oxford University Press).

Schmithausen, Lambert (1987). *Ālayavijñāna: On the Origin and the Early Development of a Central Concept of Yogācāra Philosophy* (Tokyo: International Institute for Buddhist Studies), 2 vols.

Schweizer, Paul (1993). 'Mind/Consciousness Dualism in Sāṅkhya-Yoga Philosophy', *Philosophy and Phenomenological Research* 53: 845–60.

Seager, J. R. (1995). 'Consciousness, Information, and Panpsychism', *Journal of Consciousness Studies* 2: 272–88.

Searle, John (1992). *The Rediscovery of the Mind* (Cambridge, Mass.: MIT Press).

Sellars, Wilfred (1956). 'Empiricism in the Philosophy of Mind', in Herbert Feigl and Michael Scriven (eds.), *The Foundations of Science and the Concepts of Psychology and Psychoanalysis* (Minneapolis: University of Minnesota Press), 253–329.

Sellars, Wilfred (1963). *Science, Perception and Reality* (London: Routledge & Kegan Paul).

——(1971). 'Science, Sense Impressions, and Sensa', *Review of Metaphysics* 24: 391–447.

Sen, Prabal Kumar (2003). *Nyāyasūtras with Nyāyarahasya of Rāmabhadra Sārvabhauma and Ānvīkṣikītattvavivaraṇa of Jānakīnātha Cūḍāmaṇi* (Kolkata: The Asiatic Society).

Shapiro, Lawrence (2004). *The Mind Incarnate* (Cambridge, Mass.: MIT Press).

Shoemaker, Sydney (1968). 'Self-Reference and Self-Awareness', *Journal of Philosophy* 65/19: 555–67; repr. in his *Identity, Cause, and Mind* (Cambridge: Cambridge University Press, 1984).

——(1984). 'Personal Identity: A Materialist's Account', in S. Shoemaker and R. Swinburne, *Personal Identity* (Oxford: Basil Blackwell), 67–132.

——(1996). *The First-Person Perspective and Other Essays* (Cambridge: Cambridge University Press).

——(1999). 'Self, Body, and Coincidence', *Proceedings of the Aristotelian Society*, suppl. vol. 73: 287–306.

——(2002). 'Kim on Emergence', *Philosophical Studies* 108: 53–63.

——(2007). *Physical Realization* (Oxford: Oxford University Press).

Shoemaker, S., and Swinburne, R. (1984). *Personal Identity* (Oxford: Blackwell).

Shukla, Badrinath (1984). '*Nyāya-śāstrīya-vicāra-paddhatyā dehātmavādasya sambhābhanā*', *Sarasvatī Suṣamā* 38: 121–4. Translated as '*Dehātmavāda* or the Body as Soul: The Exploration of a Possibility within Nyāya Thought', *Journal of the Indian Council of Philosophical Research* (1991): 1–17.

Sider, Theodore (1997). 'Four-Dimensionalism', *Philosophical Review* 106/2: 197–231.

——(2001). *Four-Dimensionalism: An Ontology of Persistence and Time* (Oxford: Clarendon Press).

——(2002). 'Review of Lynne Rudder Baker, *Persons and Bodies*', *Journal of Philosophy* 99: 45–8.

——(2006). 'Bare Particulars', *Philosophical Perspectives* 20: 387–97.

Siderits, Mark (2003). *Personal Identity and Buddhist Philosophy: Empty Persons* (Aldershot: Ashgate).

Siderits, Mark, Thompson, Evan, and Zahavi, Dan (eds.) (2011). *Self, No Self?* (Oxford: Oxford University Press).

Silberstein, Michael (1998). 'Emergence and the Mind-Body Problem', *Journal of Consciousness Studies* 5/4: 464–82.

——(2006). 'In Defence of Ontological Emergence and Mental Causation', in Clayton and Davies (2006: 203–26).

Silberstein, Michael, and McGeever, John (1999). 'The Search for Ontological Emergence', *Philosophical Quarterly* 49: 182–200.

Simons, Peter (1994). 'Particulars in Particular Clothing: Three Trope Theories of Substance', *Philosophy and Phenomenological Research* 54: 553–75.

Smart. J. J. C. (1959). 'Sensations and Brain Processes', *Philosophical Review* 68: 141–56.

——(1962). 'Brain Processes and Incorrigibility', *Australasian Journal of Philosophy* 40/1: 68–70.

——(1981). 'Physicalism and Emergence', *Neuroscience* 6: 109–13.

——(2008). 'The Identity Theory of Mind', in Edward N. Zalta (ed.), *The Stanford Encyclopedia of Philosophy* (Fall 2008 Edition), URL = <http://plato.stanford.edu/archives/fall2008/entries/mind-identity/>.

Smith, Brian K. (1989). *Reflections on Resemblance, Ritual and Religion* (New York: Oxford University Press).

Smith, David Woodruff (2005). 'Consciousness with Reflexive Content', in Smith and Thomasson (2005: 93–114).

Smith, David Woodruff and Thomasson, A. L. (ed.) (2005). *Phenomenology and Philosophy of Mind* (Oxford: Clarendon Press).

Solomon, Esther A. (1977–8). 'Bhaṭṭa Udbhaṭa', *Annals of the Bhandarkar Oriental Research Institute* 58–9: 986–97.

Sorabji, Richard (1980). *Necessity, Cause and Blame* (London: Duckworth).

——(2002). *Emotion and Peace of Mind: From Stoic Agitation to Christian Temptation* (Oxford: Oxford University Press).

——(2003). 'The Mind-Body Relation in the Wake of Plato's *Timaeus*', in Gretchen Reydams-Schils (ed.), *Plato's* Timaeus *as Cultural Icon* (Bloomington, Ind.: Notre Dame Press): 152–62.

——(2005). *The Philosophy of the Commentators, 200–600 AD* (London: Duckworth), 3 vols.

——(2006). *Self: Ancient and Modern Insights about Individuality, Life, and Death* (Chicago: University of Chicago Press).

——(2010). *Philoponus and the Rejection of Aristotelian Science* (2nd edn., London: Institute of Classical Studies).

Sosa, Ernest (1987). 'Subjects among other Things', *Philosophical Perspectives* 1: 155–87.

Spence, A. (1996). 'Free Will in the Light of Neuropsychiatry', *Philosophy, Psychiatry and Psychology* 3: 75–90.

——(2001). 'Alien Control: From Phenomenology to Cognitive Neurobiology', *Philosophy, Psychiatry and Psychology* 8: 163–72.

Śrīdhara (1916). *The Padārtha-dharma-saṃgraha with the Nyāya-kandalī of Śrīdhara*, trans. into English by Ganganatha Jha (Benares: E. J. Lazarus).

——(1977). *Nyāya-kandalī*, with Hindi trans., ed Durgadhara Jha (Varanasi: Sampurnanand Sanskrit Vishvavidyalaya, Ganganatha Jha Granthamala).

——(1984). *Nyāya-kandalī*, ed. V. P. Dvivedin in *The Bhāṣya of Praśastapāda together with the Nyāya-kandalī of Śrīdhara* (Delhi: Sri Satguru Publications) (1st pub. Benares, 1895).

Stcherbatsky, Theodore (1923). *The Central Conception of Buddhism and the Meaning of the Word 'Dharma'* (London: Royal Asiatic Society).

——(1962). *Buddhist Logic* (repr. New York: Dover Publications) (1st pub. Leningrad: Academy of Sciences of the USSR, 1930).

Steel, Carlos (1978). *The Changing Self: A Study of the Soul in Later Neoplatonism: Iamblichus, Damascius, and Priscianus* (Brussels: Koninklijke Academie voor Wetenschappen).

Stein, Nathanael (2011). 'Aristotle's Causal Pluralism', *Archiv für Geschichte der Philosophie* 93/2: 121–14.

Stephens, G. L., and Graham, G. (2000). *When Self-Consciousness Breaks: Alien Voices and Inserted Thoughts* (Cambridge Mass.: MIT Press).

Sthiramati (2007). *Sthiramati's Triṃśikā-vijñapti-bhāṣya: Critical Editions of the Sanskrit Text and its Tibetan Translation*, ed. Hartmut Buescher (Sitzungsberichte/Österreichische Akademie der Wissenschaften, Philosophisch-Historische Klasse; Vienna: Verlag der Österreichischen Akademie der Wissenachaften).

Stoljar, D. (2001). 'Two Conceptions of the Physical', *Philosophy and Phenomenological Research* 62: 253–81.

Stone, Jim (1988). 'Parfit and the Buddha', *Philosophy and Phenomenological Research* 48: 519–32.

Storbeck, Justin, and Clore, Gerarld (2007). 'On the Interdependence of Cognition and Emotion', *Cognition and Emotion* 21/6: 1212–37.

Stout, G. F. (1921). 'The Nature of Universals and Propositions', *Proceedings of the British Academy* 10: 157–72.

Strawson, Galen (1989). 'Red and "Red" ', *Synthese* 78: 193–232.

——(1999a). 'The Self', in Shaun Gallagher and Jonathan Shear (eds.), *Models of the Self* (Thorverton: Imprint Academic).

——(1999b). 'The Self and the Sesmet', *Journal of Consciousness Studies* 6: 99–135.

——(2006). 'Being Realistic: Why Physicalism Entails Panpsychism', *Journal of Consciousness Studies*, 13/10–11: 3–31.

——(2007). 'Selves', in Brian P. McLaughlin and Ansgar Beckermann (eds.), *The Oxford Handbook of Philosophy of Mind* (Oxford: Oxford University Press): 541–64.

——(2008). *Real Materialism and Other Essays* (Oxford: Clarendon Press).

——(2009). *Selves: An Essay in Revisionary Metaphysics* (Oxford: Clarendon Press).

Strawson, Peter F. (1963). *Individuals* (New York: Anchor Books).
——(1966). *The Bounds of Sense: An Essay on Kant's 'Critique of Pure Reason'* (London: Methuen).
——(1974a). 'Imagination and Perception', in his *Freedom and Resentment* (London: Methuen).
——(1974b). *Subject and Predicate in Logic and Grammar* (London: Methuen).
——(1974c). 'Freedom and Resentment', in his *Freedom and Resentment* (London: Methuen).
——(1985). *Skepticism and Naturalism: Some Varieties* (New York: Columbia University Press).
——(1992). 'Freedom and Necessity', in his *Analysis and Metaphysics* (Oxford: Oxford University Press): 133–42.
Stroud, Barry (2004). 'The Charm of Naturalism', in Mario De Caro and David Macarthur (eds.), *Naturalism in Question* (Cambridge, Mass.: Harvard University Press).
Taber, John (1990). 'The Mīmāṃsā Theory of Self-Recognition', *Philosophy East and West* 40: 35–57.
——(2003). 'Dharmakīrti Against Physicalism', *Journal of Indian Philosophy* 31: 479–502.
Tamura, Suzuko (2000). "Imperative Expressions in the Saru Dialect of Ainu," in *The Ainu Language*. ICHEL Linguistic Studies v.2 (Tokyo: Sanseido).
Taylor, C. C. W. (2008). *Pleasure, Mind, and Soul: Selected Papers in Ancient Philosophy* (Oxford: Oxford University Press).
Taylor, Charles (1989). *Sources of the Self* (Cambridge, Mass.: Harvard University Press).
Taylor, Richard (1966). *Action and Purpose* (Englewood Cliffs, NJ: Prentice-Hall).
Thakur, Anantalal (2003). *Origin and Development of the Vaiśeṣika System. History of Science, Philosophy and Culture in Indian Civilization*, ii/4 (Delhi: Centre for Studies in Civilizations).
That, Le Manh (1974). 'The Philosophy of Vasubandhu'. PhD Thesis, University of Wisconsin.
Thompson, Evan (2007). *Mind in Life: Biology, Phenomenology, and the Sciences of Mind* (Cambridge, Mass.: Belknap Press).
——(2011). 'Self, No Self? Memory and Reflexive Awareness', in Siderits, Tillemans, and Zahavi (2011: 157–76).
——(2014). *Waking, Dreaming, Being: New Light on the Self and Consciousness from Neuroscience, Meditation and Philosophy* (New York: Columbia University Press).
Tillemans, Tom J. F. (1995). 'On the So-called Difficult Point of the *apoha* Theory', *Asiatic Studies/Études asiatiques* 59: 854–89.
——(1999). *Scripture, Logic, Language: Essays on Dharmakīrti and His Tibetan Successors* (Boston: Wisdom Publications).
Treisman, A., and Gelade, G. (1980). 'A Feature-Integration Theory of Attention', *Cognitive Psychology* 12: 97–136.

Tsakiris, M. (2010). 'My Body in the Brain: A Neurocognitive Model of Body-Ownership', *Neuropsychologia* 48: 703–12.

——(2011). 'The Sense of Body Ownership', in Gallagher (2011).

Tucci, Giuseppe (1923). *'Linee di una storia del materialismo indiano', pts. I, II, III, Atti della Reale Accademia nazionale dei Lincei*, ser. 5, v. 17, fasc. 7 (Rome: Giovanni Bardi), 242–310.

——(1929). *'Linee di una storia del materialismo indiano', pt. IV and appendices, Atti della Reale Accademia nazionale dei Lincei*, ser. 6, v. 2, fasc. 10 (Rome: Giovanni Bardi), 667–713.

Tuske, Joerg (2011). 'The Concept of Emotion in Classical Indian Philosophy', in Edward N. Zalta (ed.), *The Stanford Encyclopedia of Philosophy* (Spring 2011 Edition), URL = <http://plato.stanford.edu/archives/spr2011/entries/concept-emotion-india/>.

Tzohar, Roy (2011). *Metaphor (upacāra) in Early Yogācāra Thought and its Intellectual Context.* Columbia University PhD Dissertation.

Udayana (1967). *Pariśuddhi*, in Anantalal Thakur (ed.), *Nyāya-darśana* (Darbhanga: Mithila Institute).

——(1986). *Ātma-tattva-viveka*, ed. V. P. Dvivedin and L. S. Dravida, *Bibiotheca Indica* 170 (Calcutta: The Asiatic Society).

——(1971). *Kiraṇāvalī*, ed. Jitendra S. Jetly (Baroda: Oriental Institute).

Uddyotakara (1997). *Nyāya-vārttika*, ed. Anantalal Thakur (Delhi: Indian Council of Philosophical Research).

Vācaspati (1980). *Bhāmati*, in Jagdish Lal Shastri (ed.), *Brahmasūtra-śāṅkara-bhāṣyam* (Delhi: Motilal Banarsidass).

——(1996). *Nyāya-vārttika-tātparya-ṭīkā*, ed. Anantalal Thakur (Delhi: Indian Council of Philosophical Research).

Van Cleve, James (1990). 'Mind-Dust or Magic? Panpsychism Versus Emergence', *Philosophical Perspectives* 4: 215–26.

Van Inwagen, Peter (1997). 'Materialism and the Psychological-Continuity Account of Personal Identity', *Philosophical Perspectives* 11: 305–19.

Varela, Francisco (1996). 'Neurophenomenology: A Methodological Remedy to the Hard Problem', *Journal of Consciousness Studies* 3: 330–50.

Varela, Francisco, Thompson, Evan, and Rosch, Eleanor (1991). *Embodied Mind: Cognitive Science and Human Experience* (Cambridge, Mass.: MIT Press).

Vasubandhu (1925). *Vijñapti-mātratā-siddhi: Deux Traités de Vasubandhu: Viṃśatikā et Triṃśikā*, ed. Lévi Sylvain (Paris: Bibliothèque de l'École des Hautes Études).

Vātsyāyana (1997). *Nyāya-bhāṣya*, in Anantalal Thakur (ed.), *Gautamīya-nyāya-darśana with Bhāṣya of Vātsyāyana* (Delhi: Indian Council of Philosophical Research). Translation: Mrinalkanti Gangopadhyaya, *Gautama's Nyāya-sūtra with Vātsyāyana's Commentary* (Calcutta: Indian Studies, 1982).

——(1973). *Abhidharma-kośa with Abhidharma-kośa-bhāṣya*, ed. Dwarikadas Shastri with Yaśomitra's *Sphuṭārtha* (Varanasi: Bauddha Bharati).
——(1975). *Abhidharma-kośa with Abhidharma-kośa-bhāṣya*, ed. Prahlad Pradhan (Patna: K. P. Jawaswal Research Institute); (2nd edn.), ed. Aruna Haldar.
——(1988–90). *Abhidharma-kośa with Abhidharma-kośa-bhāṣya*. Translation: Louis de la Vallée Poussin into French, and retranslated into English by Leo M. Pruden, 4 vols (Berkeley: Asian Humanities Press, 1988–90).
——(2008). *Pañca-skandhaka*, ed. Xuezhu Li and Ernst Steinkellner (Vienna: Austrian Academy of Sciences Press).
Velleman, David (2005). 'The Self as Narrator', in John Christman and Joel Anderson (eds.), *Autonomy and the Challenges to Liberalism* (Cambridge: Cambridge University Press), 56–76.
Vendler, Zeno (1979). 'Vicarious Experience', *Revue de metaphysique et de morale* 18/2: 161–73.
Viśvanātha Nyāyapañcānana (1985). *Nyāya-sūtra-vṛtti*, in *Nyāya-sūtra, with Vātsyāyana's Bhāṣya, Uddyotakara's Vārttika, Vācaspati Miśra's Tātparya-tīkā and Viśvanātha's Vṛtti*, ed. T. Nyayatarkatirtha and A. Tarkatirtha (Calcutta: Calcutta Sanskrit Series nos. 18–19; 2nd edn.: Delhi: Munshriram Manoharlal).
Vyomaśiva (1983). *Vyomavatī*, ed. Gaurinath Sastri (Varanasi: Sampurnanand Sanskrit University).
Waldron, William S. (2002). 'Buddhist Steps to an Ecology of Mind: Thinking about "Thoughts Without a Thinker" ', *Eastern Buddhist* 34/1: 1–52.
——(2003). *The Buddhist Unconscious: The Ālaya-vijñāna in the Context of Indian Buddhist Thought* (London: Routledge).
Wallace, Alan (ed.) (2003). *Science and Buddhism: Breaking New Ground* (New York: Columbia University Press).
——(2007). *Contemplative Science: Where Buddhism and Science Converge* (New York: Columbia University Press).
Walshe, Maurice O'C. (1995). *The Long Discourses of the Buddha: A Translation of the Dīgha Nikāya* (Boston: Wisdom Publications).
Watson, Alex (2006). *The Self's Awareness of Itself. Bhaṭṭa Rāmakaṇṭha's Arguments Against the Buddhist Doctrine of No-Self* (Vienna: Publications of the De Nobili Research Library).
——(2010). 'Bhaṭṭa Rāmakaṇṭha's Elaboration of Self-Awareness (*svasaṃvedana*), and How it Differs from Dharmakīrti's Exposition of the Concept', *Journal of Indian Philosophy* 38: 297–321.
Westerhoff, Jan (2009). *Nāgārjuna's Madhyamaka: A Philosophical Introduction* (New York: Oxford University Press).
Weyl, Hermann (1954a). 'Address on the Unity of Knowledge'; repr. in K. Chandrasehharan (ed.), *Gesammelte Abhandlungen* (1968), iv. 623–30.

——(1954b). 'Insight and Reflection'; repr. in T. L. Saaty and F. J. Weyl (eds.), *The Spirit and Uses of the Mathematical Sciences* (New York: McGraw-Hill, 1969), 281–301.

Williams, Bernard (1973a). 'Imagination and the Self', in his *Problems of the Self* (Cambridge: Cambridge University Press), 26–45.

——(1973b). 'Are Persons Bodies?', in his *Problems of the Self* (Cambridge: Cambridge University Press), 64–81.

——(2002). *Truth & Truthfulness: An Essay in Genealogy* (Princeton: Princeton University Press).

Williams, D. C. (1953). 'The Elements of Being', *Review of Metaphysics* 7: 3–18.

Williams, Paul (1998). *The Reflexive Nature of Awareness: a Tibetan Madhyamaka Defence* (Richmond: Curzon).

Williford, Kenneth (2011). 'Pre-reflective Self-Consciousness and the Autobiographical Ego', in Jonathan Webber (ed.), *Reading Sartre: On Phenomenology and Existentialism* (London: Routledge), 195–210.

Wilson, Jessica (2005). 'Supervenience-based Formulations of Physicalism', *Noûs* 39/3: 426–59.

Wittgenstein, Ludwig (1960). *Preliminary Studies for the 'Philosophical Investigations', Generally Known as the Blue and Brown Books* (Oxford: Blackwell).

——(1975). *Philosophical Remarks* (Chicago: University of Chicago Press).

Wong, Hong Yu (2006). 'Emergents from Fusion', *Philosophy of Science* 73: 345–67.

——(2010). 'The Secret Lives of Emergents', in Timothy O'Connor and Antonella Corradini (eds.), *Emergence in Science and Philosophy* (London: Routledge), 7–24.

Yablo, S. (1992). 'Mental Causation', *Philosophical Review* 101: 245–80.

——(1998). 'Does Ontology Rest on a Mistake?', *Proceedings of the Aristotelian Society*, suppl. vol. 72: 229–46.

Yao, Zhihua (2005). *The Buddhist Theory of Self-Cognition* (London: Routledge).

Zahavi, Dan (1999). *Self-Awareness and Alterity: A Phenomenological Investigation* (Evanston: Northwestern University Press).

——(2002). 'First-Person Thoughts and Embodied Self-Awareness: Some Reflections on the Relation between Recent Analytical Philosophy and Phenomenology', *Phenomenology and the Cognitive Sciences* 1: 7–26.

——(2004). 'Phenomenology and the Project of Naturalization', *Phenomenology and the Cognitive Sciences* 3: 331–47.

——(2005a). *Subjectivity and Selfhood: Investigating the First-Person Perspective* (Cambridge, Mass.: MIT Press).

——(2005b). 'Being Someone', *Psyche* 11: 1–20.

——(2011). 'Unity of Consciousness and the Problem of Self', in Gallagher (2011: 316–35).

Zanon, Jacopo (2012). "Interpretation of the I-pronoun in Contexts of Subordination in the Hindi Language," Università CáFoscari Venezia Laurea Dissertation.

Zimmerman, Dean W. (2003). 'Material People', in M. J. Loux and D. Zimmerman (eds.), *The Oxford Handbook of Metaphysics* (Oxford: Oxford University Press).

Index

Printed and bound by CPI Group (UK) Ltd, Croydon, CR0 4YY